Mirror On

1940

Cover photo: Troops evacuated from Dunkirk, 31st May 1940.

ISBN: 978-1-9993652-7-1
© Newspaper Yearbook 2023
All Rights Reserved

INDEX

JAN — PAGE

3rd	Hitler Threat To Finns	7
6th	Belisha Resigns	8
10th	"I Haven't Told You Enough," Says Premier	9
11th	R.A.F. In 2 Fights: Isle Raided	10
12th	6 Air Raids On Britain	11
13th	Heroes Of B.E.F. Raid Decorated	12
23rd	Black-Out: How Raider Sees Us	13
26th	Wrecked - Saved By Bride	14
29th	Rail Hold-Up Goes On	15
31st	England Will Get War Now	16

FEB

2nd	War Deal Suspends Officers	17
3rd	Glut Of Bacon - 2d Off	18
5th	Murder Men Saved By Trawler	19
6th	Big Meat Muddle Is Growing	20
7th	150 Police Guard I.R.A. Prison	21
8th	Gaol For Waste	22
13th	When The Bombs Drop	23
16th	Parents To Pledge On Billets	24
20th	Navy Broke Law, Norway Accuses	25
24th	Daddy's Medal	26

MAR

1st	Italy Hit: Navy Ban Coal	27
5th	Threw Bomb Overboard - "Nowt"	28
9th	Hitler Orders Ribbentrop To Rome	29
11th	Finns Talk Peace In Moscow	30
13th	Reds Say Peace Is Signed	31
14th	Assassin Shoots Minister, Kills Knight	32
18th	Duce, Hitler Meet Today	33
23rd	Nazis' New Balkan Demand	34
25th	Britain's New Sea Bid	35
26th	Allies Fight If Russians March	36

INDEX - 2

APR
		Page
4th	Churchill War Leader In New Cabinet	37
5th	Race To Build Ships	38
8th	Big Trade War Talk Today	39
9th	4 Nazi Ships Torpedoed Off Norway: One Troopship	40
11th	Allies In 2 Norway Ports	41
13th	50 Faced 2,000 / Fleet Waits / Air Base Raid	42
20th	Swim For It: Hardy Last Word	43
22nd	Our Tanks Take Town Near Oslo	44
23rd	B.E.F. Success In Norwegian Fights	45
24th	Victory Budget Taxes All Sales	46

MAY
3rd	Ten Days, Says Rome: Navy Watch	47
8th	Who Held Back Navy? Admiral Hero Asks	48
14th	Battle Of 2,000 Tanks Raging	49
18th	Conquer Or Die Order By Gamelin	50
21st	Germans Thrust At Channel	51
22nd	Amiens Burns As B.E.F. Fight For Ports	52
24th	B.E.F. In Boulogne Night Battle	53
27th	Ironside Is Home Defence Chief	54
29th	Great R.A.F. Attack To Help B.E.F.	55
30th	B.E.F. Battle On As Navy Cover Dunkirk	56

JUN
1st	B.E.F. Rearguard Men Arriving Back	57
3rd	Navy Fights To Save The Last Thousands	58
5th	We Never Surrender	59
14th	Reynaud's Final Call To U.S.	60
15th	French Hold On, Repulse Attack	61
17th	French Cabinet Shocks: Petain Premier	62
19th	Leadership, Give Us Leadership	63
24th	Petain Yields France - Leader Here To Fight On	64
25th	Petain Gives In To Italy, Too	65
29th	Families To Get Order To Move	66

INDEX - 3

JUL		Page
8th	French Planes In Gib. Raid	67
9th	2oz. Tea Ration From Today	68
12th	By Order	69
13th	R.A.F. Strike Back In Storm	70
19th	Plans To Beat Winter With New Loaf, Sugar And Tea	71
20th	Dunkirk Fighter New C-In-C	72
24th	How Your Tax Will Be Stopped Off Pay	73
26th	Soldiers Sang As Bombed Liner Sank	74
27th	Sea Blitz New Nazi Attack	75
31st	Army Men Get VC	76

AUG		
1st	Warships Chase Sea Raider	77
6th	Why Hitler Has Waited So Long	78
10th	16 Warplanes Gift By M.P.	79
12th	60 Fall To R.A.F. And Guns	80
13th	Nazis Raid Naval Port 39 Down	81
14th	Yesterday's Total 69	82
17th	Raiders Bomb London Suburbs And Gun Streets	83
19th	140-16: R.A.F.'s Biggest Victory	84
22nd	Planes Dive To Gun Women	85
24th	2 More VCs	86

SEP		
2nd	Children's Ship Torpedoed - All Saved	87
4th	Britain Gets 50 Destroyers: U.S. 8 Bases	88
5th	London Barrage Beats Attacks	89
9th	Second Night In Battle Of London	90
14th	King And Queen In Palace, Bombed	91
19th	R.A.F. Bag 46 In 5 Attacks	92
23rd	83 Children Die As Huns Sink Liner In Storm	93
24th	De Gaulle Leads Swoop On Port: Navy Opens Fire	94
26th	Bid For Dakar Abandoned	95
28th	130 Down In Day War	96

INDEX - 4

OCT — Page

1st	School First Aid Plan	97
2nd	First Women To Win GM	98
3rd	Chamberlain To Leave War Cabinet	99
5th	Japan Threat Of War On U.S.	100
7th	He Refused To Funk - Fired By Govt.	101
11th	U.S. Act To Foil Nazis	102
14th	Navy Fight Near Malta	103
17th	I Won't Let Them Hurt You	104
19th	Rumania Looted Of Arms	105
23rd	Fight Britain - Hitler To France	106

NOV

2nd	Naval Chiefs In Greece	107
4th	Town Cut Off By Greeks	108
8th	Eire Would Fight For Her Bases	109
14th	Navy Hit Italy Two Smashing Blows	110
15th	Nazi Aim: Bully Turks	111
16th	Everyone To Fight Hitler	112
20th	War Work For 500,000 Women	113
25th	Axis Drag In Slovaks	114
26th	Hang A Looter	115
30th	The Kings Pilots	116

DEC

3rd	Profiteers In Death	117
4th	Nazis Claim 19 Sunk In One Day	118
5th	Duce's Army Quits 3 Towns	119
6th	Ships Save Italians In Retreat	120
10th	British Launch Desert Attack, Take 1,000 Wops, Kill C.-In-C.	121
13th	20,000 More Prisoners Captured In Sidi Barrani Victory	122
14th	R.A.F. Blitzes Frontier	123
16th	We Invade Libya - By Bayonet	124
21st	Bardia Ringed - Told Yield	125
23rd	Halifax To Go To U.S.	126

THE DAILY MIRROR, Wednesday, Jan. 3, 1940.

Daily Mirror

No. 11,254   ONE PENNY
Registered at the G.P.O. as a Newspaper.

THE FOOLISH BURGIN

Mr. Leslie Burgin.

MR. BURGIN, the Minister of Supply, cannot supply the Army with the oil lamps it needs.

So now he asks the public to give him 24,000 oil lamps which are urgently needed to light Army huts.

Mr. Burgin has been Minister of Supply since last June, and you might have thought that in that time his department would have found time to order the necessary lamps.

No. The Supply Minister is "the foolish Burgin" caught with his lamps un-trimmed.

The stocks in the wholesalers' and retailers' stores are now exhausted and Mr. Burgin has to appeal to your generosity.

An official of one of the largest oil lamp manufacturers in the country said last night:—

"Had we been warned last September that something like fifty times our usual annual output would be wanted, we could have arranged to make the lamps even in a few months."

Carriage Paid!

If you have an oil lamp you are asked to hand it to the nearest military station or send it, carriage paid, to the Central Ordnance Depot, Didcot, Berks.

Carriage paid!

Mr. Burgin, Minister of Supply, you might at least have supplied your benefactors with the postage stamp.

And if you are running short of guns, call on the householders again. We might supply you, carriage paid, with the old blunderbuss that hangs in the hall or the primitive pistol grandfather carried in the Crimea.

ADMIRAL GETS A NEW POST

ADMIRAL Sir Henry Brownrigg, Commander-in-Chief the Nore, until last month, has been appointed Director of Greenwich Hospital.

The previous director of Greenwich Hospital received a salary of £1,700 a year.

The standard rate of pay for an Admiral is £2,920 a year.

As director of the hospital—which is a hospital only in name—Admiral Brownrigg will have the disposal of an annual revenue of more than £200,000.

This money drawn from property rents and funds, is paid out in pensions to ex-Naval men every year.

HITLER THREAT TO FINNS

GERMANY will support Russia in her war on Finland if British soldiers appear on Finnish soil or should munitions from the Allies reach "decisive proportions."

This, according to an Associated Press dispatch last night, was the view expressed by "authoritative sources" in Berlin.

These sources were quoted as "watching very closely what kind of aid Britain was giving to Finland."

"Stalin Request" Denied

German authorities, it was said, believe that the Western Powers have no unselfish interest in Finland, but merely want to use the little Republic as a pawn in the game against Germany.

"Authoritative sources" are reported to have "added sarcastically" that if British aid to Finland proved on a par with that to Poland, then Germany had absolutely no objections.

Earlier, Berlin described as "ridiculous" a report that Stalin has asked Hitler for 200,000 expert engineers and technicians to reorganise the entire Soviet economy.

The report, attributed to the Berlin correspondent of the Danish newspaper *Politiken*, declared that Stalin's request had been made because of the unprecedented burden of the war with Finland.

'Russian Base Taken'

Furious Russian attacks were renewed yesterday as the Battle of the Mannerheim Line entered its twenty-ninth day. Troops were hurled against the centre and left wing of the Finnish defence lines.

Here, according to the Finnish communique, the attacks were repulsed.

The communique said: "Enemy attacks with tanks at Lake Latva, west of the northern point of Lake Ladoga, were repulsed.

"At Aittajoki, ten miles east of Aglajaervi (Karelian frontier), our troops captured, then lost, and finally recaptured one of the Russian bases after a battle lasting all day."

Castle Ablaze

"At sea the enemy battleship October Revolution bombarded Koivisto without any result worth mentioning."

The historic castle at Turku (Aabo) built about 700 years ago when the Swedes introduced Christianity into Finland, was set on fire by Soviet planes, but damage was not severe. Two people were killed.

Daily Mirror, Associated Press, British United Press.

ELECTRICITY PRICES UP

Increased prices in electricity for consumers in many parts of Kent were announced yesterday by the West Kent Electricity Co., Ltd.

The company state that this is due to increased costs and to the conditions arising from the war. The revised rates will come into force in quarterly accounts after March 20 and in other accounts after January 1.

3 TAKE ON 12 IN AIR

THREE British bombers on patrol to search for German warships met twelve of Germany's new long-range Messerschmitt fighters about eighty miles from Heligoland yesterday.

Though heavily outnumbered, the R.A.F. planes promptly gave battle.

Two of the British planes were lost. One Messerschmitt was shot down in flames, and two others are believed downed.

An Air Ministry announcement says:

"A formation of three R.A.F. bombers encountered a squadron of twelve Messerschmitt long-range fighters well out at sea.

One Bomber Home

"The formation gave battle to the enemy. One Messerschmitt was shot down in flames and two others were driven down and are likely to have been lost.

"One of the three bombers has returned safely, a second was shot down during the encounter and the third is missing."

The pilot of the third aircraft said on his return:

"We were going south when suddenly the look-out man shouted 'Fighters!'

"We had not seen the enemy because they came straight out of the sun.

"The first burst of enemy fire penetrated our fuselage, but did no material damage.

"We gave as good as we got.

"We found ourselves fighting about twelve of the enemy. Bullets entered our aircraft and some of them missed us by a few inches."

For nearly ten minutes this aircraft

Continued on Back Page

A Present from Joe

The German Press Attaché to Finland arrived in Helsinki yesterday with wounds in the face. He had been caught in the Russian bombing of Turku (Aabo), the Finnish port.

He was driving near the harbour when Red planes bombed the district.

He threw himself behind a heap of wood. The wood fell on him. He says seventy bombs were dropped.

WHILE HER FATHER WAITS—

Lord Redesdale photographed outside his hotel yesterday.

UNITY LIES ILL IN FRANCE

WHILE Lord Redesdale slept in a hotel lounge in a South Coast town yesterday, Miss Unity Mitford, his twenty-five-year-old daughter and Hitler's friend, lay seriously ill in a hospital on the other side of the Channel.

Lord Redesdale was worn out by all-night efforts to get his wounded daughter safely back to England and home.

After reports that a passage had been booked for her on a passenger plane from France, the machine arrived without her on board.

£500 TORCH FINE

Two years' imprisonment or a £500 fine may be shortly inflicted on persons who do not screen their electric torches, writes the "Daily Mirror" Political Correspondent.

The Ministry for Home Security will issue a stern warning on this subject.

Torch bearers will be told that they must have two sheets of white tissue paper over the bulbs of their lights and torches must be pointed downwards.

Screening paper must be white. Coloured paper has already led to accidents.

Although the maximum penalties are not likely to be imposed at once, heavy fines will certainly be inflicted.

Last night it was learned that she is expected to arrive this afternoon.

Lady Redesdale, her mother, and Deborah, her sister are with Unity in France.

Her father and brother, Flight Lieutenant Mitford, are ready to meet her when the stretcher-bearers carry her down the gang-plank into a waiting ambulance.

Two Mystery Girls

For Unity Mitford's head injury— she is stated to have been hit by a revolver shot in the neck while out walking in a park in Munich three months ago—is so serious that she can travel only in ambulance coaches.

Her wound was treated by specialists before she left Germany for Switzerland, but she is far from cured.

It may be a long time before she is able to tell the story of how she was shot.

When a little cabin plane with R.A.F. markings arrived at the airport, two pretty girls stepped from the machine—one bearing a striking resemblance to Unity Mitford.

They had flown from France that morning, and an official who was accompanying them told the *Daily Mirror*:

"These girls have been brought over here to do work of vital importance for the Air Ministry."

THE DAILY MIRROR, Saturday, Jan. 6, 1940.

Daily Mirror

No. 11,257   ONE PENNY
Registered at the G.P.O. as a Newspaper.

BELISHA RESIGNS

Stanley Is War Chief

Mr. Hore-Belisha . . . leaves the War Office and goes out of the Government.

Dispute With Generals

Mr. Oliver Stanley moves from the Board of Trade to take Mr Hore-Belisha's place.

A SENSATIONAL CHANGE IN THE WAR CABINET WAS ANNOUNCED LAST NIGHT. MR. LESLIE HORE-BELISHA, THE MAN RESPONSIBLE FOR PURGING THE ARMY COUNCIL OF ITS OLD MEN, HAS RESIGNED THE OFFICE OF WAR MINISTER. ACTUALLY, HE HAS BEEN DISMISSED BECAUSE THE GENERALS OBJECTED TO HIS REFORMS AND MADE REPRESENTATIONS TO THE PREMIER.

Hore-Belisha knew nothing of his fate until Mr. Chamberlain called him into conference yesterday. He was amazed and unhesitatingly refused the new post offered to him.

He is succeeded by Mr. Oliver Stanley, whose chief claim to fame is that he is a son of Lord Derby, himself a War Minister in the last war.

Lord Macmillan, the Minister of Information, has also resigned. The new Minister is Sir John Reith, famous first head of the B.B.C.

Sir Andrew Duncan, a leader of the iron and steel industry, becomes the new President of the Board of Trade, in succession to Mr. Stanley.

Neither Sir Andrew nor Sir John is at present in Parliament. Seats will probably be found for them.

The announcement of sensational Ministerial changes, made late last night, will stagger M.P.s of all parties, writes the "Daily Mirror" Diplomatic Correspondent. There had been no hint of differences in the Government.

The Ministry of Information, of course, has always been a weak spot in the Chamberlain administration, and Lord Macmillan's departure is scarcely surprising.

Revolt by Generals

But the resignation of the War Minister, at this stage in the war, is the biggest political sensation since hostilities began.

Despite the denials of policy differences in the letters that have passed between Mr. Hore-Belisha and the Premier, it is obvious that a War Minister does not resign unless he has been repudiated by his chief on a major issue.

It was, in fact, a revolt by the generals. Hore-Belisha's "live wire" methods, his demand for a democratic Army has roused the opposition of the military caste—the old gang of the Army Command.

The old gang took their case to the Premier, and Mr. Chamberlain, anxious to appease the generals, decided to sack his War Minister. It is the first victory of the generals.

Big Following

The Prime Minister offered Mr. Hore-Belisha another Ministerial post—almost certainly the Presidency of the Board of Trade, now vacated by Mr. Stanley. Belisha refused, he could scarcely have accepted.

The ex-War Minister has a big following in the House

Continued on Back Page

FINNS GET OUR BEST

BRITAIN is sending to Finland equipment and clothing originally intended for the British Army.

Besides helping Finland, Britain is sending arms and munitions to help Sweden's re-armament, it was announced in London last night.

Although Sweden is helping Finland, the arms and munitions sent to Sweden are for her own use.

Meanwhile the expansion of the British Army goes on and Britain's own war effort is still gathering speed.

While no details of voluntary recruitment can be published, it can be stated that the first hundred thousand has been easily passed.

National service has changed the whole character of the Army, it was stated. It has "completely democratised" the forces.

★ M. Paul Naggiar, French Ambassador to Soviet Russia, was reported last night to be following Sir William Seeds, the British Ambassador, from Moscow.

Sir William Seeds left on Tuesday, and the following day Signor Rosso, Italian Ambassador, left.

"DISSENSION IN ENEMY CAMP"

German political quarters welcomed the report of Mr. Hore-Belisha's resignation as an indication of possible dissensions in the enemy camp, and, secondly, because Mr Hore-Belisha is Jewish.

Foreign and unofficial suggestions that the resignation might portend peace overtures were considered unlikely by well-informed Nazis, in view of other developments, particularly the alleged British intention to extend the theatre of war to Scandinavia.—British United Press.

MR. OLIVER STANLEY ILL

Mr. Oliver Stanley, the new War Minister, was unable to attend the conference of the Federation of University Conservative and Unionist Associations yesterday, owing to illness.

He is in bed at his London home with a slight chill, but hopes to return to his duties in a day or two.

IT'S SOUND SLEEP THAT KEEPS NERVES STEADY

Simple Medical Facts that will help you

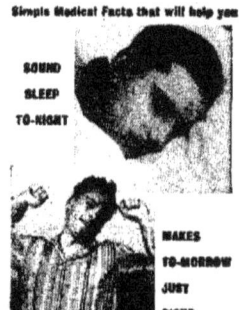

SOUND SLEEP TO-NIGHT

MAKES TO-MORROW JUST RIGHT

SLEEP DEPENDS ON NERVES

Among the aids made use of by medical science for the maintenance of the normal equilibrium in the nervous system are Calcium, Phosphorus, and Vitamin B. All these are therefore included in the scientific formula of Bourn-vita. Bourn-vita strengthens nerves while you are awake and further strengthens nerves by its ability to promote deep and restful sleep.

Still 9d per ½ lb   1/5 per ½ lb

CADBURY'S BOURN-VITA

PUTS YOU RIGHT THE NIGHT BEFORE

THE DAILY MIRROR, Wednesday, Jan. 10, 1940.

Daily Mirror

No. 11,260   ONE PENNY
Registered at the G.P.O. as a Newspaper.

"I HAVEN'T TOLD YOU ENOUGH," SAYS PREMIER

"I am certain that our people are united in their determination to win this war and to put an end to the spirit which dominates German policy. But what I am not quite so sure of is that they understand what they are up against or that we shall have to face a phase of this war much grimmer than anything we have seen yet.

"If that be so I am not blaming them. Perhaps it is because they have not been told anything about it.

"Perhaps it is the fault of the Government in general and myself in particular."

The Prime Minister in his Mansion House Speech yesterday (see Page Six).

He had been keeping things back—Mr. Chamberlain during his Mansion House speech yesterday.

BELISHA

Mr. Chamberlain made no direct reference to Mr. Hore-Belisha, but he said:—

"So long as I hold my present office and until war comes to an end, I will not be deflected nor will I shirk my inevitable responsibility in what I feel to be right no matter how difficult or even disagreeable that may be."

★

A "poison pen" attack on Mr. Hore-Belisha is reported on page 2.

Read also W. M. on "What we are up against." (Page 9.)

BRITISH LINER SUNK: WOMEN, KIDDIES SAVED

THE 10,000-ton British liner, Dunbar Castle, with 200 men and women on board, struck a mine and sank off the east coast of England yesterday.

Her master, Captain Causton, and a storekeeper were killed.

Three ships, one of them the British freighter Gowrie, were bombed and sunk by Nazi planes. Fishing smacks and two steamers were attacked in the North Sea by enemy planes.

A German plane machine-gunned and bombed a Trinity House boat taking relief crews to North Sea lightships.

The Dunbar Castle was outward bound to South Africa from London.

She had about fifty passengers, including nine children and her officers and crew numbered 150.

Survivors found drifting in two ship's lifeboats were picked up by a motor barge which brought them ashore.

At two coast towns last night men and women in tears waited for news of their loved ones.

Weeping women cried the names of their children; frantic men searched among the survivors for their wives and families.

One seaman, with water streaming from his clothes, strode ashore with a baby, three months old, in his arms. Passengers told vivid stories.

Mr. S. Jones, of South Africa, said that when the explosion occurred he was in the saloon playing cards with a young woman.

"The lights went out. I knew where the life-jackets were stacked. I got one, gave it to the girl, and got one for myself.

"When we got on deck the ship was listing over at a tremendous angle.

"The stewardesses were wonderful.

"I saw one who had much of her clothing burned off pulling one of the oars in the lifeboat. Another, after we had been picked up by a drifter, found one of the crew had been badly hurt and attended to him until we got him ashore.

"The explosion blew the foremast almost completely out of the boat.

"While we were in the lifeboat I saw one of the crew with a terrible wound on his head, who was nursing and comforting a baby."

Heroic Women

Able-Seaman Herbert Watts, of Watford, said: "When I rushed on deck after the explosion I saw that the bridge was completely wrecked and that one of the masts had fallen.

"The other crashed down on the deck as I stood there. We found the body of the captain outside his cabin door. I think he must have been on the bridge and was badly injured. He died trying to get the ship's papers.

"The engineer storekeeper, who had been badly crushed, died on board the lifeboat.

"The chief officer, Mr. Robertson, acted splendidly. He refused to leave the ship, and we had to pull him into the lifeboat by main force.

Out of the stories of calmness and heroism told by the survivors stands the tale of three heroic women.

They were three Sisters of Mercy who were among the forty-eight passengers.

Flung to the floor of their cabin by the force of the explosion, the three nuns clambered up on deck. As the crew, without the slightest trace of panic lowered the boats, the nuns calmly walked among the men, women and children waiting to be rescued.

One nun took a two-month-old baby from the arms of her mother and crooned a lullaby, while the mother adjusted her lifebelt.

Then, as the boats were lowered, and the passengers and crew took their places, one nun stood by on the sinking vessel murmuring prayers.

She refused to leave the sinking ship until the last of the dazed and injured people had been put into the boats. Then she calmly sat in the bow of the lifeboat nursing and comforting one of the children.

"All the women were calm," a
Continued on Back Page

Daily Mirror

JAN. 11

No. 11,261 — ONE PENNY
Registered at the G.P.O. as a Newspaper.

THE DAILY MIRROR, Thursday, Jan. 11, 1940.

R.A.F. IN 2 FIGHTS: ISLE RAIDED

R.A.F. planes fought two of the biggest battles of the war yesterday, one over the North Sea, the other over the Island of Sylt.

In the North Sea battle one British plane was lost; one German machine was shot down and another was forced down in Denmark. The R.A.F. machines continued their flight towards Germany.

Waves of British bombers attacked German seaplane bases on Sylt. The fight started in the early morning, continued until 7 p.m. At one time forty-five planes were seen fighting in the sky.

The attack on Sylt centred on the Hindenburg Dam, which is reported to have been damaged by bombs.

The North Sea battle was a clash between a British reconnaissance flight and a strong force of German fighters.

Our aircraft were flying 200 miles out from the English coast when the enemy fighters, diving with the sun behind them, opened their attack. The fight lasted nearly half an hour.

The attack was carried out by a number of Germany's latest and fastest fighters, twin engined, multi-gun Messerschmitt 110's.

Met the Challenge

Our aircraft met the challenge of their faster opponents by bringing the concentrated fire of guns of several aircraft to bear on the enemy fighters as they swept down to the attack. Even the heaviest close range attacks were successfully beaten off by our aircraft keeping "shoulder to shoulder" in tight and unshaken formation.

In the first wave of the fighter attack one of our aircraft was hit and dropped astern of the others. A second attack was launched immediately on this plane, which was then seen to fall into the sea.

The score was evened up a few minutes later, when an enemy fighter crashed into the water at high speed, throwing up great columns of foam within 400 yards of the nearest British aircraft.

Many of our gunners had been fir-

Contd. on Back Page, Col. 1

NOW 'MRS.', WON'T MISS RATIONS

A YOUNG Eastbourne woman faced a problem. She was about to be married and go on honeymoon, but on her ration card she was, of course, still " Miss "

How could she register at the hotel with her husband as " Mr. and Mrs." and then produce a ration card marked " Miss "?

"Doubtful Look"

The hotel people would look at them a bit doubtfully, to say the least.

So she called at the Food Control Office and asked that her ration card might be amended in advance. She explained her problem.

Satisfied with the genuineness of the application, the Controller "broke" the regulations and gave the desired amendment.

Some of the injured receiving attention at the foot of the lift shaft.

50 HURT AS LIFT CRASHES

WOMEN clasped children in their arms to save them as an Underground station lift, crowded with seventy people, swept 80ft. downward and crashed yesterday.

Fifty people were hurt—forty being taken to hospital.

The crash occurred at Hamilton-square Underground Station, Birkenhead, as home-going passenger traffic was at its height.

People were filling up the lift when suddenly it started downward. In a few seconds which seemed to the passengers like an eternity, it crashed at the bottom of the shaft.

People were knocked unconscious and flung in heaps, one on top of the other. The black-out made the confusion worse. Rescuers fell over injured people.

Baby in Arms

There were four women and two children in the lift. Most of the others were men from local shipyards.

Three of the women were together. They were Mrs. Dorothy Jump, aged twenty-three, of Daresbury-boulevard, Eastham, who broke her ankle, Mrs. Webster, her mother, who broke both legs, and a friend of hers, Miss Skerrett, of Worcester.

Mrs Jump had her two children

Contd. on Back Page, Col. 3

Women Asked to Aid Nation

THE Government are to take new steps to absorb every available man and woman into the nation's war effort, writes our Political Correspondent.

A questionnaire is to be issued in which everybody will be asked to set out what skilled work they can do.

THE GOVERNMENT SPECIALLY WANT TO KNOW THE HOBBIES OF MEN NOT NOW WORKING IN SKILLED TRADES.

A clerk, for instance, whose hobby is radio or motor-cars will be expected to hold himself in readiness to change his job.

The scheme is entirely voluntary. There is no suggestion of industrial conscription.

Nursemaids and domestic servants, for example, will be recruited for munition works.

Before that, the unemployed will, in large measure, have been brought back into industry.

IT IS HOPED, AS THE WAR GOES ON, TO TRANSFER 500,000 WOMEN NOW EMPLOYED IN NON-ESSENTIAL WORK INTO JOBS OF NATIONAL IMPORTANCE.

3 CONVICTS BREAK OUT

FORMER Dartmoor mutineer Alfred Sparks, alias Watson, was one of three convicts who escaped from Dartmoor Prison last night after a meeting in the prison chapel.

The men used an improvised rope ladder to scale the 20ft. boundary wall.

When the search in the precincts of the prison failed a police net was spread over the entire countryside. Warders searched the roads with torches and stopped all cars.

Some wooden forms and an improvised rope found lying at the foot of the boundary wall were the first indication to the prison staff that the men had got away.

Marching to Chapel

It is thought that they may have escaped when other convicts were being marched to the prison chapel to attend a choral class which is held there every Wednesday evening.

The three escaped convicts are:—

William Nolan, thirty; height, 5ft. 11in.; convicted at Kingston-on-Thames in September, 1938, for burglary and larceny.

Alexander Marsh, thirty-eight; 5ft. 4in.; convicted at Portsmouth last July for shopbreaking and larceny.

Alfred Sparks, thirty-eight; 5ft. 10in.; convicted at Kingston-on-Thames last February for house and garage breaking.

All have brown hair blue eyes and fresh complexion.

"Determined Criminal"

Sparks has been described as "a determined criminal."

He was sentenced to four years' penal servitude in 1932 for riotously damaging buildings at Dartmoor during the "mutiny."

At that trial he was stated to have escaped from Manchester Prison, but to have been recaptured the following day. When he was in Wandsworth Prison associates threw ropes over the wall, but Sparks was caught just as he was about to climb up them.

Mrs. Lillian Fish.

SCHOOL SWEETHEART DIED IN TRAWLER LEAVING HER A— BRIDE OF 6 DAYS

THEY fell in love at school. " It's just calf love—it won't last," friends said.

But their friends were wrong.

For Lawrence Fish and his sweetheart, Lillian Blackburn, were more in love with one another as they grew older.

Lawrence lived in Victor-street, Grimsby, as a schoolboy. Lillian lived just across the street. They used to walk home from school together every day, always happy and smiling.

The war came. Lawrence answered the call of the sea. He joined a trawler.

Before he went he asked Lillian to be his bride.

After two months' service at sea Lawrence was given a hard-earned leave. Just three days. They married.

Her Premonition

Back to sea he went. " I must do my bit," he told his bride. Reluctantly she let him go.

Now at nineteen, Lillian is a widow, robbed of her childhood hero by the war. He was drowned when the trawler was sunk by enemy action.

After years of courtship, marriage, and all that it means to a girl in love, had lasted only eight weeks for Lillian.

She had only lived with her husband during two short leaves—six days in all.

Tears in her eyes the young widow told the *Daily Mirror*:

" We had planned a nice little home for the end of the war. Now I shall have to spend some of my savings for furniture upon black clothes.

" But I must try to be brave as Lawrence always told me to be."

CHEAPER BATTERIES

ONE half of the torches-batteries grumble is to be met—the price is to be controlled. But there is still no guarantee, of course, that you'll be able to obtain one.

Further, foreign batteries, which are a considerable part of the supply, may be considerably dearer.

The Central Price Regulation Committee yesterday announced that retail prices of the more popular types of British batteries have been fixed as follows:—

	Pre-war price	Present price
Large torch unit cell	3½d.	4d.
Bijou battery (No. 8)	3d.	3½d.
Standard pocket lamp battery	5d.	6d.
Cycle lamp battery	8d.	9d.

Prices of other British batteries remain unchanged.

Retailers who charge more than fixed prices for British batteries may be reported to Central Price Regulation Committee.

THE DAILY MIRROR, Tuesday, Jan. 23, 1940.

Daily Mirror

JAN. 23

No. 11,271 — ONE PENNY
Registered at the G.P.O. as a Newspaper.

BLACK-OUT: HOW RAIDER SEES US

M.P.s will discuss today the mounting road toll in the black-out—just as a report is issued by the R.A.F. flyers who, for six weeks, have been flying over London by night to find out how the capital would look to a raider.

The flyers have used six planes for the night patrols, have covered the whole of the London area and are gradually patrolling the entire country. They report that, generally, the black-out is a success.

Pilots familiar with London have frequently been puzzled as to their exact whereabouts, although they knew they were over the capital.

So that although enemy planes could find their way to London with nothing to guide them from below, they could indulge only in indiscriminate bombing.

They could not hit a particular target.

Nor could the raiders be guided to London by the Thames. The R.A.F. observers report that beyond the estuary the river cannot be seen at all

Gaps In Black-Out

BUT there are gaps in the black-out curtain. The country, generally, is good. Some towns are extremely bad.

Pedestrians' torches can be seen from a considerable height, flashing miles away.

Some householders take care to hide their lights; some, particularly those whose houses back on to railway lines, do not.

Frequently the observation pilots have noticed a haze of light alongside railway lines.

This is what London looks like from the air by night:

A dense black background with instantaneous flashes going up over it all; star-like flashes from motor car lamps and torches, bigger lights from tube trains, trams and railway goods yards.

The new hooded railway signals are a great success. The red and green

Continued on Back Page

MAKES SOLDIER A ROYAL DRESS

A BRITISH soldier in the line in France is going to wear a dress designed and made by the Queen's dressmaker, Mr. Norman Hartnell.

At the same time he will put on make-up.

He is one of a concert party recruited from a battalion of the Yorkshire Regiment.

One soldier is regarded as the "beauty" of the regiment because he makes up so attractively as a young woman.

But all his personal charm could not overcome the handicap of rough ill-fitting feminine clothes.

An officer had the idea of writing to a friend who knows something of these matters.

"Yes," came the reply, "The lady" of the regiment should be fittingly dressed for the next show. Mr. Norman Hartnell agreed to produce the necessary garments.

Now everyone in the battalion is looking forward to the transformation from battle dress to beauty.

TWO BABIES

Two baby boys, born an hour or two before they were expected, have been given emergency shelter.

One was born in the Ritz Hotel, Piccadilly, before his mother could be hurried to the nursing home. The other was born in the street in Town Hall-square, Middlesbrough, before an ambulance could reach his mother.

✦ ✦ ✦

THE Ritz baby is the son of Lord Howland and great-grandson of the Duke of Bedford, whose estates are valued at £10,000,000.

Lord Howland is twenty-two years old. His wife, formerly Mrs. Clare (Brownie) Holloway, a society hostess, is thirty-five. She has a son aged eleven.

"Everything was prepared for my wife to go to a nursing home," Lord Howland said last night, "but she was taken suddenly ill and we arranged to have one of the Ritz suites turned into an emergency private ward.

"Our rooms look exactly like any others in the hotel except for the nurses who are always on hand.

£4-a-Day Suite

"We're very proud of our son and heir. At birth he weighed 6½lb. We haven't decided yet what to call him."

The suite costs £4 a day. The three rooms, decorated in nineteenth century style, overlook the Green Park.

Three bells at Lady Howland's side permit her to summon her chambermaid, her private nurses, the floor waiter.

Thick pile carpets soften the footfalls of messengers bringing choice flowers and gifts into the sickroom.

✦ ✦ ✦

THE Town Hall square baby has no name. His mother, hatless, with an old coat thrown over her thin dress, approached a special constable, whispered: "Please take me to a maternity home."

The policeman saw her distress, realised that she was shivering and afraid.

He raced to a telephone-box, summoned an ambulance and hurried back.

When he reached the woman's side her child had been born.

A blanket was brought from the police station. A police matron and a woman cleaner took care of the baby until an ambulance arrived.

"Both are doing well" the hospital reported last night.

The girl, aged twenty-two, unmarried and extremely poor, was nursing her son, heir to all the ages.

"He's a lovely boy," a nurse said. "He weighs 8½lb."

LIEUTENANT SHOT DEAD

Second-Lieutenant Michael George Sills, aged twenty-eight, of an anti-aircraft battery, was found shot dead in his hut.

At the Lincoln inquest yesterday the verdict was Death by misadventure. A medical officer said that the lieutenant's injuries suggested accidental discharge of a revolver.

ITALY: WAR MOVES

ITALY'S Cabinet met yesterday and agreed to speed up the country's preparedness for war.

Military contracts are now to have priority over civil orders—"to increase the efficiency of the armed forces in the present international situation."

Food is to be rationed. The Italians are already rationed on sugar; they get a third of the allowance issued in Britain.

The Cabinet also approved plans to economise in coal, coke and oil. Next winter no foreign coke or coal may be used for heating.

Italy is about to engage in a new search for gold. A mining company, already operating in Northern Italy, has been given further mineral rights.

Rumania Front

German armed forces, acting as railway police, have reached the Rumanian frontier, says Associated Press.

Russia, according to official information in Bukarest, has agreed to let Germany operate and police more than 200 miles of railways linking Rumania with Germany through Russian Poland.

✦ ✦ ✦

Radio Lyons, broadcasting in German last night, announced that the Germans have specially fitted out ships for the transport of troops across the Baltic—prelude to an invasion of Sweden.

U-BOAT SINKS NEUTRAL: KILLS 6

The Greek steamer Ekatontarchos Dracoulis (5,329 tons) has been sunk by a German submarine 150 miles south of the Portuguese coast.

Six of the crew were killed. Twenty-eight were saved by a Portuguese destroyer.

GIBRALTAR GUNS FIRE

The guns of Gibraltar fired yesterday. Later a destroyer and a seaplane manoeuvred around the spot where the shells were seen to fall.—Associated Press.

Dutch anti-aircraft batteries fired on a German warplane flying west between Rotterdam and The Hague yesterday. Dutch fighters went up in pursuit.

As the plane passed over the north-east coast a bomb scare was caused when a heavy object fell and damaged a building.

It is officially announced that Holland will protest to Germany over this violation of Dutch neutrality.

Holland has already protested about a German plane which flew over her territory on Saturday at Nijmegegen, Gelderland and The Hague, it was announced yesterday.—British United Press.

Holland Protests to Berlin

Miss O. Richards

LOVERS' RING— OF WIRE

A HASTILY made "engagement" ring, fashioned from a scrap of wire from a plane, has brought romance to Miss Olga Richards, twenty-two-year-old variety actress from Chingford (Essex), now in France with the "Hello Happiness" Company to entertain the B.E.F. and Air Force.

It was given her by a squadron leader who will soon make her his bride.

Two weeks ago, after a cold journey from England, the company arrived late at night at a town in the B.E.F. area, where they were to give the first of a series of shows.

But the E.N.S.A. arrangements had broken down. There was no one to meet the shivering players at the station, and they had no idea where to go.

Then Olga, a pretty brunette, saw a trim figure in the uniform of an R.A.F. officer. She ran to him and he gave a delighted smile of recognition.

It was a handsome young squadron leader whom she had met once before at a party in England just before war broke out.

She knew he was somewhere in France, but had never expected to see him again.

On Leave Soon

"For heaven's sake get us out of this jam," she implored the squadron-leader.

He did. He took charge of the whole company, and after vainly searching every hotel in the town for accommodation, took them out to his village, saw that they had hot food and put them to bed in tents.

The next day E.N.S.A. officials made a belated arrival, and the series of shows began. Every night the squadron-leader saw the show from the front row of the stalls.

On the company's last night in the town the squadron-leader asked Olga to marry him.

A very happy Olga said at her hotel at Air Force headquarters last night: "The squadron-leader goes on leave in ten days.

"By that time I shall be back in England, and we are to be married as soon as possible.

"We are very much in love and are both very happy."

NAVAL TRAWLER PRESUMED LOST

H.M. Trawler Valdora, temporary skipper Albert Potterton, R.N.R., is overdue and must be presumed to have been sunk.

Valdora was manned by a crew of nine ratings. The next of kin have been informed.

This announcement was made by the Admiralty last night.

13

THE DAILY MIRROR, Friday, Jan. 26, 1940.

Daily Mirror

JAN. 26

No. 11,274   ONE PENNY
Registered at the G.P.O. as a Newspaper.

Folly

MOTHERS BRING CHILDREN BACK TO DANGER

ASTONISHING figures of the numbers of evacuated children and mothers who have now returned to their homes in the danger zones were given in the House of Commons last night.

Of the 734,883 children who left home without their mothers, 315,192—nearly half—had returned by January 8.

There were 260,276 who were accompanied to safety by their mothers. Now 223,381 have gone home.

✦ ✦ ✦

Mothers evacuated totalled 166,206, and 145,681 have returned.

The figures are eloquent. It is the mothers who have taken their children back into perilous areas.
THIS IS FOLLY.

VICTORY ONLY IF WE ATTACK

"The only way to bring about the defeat of Germany is by overwhelming blows on land and sea and in the air."

THE President-elect of the Federation of British Industries, Colonel Lord Dudley Gordon, stated this in London yesterday.

"Economic warfare cannot be final except, perhaps, after a long period of years," he added.

"Nevertheless, our trade effort can have immeasurable results. Many of us have been accustomed to think of trade as something which flourishes in peace and languishes in time of war.

"That does not apply in the present advantageous position of Britain, and we should do all that is possible to eliminate the feeling of doubt abroad that we cannot maintain our export trade."

The tendency of other countries to look on Britain as in the front line of the war and unable to continue ordinary trade activities was due to German propaganda, he told a meeting of the Incorporated Sales Managers Association.

It Will Be a Hard War—
Sir N. Henderson

IT is going to be a hard war. It will last a long time. It is a war in which everyone must help wholeheartedly.

Thus Sir Nevile Henderson, ex-British Ambassador in Berlin, warned Britain yesterday in a speech at Sleaford, Lincs.

Britain had a great economic advantage, he said, but there was not going to be any early collapse in Germany. Wishful thinking would not win a war.

We would have to get 20s. out of every pound, for Germany, highly organised, was getting a mark for every mark.

He described an incident illustrating Field-Marshal Goering's passion for conserving every scrap of material likely to help Germany.

He said he was with Goering in his private train in Germany and the metal stopper of a bottle fell on the floor.

It looked as if it would be overlooked, but Goering ordered a servant to pick it up, remarking that Germany fed a hundred thousand pigs from the proceeds of used metal bottle-stoppers.

Crush Bullying by
Germans—Air Chief

"SO long as the German people allow themselves to be dominated and ruled by their present leaders, then so long must we hold the German people to their share of responsibility for war.

"So long as this continues, we must fight for a peace which is going to prevent those two German characteristics — bullying domination or supine weakness — from being allowed to threaten world peace in the future."

Captain H. Balfour, Under-Secretary for Air, made this statement when addressing his constituents at Ramsgate yesterday.

Says Mother Always Right

LOVELY Zoe Gail, eighteen-year-old South African actress, now playing at a London West End night club, is worried.

She has had a proposal of marriage, but she cannot say "Yes" until her mother—who is on her way from South Africa—arrives to give her consent.

Zoe's stepfather, who is a wealthy Johannesburg stockbroker, and her mother have cabled her: "Leave everything until mother's arrival."

Zoe, star of the Paradise Club show, told the "Daily Mirror":

"I never do anything without mother's consent. I think I've got a mother complex.

"Although I am in love, I shall let mother give her decision. Maybe she thinks I'm too young to become engaged.

"I am under a solemn promise not to mention the name of the man who has proposed to me.

"I shall do as mother says. Although I know it sounds old-fashioned, mother is always right."

Miss Gail has been in England for eighteen months. She was an amateur actress in South Africa.

NAVAL CONTROL OF SHIPYARDS

MERCHANT shipbuilding is to be put under Admiralty control. It will be speeded up to create a vast merchant fleet, writes the *Daily Mirror* political correspondent.

Shipyards that have been idle for years will be put into commission.

A meeting in London of the Labour National Advisory Council next week will discuss the speeding up of the war effort.

On this body the Government, employers and trade unions are represented.

Kiss Cures Cold

New cure for colds is—kissing. "A good healthy kiss generates so much heat that it destroys germs. The University ought to advocate more kissing."

This sporting statement comes from Dr. S. L. Katzoff, a psychiatrist, intervening in the revolt of students of the University of California against the sixty-day ban on kissing imposed by the University health officers after eighteen boys and girls were reported ill with influenza.—Associated Press.

R.A.F. PLANE SHOT DOWN

A British plane, which left its base in France yesterday to carry out a reconnaissance flight over North-west Germany failed to return, it was announced last night.

Berlin said that the plane was shot down over Duisburg, a Rhineland port with extensive docks and harbour accommodation, and claimed to be the largest inland port in the world.

WRECKED —SAVED BY BRIDE

ELEVEN men, survivors of a Swedish ship lost after an explosion, landed on a deserted islet off the Western Scottish coast—and were given a village wedding feast, to save their lives.

For days they had drifted in an open boat through icy seas. Three of them were gravely injured; all were exhausted, hungry, cold.

Boys in an island village two miles across the bay saw lights on the deserted isle, rowed out, saved the crew and brought them back to the village.

In the tiny Highland hamlet of eight houses there was little food for eleven starving men.

So, to end their hunger, a village bride gave them the wedding breakfast the islanders would have eaten in her honour next day.

The survivors were from the Swedish steamer Gothia. Three men were killed when she blew up.

The rest put off in two ship's boats. One with ten men aboard has not since been seen.

The other, with its eleven

Continued on Back Page

HITLER MEN RECALLED

GERMAN ministers to Rumania, Hungary, Yugoslavia, Greece and Bulgaria were summoned last night to Berlin for conferences, says a report from Budapest, Hungarian capital.

Germany has not demanded an increase of her oil quota from Rumania, it was officially announced in Bukarest, the Rumanian capital, last night.

Earlier it was reported that Germany had warned Rumania that she must send more oil to the Reich.

It was added that the German Government had told Rumania it would be forced to seek "other methods" if Rumania failed to ship oil more freely than the present total of 130,000 tons of raw oil a month.

£500,000 for Food

The German-Turkish agreement provides for the liquidation of £500,000 worth of German goods in Turkish warehouses. Turkey will send Germany foodstuffs in exchange.

Germany and Russia are reported to have signed a secret treaty in October. Russia promised to re-ship to Germany 35 per cent. of her imports of raw materials.—*Associated Press Exchange, British United Press.*

GERMANS SCUTTLE TRAPPED FREIGHTER

"THE German freighter Albert Janus (1,600 tons) was scuttled after being intercepted by one of our patrol ships," said the French war communique last night.

"A U-boat was successfully attacked by one of our patrol ships."

136 STUDENTS EXECUTED

Mr. Chamberlain told the House of Commons yesterday that the Government had received a report of the execution of 136 Polish students, some as young as twelve or thirteen, by the Germans.

Lieut. K———, of the ——— Regiment, stationed at ———, says

When I've only a minute for a stand-up meal it's

Fry's SANDWICH CHOCOLATE

2D AND 4D

THE DAILY MIRROR, Monday, Jan 29, 1940.

Daily Mirror

JAN. 29

No. 11,276 ONE PENNY
Registered at the G.P.O. as a Newspaper.

She's Hot on Ice

Skating on the Serpentine, the first time skating has been possible there for many years.

This picture was taken during Britain's cold spell which began last month.

Now turn to the middle pages for more pictures.

RAIL HOLD-UP GOES ON

BRITAIN'S railways yesterday suffered the biggest hold-up of the century. Some long-distance trains were more than twelve hours late; one London train took two hours to travel eleven and a half miles. Three trains were " lost."

The Night Scot from Glasgow was due at Euston at 6.42 a.m. It arrived at 5.50 p.m.

After it had crossed the Scottish-English border long halts were made in the middle of the night. It was not until daybreak that the passengers were aware that the train was so far behind time.

Passengers who had been asleep woke up with the dawn, washed and prepared for their arrival at Euston. Then they learned that they had not yet arrived at Preston.

The train's progress became even slower as the day wore on.

One young mother with two children had left Greenock, Renfrewshire, at 7.50 on Saturday night, and arrived in London nearly twenty-four hours later, instead of the scheduled eleven hours.

At 5.10 p.m.—nearly twelve and a half hours late—the Scottish Royal Mail steamed into Euston. A Post Office employee working on the train said, " We left Aberdeen at three o'clock on Saturday afternoon. Once we were held up for three hours; another time it took us nearly an hour to travel about 100 yards."

Two hours to do a journey of eleven and a half miles—that was the experience of about 100 passen-

Continued on Back Page

ROOFS OF 40 HOMES FALL

ROOFS of forty houses crashed in, in Inkerman-street, Aston, Birmingham, yesterday—but no one was injured.

One hundred and fifty people had to take shelter elsewhere.

Many people escaped unhurt because the roofs did not all fall in at the same time.

When the first roof crashed—at a house in Oxford-place—neighbours hurried out to help the occupants. Other roofs fell in at intervals.

Several people helping to save friends' furniture from the damaged houses had to dash home when their own roofs fell in.

A paralysed woman, Mrs. Hill, seventy-one, who lives in one of the houses, was carried from her home in an armchair and taken to the infirmary in a motor-van.

Furniture Problem

Mr. Harold Ashford, who lives in the house where the first roof fell took place, said:

"I don't know how to get my furniture out, because if we go into the house debris immediately starts falling."

Emergency arrangements were made by the Birmingham Corporation Estates Department for some of the occupants to be housed in municipal flats in Emily-street.

Several lorries were used to remove furniture from the damaged houses to the flats.

Others took refuge with friends.

OUR MILLIONS FOR U.S.

The U.S. Treasury revealed last night that in October, Great Britain and France spent about £30,000,000 of their assets in America in war purchases.

The November figure will probably be £125,000,000.—Exchange.

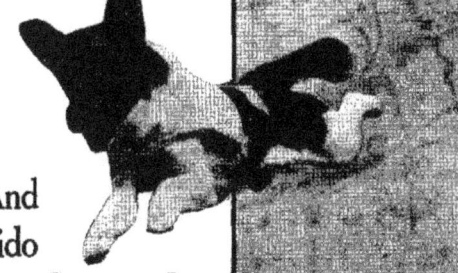

And Fido Can Step on It

FOUR RED DIVISIONS CRUSHED

FINNS claim to have inflicted a crushing defeat on the four Red divisions which had been battering their lines north-east of Lake Ladoga all last week in an effort to outflank the Mannerheim Line.

While no official estimate of the Russian casualties was available yesterday, Finnish soldiers believe that only a fraction of the Red troops escaped from the trap into which Mannerheim's generals led them.

Huge masses of booty were seized by the Finns.

Observers believe it is merely a question now whether the Red Army is able to withdraw from this sector in time to escape annihilation.

Red aviation has been quiet in the past three days and the Finns believe that the presence of Sir Walter Citrine's Trade Union Council delegation may be partly responsible for this lull.

Russian air activity yesterday was confined to the north. Material damage was slight, and the bombs killed only one civilian and wounded three.

Circles in Tallinn, which claim to have connections with leading Soviet politicians in Moscow, declare that Finland, if the war ends with a Russian victory will be colonised by Russians.

Both Stalin and Molotov are said to have radically altered their original plan which was to have established a Soviet Finland with a Government in Helsinki and have now decided that if the Russians succeed in occupying Finland, the inhabitants will be deported to various districts in Russia in the same way as was done years ago with the Finnish population in the Russian frontier districts.

Those Finns who are considered most dangerous will be sent to Siberia.

Associated Press, British United Press and Exchange.

PLANE LIFTED TOP OFF 2 HOUSES

FROM OUR OWN CORRESPONDENT

EXETER, Sunday.

A PILOTLESS R.A.F. plane crashed today into two Exeter houses, lifted off the top storeys of both homes, wrecked the bedroom in which a young bank clerk lay ill and left two families unhurt.

Three miles away, in a small forest near the village of Ide, two R.A.F. men parachuted to safety. A third, the pilot, came down in a timber yard.

All three had leaped for their lives when the plane seemed certain to crash.

When it plunged into two houses in Woodville-road the occupants, Mr. and Mrs. A. Royston and their guest, a young bank clerk, and Mr. and Mrs. Reed and their two young children, thought that air raids had begun.

So did the neighbours. " My husband and I and my baby Vicki—she's two and a half—were in the front room when a great shadow darkened the sky," said Mrs. E. Long, who lives opposite.

Crash and Roar

" There was a crash and a roar. The two houses opposite seemed to tumble down.

" I grabbed my baby. 'It's a bomb,' I screamed.

" The baby repeated after me, 'A bomb, a bomb—what's a bomb, mummy?'

" Then I looked out of the window and saw the wrecked plane and the people running out of the houses."

Mr. and Mrs. J. Condliffe, who also live opposite the wrecked houses, were dozing off after a cup of tea when the crash occurred.

" I heard the drone of a plane," said Mr. Condliffe. " Glancing out of the window I saw that it was coming straight for us.

" We dashed out, and reached the road as the plane crashed.

" I ran into the house and shouted: 'Is everyone all right?' Mr. and Mrs. Royston and their twelve-year-old son dashed out. Just then a pyjama-clad figure appeared at the top of the stairs—it was the sick bank clerk.

" Blinded by petrol fumes and covered from head to foot with plaster, he stumbled to the foot of the stairs.

" He was calm and made a joking remark. His chief concern seemed to be for his lost spectacles."

ESCAPE

"WEIGH anchor." The 8,245-ton Dutch tanker Mamura was preparing to move to a new berth off the south-east coast last night.

As the chain rattled in, it exploded a mine. A huge column of water roared up just ahead.

But the mine was several fathoms down. This depth deadened the blast.

The Mamura was undamaged.

If the captain had steamed a yard or two ahead before dropping anchor, he would have been right over the mine.

Four of his crew were treated on shore for slight injuries and shock.

Daily Mirror

DAILY MIRROR, Wednesday, Jan. 31, 1940.

No. 11,278 — ONE PENNY
Registered at the G.P.O. as a Newspaper.

JAN. 31

DEMANDS SECRECY FOR 'WREN'

Constance Moorat, the Admiralty woman dispatch rider, photographed yesterday.

A "WREN" dispatch rider who punched a policeman and knocked his helmet off was fined 40s. at Westminster Police Court yesterday for assault.

For a traffic light offence she was fined 30s.

When the woman—Constance Helena Margaret Moorat, aged twenty-five, whose address was given as Room 12, West Block, The Admiralty—stepped into the dock in her blue W.R.N.S. uniform a naval lieutenant-commander asked that " anything that might come out" should be withheld from the Press.

"You must leave that to the discretion of the Press; they will act quite properly," replied the magistrate, pointing out that he had no authority to control the Press

"Don't Report It"

Afterwards reporters were approached by the officer who urged that the case should not be reported. When the *Daily Mirror* representative agreed to pass the request to his Editor, saying it was most improbable he would accede to it, the officer remarked: "I must get into touch with Sir Walter Monckton"—the Chief Censor.

Soon afterwards a telephoned request was made by the Admiralty to the "Daily Mirror" asking that all mention of the case should be kept out of the paper.

The *Daily Mirror* considers that nothing stated in court could be of the smallest assistance to the enemy But for efforts to prevent publication the case differed only in details from assault charges heard daily

And as the case is of public interest, the "Daily Mirror" has no intention of suppressing it.

Moorat pleaded guilty.

Police-Constable John Shorto, on duty at the Knightsbridge junction with Sloane-street, saw a motor-cycle driven towards Kensington fail to stop as traffic lights changed from amber to red, thus causing severe dislocation.

Moorat, the rider, said: "I am allowed to cross the lights."

"I told her she would be reported," continued the officer, and she said: 'Your girl must have let you down last night.'

"Wanted Revolver"

"She hit my books from my hand. As I bent to pick them up she knocked my helmet off. She hit me three times across the face with her clenched fist."

The blows hurt, but he was not bruised.

When told that she would be arrested, she said: "We are going to be issued with revolvers. I wish I had mine now. It would be useful."

Moorat said she was sorry that eagerness to execute orders had caused her to commit the offences.

"May I apologise? The dispatch was urgent; it really was a matter I could not delay any further."

Moorat was driven from the court in a car with another Wren of similar rank, the lieutenant-commander, and a Wren officer.

★ See Cassandra—page 10.

Coal Ration Now Two Cwt.

Coal deliveries to householders are to be restricted to two cwt. a week, except by licence in hardship cases.

Instructions to this effect have been given by the Mines Department to local fuel overseers all over England.

Hospitals and similar essential institutions will receive adequate supplies.

The coal ration dated originally from October 1, 1939, and at first consumers could obtain 75 per cent. of their previous year's purchase.

Coal trains began running into London again yesterday. Normal running, it is hoped, will be nearly re-established today.

PLANE TO DROP FOOD

A DRAMATIC appeal for food supplies was made to the *Daily Mirror* last night by Miss A. Griffin, manageress of a Crawford, South Lanarkshire, hotel where more than seventy men, women and children, passengers from a London-bound train and motor-coach are stranded.

An aeroplane may fly over the isolated village today and drop packages of food for the marooned travellers and villagers who have been cut off from the outside world for three days.

"Our plight has become serious," said Miss Griffin. "We have no means of getting food through and we cannot get bread or milk.

"I have asked for an aeroplane to be sent with food supplies if there is no sign of the weather situation being overcome.

Three-day Ordeal

"Fortunately we had good stocks of tinned milk in the hotel and have been able to carry on so far despite the large number of enforced guests.

"The last three days have been an ordeal for the hotel staff as well as for our visitors from the trapped London train and coach."

Although its population has been increased by hundreds of workmen brought down to open the blocked

Contd. on Back Page, Col. 4

AND HE SPOKE OF MERCY

TWENTY-FOUR men of a British steamer sunk by a Nazi plane sprawled helpless with injuries and cold on small rafts swept by wild seas.

Above them a Nazi plane circled and dived, death cracking from its machine-guns.

The men did not look up. Helplessness numbed them. They lay limp on the rafts, or sat with their heads in their hands.

One by one death took them. One by one they rolled off into the sea. Until only three were left.

The men on the rafts were the crew of the London steamer Stanburn. The story of their death was told when the steamer Gripfast, of Newcastle, struggled into harbour yesterday.

The Gripfast was also attacked, and the crew of seventeen machine-gunned as they crowded one small boat. But later they went back to their ship.

"Frozen Numb"

The master of the Gripfast, Captain Allen, said: "We saw the plane drop two bombs on the Stanburn.

"Both her lifeboats were smashed, and her crew scrambled on to little rafts—seven or eight on each. Most were wearing only a thin singlet and dungarees. One man was naked.

"We went to try to pick them up while the plane sprayed bullets.

"Kneeling on one raft was a man who slowly lifted his head. We hailed him. He raised his arms. We threw him a line—but it just trailed across his hands which were covered with blood. The waves were as big as houses."

The Gripfast fought twenty hours to reach a little harbour. As, with plates stove-in, she rolled helplessly aground on rocks, her wounded were brought ashore.

And the first was Larry Thomas, of Cardiff, sixteen, messboy.

In his thigh was a German bullet. He had been shot while in the boat.

★ In his speech last night, Hitler said: "The British walk around with the Bible in their hands, but they treated Germany without any feeling of mercy."

ENGLAND WILL GET WAR NOW
—Says Hitler

"AFTER Munich I wanted to talk, to go on negotiating. They wanted war. Very well, now they will get a fight. It will be England's turn to see what war is like."

Hitler roared out that threat in the Sports Palast, Berlin, last night—the seventh anniversary of his rise to power.

It was a bitter attack on England, on "old man Chamberlain" and on Churchill.

"We can assure Churchill that we know what Britain and her friends have done in the last five months, but I doubt if he knows what we in Germany have done in the past five months.

"We have done tremendous work, so much that it overshadows the past five years. Our armament is now running according to plan. Our foresight is bearing fruit, such good fruit that the enemy is now beginning to copy. But they are poor copyists."

Hitler began with his usual recitation—the evils of Versailles. Then he spoke with heavy sarcasm of England fighting for ideals—"she always fights for ideals"—and his frequent references to the "Bible-reading Chamberlain" were greeted with loud guffaws.

"When Chamberlain stands up as a preacher and proclaims his stupid war aims I say: You betray yourself. For 300 years your statesmen have been explaining that England went to war only for God and religion.

"English history is one series of rapine, plunder, blackmail and terror.

Says "I Warned"

"If Chamberlain walks with a Bible, it is the same as if the devil was studying the prayer book.

"Churchill expresses what old Mr Chamberlain thinks to himself: 'Our goal is the destruction and extirpation of Germany.'"

All this was in the true Hitler opening strain. His voice was low, he stuttered slightly, then the voice rose to a shriek as he launched one tirade after another against England.

"In 1938 the old, well-known warmongers in the Western Powers came to power again. I raised my warning voice

"In 1939 they wanted war. They did not want an understanding.

"All right then. They have got war.

"I can tell England and France that they, too, will get battle as our other enemies have.

"Germany and Italy are still close friends.

"I attempted last year to forestall

Contd. on Back Page, Col. 2

GERMANS LAND IN LUXEMBOURG, ESCAPE

A GERMAN warplane landed at Hosingen, Luxembourg, about two miles from the German frontier (reported Associated Press last night).

The crew of three asked Luxembourgers where they were. When they were told, they jumped into the plane and took off for Germany.

LOVE BEATS LEAVE BAN

ALTHOUGH leave from France has been stopped because of the weather, a young member of the R.A.F. flew home yesterday in the special messenger plane—so that he can be married tomorrow.

His wedding had twice before been postponed. Once when the aircraftman was drafted abroad and once when his leave was stopped.

The new stopping of leave brought the prospect of a third postponement and visions of a sobbing bride.

But the R.A.F. has a heart. A report of the special circumstances of the case was placed before O.H.Q. and a swift decision was made—the man was to be given every possible facility to get home, weather or no weather. Cupid, it was apparently felt, could be trifled with once too often.—*Exchange*.

BROADCAST CANCELLED

RADIO programmes to the B.E.F., which are broadcast by the B.B.C. on 342 metres, were suddenly cancelled last night.

An official told the "Daily Mirror": "I am sorry, but we can give no reason for the suspension of the programme. As far as I know the cancellation is for tonight only."

The B.B.C. announced last night that Mr. F. W. Ogilvie, the Director-General, is visiting the B.E.F. to get a first-hand impression of the tastes of the troops, and the conditions in which they are able to listen.

He is also meeting representatives of the French broadcasting authorities to discuss matters of mutual interest.

SCHUSCHNIGG IN MUNICH

Dr. Schuschnigg has been moved to Munich, states Paris Radio, according to a message from Berne.

His left side is reported to be paralysed and he is nearly blind in the left eye.

Daily Mirror

DAILY MIRROR, Friday, Feb. 2, 1940.
No. 11,230 — ONE PENNY
Registered at the G.P.O. as a Newspaper.

Meet Mr. Skotnicki

WAR DEAL SUSPENDS OFFICERS

TWO Army officers have been suspended by the War Minister pending an inquiry into the supply deal revelations made in the House of Commons by Mr. Burgin, the Minister of Supply, after the matter had been raised by Mr. Ernest Thurtle, M.P.

"In view of the allegations made publicly against two military officers," Mr. Oliver Stanley, the War Minister, said in the House of Commons yesterday, "I propose to institute an inquiry at once."

Mr. Thurtle claimed and Mr. Burgin did not deny that a man with a prison record, Charles

(Continued on Back Page)

TRAIN TRAPS GIRL

GOING home from her work in the black-out, Miss Kathleen Phelan, of Clifford-road, Hounslow, Middlesex, stepped between two coaches of an electric train at Boston Manor (Piccadilly Line) station.

As the train gathered speed, she ran forty yards between the rails. Then the train was stopped by a passenger who heard her screams.

And yesterday she was back at work as usual, serving customers in a Brentford cafe.

"I Held On"

She said yesterday: "I thought I was getting into a carriage. Instead, I fell feet first to the rails and before I could get out, the train started.

"I held on to a pipe and ran screaming between the rails with the train. Then it stopped and I climbed on to the platform just as station officials were rushing to find me.

"I don't know how I kept off the live rail. I was told that if the train had left the station I should have been killed.

"I escaped with cuts on one leg and they treated me at the station. I would not go to hospital as I wanted to be at work next day.

"My boss wanted me to stay at home and rest, but I thought if I came to work I would not feel the shock so much."

Charles Kinsler Skotnicki—a "Daily Mirror" picture taken in his office in Piccadilly, London, where he spent the day doing business.

EX-KAISER: JOIN TO FIGHT RUSSIA

THE ex-Kaiser believes that Germany, Britain and France should cease fighting each other and join to fight Russia.

This opinion is expressed in a letter to Mr. Poultney Bigelow, his friend for many years, which Mr. Bigelow made public last night in New York.

The ex-Kaiser wrote from Doorn on January 16:—

"The magnificent stand of the Finns has smashed the nimbus of Bolshevism and set people thinking, with the result that the wish for peace is gaining ground.

"The belligerents should stop fighting and join their forces to help the Finns.

"They should fight in one line to rid the world and civilisation of Bolshevism."

The ex-Kaiser is now a haggard old man of eighty-one. Anxiety has recently been felt for his health, weakened by his worrying over the war.—Associated Press.

MEAT BY PARACHUTE

Meat rations were on Wednesday dropped by parachute to an Army unit in Scotland cut off by road and rail.

Colonel Hayley, D.S.O., O.B.E., the War Office official who, it is alleged, in Parliament, introduced Mr. Scott—or Skotnicki—to Ministry of Supply officers. They, in turn, introduced him as a financial agent to Government contractors.

THE KING'S COLD

The King has a slight cold, and is confined to his room, it was officially announced at Buckingham Palace yesterday.

The *Daily Mirror* understands that the King is remaining in his room as a precautionary measure, and that the cold is of such a slight nature that he hopes to be about again, carrying on his normal duties, in a day or two.

94 BRITISH SEAMEN PRISONERS

THIRTY survivors from the British submarine Undine, thirty-seven or thirty-nine from the Starfish and twenty-seven from the auxiliary cruiser Rawalpindi are now interned in barracks in the town of Spangenberg, south of Cassel, it is learned in Berlin.

Nothing can be learned about any survivors from the submarine Seahorse, and it is believed that the whole crew perished.

Lord Haw-Haw broadcast last night a further list of submarine survivors. They are:—
Chief Petty Officer E. A. Evans, born May 15, 1903, in Plymouth. Naval badge SM34916.
Stoker Evan Wellis, born February 23, 1916, at Tylorstown, Glamorgan, South Wales. Naval badge BK87232.
Stoker (First Class) Ronald Bowrer, born April 12, 1917, at Gillingham, Kent. Naval badge CK86189.
Seaman Patrick Graham, born August 2, 1916, at Downpatrick, Ireland. Naval badge DJ128563.

U.S. TAKES 30,000 JEWS

The U.S. Immigration Bureau reports to Congress that 82,998 alien immigrants were admitted in the year ended July 1, compared with 67,895 the previous year.

Immigrants from Germany numbered 33,515, of whom the bureau listed 30,096 as Jews.

NAVAL CAPTAIN FOUND DEAD

CAPTAIN Charles Ernest Hotham, Captain of the Fleet on the staff of Admiral Sir Dudley Pound, was found dead yesterday in his rooms at Valetta, Malta.

Captain Hotham was appointed to the staff of Sir Dudley, Mediterranean Commander-in-Chief, two years ago.

Previously he had been flag captain, and chief staff officer on the Yangtze command, where he was in command of H.M.S. Bee.

After the war Captain Hotham, who was awarded the D.S.C., was appointed navigator of the Admiralty yacht.

Third Officer —————— W.R.N.S. stationed at ————— says

When I've only a minute for a stand-up meal it's

Fry's SANDWICH CHOCOLATE

2d AND 4d

Daily Mirror

DAILY MIRROR, Saturday, Feb. 3, 1940.

No. 11281 — ONE PENNY
Registered at the G.P.O. as a Newspaper.

B.E.F. Told to Save

All over the B.E.F. area notices have been posted telling all ranks: "Fight waste as you would fight the enemy," and reminding them that the war is costing £6,000,000 a day. "Do not forget," say the notices, "that your families at home are rationed, and extravagance in the field is a disgrace when families at home are short of anything."

NEW LOVE CANCELS WEDDING

ON the eve of her marriage to a flying officer, titian-haired Ursula Gillespie, film and stage actress, told the "Daily Mirror" last night that she had cancelled her wedding.

She has fallen in love with another man.

The engagement of Miss Gillespie, daughter of a dentist, of Chirton, Clifton-road, Newcastle-on-Tyne, to Flying-Officer Brian Peter Hosewood Page, of Sutton, Surrey, was announced some weeks ago.

The wedding should have taken place at St. George's Church, Newcastle, today.

She said Flying-Officer Page had travelled north after the wedding had been cancelled, but she would not reveal the reason for his visit.

"The wedding is definitely off," she said. "I am not marrying anyone tomorrow anywhere.

"I have nothing to say about any new romance."

In Car Accident

Miss Gillespie's sister said: "My sister cancelled the arrangements for the wedding less than a week ago.

"She is planning to marry someone else in the near future, but we do not think it fair at the moment to reveal his name."

Last June Miss Gillespie was awarded £624 and agreed special damages of £240 for injuries she received in an accident when she was travelling in a car driven by her father.

ALIENS GET THE BEER

ALIENS detained in this country are to be allowed new privileges, the Home Secretary announced yesterday.

They will be allowed a pint of ale every day; or, if they prefer it, stout, cider or a half bottle of wine.

The prisoners—all will also be allowed to wear their own clothes, to write and receive letters, to smoke and to do work for wages.

✦ ✦ ✦

CONTRAST: Until war began, wounded men of the last war in the Star and Garter Home, Richmond, were given a pint of beer every day. When war was declared the beer was stopped for economy reasons. There were protests.

Now the men get their beer three days a week.

✦ ✦ ✦

QUESTION: Is it better to be an enemy alien of this war than a wounded British soldier of the last?

Film actress Miss Ursula Gillespie, who was to marry Flying-Officer Brian Peter Hosewood Page, of Sutton, Surrey, announced last night that the wedding will not take place.

Czech Anthem Stops Radio

A CZECH actor silenced a German station broadcasting a play from Prague last night.

He was taking part in the broadcast and began to declaim the Czech national anthem, "Where is my home?"

Immediately the station closed down. Three minutes later it came on the air again—with a talk on the Arctic.

✦ ✦ ✦

The Vatican radio station was heavily jammed.

A German speaker said the Totalitarian State was trying to widen the distance between the believer and the priest.

"But here," he said, "totalitarianism has arrived at its end."

Immediately jamming began.—(Associated Press messages.)

BOOMPS FOR LADY ASTOR

AN eighteen-year-old Ajax rating, Leslie Bradley, of Louth, Lincs, danced the "Boomps-a-Daisy" with Lady Astor at a celebration ball at Plymouth Guildhall last night.

He did not know who his partner was until the dance was over, and then at her request he told her the story of the battle with the Graf Spee.

Leave Celebration

The Ajax men were celebrating the news that 300 of them are to go on a fortnight's leave on Monday.

The news was given to the crew as they left the ship. The rest of the men will have their leave when the first batch returns.

More than a thousand people feted the men at the ball. Lord and Lady Astor, who are Mayor and Mayoress of Plymouth, entertained officers to dinner and later went with them to the ball.

GLUT OF BACON —2D. OFF

BY A SPECIAL CORRESPONDENT

BACON AND HAM PRICES WILL BE REDUCED NEXT WEEK BY AN AVERAGE OF 2D. A LB.

That official announcement last night reveals the muddle of the existing bacon rationing plan.

The Ministry of Food declared that bacon was scarce before Christmas, but since then imports have come forward with remarkable regularity.

It was added that "it must not be assumed that the present large supplies and low prices can be maintained for more than a short time."

The fact is that shopkeepers have had so much surplus bacon, unsaleable

Continued on Back Page

IT ISN'T THEIR WAR

A SHIP'S lifeboat with a tattered canvas for a sail and twenty exhausted men lying along the thwarts, headed through the mists of an Irish channel.

A motor-boat hailed them, threw them a rope . . . and another Atlantic voyage was over.

For five days and nights the seamen had fought their way through a storm; hungry, thirsty, cold. They started out thirty-three strong. Five of them went mad and died. Eight more died of exposure. And twenty of them came back.

Their ship, the Greek steamer Eleni Stathontas (9,000 tons) was torpedoed without warning in the Atlantic last Sunday morning.

The crew took off in two lifeboats. One of the boats was caught and cut in two by the still-turning propeller, and all thirty-three men crowded into one little boat.

Men Went Mad

One of them was an Irishman, Michael Ryan, of Tullabrack, County Limerick. The rest were Greeks.

"There were some dry biscuits in that boat," Ryan said yesterday, "a tin of water and some corned beef—for thirty-three of us.

"By Tuesday our rations were exhausted, and as night fell two men went mad.

"They died soon and we quietly slipped them overboard and rowed on. Next morning the horror increased. Three more men began to rave.

"They died, too, and we buried them as the gale roared.

"By now the younger men were in a pitiable condition. Men died where they sat and there was nothing you could do to help them.

"During Wednesday night we saw a trawler and I signalled to her with a police whistle. But she put out her lights and sailed away.

"When dawn broke on our last day we saw a sailing vessel.

"I and seven others leaped to the oars and pulled towards the ship . . . but she vanished.

"We kept on sailing and hours later I saw land and a village on a foreland, and I knew we had made Ireland."

The master of the ship, Dimitrios Gradson, was one of the survivors. He said:

"I am a neutral. But surely this is not war. It is murder."

I HAVE 'PEACE-TIME SLEEP' AT A PEACE-TIME PRICE...thanks to BOURN-VITA

When you've plenty to worry about there's all the more reason to feel equal to it. Don't walk about feeling like a blackout in a coal-cellar — it hinders you and everyone else. Make sure of sound *natural* (NOT drugged) sleep. *That's* the best nerve-tonic that ever was invented.

MORAL: Start Bourn-vita to-night!

9d PER ¼ LB • 1/5 PER ½ LB

CADBURY'S BOURN-VITA STILL AT PEACE-TIME PRICE

DAILY MIRROR, Monday, Feb. 5, 1940

Daily Mirror

No. 11,232   ONE PENNY
Registered at the G.P.O. as a Newspaper.

Gas Mask Service Stations

Service stations for testing gas-masks are shortly to be set up all over the country, writes the "Daily Mirror" Political Correspondent. These centres will be under the control of local authorities.

Anyone who has a defective mask will be able to take it to the local centre for examination. If the defect is due to deterioration, the damage will be repaired or a new respirator issued free.

Gas masks are likely to suffer from wear and tear.

BURGIN: VOTERS WANT TO KNOW

MURDER MEN SAVED BY TRAWLER

FIVE men in a Nazi murder plane, realising that their shattered machine could not carry them home, deliberately crashed near one of the unarmed British trawlers they had been attacking—and four of them were saved from the sea.

The fifth died in the sea before he could be rescued. One died of multiple wounds in the trawler.

Three more, two of them wounded, were landed at Grimsby yesterday by the trawler Harlech Castle, whose crew told the story of the rescue.

The German bomber, one of twenty that raided the English coast on Saturday, bombing and machine-gunning defenceless ships, was furiously attacked by a British fighter.

"We knew we could never reach Germany again," one of the wounded airmen said last night as he lay, bandaged, in a bed in the Harlech Castle.

"I sighted a trawler and pointed it out to the pilot.

"He said, 'I will land near the trawler. When we touch water, jump into the sea. The British will save us.'

"We jumped and four of us were picked up. The other man was lost."

Skipper Thomas Trendall, of the Harlech Castle, telling the story of the rescue, said:

"We saw the air battle and the German machine dive down to the water quite near us.

"Before we could reach them the machine had sunk, but the Germans were left struggling in the water.

"They were wearing life-jackets which kept them afloat. I manoeu-

Continued on Back Page

Arline Judge.

NO GLAMOUR AS HIS WIFE —£62,500

FROM JOHN WALTERS
("Daily Mirror" Correspondent)
New York, Sunday.

MILLIONAIRE U.S. playboy Daniel Reid Topping, was entranced by Arline Judge, known as Hollywood's shapeliest actress, and married her.

But when she gave up her career to give him a family he decided Arline Judge was more glamorous than Mrs. Daniel Topping, mother of his son.

That is Arline's explanation of the change that has caused her to sue him for divorce alleging "intolerable cruelty."

She is receiving a settlement of £62,500 and the divorce is expected to become final next April.

Convent Girl

Arline, ex-convent girl, will also get full custody of their two-year-old son. Topping's name has recently been romantically linked with that of skating star Sonja Henie.

Of this Arline told me:—

"I am very fond of Sonja, and if Dan interests her in the romantic way, I hope he will be very happy. I cannot think of a nicer girl for him to be interested in."

Arline married Topping the day she divorced screen actor Wesley Ruggles.

Stalin Sends Hitler Bear, Goering Caviare

Caviare for Goering . . . a bear for Hitler.

These are the "supplies" now reaching Germany from Russia.

The caviare is sent daily by air, according to Paris radio. Caviare has always been a passion with Goering.

"This is the only supply arriving punctually from Russia," the Paris announcer said last night.

The Russian bear from the wild Siberian forests will be flown to Germany on Tuesday. It will be put in the Berlin zoo.

The animal is a rare specimen seldom seen in captivity.—British United Press.

£250,000 GRAIN FIRE

A FIRE yesterday at a large grain store at Newhaven, Sussex, known locally as "Stricklands Granary," destroyed foodstuff valued at £250,000.

Two fire brigades, helped by the pumps of two tugs lying in the harbour and others worked by auxiliary firemen and the fire staffs of local firms, fought hard to save the grain.

Several Men Hurt

After about three hours the fire was got under control, but by then the roof had fallen in. The noise of the crash was heard five miles away.

The cracking of red hot slates sounded like pistol shots and the heat could be felt a hundred yards away.

Several men were injured by blazing tiles which fell from the roof.

The Brighton and Newhaven fire brigades were still standing by hours afterwards to prevent the smouldering grain flaming up again.

THE KING AT WINDSOR

The King and Queen spent the week-end at Windsor, and attended morning service at the Royal Chapel, Windsor Great Park, yesterday. The King has now completely recovered from the cold which kept him indoors for two days last week.

HE DIED FOR CHILDREN

A DOCTOR gave his life for his children yesterday when his car ran into a deep stream by the Petworth-Chichester road.

Dr. Stephen Pegum, of Selsey-avenue, Bognor Regis, was driving down a half-mile slope when the accident occurred.

The car plunged into the stream where it was 4ft. deep. Dr. Pegum was flung against the windscreen and injured his head severely.

His only thought was for his children.

Dazed by his injury, he staggered from the car, then lifted out his children and carried them through the water to safety, helped by Mr. Rex Vicat-Cole, sixty-nine, an artist.

No sooner were his children safe than Dr. Pegum collapsed in the water. He died while being taken to hospital in another car.

Soon afterwards Mr. Rex Vicat-Cole collapsed in the garden of his home at Up-Waltham. He was found there by his son, and died later.

Landscapes in London—Hyde Park, Kensington Gardens and the Thames —made the name of Mr. Rex Vicat-Cole, third of four generations of painters, well known in the world of art.

Educated at St. John's Wood Art School, he exhibited at the Royal Academy for nearly forty years. He was also author of several books on art.

GIRLS' SCHOOL BLAZE

Banbury Municipal School, which has about 800 pupils, including evacuees from Fulham Girls' High School, was badly damaged by fire yesterday.

Auxiliary firemen helped the Banbury brigade to fight the fire, which, it is thought, may have started in a laboratory.

FROM OUR SPECIAL CORRESPONDENT
LUTON, Sunday.

THE local Labour Party at Luton, Mr. Burgin's hat-making constituency in Bedfordshire, held an emergency meeting this afternoon.

The main topic of discussion was the Scotnicki affair—the House of Commons admission by Mr. Burgin, Minister of Supply, that Charles Kingsley Scott or Scotnicki had been introduced as a financial agent by Army officers, although he was a man with a prison record.

In an exclusive statement published in his name in the Sunday Pictorial today, Mr. Scott said:

"Ten years ago . . . the firm of solicitors who handled my affairs were Messrs. Denton, Hall and Burgin. And Mr. Leslie Burgin was a member of that firm.

"When he was fighting his election at Luton, two of my cars were used for transporting electors on polling day."

"Came as Shock"

When the Labour Party meeting ended today, Mr. J Roberts, the chairman, issued this statement:

"The reported connection, long ago as it seems to be, between Mr. Burgin and this man who was later convicted, has come as a shock and a surprise to the people of this town.

"I can tell you that the Luton Labour Party will not let the matter rest. We shall discuss the whole affair at tomorrow's annual meeting of the party, and, if necessary, ask Mr. Burgin for an explanation."

Mr. Kerran, prospective Labour candidate for the division, said:—

"I feel that the whole affair requires urgent investigation, and I feel sure that the Labour Party in the House will press for an explanation."

Conservative circles here, torn between loyalty to the National Government and sympathy with their Liberal member, were cautious.

"We are watching this with interest," one of the party chiefs said tonight, "we must see how the cat jumps."

SOLDIERS JUMP FROM TRAIN AT TUNNEL

Two soldiers under escort escaped from a London-bound train yesterday when it pulled up near Watford tunnel, scene of the landslide earlier in the day (reported on page 3).

The men, eluding their escort, jumped from the carriage, scrambled up the embankment and dashed across fields beside the track.

The train continued its journey. A description of the men has been given to the Herts police.

NEW HOUSE DEATH RIDDLE

A middle-aged man with one ear cut off was found lying dead in a partly-built house at Havering-gardens, Chadwell Heath (Essex) yesterday.

Police found the man had died from extensive knife wounds, which they believe were self-inflicted.

Early this morning the man had not been identified.

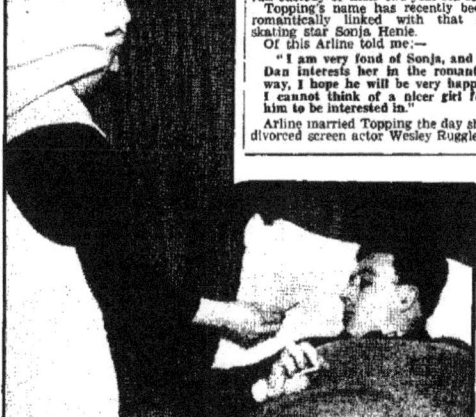

A nurse in Whitby Cottage Hospital gives a captured German airman a cigarette and a light for it.

Daily Mirror

DAILY MIRROR, Tuesday, Feb. 6, 1940.

No. 11,283 — ONE PENNY
Registered at the G.P.O. as a Newspaper.

Sign with Your Butcher Now

You will hear this week the date on which meat rationing will begin. And you will also probably learn the amount of the ration.

So if you have not yet registered with a butcher, you should do so without delay.

The Ministry of Food pointed out yesterday that until the number of consumers with each retail butcher is known, it will be almost impossible to arrange adequate distribution of supplies.

BIG MEAT MUDDLE IS GROWING

BY A SPECIAL CORRESPONDENT

BRITAIN is in the grip of the Great Meat Muddle. As the Ministry of Food announced yesterday the appointment of two new meat directors, Mr. H. S. Turner and Mr. R. S. Forsyth, it was admitted that the Ministry's meat distribution plans have broken down.

In one district after another butchers are closing their shops. They have no meat to sell.

Throughout the country farmers and butchers are meeting in protest; shopkeepers are explaining and apologising to the public.

Many cannot supply their customers at all. Others are shutting shop because they refuse to sell the poor quality meat that is offered them.

In Sheffield, where hundreds of homes went without their Sunday joint, butchers decided to remain closed on Monday and Tuesday each week.

Decided to Close

In Portsmouth only two beasts were sent into the city last week, against the normal pre-war supply of between three hundred and three hundred and fifty.

Butchers from Trowbridge and Stratford-on-Avon, who serve a population of 50,000 people, decided to close their shops today as a protest against the bad quality of meat allocated to them by the Minister of Food.

"When the butchers saw the quality of the lamb they were supposed to accept for sale they unanimously decided to close every butcher's shop in West Wiltshire tomorrow," Mr. F. P. Garlick, a leading butcher, said last night.

"They want me to pay 9d. a lb. for it. The Ministry of Food officials said unless we accepted the lambs we could have no meat, but that could not induce any decent butcher to take such stuff."

Mr. Garlick took a *Daily Mirror* representative to the Trowbridge Market Hall, where lambs were laid on a grubby-looking cement floor, usually a market place for cheapjacks to sell their wares.

No Shops Open

In Leamington, Warwick, Kenilworth and district butchers' shops are to close three days a week because of difficulties in the distribution.

In Cumberland the position is so grave that yesterday in Carlisle not a butcher's shop was open. They had no meat.

One Manchester butcher said: "We are handling meat of a quality not seen on our counter since the last war. Usually we get lambs of 30 to 35lb., now we are getting them up to 50lb.—when we can get them at all."

"A lot of Manchester butchers were closed from Monday to Thursday because they could not get supplies."

Because their faith prohibits the

Contd. on Back Page, Col. 1

BURGIN SEES THE KING

Mr. Leslie Burgin, Minister of Supply, went to Buckingham Palace and had an audience with the King yesterday.

SHE SENT A LOVE-LETTER...

BY A SPECIAL CORRESPONDENT

MABEL RODDICK, aged eighteen, a tailoress, finished the Army tunic she was sowing and slipped a note inside a pocket; a letter asking the soldier who wore the tunic to write to the girl who made it.

Mabel laughed to her friends. "It's a silly sort of thing to do," she said. "Still . . . you never know."

Mabel's note was answered a few days ago. George Norris, aged twenty, of the Royal Corps of Signals, found the letter in his tunic pocket, wrote to ask the writer to meet him.

Mabel read and laughed again. A different laugh this time.

"Come and have tea with me," she wrote back.

And this is why she laughed:—

* * *

They met yesterday in Mabel's home in Caledon-road, East Ham, E.

And Mabel, admiring the handsome young soldier, smiled up at him and said:

"Oh, George. You are just a generation late."

"That letter was meant for your father and the men who fought with him."

Her letter was written in 1917. Mabel Roddick, the girl tailoress, has become Mrs. Mabel Young.

She's forty-one years old now. She has a daughter aged twelve.

"The joke's on both of us," said George. "Of course, I thought I was going to meet a young girl.

"Still it'll be fun being a brother to the family. It's strange to think that Mrs. Young made the tunic before I was born.

"My father served in France in the

Contd. on Back Page, Col. 5

...ris Young (wearing military tunic); her mother, Mrs. M. Young and George Norris (owner of the tunic). Mrs. Young tailored it twenty-three years ago—slipped a note in the pocket which Norris answered just the other day.

MINESWEEPER SUNK: 54 LOST

THE commanding officer and fifty-three men are believed to have been lost from the minesweeper Sphinx (875 tons), which sank in heavy weather while being towed into port with her engines disabled.

She had been damaged by enemy air attacks on Saturday. Big seas were running when the tow parted, and finally the ship capsized, says the Admiralty communique.

Four Officers, 45 Ratings Missing

Commander J. R. N. Taylor and four ratings are known to have lost their lives. Four officers and forty-five ratings are missing and are feared to have been lost.

Next of kin have been informed. The survivors—two officers and forty-four ratings—have been landed.

The Sphinx was completed last July, built by William Hamilton and Co., Port Glasgow, at a cost of more than £100,000.

She had a designed speed of seventeen knots, carried two 4in. high-angle guns and five smaller weapons.

BABY 'MEDICINE' IS POISON

LATE last night there had been no response to the broadcast SOS for the man who was sold a bottle of poison in a Guildford chemist's shop earlier in the evening in mistake for dillwater, common remedy for children's digestive troubles.

The man was served with compound linctus of codeine, which, if given to a baby in quantities usual for dillwater, would probably be fatal.

"The mistake," said the chemist, "occurred through putting wrong labels on bottles of the same size.

"Anyone who has used dillwater will at once notice the difference."

SHAVED IN PUBLIC

Although the Germans have been clearly warned not to have any relations with prisoners of war, Frau Wiederroth, of Scershausen, carried on relations with a Polish prisoner.

Revealing this in an official communique, the district superintendent of the Nazi Party declares:

"In order to make an example of her, I called on her myself and personally shaved off her hair in public."
—Exchange.

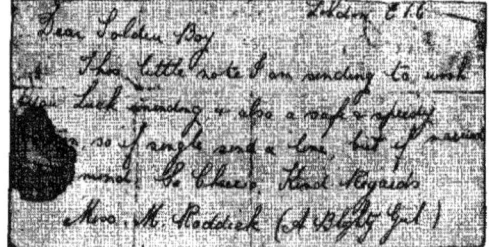

WRECKED CAR ON ENGINE— TWO ESCAPE

A CAR in which were a man and his daughter was struck by a goods train on a railway crossing at Wymondham (Norfolk) last night.

The car, still upright, was carried on the front of the engine for 200 yards, with the occupants still inside it.

When the train stopped the car was a wreck, but all the couple had were minor injuries.

They were Mr. G. W. Rackham and his daughter Joy, of Stanfield Hall, Wymondham. They were crossing the L.N.E.R. line at Browick-road, Wymondham, when the car was struck.

Mrs. Steward, another daughter of Mr. Rackham, told the *Daily Mirror* last night. "The crossing gates were open. When the train hit the car my father and sister remained inside.

"Fortunately the car kept upright. Father was cut and bruised and my sister is suffering from shock.

"They were brought home in another car. Their injuries are not serious."

FINLAND— ALLIED TALK

THE war in Finland and questions of supply were discussed when the Supreme War Council held its fifth meeting yesterday in Paris.

It was the biggest gathering of Allied war leaders yet held—"The finest war council meeting I ever attended," said M. Daladier, the French Premier. "Harmony was complete."

The meeting should have been held in London, but was transferred because M. Daladier has a fractured ankle.

Britain was represented by Mr. Chamberlain, Prime Minister; Lord Halifax, Foreign Secretary; Mr. Winston Churchill, First Lord of the Admiralty; Sir Kingsley Wood, Secretary for Air; Mr. Oliver Stanley, Secretary for War; Sir Ronald Campbell, British Ambassador in Paris; Admiral of the Fleet Sir Dudley Pound, First Sea Lord; Sir Alexander Cadogan, Under-Secretary for Foreign Affairs; General Sir Edmund Ironside, Chief of the Imperial General Staff, and Mr. H. L. Ismay, Secretary of the Committee for Imperial Defence.—British United Press.

DAILY MIRROR, Wednesday, Feb. 7, 1940.

Daily Mirror

No. 11,284   ONE PENNY
Registered at the G.P.O. as a Newspaper.

150 POLICE GUARD I.R.A. PRISON

POLICEMEN AND SCOTLAND YARD OFFICERS UNITED LAST NIGHT TO GUARD WINSON GREEN PRISON, BIRMINGHAM, WHERE TWO CONDEMNED I.R.A. MEN ARE DUE TO DIE TODAY.

When it was announced that the Home Secretary had refused a reprieve the guard was doubled; by the afternoon it was redoubled, and last night 150 policemen carried out a constant patrol round the prison.

As the guards were increased new I.R.A. bomb and fire outrages in London, Manchester and Birmingham were taking place—new threats of I.R.A. vengeance were being received.

In the condemned cells, last rites were administered to Peter Barnes and James Richards who die today for the part they played in the Coventry explosions which killed five people.

Special guards attended each member of the Cabinet last night. Every Minister had three Scotland Yard officers in attendance. Extra men patrolled Downing-street.

At the prison no chances were being taken.

No Risks Taken

It was impossible for anyone to stand outside the wall of the gaol last night for more than a minute or so, writes a Daily Mirror reporter. I tried it.

And scores of times I was surrounded by policemen who appeared to spring at me from nowhere. They did their job thoroughly.

They asked me my name, my business, searched me thoroughly and anxiously scanned all material of identification.

Tension

Even then they refused to allow me to stand in one position, pointing out that they could not take any risks.

The public living near the gaol were alive to the tension. They kept in constant touch with the police, informing them of everything that happened.

In the public houses near the gaol plain-clothes policemen were on duty. All strangers were closely observed and for this task the landlords and waiters were recruited.

(Bombs Wound Six—See Back Page)

Three Post Office workers, left to right, Alfred John Sherman, G. M. Jones and G. W. Fenn, injured—but still smiling—after the explosions at Euston Station yesterday. Another man, working with them, was loading mailbags into a van when one of them exploded in his face. (Other pictures on back page.)

STATE CAFES SOON

NATIONAL kitchens and restaurants are likely to be set up by the Government soon after meat rationing starts on March 11, writes the Daily Mirror Political Correspondent.

They will be a development of the scheme which operated towards the end of the last war.

The idea is that workers in such cities as London, Manchester, Birmingham and Glasgow will be able to get quick and cheap midday meals without having to surrender meat coupons.

Communal kitchens are becoming popular in factories and business houses where lunch hours have been cut at the request of the workers on account of the black-out.

11 a.m. to 3 p.m.

It is expected that every big concern will establish a system of factory and shop meals for the duration of the war.

The Government's national kitchen and restaurant scheme will cater for clerks and typists whose businesses do not run their own canteens.

Restaurants are expected to be set up in the busiest parts of the cities, and will be open from about 11 a.m. to 3 p.m.

There will be no meat ration for dogs, and when the rationing starts dog owners will have to feed their pets on liver, offal or horse-flesh—if they can get it.

These foods will probably be difficult to get.

Your meat ration—page 3

BABY BORN IN POLICE BOX

CRAMPED inside a police telephone box, a doctor at Swansea last night fought for the life of a mother and her unborn child.

A few minutes later the child—a girl weighing five and a half pounds—was born.

There was no room to open the door of the box, so the doctor handed the baby through the telephone slot to a waiting assistant matron.

She took the baby to a hospital a few yards away.

The doctor, Dr. Quarran Evans, resident medical officer at Swansea hospital, was in the hospital when he received an urgent call to the nearby police box. There he found Mrs. Talbot, of Argyle-street, Swansea.

"There was not enough room for the assistant matron, who had to stand outside ready for any emergency. I had to stand with one foot halfway up the wall, but we managed so well that the child was born.

"Mother and baby were taken to Tawe Lodge Infirmary, where they are doing well."

TALKERS WILL DIE

THE death penalty is soon to be imposed on those who give information to the enemy, writes the Daily Mirror political correspondent.

Under the existing regulations the maximum penalty is only a £500 fine and two years' imprisonment.

Under the new regulations those who make indiscreet statements, or lose official documents through gross negligence, will probably be liable to penal servitude.

There is no failure to take vigilant precautions against leakages, the Premier told the Commons yesterday.

The death penalty has been considered for the most serious cases, he said.

Gossip May Cost Thousands of Lives.—See page 4.

SCREAM STOPS WEDDING

From JOHN WALTERS
NEW YORK, Tuesday.

THE marriage of the novelist Ludwig Lewisohn to a woman twenty-seven years his junior was halted in a synagogue in Baltimore yesterday, when another woman, accompanied by a six-year-old boy, appeared and screamed, "This wedding can't take place!"

Lewisohn, a man of fifty-eight, who leads the Zionist movement in America, was standing with his bride, Miss Edna Manley, before the rabbi, exchanging their vows, when the woman broke in and staged a violent scene.

The woman, who had come by air from New York, cried.

"I have been his wife, his muse and soul. I have inspired all his poetry!"

The boy accompanying her fought to reach Lewisohn, shouting, "Let me come to you, Daddy!"

The bride became hysterical, and guests wept as the scene became wilder and wilder.

After an hour's postponement the wedding took place, although the protesting woman and her lawyer announced they would have Lewisohn arrested for bigamy.

More Sea Heroes Are Honoured

More of Britain's men of courage have had their bravery recognised with the award of the O.B.E., it was announced last night.

Two of them are Captain John Steward and Marine Henry Read, master and gunner of the steamer Hopestar.

Their combined courage and skill saved the ship from a long, relentless attack by a U-boat. Three times the submarine loosed torpedoes at the Hopestar.

The gunner made the U-boat dive with a well-placed shell. And not until then did Captain Steward use a smokescreen. He had refused to spoil the gunner's chance.

Another brave man honoured is Mr. Thomas Ward, chief officer of the steamer Oakgrove, sunk by enemy aircraft. When the captain was killed, Mr. Ward directed the lifeboat with such skill and coolness that he saved his men.

Heroes honoured yesterday: Stories and pictures on Pages 2 and 11.

TWO LIVES SAVED BY
1. FUNERAL
2. KNOCK-OUT

TWO men were saved from death yesterday—one by a funeral, the other by a knock-out.

Strolling across his farm, Mr. Frank Humphrey, of Brookvale Farm, Northfleet, saw a funeral passing along the roadway nearby. He stopped, took off his hat.

As he did so, the earth caved in in front of him, leaving a crater about 45ft. deep.

"That funeral undoubtedly saved my life," said Mr. Humphrey. "If I had not stopped for it I should have fallen into the crater and been buried alive."

The subsidence, it is believed, was caused by an underground spring.

The man who owes his life to being knocked out is Commander J. L. Mieville, hero of the last war, who won the D.S.O. in the Zeebrugge action.

Back on active service, he got leave this week and, on his way home to Ashenhurst Hall, near Leek (Staffs) had to stay overnight at a Leek hotel.

Draught on Face

While he was taking a bath gas began to escape from the geyser.

His senses reeling, Commander Mieville got up to open the window, but fell against the door.

The blow cut his head and knocked him out.

The fall saved him.

Although the bathroom was full of gas a draught of fresh air came under the door by which the unconscious man was lying.

It fanned the gas away from his face and kept him alive until hotel servants broke into the bathroom.

FRAMED

Among recent acquisitions by the Imperial War Museum, Lambeth-road S.E., which has recently been partially reopened, is the famous "Peace In Our Time" joint declaration signed by Herr Hitler and the Prime Minister, which Mr. Chamberlain brought back from Munich in September, 1938.

SHEEP MUST NOT SLEEP

SHEEP in Leicestershire are not allowed to sleep no matter how tired they get. Shepherds follow them around, keeping them on the move all the time.

In the Ashby-de-la-Zouch grazing lands the sheep are suffering from blindness as a result of the weather ten days ago, which makes them so giddy they want to lie down and die. Farmers are employing extra men to keep the sheep walking—and living.

In spite of these efforts, scores of ewes and lambs are dying.

Poultry are also dying in large numbers.

"Because the railways cannot guarantee deliveries of day old chicks, I have had to kill 50,000 since Christmas," Mr. W. D. Evans, of Kibworth, owner of one of the biggest hatcheries in the Midlands, told the "Daily Mirror" yesterday.

"I am cooking the chicks, mixing them with meal and giving them to the chickens." he said.

DAILY MIRROR, Thursday, Feb. 8, 1940.

Daily Mirror

No. 11,285   ONE PENNY
Registered at the G.P.O. as a Newspaper.

GAOL FOR WASTE

IF you waste food you may go to gaol. The Ministry of Food are now considering making food wastage a breach of the Defence Regulations, for which the maximum penalty is a £500 fine and two years in prison.

The waste of good food in his constituency, North Tottenham, is alarming Socialist M.P. R. C. Morrison. A dustman there recently found 20lb. of bacon rashers in a dustbin.

Within the past few days Tottenham dustmen have found in the garbage cans, seventy loaves of bread, 100 bread-rolls, 3lb. of butter in half-pound packets.

Mr. Morrison is going to ask the other Morrison —the Food Minister—to investigate the wastage.

"The more I hear of the food that is being wasted, the more appalled I become," he said to the "Daily Mirror" Political Correspondent last night.

Don't be a Waster. Don't throw good food away. If you do you will be liable to a fine and perhaps gaol—and the frugal bread and water diet.

BOY RESCUED CAPTAIN

A DECK boy, aged sixteen, of the crack Irish mail boat Munster, sunk yesterday, was the hero of his mates last night. For he had saved the captain's life.

George Cowen, of Cardiff, had only been a deck boy on the Munster for eight weeks. Yet when he was awakened by an explosion at sea he did not think first of himself.

He ran to the bridge and found that the master, Captain James Paisley, of Larkfield-road, Aigburth, Liverpool, had broken an arm in two places.

Without help he could not don his lifejacket. The Munster was sinking quickly.

But George would not jump for the
(Continued on Back Page)

Look at This Hat, Girls!

It's the very latest in steel helmets. It weighs 1lb. 2oz., compared with the standard 3lb., and it won't disturb your permanent waves.

The inventor is Mr. Albert Smith, seventy-year-old president of Bradford Chamber of Trade. He intends to send one of the hats to the Queen.

The model you see above is fitted with an ordinary hat band. Comfort is ensured by a head band made from rubber.

The cost? Probably 8s.

PARIS RAID ON SOVIET

FRENCH police made a sensational raid on the headquarters of the Soviet Russian trade delegation in Paris on Monday, it was learned in London yesterday.

The building was searched from top to bottom. The bank in the same building was also searched. Books and papers from both the bank and trade delegation were taken away.

No reason was given for the raid, which was carried out by scores of gendarmes.

On the same day, the private flat of the head of the Soviet trade delegation, who enjoys diplomatic immunity, was raided by the police. Private papers were taken away.

The Soviet Ambassador in Paris, M. Suritz, protested to the French Foreign Office.

SAFE FORCED FOR WEDDING

Safebreakers worked feverishly to crack open a safe in a Staffordshire church as a couple were married—over three hours late—only a few yards away.

The minister had lost the keys and could not get at the marriage register—hence the hurried efforts to force open the safe before six o'clock, the last legal hour for a wedding.

The couple whose wedding was so long delayed that it nearly did not take place were Miss Minnie Malkin, aged twenty-one, and Harold Greenwood, aged twenty-four, of Leek.

Though they live only a few hundred yards from Ball Haye Green Methodist Church, the ceremony took nearly four hours to complete. The couple were wed only ten minutes before six o'clock.

PARENTS' VISITS TO B.E.F. WOUNDED

RELATIVES of members of the B.E.F. reported missing are to be allowed to go to France, and go from one hostel to another behind the lines to search for them.

In the last war many men who had lost their memories remained in hospital unidentified while their parents or wives grieved for them as dead.

The Red Cross is establishing a "Missing Persons Bureau" on the lines of the Bureau at Scotland Yard. Parents who wish to trace sons will be able to write to the Red Cross, which will then organise searches. If these fail parents will be brought to France.

Those who have sons seriously wounded may also go to France to visit them and the British Red Cross has engaged a "parents' hotel" at the base to house parents.

General Sir Sidney Clive, who is Commissioner for the British Red Cross in France, revealed these arrangements yesterday.

For the Nurses

The Red Cross recognises that nurses who go out under shell fire are heroes as much as the fighters. In the past their role was taken for granted, but now an effort is to be made to give them the care they deserve.

"Two chateaux have been rented and equipped for nurses brought back from the front lines," Sir Sidney said. "Whenever a nurse shows signs of breaking under the strain, she will be evacuated to one of the rest homes where, far from the sound of gunfire and the horrors of battle, she will be given rest and treatment until she is considered fit to go up the line once again."

No 1914 Muddle

"The B.E.F. is infinitely better equipped in its medical services than in the last war," he added. "We have had time to organise, and there will not be the muddle which we saw in 1914."

The first British women ambulance drivers to serve on the Western Front are due to take up duty with the ambulance units which British women have given to the defence forces. It is expected that the units will begin functioning in France within the next few days.—British United Press.

NAZIS SUSPEND ALL LEAVE

All leave has been suspended in Germany, states Paris Radio. It adds that, according to reports from Belgium, Hitler intends to launch a large-scale attack at once.

A German Admiral stated yesterday, says the same report, that so far Germany had engaged in only guerrilla warfare, and that war from the air had not yet started.

Three of those who escaped from the Munster were Mrs. Sheila Gray and her daughters, Judy, aged two, and Anne, aged three. She and one child were in one lifeboat, and did not know the fate of the other for three hours, when she was picked up.

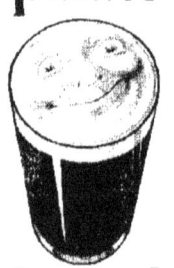

Guinness tickles the palate

—hence the smile

"I have recommended Guinness for some twenty years," writes a doctor, "especially for those who return home 'dead tired' and disinclined for food."

"Guinness sharpens up the appetite wonderfully," writes another.

Even the taste of Guinness—so clean and invigorating—helps to bring appetite. Have a Guinness after work and *enjoy* your evening meal.

The above extracts from doctors' letters are quoted by special permission.

GUINNESS is good for you

DAILY MIRROR, Tuesday, Feb. 13, 1940.

Daily Mirror

No. 11,289   ONE PENNY
Registered at the G.P.O. as a Newspaper.

FEB. 13

Soldier on Leave —Home Seized

A soldier home on short leave, his wife and six children were evicted by a sheriff's officer from their corporation house in Park-street, Airdrie, Lanarkshire, yesterday, and their furniture piled outside in the road. The soldier spent the rest of the day looking for another home.

An official of the corporation said the soldier's family had paid no rent since September 16 last year. On January 28 the warrant, which was put into effect yesterday, was granted in his absence.

Many people, added the official, thought the family of a member of the Services need not pay rent, but the Emergency Powers Act gave protection only against eviction where it could be shown that inability to pay was due to the war.

BEF NEEDS MANY MORE WORKERS

From BERNARD GRAY, "Daily Mirror" Correspondent with the B.E.F.

ON cinema screens all over Britain will shortly begin a great campaign to secure volunteers for France.

The B.E.F. wants more men. Not to fight, to work.

Thousands more men are needed for the Auxiliary Military Pioneer Corps, or labour corps, as they used to be called.

Men who can fight for their country with shovels as weapons; men who are prepared to use their muscles against the enemy.

Many more are required before the middle of summer.

There are now thousands of these "Amps," as they are known, in France.

It is a real League of Nations army. There are British, anti-Hitler Germans, Czechs, Poles, Spaniards, all supplemented by local hired French civilians who have volunteered to help with the work.

61, Going Strong

British volunteers are officially between the ages of thirty-five and fifty, but several enthusiastic "Amps" are getting nearer the sixty mark.

I heard of one man today believed to be sixty-one. He joined the Pioneer Corps because his son is in France.

"I thought I'd like to be somewhere near him," he explained.

Chinese labourers, a familiar sight in France during the last war, will not be here this time. A project to bring them to France has failed.

RATIONS FOR GERMAN DOGS

Germany has begun to issue ration cards for three kinds of dogs—thoroughbreds, dog guides for the blind, and hounds—according to Brussels radio last night.

WHEN THE BOMBS DROP

THE Nazi Government is deliberately misleading the German public into thinking they are immune from air attacks.

But the people of Britain, for their own welfare, must face the facts about bombing.

The authorities in Britain believe that if the public know the truth, they will be in less danger—if and when the bombers come—than the Germans who listen to their leaders' lies.

Constant propaganda from German radio stations tell the German public that their towns and cities are invulnerable to an attack because of the anti-aircraft, air-fighters and balloon barrages.

It is fantastic for anyone to think that every single bomber which tried to raid London or any other big town would be brought down.

The real and only answer to the bomber is the bomber—in other words, the deterrent is retaliation.

British experts point out that, no matter how strong the defenders were in anti-aircraft guns, fighters and balloon barrages, there could be no guarantee that all the raiders or even a percentage of them would be shot down.

Accuracy Impossible

One thing is certain—our defences rule out any possibility of effective target bombing.

Air attacks, if they came, could only result in indiscriminate bombing from great altitudes.

Posters advertising new flats have described London as the safest city in the world from air attack.

Very likely such a statement is true, but that does not mean immunity from bombs if air raids start.

Don't Watch Raids

It is not safe to go out into the streets, as so many people have done in the past, to watch a German bomber being fought off by our air defences.

If large-scale air raids and indiscriminate bombings should begin, a great many needless casualties would be caused by people failing to heed the most elementary rule of A.R.P.— to take shelter.

If raids are treated as spectacular events, the casualties would be tremendous.

Rhoda Mary Morgan, the dead governess.

GIRL GAVE UP WEALTHY LOVER

A YOUNG governess found dead in a car with an aircraftman had given up a wealthy man friend in favour of her 2s.-a-day sweetheart.

But the mystery of their death, clasped in each other's arms, may remain unsolved at the inquest today on Aircraftman Irwin Thomas, twenty-two, and the girl, Rhoda Mary Morgan, twenty-one, employed by Brigadier-General Hugh Cecil Cholmondeley, of Edstaston House, near Wem, Shropshire.

Irwin Thomas was known to everybody in the village of Yorton, near Wem.

He had been playing darts and dominoes in the local "pub" with his lifelong friends. A few hours later he was dead by the side of his fiancee in her employer's car, a tube leading from the exhaust into the saloon.

The car, in the garage adjoining General Cholmondeley's home, had been left with the engine running, but when the couple were found the engine had stalled.

Wedding Planned

Mrs. Griffiths, mother of a girl friend of Miss Morgan, told the Daily Mirror yesterday that the couple were to have been married soon.

"Rhoda was terribly in love with Irwin, and had thrown over a wealthy man who wanted to marry her so that she would be free to go to him."

Miss Morgan was governess to the seven-year-old daughter of General and Mrs. Cholmondeley.

"She was always a bright and happy girl, most friendly with the other members of our staff," Mrs. Cholmondeley said.

Thomas, who had known Miss Morgan for only about six months, spent a few hours before he went to meet his sweetheart for the last time in the Railway Hotel near his home at Yorton, near Wem.

"He was as bright as usual, talking about his return to camp the following day," Mrs. Robinson, the landlady, said.

NEW WAR FRONT

—Says Turkey

ARRIVAL of the Anzac troops in Egypt impressed Rumania yesterday.

There was free comment by observers on the effects of the landing on the Rumanian oil situation.

The Bukarest newspaper "Universul" said: "The Rumanian State has the right to defend our own oil industry."

Rumania called 200,000 reservists for service on March 1, which will give her 600,000 men under arms.

At Istanbul it was reported that the arrival of the Anzacs increased the belief that a new front might open in the Near East or the Balkans this spring.

Italy is speeding fortifications both in the Udine region opposite Yugoslavia and in the Brenner Pass zone opposite Germany.

Large sums earmarked for "public works" by the Italian Government at Cabinet meetings in January, are said to have been diverted for re-fortifying the Brenner Pass.

Without a thoroughly fortified Brenner Pass, it is stated, Italy cannot feel safe to pursue her neutral policy with any assurance against possible German threats.—Associated Press and Reuter.

The Anzacs Land.—See page 4.

MORE MEAT COMING SOON

ADEQUATE supplies of meat should be available for every housewife soon.

Mr. Lennox-Boyd, Parliamentary Secretary to the Ministry of Food, said so yesterday.

Cattle entries have increased more than 50 per cent. during the last two weeks compared with the preceding three weeks.

Mr Lennox-Boyd said that stories about shortages had, on investigation, disclosed only a shortage of the particular meat to which people in certain districts were accustomed.

It had been suggested in some quarters that the meat distribution had been taken from the hands of the people bred and born in the business and put in the hands of those who did not know one carcase from another.

Defends Bureaucrats

It was not fair to say that bureaucrats were controlling meat distribution because the Ministry had the experience of the trade to draw upon.

The improvement in the entries of home-killed cattle, sheep and pigs would have an appreciable effect on home-killed meat and lead to a lessening of the difficulties figuring in the public mind.

He added that the entries of calves had increased by nearly 40 per cent., sheep by 30 per cent. and pigs by over 200 per cent.

He said that the country is in a moderately secure position as regards sugar, but there is no prospect of an increase in the ration at the moment.

The position of sugar for brewing was under consideration. Any question of the restriction of brewing raised large revenue considerations.

The Government hoped a decision would be reached soon on schemes for setting up factories for processing surplus potatoes.

The Ministry of Food announced that under the meat rationing scheme purchases of meat by catering establishments will be limited to 60 per cent. of the quantities they have been in the habit of buying.

DINERS RATIONED— THEY DIDN'T KNOW IT

UNKNOWN to themselves, diners at one of London's largest hotels have undergone "voluntary rationing" for a week.

They have dined in accordance with the official rationing scheme, which cuts their consumption by 60 per cent.

"We agreed to a request from the Ministry of Food to try out rationing for a week," the manager of the Savoy Hotel told the "Daily Mirror" last night. "It has been a complete success.

"Tactful suggestions by waiters to diners brought about a larger consumption of poultry, fish and eggs."

Restaurant owners have formed no definite plans. They have been awaiting the Ministry of Food order, issued last night, which announced that catering establishments will be limited to 60 per cent. of the quantity of meat they used to buy.

DAILY MIRROR, Friday, Feb. 16, 1940.

Daily Mirror

FEB. 16

No. 11,292 — ONE PENNY
Registered at the G.P.O. as a Newspaper.

Bravo! Exeter

PARENTS TO PLEDGE ON BILLETS

CHILDREN evacuated under the Government's new scheme, to start if civilians are bombed, must stay in reception areas until told to return.

Parents will have to sign an undertaking to this effect.

- Billeting must continue to be principally in private houses and not camps.
- A roll of householders willing to share with neighbours the work in caring for the children will be set up.
- Allowances for children of fourteen will be increased to 10s. 6d. weekly.

The Queen is to send a letter of appreciation to the 250,000 householders who have had children billeted on them since the war began. It will be suitable for framing.

The Queen is sending the letter at the request of the Government, who wish the sacrifice and fortitude of the nation's "other mothers" to be recorded and remembered.

The scheme was explained last night in a broadcast by Mr. Walter Elliot, Minister of Health, after he had outlined it in Parliament.

"Winter has gripped all Europe and halted the war. But when winter passes the danger comes again. We must look ahead," he said.

In School Canteens

"We are doing everything possible to avoid difficulties.

"For example, meat meals at school canteens will not require coupons or bits of coupons from the children's ration books.

"We are asking all the householders in the receiving areas to accept enrolment as being willing to share this service with those who all winter have borne the burden of the day.

"Many countries abroad are wondering how we shall tackle our tasks in 1940. Many people at home say, 'If we could only do something to help.' You can help your neighbour, you can help the children.

"The World Watches"

"It is a gesture of solidarity which all the fighting men will understand, that the children from the cities should continue to enjoy the friendship and the comfort of the firesides in the villages and in the country towns.

"All the world is watching, and would know if we failed. All our people will be heartened, and all the people who love us and who sympathise with our cause will rejoice, when we succeed, as we mean to succeed."

Referring to the increase of the billeting allowance from 8s. 6d. to 10s. 6d. for all children over fourteen, which begins on March 3, Mr. Elliot said:—

"We are extending the billeting allowances on similar terms to those given under the Government scheme to private arrangements, even with relatives."

More than 400,000 children are still in the evacuation areas.

The new scheme will only operate "if air-raids develop on a scale involving serious and continued bombing."

GRACIE: YEAR IN U.S.

Gracie Fields landed in New York last night from the Italian liner Rex.

She told the ship reporters that she was going to spend a year in California with her parents.

She needed the holiday, her doctor had told her, because of her recent operation.—Associated Press.

To Pay If You Lose Gas Mask

Lose or damage your gas mask in future, and you will be liable for payment for a new one.

The charge will probably be based on the cost of the respirator.

Although civilian type gas masks cannot be bought, their estimated cost is 2s. 6d.

Particulars of the arrangement for replacement of gas masks will be notified to local authorities at an early date.

NAZIS' MILLION SLAVES

FIELD-MARSHAL GOERING, broadcasting last night from a secret radio station, informed the Germans that:—

A million Poles are to be transported to Germany to labour in the fields;

The price of butter is to be increased 2½d. a lb. Milk prices are to go up.

And he urged them to be patient.

"Those who have money," he said, "can buy butter. The poor can buy margarine."

He declared that the Polish labourers were not being forced to come to Germany.

In fact, they will be slaves. Already they have been told that they cannot expect the same wages as Germans since they are "an inferior race."

Theirs will be forced labour at a starvation wage; that is the price of defeat at the hands of the Nazis.

Goering's speech had been delayed a quarter of an hour. No reason was given. He spoke hesitatingly as though a stranger to his subject.

"We cannot be beaten militarily,

Continued on Back Page

O.K. TO KISS A SOLDIER—BISHOP

THE Bishop of Manchester (Dr. Guy Warman) sees nothing wrong in a girl kissing a soldier, no more than kissing a civilian.

"I don't think it is any different from kissing a policeman, or even a parson," he said at a Bury (Lancs) meeting yesterday.

"When we look around us in normal times," he said, "and see in the parks, outside garden gates, and by lamp-posts, young folk saying goodnight, we smile with a certain amount of tolerance, because most of us did the same thing ourselves once.

"We were not ashamed of it then and we are not ashamed of it now.

"Many people think it is quite possible for a girl and a boy in civilian dress to enjoy a normal friendship, but as soon as the boy dresses in uniform, then they think there is something wrong.

"I don't think so," said the Bishop.

U-BOAT WAITED —SUNK

A U-boat lay in wait for H.M.S. Exeter as she made her voyage home from South America.

But, as she lurked in the Atlantic, she sighted the meat freighter Sultan Star. She could not resist the temptation and torpedoed the freighter.

It was her last victim. The U-boat was destroyed.

So the men of the Exeter came home yesterday like this man—all smiles . . . with "thumbs up."

Their ship battered, shell-fragment holes pitted in the bridge, the funnels patched, holes in the deck.

But a conqueror.

And the men conquerors. Smiling long and broadly. Now read the story of the home-coming, and see the pictures on pages 10 and 11.

8,000 PLANES NEEDED

According to the *New York Herald-Tribune* Allied agents told the Secretary to U.S. Treasury that the Allies must have about 3,000 pursuit planes and over 5,000 bombers within eighteen months.

The agents asked for the latest American pursuit plane types.

ROOSEVELT MAKES A MYSTERY

Escorted by two destroyers, President Roosevelt sailed from Pensacola, Florida, in the U.S. cruiser Tuscaloosa yesterday for an unknown destination. He may be going to a secret rendezvous for highly confidential talks with British, French and Italian officials.

Has he a secret rendezvous somewhere at sea or are Allied representatives going to meet him at some West Indian port?

Washington recalled a rumour of several weeks ago, denied at the time, that the President had a plan for a high seas meeting with foreign leaders to discuss world peace and the restoration of economic stability among the nations, cables John Walters, "Daily Mirror" New York correspondent.

The perfect emergency ration

Fry's Sandwich Chocolate

2d and 4d

DAILY MIRROR, Tuesday, Feb. 20, 1940.

Daily Mirror
No. 11,295 — ONE PENNY
Registered at the G.P.O. as a Newspaper.

Workless for Arms Jobs

EVERY employment exchange in Britain has been told by the Ministry of Labour to search the registers for men apt enough to learn a new trade.

Men are being given training as engineers, for armament work, at fourteen Government centres. Their ages range up to forty-five.

Among future munition workers at one centre are a butler from a ducal mansion, a forty-four-year-old waiter who had worked for ten years in exclusive hotels in the West End of London, a crooner from a Blackpool dance band, tap dancers and professional musicians.

Married men receive unemployment allowances for their wives and families while at a centre. All men receive board and lodging.

It is hoped to supply this year 40,000 draughtsmen, fitters, turners, instrument makers, machine operators, sheet metal workers, and electric and oxy-acetylene welders.

NAVY BROKE LAW, NORWAY ACCUSES

AN anti-British speech, revealing how fearful Norway is of offending the Nazis, was made in the Norwegian Parliament last night when the Foreign Minister, Professor Koht, accused Britain of breaking international law when the Navy freed the captives of the Altmark.

He disclosed that, contrary to British belief, the Altmark did not call at Bergen, the Norwegian port.

She was stopped, he said, by a Norwegian torpedo-boat, whose captain was informed that the Altmark carried anti-aircraft guns, and was satisfied that " she was what she purported to be."

Another torpedo-boat was sent out and met the Altmark north of Bergen.

"This time," said Professor Koht, " she refused inspection and with full rights."

He said that the Altmark did not use her radio after she had been told not to do so.

"On February 16," he added, " I heard that British aeroplanes had been sighted near Bergen. These were the planes which reported to the British Navy where the Altmark was.

"The British probably knew what the ship had done earlier, for they knew what we did not know—that there were many British prisoners aboard."

Professor Koht, says Associated Press, then repeated the Norwegian account of the incident in the fjord.

"Had All Rights"

"The following morning," he said, " the Norwegian Government prepared to protest against this illegal procedure, which is against international law."

He said the British Minister in Oslo, Sir Cecil Dormer, " tried to give a defence of the British action. He said the Altmark had prisoners aboard and we should have stopped the ship

"To this the answer was that the ship in any case had all rights to navigate through Norwegian territorial waters.

"The Norwegian officer in charge of the torpedo-boats said the same to British officers."

Then Professor Koht made a startling statement on international law.

"There is no international rule," he said, " which forbids a Power at war from transporting prisoners through a neutral area."

That suggestion is contrary to all accepted interpretations of the law. Professor Koht said the British Minister declared that the Germans had sunk British merchant ships in

Continued on Back Page

★ Roosevelt as Judge? ★

Norway's trade shipping journal suggests that President Roosevelt should be asked to mediate in the Altmark dispute and that he might preside over a court of arbitration.

"I have no knowledge of the suggestion," Mr. Cordell Hull, U.S. Secretary of State, said last night.

✦ ✦ ✦

Moscow Radio last night quoted Norway's Premier Hambro: "The Altmark incident has achieved results months of sea warfare could not accomplish"; added that Norwegian ships might refuse to trade with Britain, which is Germany's object.

FIRST B.E.F. BRIDEGROOM

From BERNARD GRAY,
"Daily Mirror" Correspondent with the B.E.F.

THE first B.E.F. marriage has been celebrated in the office of a French village Mayor, with the officers of the famous Welsh Guards standing outside to cheer their man as he emerged with his bride

The girl was a Polish refugee, with no hope of a real home until Corporal Marcel Amerlinck, of the Welsh Guards, came along. They fell in love decided to wed.

But there were snags, religious and legal.

In the end the legal authorities relented.

A few minutes after the wedding the lovers had to part—he for duty, she to return to her work on a farm. But they were reunited that night in the bridegroom's farmhouse billet.

There, each night, they sit and talk in French. She calls him sergeant now, for the Army gave him a present of promotion.

The one-time refugee is now looking forward to days of happiness in Britain.

" My people at home in Cardiff are waiting for her to go to them," the sergeant said

Lieutenant W. J. K. Shaxby, R.N., and his bride—a picture taken at their wedding, which took place on board ship.

157 ARE LOST IN SUNK DESTROYER

H.M. destroyer Daring has been torpedoed and sunk. Nine officers and 148 men are missing, feared lost. Only one officer and four ratings have been picked up.

Among the missing is the commander of the destroyer, Commander S. A. Cooper.

The Admiralty announced the sinking yesterday, and stated that the next-of-kin had been informed.

The Daring was of 1,375 tons. She was Britain's sixth destroyer loss of the war.

The German High Command communique yesterday claimed the sinking of a destroyer—later Berlin said it was the Daring

The full claim was: "In various sea areas four enemy convoys were successfully attacked by U-boats. Out of three convoys, steamers and tankers, and out of a fourth, a destroyer which belonged to forces safeguarding the convoy, were sunk."

The Admiralty said the total German claim was " fantastic—as German claims usually are."

The mother of Lieutenant W. J. K. Shaxby, one of the Daring victims, said last night: " War has robbed both my daughter-in-law and me of a husband. My husband, Captain Richard Shaxby, died recently from neurasthenia contracted in the last war."

Lieutenant Shaxby was married to Miss Anthony Stanfield-Hill, of Sydney, N.S.W., at sea in the summer of 1936. They had no children.

Comdr. Cooper, at sea

H.M.S. Daring was a destroyer of the Defender class, completed in 1932.

TURKEY'S BIG DEFENCE MOVE

THE Turkish Cabinet has decided to put into force the National Defence Law.

The application of this law is held in Ankara to mean that Turkey feels that either she or her Allies are threatened in the Balkans or the Near East.

The new law issued yesterday contains measures for strengthening Turkey's military defences, for the control of imports and exports, and for the reorganisation of various industries to supply the needs of the Turkish armed forces.

It also provides for severe measures to prevent speculative activity harmful to the country's military and economic integrity.—British United Press.

Summer Time on Sunday

When Summer Time starts on Sunday, black-out time will remain half an hour after sunset.

Normally, lighting-up time in winter is half an hour after sunset, and in summer time, an hour after. This year, however, no such order has yet been made.

Mother Said

REJOIN ARMY OR STARVE

A MOTHER whose twenty-year-old son was an absentee from the Army refused to give him food, told him his place was back with his regiment and that he must go back or starve.

The son, Edward Davenport, aged twenty, stationed at Wellington Barracks, Bury, Lancashire, pleaded guilty at Bolton yesterday to stealing 2s. 1d. from a gas meter and £1 from a house in Holden-street, Bolton. He had been an absentee from his depot since February 5.

Mrs. Sarah Davenport, of Slaterfield, Bolton, the mother, said " I kept him without food, which was only right. His place was back in the Army."

Davenport told a detective that he was hard up and had to have something. He said he was prepared to repay the money.

At Meal Times

He was bound over for six months, ordered to pay 10s. costs, and handed over to a military escort.

Mrs. Davenport told the " Daily Mirror": " Perhaps there are not many mothers who would starve their sons to make them return to their depots. But I say that if they join the Army they must make the best of it.

" Whenever I started to prepare the meals he would leave the house because he knew I would not give him anything

" He told me before he was taken back by the escort that I had done the right thing. It will make a man of him.

" At New Year when he was a day over his time I told the authorities to come and fetch him."

Mrs. Davenport's eldest son is also in the Army and another is joining soon

DARTMOOR MAN CAUGHT AT 1 a.m.

After escaping from Dartmoor Prison yesterday, James Hall, alias George Swift, aged thirty-one, was recaptured at 1 a.m. today.

Nine hours' liberty ended when he walked into the arms of two police officers at Moreton Hampstead, fifteen miles from where he got away.

Hall escaped from a working party in the prison gardens.

Prison officers on horseback joined in the search for him.

DAILY MIRROR, Saturday, Feb. 24, 1940.

Daily Mirror

No. 11,299   ONE PENNY
Registered at the G.P.O. as a Newspaper.

2 MORE U-BOATS SUNK

Two German submarines were bombed and sunk in the North Sea on Wednesday by R.A.F. reconnaissance planes, it was revealed this morning.

Ship rams U-boat — see back page.

THE British Navy is tightening its grip on the seas of the world.

In the Arctic Ocean, outside the Russian port of Murmansk, a line of British and French warships stretches westward to the coast of Norway.

They hunt submarines—and they intensify the blockade against Germany.

German ships, it is believed, are dodging the British control in northern waters. They load Russian oil in Murmansk, then sneak home along the neutral Norwegian coast.

The Allied Fleet will seize these oil tankers, if they now dare to emerge, before they enter a sheltered area.

Already they have captured one prize.

"British warships operating off
(Continued on Back Page)

SWOOPED ON £4,000,000

By JOHN WALTERS

NEW YORK, Friday.

REVELATIONS made in Washington today show how valueless was the Isolationist propaganda against the British search of American air mails at Bermuda.

Senator Pepper, of the Senate Foreign Relations Committee, said that:—

Between £3,500,000 and £4,250,000 sent to Germany by Nazi sympathisers in America has been found and confiscated in the air mail.

Senator Pepper, who said he had obtained these figures in the most careful investigation, added: "This money, mostly in big denomination dollar bills, has been leaving America in a steady stream.

"Most, if not all, of it, has been found by the British at Bermuda."

These disclosures have done much to change the views of Americans, at first angered by propaganda stories of a British deliberate hold-up of mails.

The other Isolationist complaint that the pilot of the U.S. plane was forced to hand over the mail at the point of a British bayonet was also denied by the State Department at Washington today.

DADDY'S MEDAL

Amidst the Brave Company of Men of H.M.S. Exeter and H.M.S. Ajax, to whom the King did honour yesterday, stood one woman . . . Mrs. W. H. Russell.

On her breast the King, emotion showing in his face, pinned the Conspicuous Gallantry Medal won by her husband, Marine Russell.

And later, the sharp eyes of her baby saw the glint of the medal. "That's Daddy's medal," said the mother.

"I think you're wonderful," the Queen told Mrs. Russell, as she took the hand of the child whose father died.

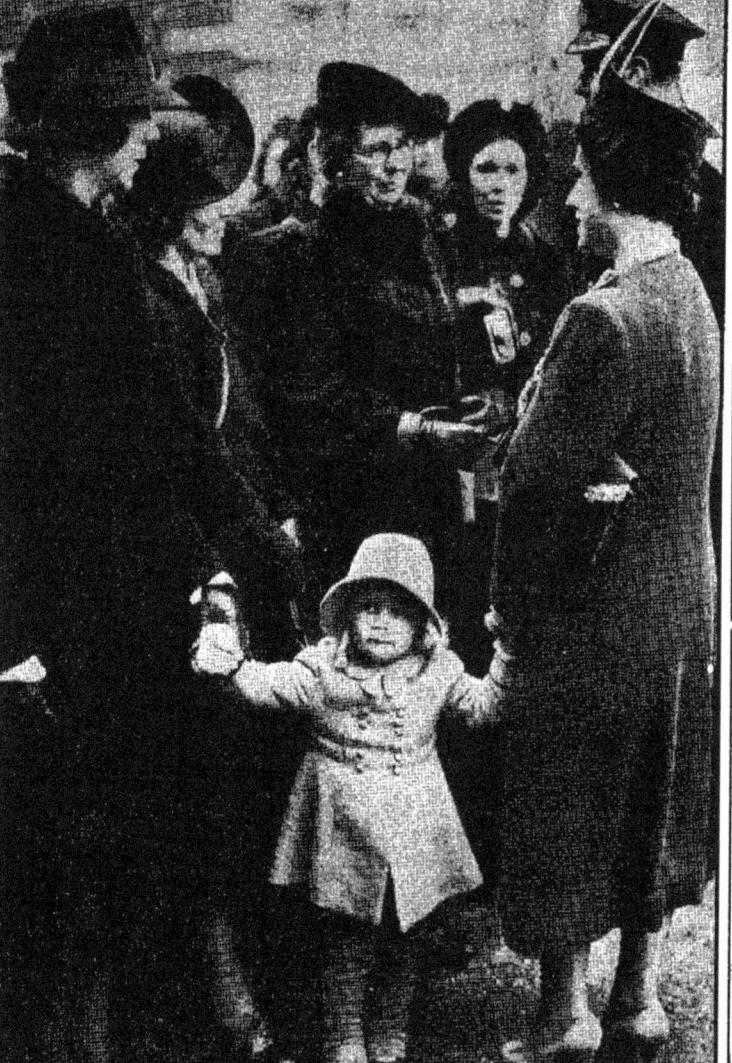

The seaman Winston spotted. —Page 3.

Hushed crowd salute widow, and Mr. Churchill's speech.—Page 5.

Other pictures. — Pages 10 and 11.

IF IT'S CHOCOLATE THEN IT'S FOOD

There's a glass-and-a-half of fresh, full-cream milk in every ½ lb block of Cadbury's Milk Chocolate. It's the world's most delicious way of giving yourself quick energy.

CADBURY'S
MILK CHOCOLATE
'feeds you on your feet'

Daily Mirror

DAILY MIRROR, Friday, March 1, 1940.

1,304 — ONE PENNY
Registered at the G.P.O. as a Newspaper.

Her Hand Was Put in Boiling Water

Joyce Field, aged six, sleeping at peace last night in a home Birmingham police found for her. She had found refuge from a cruel stepmother who put her hand in boiling water. (Story on page 3.)

MERCY RIDE IN SNOW

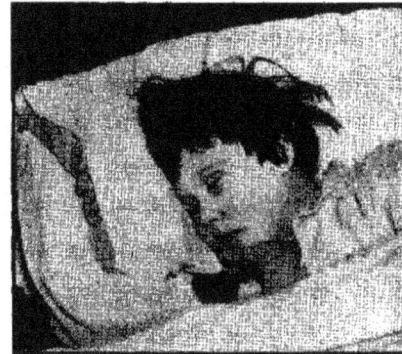

A YOUNG nurse who had never been on horseback in her life before, rode through snow with a sick baby in her arms as soldiers hewed a way for her out of huge drifts.

The struggle went on for hours, miles.

She was fighting for a life against cold and time. And her fight was in vain. Her heroism—an episode of Britain's January cold spell—has now been revealed with the death of the child.

Her horseback ride was the only way she could get three months' old Edwin Clarkson from his lonely farm home on East Witton Fells, North Yorks, to the hospital for an operation which was the only possible means of saving his life.

The heroine was Miss Shepherd, nurse in charge of the lonely district. Her home was formerly at Ruislip, and she then lived at Harrow before going North.

With Dr. George Cockroft, of Middleham, she fought her way to the farm. An examination revealed the need for an immediate operation. But the hospital at Darlington was twenty-five miles away.

The young nurse took a quick decision. She had never ridden a horse before. But it was the only way to take the child from the moors—so she would carry it on horseback.

The baby was well-clothed and pinned into a blanket, placed into a pillowcase, and finally wrapped up in brown paper.

Soldiers carried spades to dig a way and buckets of ashes to prevent the horse slipping. And the heroine on horseback followed, with the doctor walking behind her.

Later she said: "As the little procession wended its way it seemed reminiscent of the flight into Egypt."

Lone Battle

Nurse Shepherd never faltered on the long cold miles to a main road where a car awaited them.

This was not the only brave action of Nurse Shepherd during the cold spell.

This girl, who looks frail, who is under 5ft. in height, fought the snow again to deliver a child born on a farm over the fells nine miles away.

It was at 2 a.m. on a pitch black night that the call came.

With a stick in one hand and her midwifery bag in the other she set off to walk.

On the moors the snow was deeper than the stick. She became so tired that she had to drag the midwifery bag behind her.

In three and a half hours she covered only three miles. Her clothes were sheeted in ice.

When she could hardly get any further, the farmer arrived on horseback. Together they got to the farm. The child was born, the nurse using lemonade bottles as hot-water bottles.

Next day she rode seventeen miles for medical supplies. The snow kept balling under the horse's hooves. She used her surgical scissors to clear it.

Tipped and she fell
Middleham.

FIRE DEATH MYSTERY

SCOTLAND Yard detectives went to Peterborough, Northants, last night to investigate the death of Mrs. Elizabeth Grace Hadman, who was found dead after a fire at her cottage home on Wednesday.

When a doctor examined her charred body last night he found she had a severe head wound.

Mrs. Hadman lived with her husband and four children in a cottage in Lower Lodge, Chesterton, near Peterborough.

Heard Screaming

On the morning of the fire her husband got up at about 4 o'clock, lit the fire, took her a cup of tea and then went to work.

Shortly afterwards, his brother, who lives next door, heard the children screaming, jumped out of bed, and saw dense clouds of smoke coming from his brother's house.

He rushed out, and got the four children—aged ten, eight, four, and eleven months—out of the cottage, and then sent for the fire brigade.

Their mother's body was found by the firemen.

SOVIET CHIEF SACKED

M. V. Potemkin, Soviet Assistant-Commissar for Foreign Affairs, has been "relieved of his post," according to the Moscow radio.

He is to become Commissar for Education, the wireless stated.—British United Press.

HERRINGS UP 1d. A LB.

The retail price of herrings is to be raised from 6d. to 7d. a lb. from Monday, says a Ministry of Food announcement.

AND THEY ARE BRITONS

AN attempt to introduce German peace propaganda into this country is being made by a group of Fascists headed by Lord Tavistock.

A leaflet, setting out the supposed German terms for peace has been prepared.

The group responsible for the leaflet call themselves the British Council for Christian Settlement in Europe. It is a Fascist organisation.

Its chairman, Lord Tavistock, after dabbling with Communism, Pacifism and Social Credit, became interested in Fascism and National Socialism.

The secretary is Mr. John Beckett, who was a prominent member of the British Union of Fascists until 1937. He then left, with Mr. William Joyce, to form the National Socialist League.

Joyce left England for Germany just before war broke out, and is employed by the Nazis to broadcast anti-British propaganda.

Familiar Nazi Lines

Treasurer of the British Council is Captain Gordon Canning, a member of the Link, the pro-Nazi organisation dissolved when war began. He is, or was, a member of the British Union of Fascists.

A prominent member of the group is Ben Greene, a National Socialist propagandist.

The peace terms, according to Lord Tavistock, were drawn up after consultation with the German Legation in Dublin.

"I showed them to Lord Halifax, who criticised them as being rather vague," he said yesterday.

The terms contained in the leaflet are on familiar Nazi lines. They say that Germany really only wanted to build up "a great civilisation," and that if she made mistakes, Britain misunderstood them.

But poor "misunderstood" Germany wants peace on terms that will ensure a "reconstructed," that is, Nazi-controlled, Czech State, and is not prepared to have any "interference" with the German hold over Austria.

"I have prepared the leaflet giving the main points of the proposals," Lord Tavistock said last night, "but no definite plans have yet been made for its distribution."

These "peace proposals" are, of course, not peace terms at all.

They are a piece of German propaganda fostered by Hitler's admirers in this country.

ITALY HIT: NAVY BAN COAL

TODAY British and French warships will impose a new blockade on Germany. They will seize and capture cargoes of German coal on their way to Italy.

The Italian Government, says the "Daily Mirror" Political Correspondent, are expected to protest in the strongest terms and to take immediate action.

In Rome it will be claimed that the stopping of the German coal is an offence against international law. But Britain and France believe they are firmly within their rights in holding up German goods carried by ships of any nationality.

Italy is already taking steps to find new coal supplies. She is negotiating with America, writes the "Daily Mirror" New York correspondent, for the purchase of 4,000,000 tons of coal, at a cost of £4,000,000.

It is doubtful if she can afford to pay for American coal, since she has little foreign currency, and what she has she must conserve.

But coal she must have. She imports 12,000,000 tons every year; 60 per cent. from Germany, the rest largely from Britain.

"Brutal"

Some of the German coal can go by rail through Austria into Italy. But Germany is short of railway trucks and rail passage is expensive. Much of the imports from Germany go through Holland into Rotterdam and then by sea to Italy in Dutch ships.

From today the coal trade will be stopped. Italy has now refused to increase her imports of British coal.

Her indignation at the new blow to her coal trade with Germany was expressed yesterday in Mussolini's newspaper, Popolo d'Italia, which declared:

"The English are breaking international law in a brutal and constant manner."

The Italian Press, too, gave great prominence yesterday to American protests against the British blockade, although it was complained that the Americans are making mock protests.

"Eighty per cent. of the people in America," one writer said, "eagerly desires an Allied victory."

DARDANELLES— ROME REQUEST

AN inspired statement circulated in Rome yesterday says that Italy may claim from Turkey the right to dispatch warships through the Dardanelles to the Black Sea to protect traffic.

The immediate cause of the statement is said to be an unconfirmed report that Britain has already sought the permission of the Turkish Government to make such a move.

Entrance of warships to the Dardanelles is subject to the Montreux Convention, which gives Turkey the right to ban or permit the passage of warships.

"It is evident," the Rome statement said, "that Italy must preoccupy herself with the safety of her own traffic.

"Italy could not stay indifferent to anything touching the Near East and Balkans."—Reuter.

Sold!

For under 10,000 pesos—about £1,000—the wreck of the Admiral Graf Spee has been bought by Senor Julio Vega Helguera, head of a Montevideo firm of food importers.

The German Legation in Montevideo has reported the transaction to the Uruguayan Foreign Ministry.—Reuter.

Sub Leader ———, stationed at ———, say:

When I've only a minute for a stand-up meal it's

Fry's SANDWICH CHOCOLATE

2d AND 4d

Daily Mirror

DAILY MIRROR, Tuesday, March 5, 1940.

No. 11,307 — ONE PENNY
Registered at the G.P.O. as a Newspaper.

Captain C. P. Davis.

Mr. David Behar

2 BROTHERS, EX-MAYOR ARE SACKED

THREE men, sacked by the Minister of Supply, declared last night that they were astonished when the Minister told them they must go. The men are:

David Behar, aged thirty-five, prospective Conservative candidate for Dartford;
His brother Robert Behar, aged thirty-nine; and
Captain C. P. Davis, five times Mayor of Deal, Conservative candidate for North Hammersmith, anti-Dora campaigner.

The brothers Behar, in the uniforms of staff captains, walked out of the gallery of the House of Commons after Mr. Burgin, the Supply Minister, had announced that they must quit the Ministry and that their recommendations for Army commissions were withdrawn.

Mr. Burgin had been asked if they had been recommended for Army commissions to enable them to serve in the Ministry of Supply. He replied:

"I have come to the conclusion that these two gentlemen should not continue to serve on the Ministry of Supply, and have so informed them."

Mr. Ede: Do you know that these two gentlemen are still wearing military uniform, and will you tell the War Office that they are not being recommended for commissions?
Mr. Burgin: Yes.

Liaison Officer

Mr. Ede asked what Captain Davis's duties were in the Ministry and if he knew that Captain Davis had had previous business relations with the Behars.

Mr. Burgin said Captain Davis was a liaison officer, and his job was to speed up the movement of material to and from the filling factories.

He had now told the War Minister —who was considering what action to take—that Captain Davis would no longer serve the Ministry of Supply.

Mr. David Behar, the younger of the Behar brothers, lives in a luxury flat in Berkeley-square, W., has a suite of West End offices, is chairman of Gillow and Gillow, auctioneers and estate agents, and a director of a

Continued on Back Page

ITALY DEFIES COAL BAN

SIX Italian ships, loaded with German coal, sailed from Rotterdam yesterday in defiance of Britain. Five others were expected to sail last night.

Others may leave today.

There were twelve Italian ships loading German coal at Rotterdam during the week-end.

Four of them—the Orata, Pelcen, Liana and Numidia—sailed shortly before midnight on Friday, but returned to their berths on Saturday.

It was reported they were awaiting new instructions from the Italian Government.

Reports from Amsterdam said that the British Government has given sanction for the passage of further ships carrying German coal to Italy are without foundation, it was stated officially by the Ministry of Economic Warfare last night.

"Manifestly Abusive"

Britain's blockade of German coal exports to Italy may lead to a rupture of the Italo-British "Gentlemen's Agreement" regulating the two countries' Mediterranean relations, warns a vigorous Italian Note of protest which reached London yesterday.

The Italian Note goes beyond a formal protest on coal stoppage, and strikes at contraband control generally and tampering with mail.

The Note said the submission of all maritime traffic of non-belligerent countries to contraband control "is manifestly abusive."

The British blockade of German exports was objected to because it "profoundly disturbs the mechanism of international exchange, suppresses the sources of supply and reduces the possibilities of production of non-belligerent States."—Associated Press and Exchange.

U-BOAT SUNK BY R.A.F.

A U-BOAT was yesterday attacked in Schilling Roads by an R.A.F. plane and is believed to have been destroyed.

Schilling Roads is near the mouth of the Elbe, not far from Cuxhaven. The aircraft was on reconnaissance duty when the submarine was sighted in shallow water on the surface.

Four bombs were dropped, one of which registered a direct hit between the conning-tower and the stern.

After the attack the submarine was seen to be enveloped in a cloud of greyish black smoke, with only the upper part of its conning-tower visible above the water.

An Admiralty statement last night reveals that of the six German ships which tried to make a dash home from Vigo, northern Spain, a fortnight ago, three were captured by British and French Navies, one scuttled herself, one was wrecked at the northern end of the Norwegian territorial corridor, and only one got home.

The communique adds:

"The week February 26 to March 3 has been exceptional for the British Navy and its handling of commerce. The total loss of British tonnage was only 1,886 tons.

"On the other hand four German ships, totalling 18,490 tons, have scuttled themselves to avoid capture."

10,000-TON STEAMER LOST—CREW SAVED

FIFTY-SIX members of the crew of the 10,000-ton London steamer Pacific Reliance, sunk off the West Coast yesterday, were landed at a fishing port in Cornwall last night.

One of the crew told the *Daily Mirror*: "A terrific explosion almost tore the ship in two. We took to the boats.

"Fortunately the weather was calm and shortly after the ship sank an R.A.F. reconnaissance plane appeared. She gave our position to a small coasting steamer, the Macville."

ARMY CAMP BLAZE

Fire brigades from Purfleet, Grays and Tilbury, as well as A.F.S. men, were called out last night to help troops fight a fire at a military camp at South Ockendon, near Grays, Essex.

The fire involved wooden buildings and was so fierce that the glare could be seen for miles around. It was under control in two hours.

THREW BOMB OVERBOARD— "NOWT"

BRAVING German bullets which were sweeping his ship in the North Sea, a trawler's fireman picked up an incendiary bomb which had fallen and threw it overboard.

And all twenty-eight-year-old Joe Utting, who lives at Toll-square, North Shields, had to say when congratulated by the skipper and his shipmates, was:

"IT'S NOWT."

And "It's nowt" is all Joe Utting, of the North Shields trawler, Ben Vurie, said to the "Daily Mirror" yesterday.

Skipper George Charlton, of Belkwall Green, North Shields, said:—

"Joe has been dodging people who wanted to talk to him about his exploit ever since we reached port."

Yet the first V.C. was awarded to a midshipman who, during the Crimean War, threw overboard a live shell.

Swept by Bullets

Joe was dashing off to undergo a gunnery course when a *Daily Mirror* reporter saw him, and when the Ben Vurie next puts to sea, she will carry a gun with him as one of her gunners.

"We don't think Joe's action was nowt," said Skipper Charlton. "It was heroic.

"The German aeroplane was sweeping the ship with her machine-guns when he ran from the galley alleyway, where he was sheltering, got into the small boat into which an incendiary bomb had fallen and heaved it into the sea.

"Utting did not know whether the bomb was an explosive or an incendiary bomb. He just knew it was a bomb and that the ship was in danger."

Saved the Ship

"An explosive bomb dropped near the ship and lifted her stern out of the water. But for Utting's quick action, the ship would in all probability have been set on fire.

"The plane released a shower of about a dozen incendiary bombs. Two fell in the ship."

"I ran to the scuppers and tried to get the other one, but a shower of sparks from the bomb prevented me getting near. Just then the ship dipped and shipped some water, which extinguished the bomb."

Another member of the crew, seventy-year-old deck-hand Owen Rowlands, of South Shields, who was made prisoner by the Germans in the last war, said—

"I have seen many plucky actions, but Utting's was the bravest."

ARMY RELEASES 29,000 WORKERS

To give full scope to Britain's industrial war effort, and so that essential industries shall not be dislocated, the Army has released 15,000 reservists for three months.

This comb-out for men who are valuable to industry has also released 3,000 Territorials and 11,000 others.

Machinery has also been set up to secure postponement of calling-up of men vital to industry.

OVER FRONTIER BY MISTAKE

Two English soldiers crossed the Franco-Belgian frontier yesterday by mistake. They entered an estaminet at Templeuve and asked for a cup of coffee. There they learnt their mistake and were arrested.—Reuter.

Give Her Pickles

A bottle of pickles may be the most suitable gift for some young men to take to their girl friends.

In a report to the "Journal of Heredity," Dr. S. Davidenkov, of Leningrad, declared that he had found in some families an inherited inability to eat anything sweet.

Pickles, sour potatoes, cranberries and rye bread were delicacies to such people, he said.— Associated Press.

ACCUSED OF MURDERING WIFE IN FIRE

WHILE he was milking cows in his shed with his brother, Arthur Charles Hadman was arrested last night by Scotland Yard men and charged at Stangrounds (Hunts) police station later with the murder of his wife, Grace Elizabeth Hadman.

Mrs. Hadman was found dead in the burned-out sitting-room of her cottage at Chesterton, near Peterborough, after her four children had been rescued from the fire just in time by their father.

Hadman will be brought before a special Court at Old Fletton this morning.

With His Brother

The officers who took him to the station were Chief Inspector Bridger and Sergeant Marshall, of Scotland Yard; Superintendent Hodson, of the Hunts Police; and Patrol-Driver Douglas.

Hadman was with his brother when the officers arrived. He was in his working clothes, without a coat, and wore rubber boots. The officers had a few minutes' talk and took him aside.

Patrol-Driver Douglas then went to the cottage 100 yards away and brought his coat, and Hadman was driven away in the police car.

(A picture of Hadman leaving the cowshed after his arrest is on back page.)

HIS FATHER'S KIT BAG

WHEN Colin Little, aged nineteen, joined the Royal Artillery at the Territorial headquarters in Biggleswade, Beds, they issued him with a kit-bag.

It was not new, and as he turned it outside in he saw a name and a number. The surname was his own.

He found that he had been given the kit-bag his father carried through the last war.

His father, Mr. Herbert Little, of Biggleswade, handed back the kit-bag at Felixstowe in 1919.

DAILY MIRROR, Saturday, March 9, 1940.

Daily Mirror

No. 11,311 — ONE PENNY.
Registered at the G.P.O. as a Newspaper.

HITLER ORDERS RIBBENTROP TO ROME

AS GERMAN PRESSURE ON SWEDEN BEGAN TO SHOW RESULTS YESTERDAY IN A STIFFENING OF SWEDEN'S REFUSAL TO AID THE FINNS, HITLER SWUNG HIS DIPLOMATIC FORCES TO A NEW FRONT.

He ordered Ribbentrop to Rome to see Mussolini and Count Ciano. Ribbentrop leaves today by special train.

"This short visit," said the German radio last night, "is another visible proof that the axis was never weakened or broken."

And Berlin announced that Ribbentrop would discuss with the Duce the Sumner Welles visit and the Swedish mediation in the Finnish war.

In fact, writes the "Daily Mirror" Political Correspondent, Ribbentrop goes to Rome in an attempt to smash the proposed trade pact between Britain and Italy.

Hitler knows he must stop the deal by which Welsh coal will be exchanged for Italian munitions and machinery

Italy Must Choose

The trade pact has already been initialled and is now delayed until a solution is found to the dispute over the German coal now held by Britain

And Ribbentrop visits Rome as the Duce hesitates. Italy must either openly join forces with Hitler or enter into trade relations with Britain.

Mussolini is known to favour the Nazis. But his power in Italy is waning. He cannot count on the united support of the Italian people and an unpopular move might end his career.

Reports that M. Svinhufvud conferred with Government officials in Berlin (see column 4) were denied in Berlin. A spokesman said:

"All we know is that he is on his way to Italy for his health. Of course, he may undertake some other business there."

Von Ribbentrop and Hitler, it is understood, conferred at the Chancellery last night on the subject of the German Foreign Minister's visit to Rome.

PLANE ATTACKS BELGIAN BOATS

THREE Belgian fishing boats reported yesterday that they had been machine-gunned from the air last night in the North Sea, opposite Zeebrugge. — Associated Press.

WINSTON—20 DAYS' GRACE

The Appelate Division of the New York Supreme Court yesterday gave Mr. Winston Churchill twenty days to answer a £250,000 slander suit brought by William Griffin, a New York newspaper proprietor.

The action was based upon an alleged denial by Mr. Churchill of an interview in 1936 with Griffin when Mr. Churchill was said to have asserted: "It was all a mistake for you (the United States) to enter the world war"—Associated Press

LADY HAW-HAW

Meet Lady Haw-Haw, wife of the hypocritical "Hamburger." Hers is the voice you hear every night announcing the programme.

Picture above shows her as a ballet dancer and (below) a studio portrait.

TELLS ON RADIO OF GAY NAZI LIFE

THE mysterious woman who broadcasts on the Hamburg radio, and has become known as "Lady Haw-Haw," is, in fact, entitled to that name, for she is the second wife of the man who, during the past six months, has made for himself the most outstanding name in broadcasting.

Lady Haw-Haw was before her marriage two years ago Miss Margaret White, known to her friends as Margot. She is the daughter of Mr. and Mrs. E. R. White, who now live at Bellott-street, Cheetham Hill, Manchester.

Lady Haw-Haw has several times

Contd. on Back Page, Col. 4

SHIP SUNK: 68 SAVED

Seventeen European and fifty-one Lascar members of the crew of the Harrison Line steamer Counsellor (5,068 tons), of Liverpool, were landed at a north-west coast port yesterday after their vessel had been sunk by an explosion.

SWEDES WARN ALLIES, FINNS

SWEDEN'S Government has decided that any attempt to land troops or to send troops through Sweden will be opposed by force—a warning to the Allies that no armed help to Finland can go that way.

The Swedes deny that they are putting pressure on Finland to yield to the Russian demands, but they have hinted that if the Finns refuse, the Swedish volunteers will be withdrawn.

In Stockholm it is believed that a general mobilisation will soon be ordered.

Direct negotiations between M. Paasikivi, the former Finnish Minister in Stockholm, and Mme. Kollontay, the Soviet Minister in Stockholm, will be begun in Stockholm today, says a British United Press from Stockholm.

A Reuter message, however, says that peace talks between Finland and Soviet Russia will probably be held in Tallinn, the Estonian capital, or Riga, the Latvian capital.

Terms Rejected

Mr. Steinhardt, U.S. Ambassador in Moscow, conferred yesterday with M. Molotov, Soviet Commissar for Foreign Affairs.

Mr. Steinhardt also met the Swedish Minister.

The Finnish ex-President Svinhufvud, one of the "peace" delegates, flew yesterday from Stockholm to Berlin.

He went at once to the German Foreign Office where he is believed to have seen Von Ribbentrop in the company of the Swedish Minister in Berlin

In Helsinki it is unofficially reported that the terms have already been flatly rejected

The Allies, said a Paris spokesman, will continue to give Finland aid should she decide to fight "to the bitter end."

Field-Marshal Mannerheim had a long conversation at his headquarters yesterday with members of the French military mission now in Finland, says a Reuter message from Rome.

R.A.F. PLANE BOMBS 3 NAZI PATROL SHIPS

Just what one R.A.F. warplane did to a Heinkel seaplane and three German patrol ships before he "called it a day"—and carried on with his job, reconnaissance. . . .

AN R.A.F. pilot, flying near the Island of Borkum, enemy naval base, spotted a Heinkel 115, a long-range seaplane, about a mile ahead.

He overtook it and attacked from dead astern, hitting the enemy's fuselage from 150 yards.

At fifty yards' range the attack was pressed home. The German rear gunner was silent. He had either been disabled or killed.

One of the British crew signalled his gun had jammed. The pilot flew into a cloud so that the gun could be cleared.

With all his guns again serviceable, the pilot emerged and saw his opponent below him. He dived to renew the fight at close range, and the damaged Heinkel was driven to find safety in cloud.

Soon afterwards the pilot saw

Contd. on Back Page, Col. 3

WHY 1,500,000 MORE HAVE JOINED THE COCOA ARMY

EVER since the war began the demand for Cocoa has risen steadily. About 5½ million cups a day were drunk in peace-time—over 7 million cups a day now.

Why is this?

There is a simple answer. People everywhere are finding out what the Royal Navy knew over a century ago when Cocoa was first issued as an official ration. It is the ideal drink for anyone who is doing a real job of work. It's a drink that is also a food, full of warmth and steaming cheerfulness.

In hard civilian jobs, among our troops, in the Merchant Navy—everywhere COCOA is coming in with a swing. You will not need to ask why. Just try it for yourself and you will find what we mean when we say,

"A cup of cocoa is a cup of food"

CADBURY'S

BOURNVILLE COCOA

DAILY MIRROR, Monday, March 11, 1940.

Daily Mirror

MAR 11

No. 11,312 ONE PENNY
Registered at the G.P.O. as a Newspaper.

Not to Wed —Yet

Glamour girl Norma Hoskin.

ROME WON'T FIGHT

Rome Radio commenting on Ribbentrop's visit announced this morning: "Suppositions that as a consequence of the negotiations Italy intends to change the attitude taken after the beginning of the war are without foundation."—Reuter.

TODAY Von Ribbentrop, the German Foreign Minister, now in Rome, will have an audience of the Pope.

Ribbentrop will almost certainly attempt to conciliate the outraged feelings of the Vatican by promising to modify or even stop the persecution of Roman Catholics in conquered Poland.

If the move succeeds the way will be clear for Hitler's big plan—an Easter peace move supported by the Pope and President Roosevelt.

As Von Ribbentrop arrived in Rome yesterday he learned that Britain had released the Italian ships carrying coal from Germany.

Italy Pleased

He found that the tension between Britain and Italy had been eased, and the Italian Press full of praise of England.

Within an hour he was in conference with Mussolini. The talk lasted an hour and a quarter and will be continued today.

Later Von Ribbentrop saw Count Ciano, the Italian Foreign Minister.

Ciano's newspaper "Il Telegrafo" says that during the conversations only Ribbentrop spoke. Mussolini and Ciano listened and were silent.

The opportunity for German mischief-making vanished as Britain announced the release of the thirteen coal ships. All Italy was relieved and pleased.

"This is an act of goodwill," was the general newspaper comment; and the Rome radio announcer, speaking in German, said, "There is now no longer a difference of opinion between Italy and Britain."

Certainly, the British decision will make it easier for Mussolini to say "No" to German plans and for Ciano to give Ribbentrop advice.

With Ribbentrop in Rome, Hitler made a strange faltering, short—it lasted only fifteen minutes—speech in Berlin.

He talked of the German statesmen of the past who were loved by the gods "only because they attempted to achieve the impossible," and of the blood "that has united Germany for better or for worse."

The speech is on page 2.

★ They Ignored Him

Budapest Radio, generally very pro-German, almost ignored Hitler's speech. In the middle of the news bulletin the announcer merely said: "Hitler spoke today," and went on with the rest of the news.

FINNS TALK PEACE IN MOSCOW

FINLAND ADMITTED LAST NIGHT THAT FOUR FINNISH DELEGATES HAVE BEEN IN MOSCOW FOR THE PAST FIVE DAYS TO DISCUSS PEACE TERMS WITH THE KREMLIN.

"The delegation has had two or three interviews with Soviet Government representatives," the official Helsinki statement said last night. "The Finnish delegates took note of the Soviet peace conditions.

"No decision has been taken up to the present."

One Finnish general, shown a copy of the statement last night, declared in disgust: "And we have been fighting for three months for this."

Finland's delegates in Moscow are the Premier, M. Ryti, Stalin's old acquaintance, M. Paasikivi, General Walden, representing Marshal Mannerheim, and M. Voionmaa, a Finnish M.P.

The Russian terms are not officially announced, but one report says the time limit for Finnish acceptance is fixed for tomorrow.

Rome radio says Finland is prepared to hand over part of the Karelian Isthmus and the Petsamo district, but refuses to give up Hangoe, the fortified port commanding the entrance to the Gulf of Finland.

A British United Press message from Stockholm says it is reported that Finland has sent the Russian terms to Britain and France and has asked the Allies what they will do if she refuses the conditions and decides to fight on.

In fact, writes the "Daily Mirror" Political Correspondent, there is no doubt that if the Finnish Government appeals for greater support within the next forty-eight hours, it would be forthcoming.

But Germany and Sweden are putting tremendous pressure on Finland to accept the Russian terms.

Hitler knows the danger. He fears that Britain and France will send an expeditionary force to help Finland, and he knows he cannot count on Russian support this summer.

Stalin, too, is anxious to avoid open warfare with the Allies.

But he knows that Britain is still

Continued on Back Page

PRODUCER'S NO TO HER ROMANCE

From JOHN WALTERS

NEW YORK, Sunday.

A LONDON showgirl and her wealthy undergraduate fiance, both aged twenty-one, had to abandon their wedding plans today, after they had already obtained the licence—because her producer objects.

They are Miss Norma Hoskin, appearing in an American version of the Folies Bergeres, and Frank Boylan, of Harvard University. He fell in love with her three years ago when he saw her on the stage at the Prince of Wales Theatre, London.

Yesterday they gave notice to marry, but today producer Clifford Fischer, who acts as Norma's guardian, stepped in.

"I'm compelled to stop their romance," he said. "Firstly, I cannot release Norma from the show; secondly, she's in the United States under a 500 dollar bond I posted myself which makes me responsible for her."

"I'm very upset, but there's nothing to be done but to postpone the wedding," wept Norma.

Boylan told me that he lost track of Norma after their meeting three years ago until he saw her picture outside a Boston theatre the other day, and found her backstage the same night.

"I'm still determined to wed Norma some day," he said.

Norma's parents live in Australia.

ADAM ARRESTED

From JOHN WALTERS

NEW YORK, Sunday.

EPSTEIN'S famous statue "Adam" was taken into custody here today through failing to show visible means of support.

Adam arrived last week from England, but no one claimed him, although it is believed that a "guardian" is following by another boat.

When they seized Adam today, the Customs officers stated that the United States Government could keep him unless a claimant turns up.

SCUTTLED NEW SHIP

THE Germans have brought their scuttling score to thirty-four. It was announced last night that another German ship has gone to the bottom.

The victim of the latest suicide of the sea is a brand new motor vessel, the Hanover, a 5,600-tonner, which was built last year.

She was plying confidently enough between the West Indian islands of Santo Domingo and Purto Rico a few nights ago when the inevitable British warship—a cruiser—came on the scene.

Then the German crew got busy. Not with screened guns or other secret weapons, but with the fire-raiser's paraphernalia, combined with some German nautical "plumbing."

What with fire raging on top of her, and water rushing into her innards, the Hanover hadn't much of a chance. And, of course, the crew, in the circumstances, scuttled, too—scuttled off in their small boats.

She belonged to the Norddeutcher Lloyd Co.

Pink Form Was Just a Pink Slip

Members of the Auxiliary Territorial Service will show their pink forms whenever called upon to do so.

This appeared on the notice board at the A.T.S. headquarters of a certain command.

The A.T.S. girls are issued with pink-coloured leave passes, but they wondered what the real meaning of the notice was.

"Someone was trying to be funny," an official of the A.T.S. told the "Daily Mirror" yesterday.

TWO EVACUATED BOYS MISSING

TWO boys evacuated to Lewes, Sussex, were missing last night from their billets.

The boys, John Gibbs, twelve, of Larnaca-street, Bermondsey, London, S.E., and Dennis Burns, ten, of Tanner-street, Bermondsey, left their billets at about 2.30 saying that they were going for a walk up the river.

HOT-WATER BOTTLE UNDER SKELETON

A RUBBER hot-water bottle, filled with water, lay under the skeleton of a man found in bushes at the foot of a 400ft cliff at Folkestone yesterday.

Discovery was made by two schoolboys in The Warren, a popular rambling ground.

Police think the man had been dead more than two years.

Small pieces of clothing were still on the skeleton. The man wore boots in a good state of preservation, but there were no clues as to his identity.

Bushes and branches of trees had to be cut away before the police could remove the skeleton.

About 300 yards away is a tea chalet frequented by thousands of people during the spring and summer months.

The presence of the hot-water bottle upsets the theory that the man may have fallen over the cliff and not been seen.

DAILY MIRROR, Wednesday, March 13, 1940.

Daily Mirror

MAR 13

No 11,314 ONE PENNY
Registered at the G.P.O. as a Newspaper.

Roosevelt Wants Easter Truce

From JOHN WALTERS
New York, Tuesday.

PRESIDENT ROOSEVELT has instructed his "big four" in Europe, Sumner Welles, Myron Taylor and Ambassadors Kennedy and Steinhardt to do everything possible to secure an Easter truce in Europe of thirty to sixty days, according to reports in Washington tonight.

The thirty-day truce proposal was first made by Senator Key Pittman. Now it is believed the President is behind it.

Many Americans who sympathise with the Allied cause are becoming increasingly suspicious of Welles's mission and the activities of other American diplomats in Europe, fearing they are trying to bring about another Munich.

"Mean Hitler Victory"

New York Herald Tribune says today: "Thirty-day armistice in the West now would mean Hitler has won the war.

"Surely the President does not wish to repeat on a far grander scale the experience of September, 1938, when, with the world seemingly on the brink of war he summoned Hitler to negotiate. Negotiations took place, and Czechoslovakia was laid upon the altar as a result.

"Now the President is again getting the United States into Europe, and a good many Europeans are anxiously asking whether he knows what he is doing there. So are a good many Americans."

HER MA TOLD NAVY

SHE started as a prospective mother-in-law should—by having her own way. And none was so pleased as the bridegroom when she got it.

For Able-Seaman Roy Hellon's wedding had been postponed five times through his leave being stopped. A sixth disappointment seemed inevitable.

But the bride-to-be's mother, Mrs. Barratt, of Cambridge-street, Plymouth, wouldn't stand for it.

"Can't postpone wedding again. Must take place this time" she telegraphed to the captain of Roy's ship.

It worked. Roy and her daughter Elizabeth were married at Plymouth yesterday

500-Mile Trip

The wedding was first planned for December 28. After the five postponements it was fixed for 2 p.m. yesterday.

After Mrs. Barrett's successful ultimatum, Roy started a 500-mile trip from a Scottish port for Plymouth.

When he got to Paddington he wired Elizabeth saying he could not get there in time.

Elizabeth went round the town on her bicycle telling the guests that the time had been altered from 2 p.m. to 4 p.m.

Roy's train did not arrive at Plymouth until 3.30. He got a taxi.

Mrs. Barrett told the *Daily Mirror*: "When Roy sent the telegram saying he still could not get leave and would we postpone the wedding until Thursday, I thought it had gone a bit too far.

"I decided to send a telegram to his captain and see what he could do about it."

Able-Seaman Roy Hellon and his bride, married at the sixth attempt, because mother-in-law told the Navy: "The wedding's got to take place."

REDS SAY PEACE IS SIGNED

FINLAND, IN A DRAMATIC MESSAGE THIS MORNING, DENIED A MOSCOW REPORT THAT PEACE HAD BEEN SIGNED AND THAT FIGHTING WOULD END AT NOON TODAY.

Russia claimed that the Finnish delegation had signed a treaty on these terms.

1. Russia gets the entire Karelian Isthmus including Viborg (Viipuri), the area round Lake Ladoga and parts of Eastern Finland;
2. Hangoes and the territory around it will be leased to the U.S.S.R., and Russia will build submarine bases there;
3. Finland undertakes not to maintain any warships in this area except small patrol ships;
4. The Soviet Union undertakes to withdraw its troops from the Petsamo district;
5. The Soviet Union will have the right of free transit from Petsamo to Norway and vice versa;
6. In the course of the year 1940 a railway is to be built through Northern Finland;
7. The peace treaty is to be ratified in three days in Moscow.

Even if the Finnish delegates signed in Moscow, the peace terms may not be accepted by Finland.

The Finnish Parliament, meeting in secret last night, stormily debated the terms, which must be ratified by the Finnish M.P.s.

There is a further barrier to acceptance. It is possible that the Army and Marshal Mannerheim will reject the agreement, call for Allied aid and fight on.

If the Moscow peace report is correct the war that began with the Russian invasion on November 30 ends today after three and a half months of desperate fighting.

Appeal to Workers

The main theatre of war has been the Karelian Isthmus, now ceded to the Russians—a sixty-mile corridor between the Gulf of Finland and Lake Ladoga opposite Leningrad.

Fighting last night was reported to be slackening, but there were no indications on the fronts that the war was about to end.

Mr. Chamberlain will make a statement today on Russo-Finnish talks. There is considerable opposition to Britain's action and a debate will be arranged.

How strong the Allied help to Finland would be was revealed in a startling speech in the French Chamber yesterday by Premier Edouard Daladier.

He announced that 50,000 British
(Continued on Back Page)

R.A.F. BOMBER SINKS A SUBMARINE

THE pilot of an R.A.F. bomber who attacked single-handed a German submarine at the entrance to the Schillig Roads yesterday afternoon, has reported that before flying off he saw the bow and stern of the U-boat sticking out of the water, with the centre part submerged It is believed that the U-boat sank soon afterwards.

The incident occurred during an R.A.F. reconnaissance flight over the Heligoland Bight, and not far from where a U-boat was bombed and destroyed a week ago.

The submarine was going slowly along the surface when it was sighted by the aircraft which had just emerged from a low layer of clouds.

The bomber immediately crossed the submarine and dropped four 250lb. bombs, one of which was seen to hit the vessel just ahead of the conning tower. A second hit is also believed to have been registered.

Another of our aircraft engaged on reconnaissance a few hours later saw a number of patrol vessels in the area where the attack had been made.

More Than 50

Shillig Roads are in the mouth of the River Elbe, between Bruenesbuttel and Cuxhaven.

Considerably more than fifty U-boats are believed to have been sunk altogether, and many badly damaged.

The one which was attacked by an R.A.F. machine in Shillig Roads last week was also sunk by a direct hit between the stern and the conning tower.

It was in the Shillig Roads, too, that the R.A.F. dropped bombs on a pocket battleship, believed to be the Admiral Scheer, in the first few days of the war.

BEHAR BROTHERS RESIGN

Mr. David Behar and Mr. Robert Behar, the brothers sacked by Mr. Burgin, Minister of Supply, at the beginning of the month, have given up their Army commissions.

The official *London Gazette* last night announced their appointments as second lieutenants in the Royal Artillery, and their resignations.

NO MORE BAD OFFICERS

"I SAW men killed in the last war because they had been allowed to go out under commanding officers who were not up to the job. I am determined to see that that shall not happen again."

This pledge, greeted by a storm of cheers, was given last night by Mr. Oliver Stanley, the War Minister, in the House of Commons.

Mr. Stanley was replying to the debate on the Army Estimates (reported on page 2).

He added that no commanding officer should be allowed to take troops to France, whatever their merits may have been in the past, unless those who are responsible for the job are convinced that he is competent to do the job.

"Democratisation of the Army," he said, "must mean equal opportunity for all, going through the ranks to get a commission. What we can never allow it to mean is a reduction in the authority of those officers when once their commission has been granted.

"If democratisation means that, I should regard it as a catastrophe for the Army."

Sir H. Morris Jones said Mr. Stanley had not paid special tribute to the work done by Mr. Hore Belisha during the two years he was War Minister.

Mr. Stanley said "We do not come here as a mutual admiration society." When members read the Official Report they would see that he had gone out of his way to pay tribute to his predecessor's work.

BIG DANGER OF BOMBING

IF you live in an evacuation area, don't bring your children home for the Easter holidays.

The Minister of Health has issued a warning to this effect. He says that it is in the interests of safety that parents should not bring their children home to areas that have been evacuated.

He adds that it is the view of the Government that the danger of air attack must be regarded as more serious during the period covered by the usual school holidays at Easter than it was at Christmas.

A good many children were brought back at Christmas but the Minister recognises that the risk was not so great then

"The responsibility for dangers which may ensue upon failure to act on this advice must rest with the parents" says the Minister.

White Ties Will Help Us Win the War

Sir John Reith, Minister of Information, congratulated the Cinematograph Exhibitors' Association last night—because they had made their banquet at Grosvenor House, London, "a white tie affair."

"It is the first time I have worn a white tie since the war started," he said. "I think the policy of wearing a white tie is right and proper and does us all good."

The menu was oysters, hors d'œuvres, smoked salmon, consomme cream soup, salmon, braized ox tongue and spinach, chicken salad, potatoes and peas and sweet.

DAILY MIRROR, Thursday, March 14, 1940.

Daily Mirror

No. 11,315   ONE PENNY
Registered at the G.P.O. as a Newspaper.

ASSASSIN SHOOTS MINISTER, KILLS KNIGHT

SIR MICHAEL O'DWYER, AGED SEVENTY-FIVE, GOVERNOR OF THE PUNJAB DURING THE AMRITSAR RIOTS IN 1919, WAS SHOT DEAD BY AN INDIAN GUNMAN AT A CROWDED MEETING IN CAXTON HALL, WESTMINSTER, YESTERDAY.

The gunman fired first at Lord Zetland, Secretary of State for India, and slightly wounded him. Then, as they rose to reach him he turned his gun, shot and wounded Lord Lamington, aged seventy-nine, ex- Governor of Bombay, and Sir Louis Dane, aged eighty-four, another Punjab ex-Governor.

Nearly 300 men and women had heard Sir Percy Sykes address the meeting of the East India Association in the Tudor Room of Caxton Hall.

Lord Zetland was in the chair. The meeting was about to close and Lord Lamington had risen to propose a vote of thanks, when a thick-set Indian rose, walked to the Press table, pulled out a revolver and fired.

As the first two shots were fired Lord Zetland toppled over and collapsed on the arms of his chair.

Sir Michael O'Dwyer jumped up. Two shots entered his heart and he fell back dead.

Assassin Fired
Six Shots

The assassin fired six times. With his last two bullets he wounded Lord Lamington and Sir Louis Dane, who had been sitting at each end of the front row of the audience.

Sir Louis was hit in the arm; Lord Lamington's right hand was shattered.

For a shocked second no one moved. The assassin turned, shouted "Make way, make way," and dashed down the aisle.

Two men, one of them in uniform, jumped on a man and threw him. Then men and women jumped to their feet, shouted, "Murder, police . . . a doctor."

A woman doctor, Dr. Grace

(Continued on Back Page)

Sir Michael O'Dwyer—died with two bullet wounds in his heart.

Thirty-seven-year-old Indian, Mahomed Singh Azad, leaving the Caxton Hall with police. He was charged last night with the murder of Sir Michael O'Dwyer and with wounding Lord Lamington, Sir Louis Dane and Lord Zetland by shooting them with a revolver.

Lord Zetland—a bullet grazed his ribs, and he fell

Lord Lamington was shot in the hand.

FINN, SWEDE, NORWAY PACT

A CONFERENCE between Finland, Sweden and Norway for the conclusion of a treaty of defensive alliance will be opened immediately, declared M. Tanner, the Finnish Foreign Minister, in Helsinki last night.

M. Tanner stated that the war with Russia had prevented the investigation of the possibilities of such a pact, which he said " will secure the frontiers and the independence of these three nations."

Soviet-Rumanian Treaty

He added that it had been agreed by the Governments of the three countries that now a Russo-Finnish peace has been re-established, the question of an alliance should be investigated.

Plans for a non-aggression pact between Russia and Rumania were reported in Bukarest, Rumanian capital, last night to be under consideration. The talks would be held in Berlin.

A military commission composed of high-ranking Rumanian Army officials is at present in Berlin. The Rumanian delegation is reported to have left for Berlin secretly, says the Associated Press.

Sweden to Rebuild Finn Front—Page 3.

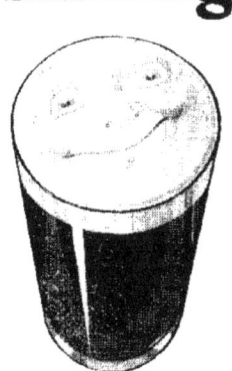

Keep smiling

Guinness is good for you

DAILY MIRROR, Monday, March 18, 1940.

Daily Mirror

No. 11,318 — ONE PENNY
Registered at the G.P.O. as a Newspaper.

MAR 18

DUCE, HITLER MEET TODAY

First Civilian Killed in Biggest Air Raid of War

MAKING its biggest raid on Britain since the war began, Hitler's air force bombed Scapa Flow, killing a civilian.

The raid began in twilight and ended in darkness on Saturday night.

R.A.F. fighters beat off Heinkels from the Forth Bridge. The Germans never got within bombing distance of it.

Dropping more than 100 bombs in eighty-five minutes, fourteen planes attacked the fleet anchorage at Scapa Flow.

They hit only one warship, inflicting minor damage and caused seven naval casualties.

But bombs which were dropped on land damaged five cottages in the little village of Bridge of Waith, near Stromness. Seven civilians were wounded.

Dived into Ditches

The civilian killed was a man who was hit as he stood at the door of his house in Bridge of Waith.

He was James Isbester, aged twenty-seven, an Orkney County Council employee, married, with one child.

One house in the hamlet was completely wrecked, and a woman crawled unaided from the debris. Flashes of gunfire during the raid lit up a large area of the countryside and the heather covered hills were set ablaze by incendiary bombs.

There are huge craters in the earth in the Bridge of Waith district, where people threw themselves into ditches to avoid the debris, which shot 40ft. in the air.

One of the raiders was shot down and others were believed damaged, said the Admiralty communique yesterday announcing the raid.

The communique said that fourteen machines "reached the objective."

And they were met with a blaze of

Contd. on Back Page, Col. 1

R.A.F. Bomb Patrol Ships

During a daylight reconnaissance of the Heligoland Bight, R.A.F. planes bombed German naval patrol vessels. These vessels were sighted at points between Borkum and Heligoland.

One of the ships in the German formation was partly lifted out of the water by the bomb explosions.

Two enemy aircraft which were attacking ships off the east coast of Scotland were intercepted and attacked yesterday by R.A.F. fighters and pursued into the clouds.

Damage is believed to have been inflicted on both German planes, says an Air Ministry statement.

BABY FOR PRUNELLA

LADY David Douglas-Hamilton, leader of the Women's League of Health and Beauty, who has often been described as "the perfect woman," is expecting a baby in June.

It will be the "ideal baby." Lady David Douglas-Hamilton has her own ideas on how a baby should be reared to ensure perfect fitness and health.

She was formerly Miss Prunella Stack, Britain's leading "keep-fit" girl.

This is what she has said of her own upbringing:—

"From babyhood I was brought up in a perfectly natural way. My mother did not believe in fads or fancies. I do not believe in them either.

"At the age of five I was a member of my mother's first juvenile physical training class.

"Before I was six I had been hardened to the idea of fresh air and cold water. Cold baths were such fun.

"Ever since I can remember I have eaten fruit at every meal."

At the time of her marriage in October, 1938, to Lord David Douglas-Hamilton, she was twenty-two. Her husband is the youngest son of the late Duke of Hamilton, who died on Saturday.

The Women's League of Health and Beauty had more than 140,000 in Great Britain alone when the war broke out and branches all over the Empire.

GIRL SHOT IN FUN PARK

RUSHING up to her sailor friend at a Blackpool shooting gallery last night a sixteen-year-old girl was accidentally shot in the stomach by him as he turned to greet her.

Late last night the sailor, Walter Stanley Parkinson, sat by the bedside of the girl—Barbara Bowman, of Cumberland - avenue, Blackpool — as she lay seriously ill in hospital.

She had undergone an operation by which the bullet was removed.

The accident occurred in Luna Park and crowds saw the girl crumple up and fall to the floor.

"If she had arrived a fraction of a second later it would not have happened," said Mrs. J. Hudson, who was in charge of the shooting gallery. "It was the last shot in the gun."

MUSSOLINI AND HITLER WILL MEET THIS MORNING IN A SECRET RETREAT ON THE ITALIAN SIDE OF THE BRENNER PASS.

The Duce suddenly left Rome yesterday by special train, accompanied by Count Ciano, his son-in-law Foreign Secretary, and by Von Mackensen, Germany's Ambassador in Rome. Ribbentrop is believed to be travelling with Hitler.

No explanation of the meeting was given in Rome or Berlin, but the Rome Radio announcer, commenting on the second visit of Mr. Sumner Welles, said:—

"Public opinion expects mediation and even peace proposals, especially now that Germany has prevented the war spreading to the north."

Ribbentrop Carried Peace Plan

The meeting is almost certainly a new attempt by Hitler to secure a peace that will leave him with his spoils.

The move began when Ribbentrop visited Rome, bearing with him a draft peace plan.

That plan, it is believed, was submitted to Mr. Sumner Welles when he reached Rome after visiting Berlin, Paris and London.

What Mr. Welles said is not known, but the result is Mussolini's dash to the German frontier to meet Hitler.

It may be that he is carrying a revised peace plan backed this time by President Roosevelt.

In Paris last night it was reported that Mussolini will tell Hitler that his peace terms are quite unacceptable and will urge him to revise them so that they can receive the approval of President Roosevelt.

It is significant that Mr. Sumner Welles is reported to be delaying his departure from Italy.

He was due to leave Naples tomorrow on board the Italian liner Comte de Savoia. He changed his plan so that he would leave on Wednesday from Genoa.

In Rome last night, says Exchange, it was announced that the sailing of the Comte de Savoia is

Contd. on Back Page, Col. 5

MEETS HUSBAND FRANCO SPARED

FROM JOHN WALTERS
New York, Sunday.

BLONDE actress Edith Dahl, whose beauty caused General Franco to spare the life of her daring airman husband, was reunited with him here today when he landed from Spain after a three-year parting.

"My darling, at last—at last," sighed Edith. "Don't let me lose you again," said Harold, as he stroked her hair and told her how he owed his life and freedom to her.

When, as a flyer for the Loyalists, this thirty-year-old American was captured by the rebels and marked for execution, Edith sent a letter and photograph to Franco begging that her husband's life be spared.

Today Harold told me as he held his wife's hand: "There is no doubt Edith's letter and photograph saved me from being shot by an execution squad. Three days after I was sentenced to die the sentence was unexpectedly commuted and while serving a term of life imprisonment I was suddenly told I would soon be free."

B.E.F. Leave Is Stopped Again

B.E.F. leave has been held up owing to unforeseen delay. Normal leave will be resumed as early as possible, says the War Office.

Leave was suspended on January 14 and resumed on a limited scale three days later. The big freeze-up at the end of January caused another brief postponement of leave for B.E.F. and R.A.F. men in France.

There was another postponement on March 1 because of "unavoidable delays." Men due to cross from France had to wait until stormy conditions abated.

CABINET RESHUFFLE

BY OUR POLITICAL CORRESPONDENT

IMMEDIATE changes are expected in both the British and French Cabinets.

Mr. Chamberlain is almost certain to approach the Liberal and Socialist leaders, ask them to reconsider their decision of last September, when they refused to enter the Cabinet.

The Socialists will decide to remain in Opposition.

Sir Archibald Sinclair, leader of the Liberal Opposition, may, however, join the Cabinet. His recent speeches on the need for Allied unity in resisting aggression have been applauded by Members of all parties.

Sir Kingsley Wood, Air Minister, and Lord Chatfield, Minister of Defence, may be involved in the Cabinet reshuffle.

Mr. Burgin is expected to remain.

Gamelin: New Post?

Mr. Chamberlain will probably consider his Cabinet reshuffle during the Easter recess, and announce his decision just before Parliament meets on April 2.

In France, Premier Daladier is also considering new men for his Cabinet. M. Blum, Socialist leader, is likely to be asked to join; M. Laval, ex-Premier, may become Foreign Secretary.

It is believed that General Gamelin, now Commander-in-Chief of the Allied Armies in France, will become Daladier's new War Minister.

The German radio announced last night: "Mr. Winston Churchill has left London hurriedly for Paris."

The Admiralty refused to comment on that statement.

AMBULANCE EXPLODES

Ten persons, including four policemen, were injured by an explosion after the petrol tank of an ambulance caught fire last night at a garage of the St. John Ambulance Brigade in Ladywood-road, Edgbaston, Birmingham.

33

DAILY MIRROR, Saturday, March 23, 1940.

Daily Mirror

No. 11,322 — ONE PENNY
Registered at the G.P.O. as a Newspaper.

MAR 23

She Died for Hitler

HUNS SINK SEVEN

GERMANY is seeking vengeance for the Sylt raid by hitting back savagely — at the neutrals.

Seven small neutral ships have been sunk by U-boats without warning in the last two days. These lawless attacks cost many lives, including that of a woman.

None of the torpedoed neutral ships was in convoy. U-boats are afraid to attack convoys guarded by anti-submarine forces.

Instead, innocent neutrals, sailing independently on lawful voyages, are sunk so that Germany can claim a success and the bell of the useless liner Bremen be sounded on the Nazi radio.

All the neutral ships were small vessels. Only one was over 2,000 tons.

Six Were Danish

Six were Danish — Bothal (2,109 tons), Viking (1,158 tons), Christiansborg (1,929 tons), Minsk (1,229 tons), Charkow (1,026 tons) and the Algier (1,654 tons). The seventh Svinta (1,267 tons) was Norwegian.

In all, forty-six neutral citizens have been killed in this latest burst of German sea savagery.

It is thought that U-boats have been sent out with instructions to sink ships at all costs, to offset Germany's unpleasant experiences of the last few days.

It was revealed yesterday that Norway delivered a protest to Germany on March 8 against the sinking of Norwegian ships bound for neutral ports and neutral ships bound for Norway.

The note, it was officially stated, urged that the questions "should be discussed as soon as possible by representatives of the two countries with a view to rendering Norwegian sea traffic less dangerous and ensuring that Norway receives her supplies."

Jump Into Sea

"The Norwegian Minister in Berlin has therefore asked the German Government to inform him if they also desired such talks."

Twenty survivors from the Algier — nineteen crew and a woman — jumped into the sea when their ship was struck. The vessel sank in three minutes.

When they were landed at a British port yesterday, they said that other four of the crew and a woman passenger were believed to have been killed by the explosion.

The Viking was torpedoed as she was about to send aid to the sinking Bothal.

Five survivors from the Bothal and two from the Viking were clinging to a raft.

An R.A.F. plane saw them and directed ships to their rescue.

Ten German bombers which attacked a convoy on Wednesday night fled when chased by two fighter planes. Yesterday the pilot of a British fighter said that after he attacked one of the Heinkels it

(Continued on Back Page)

Lovely victim of Hitler's ambition—La Jana, world-famous dancer—is dead.

Determined to force German culture into occupied Poland, the Fuehrer sent his favourite there on a command tour. She caught a chill—and was rushed to her luxurious home in Berlin—where double pneumonia set in.

The pride of Germany, with her glowing amber-coloured skin (which she covered daily with olive oil), was a close friend of ex-Crown Prince Little Willie.

She scored a big success on her first visit to England in 1932 and later appeared in the Cochran revue, "Streamline."

WE TORPEDO FIRST SHIP

FIRST case of a German merchant ship being torpedoed and sunk by a British submarine—and, incidentally, the first blow at Germany's iron trade from the Norwegian port of Narvik—was announced yesterday.

But in accordance with international law, the submarine provided for the safety of the crew and allowed them to go, except the first engineer, who was taken prisoner.

The Admiralty announcement yesterday said: "On the evening of Thursday, March 21, one of his Majesty's submarines intercepted the German ship Heddernheim (4,947 tons).

"She has reported that the crew are safe and that she has sunk the ship."

The Heddernheim was carrying iron ore. M.P.'s recently complained that the ore route from Narvik was the biggest loophole in the British blockade.

Thirty-six members of the crew of the Heddernheim, who were taken to Skagen, near the northern tip of Jutland, left for Germany yesterday.
—Foreign messages from British United Press.

NAZIS' NEW BALKAN DEMAND

HITLER has warned King Carol of Rumania that Rumania must:—

Lower the exchange value of the Rumanian lei in relation to the mark. (This has already been altered twice in Germany's favour.)

Speed up oil production.

Increase the volume of trade between the two countries and improve transport.

Speed up agricultural production.

While these demands—contained in a twelve-point note—were being handed to the Rumanian Government yesterday by Dr. Clodius, the German economic expert, King Carol re-emphasised Rumania's determination to defend her frontier.

Addressing Crown Prince Michael and a delegation of Senators, King Carol declared that the nation would defend her frontiers "with all her energy in the conviction that they represent the sacred rights of the nation."

Minister Attacked

"All Rumanian activity at present should be dominated by meeting the needs of the armed forces, and all efforts and sacrifices should be made for national defence," said the King.

"Today there exists only one word of command, one purpose—that of conserving the integrity of Rumania."

The German Note, it is suggested in circles close to the German legation in Bukarest, may lead to the resignation of M. Tatarescu's Government.

The Note makes a sharp attack on M. Ion Christu, the new Rumanian Minister of Foreign Trade—an office created by royal decree in the middle of last month—for his part in shaping Rumania's recent economic policy.

Before his appointment Christu had been head of the Economic Department of the Foreign Ministry since 1934.

Ribbentrop Visit?

Ribbentrop, according to Rome radio, will soon again be on the move. He is expected to visit Belgrade, capital of Yugoslavia, Bukarest and other Balkan countries.

With this report came a statement that Count Teleki, Hungarian Prime Minister, will arrive tomorrow in Rome, to be received by the Duce and Count Ciano and also visit the King and the Pope.

Turkey, without explanation, yesterday ordered nine Turkish freighters to return immediately to their home ports from the Mediterranean.
—Foreign messages from British United Press, Associated Press, Exchange and Reuter.

TRADE MISSION COMING

A Rumanian trade delegation is leaving for London next week to negotiate a new payments agreement, says Reuter.

PARIS GOVT. MAJORITY—1

FRANCE'S new Premier, M. Reynaud, decided late last night to ride the storm over his two-day-old Government.

In face of a majority of only one vote after he had put a win-the-war statement to the Chamber yesterday afternoon, he called his Cabinet together to consider the question of resignation.

Later came the announcement that the Reynaud Cabinet had decided to defy opposition in the Chamber and remain in office.

M. Daladier, the former Premier and War Minister, is a member of the new Government. He remains War Minister.

The new Premier captured the support of the Socialists. But he was attacked by the Radical Socialists (Liberals) and the Right Wing.

The vote was 268 in favour and 156 against. But there were 111 abstentions, which M. Reynaud took into account against the votes in his favour.

"Rouse Our Strength"

The Socialists, who have three representatives in the Cabinet, said their co-operation had been loyally given to provide the country with all possible means to obtain a just and lasting peace in the shortest possible time, and with the fewest sacrifices.

But Radical Socialist speakers scathingly criticised the Cabinet's composition, as well as the "vagueness" of the Premier's statement.

This is what M. Reynaud said:

"In this total warfare, everything is at stake. To win is to save all; to succumb is to lose all.

"The new Government has no other reason for its existence than to arouse, to muster and to direct all the strength of France to fight and win and to crush treason from wheresoever it may come."

He added that France's "rhythm" was too slow, and declared the new Government would rouse the nation.

But critics said he had produced a Government according to the old party formula, though it was on a wider basis than Daladier's.
—(Reuter, British United Press, Associated Press.)

LOVED BY 11 WIVES

From JOHN WALTERS
NEW YORK, Friday.

HIS widow and seven of his ten former wives wept as they followed the remains of Frank Warren to the grave at Straight Creek, Kentucky, today.

All heavily veiled, the eight women interrupted the graveside prayers with such cries as:

"He was a grand man, he was," and "Never did such a good husband live."

Warren died at the age of seventy-four after a busy life of marriage, divorce and re-marriage. But though eleven times wed, he had only four children.

A dweller in the mountains of Kentucky, notorious for child brides, Warren lived up to its tradition by marrying girls between the ages of thirteen and sixteen.

He was a regular sheikh," Joe Asher, father-in-law number six, told me over the telephone.

"He broke the hearts of ten wives by forcing them to divorce him.

"His youngest bride was under thirteen when he married her. His widow Cynthia is only sixteen now."

IF IT'S CHOCOLATE THEN IT'S FOOD

There's a glass-and-a-half of fresh, full-cream milk in every ½ lb block of Cadbury's Milk Chocolate. It's the world's most delicious way of giving yourself quick energy.

CADBURYS
MILK CHOCOLATE
'feeds you on your feet'

DAILY MIRROR, Monday, March 25, 1940.

Daily Mirror

No. 11,323   ONE PENNY
Registered at the G.P.O. as a Newspaper.

MAR 25

BRITAIN'S NEW SEA BID

The Rich Man Goes to Sea—in Trawler

HERE is a picture of a wealthy man off to sea.

With a sailor's bag over his shoulder, a 1s. 11d. cap on his head and a sixpenny pipe in his mouth, he is obviously not joining a luxury liner.

Mr. Harold Anselm Vernon, ex-big game hunter, is, in fact, off to join a trawler in which he is gunner and "spare hand."

He says it is the only way he can get at the Germans and do something useful.

So he has left his flat in Regent's Park, closed his country house, and gone to live in lodgings at Lowestoft.

He allows himself only one of the many luxuries he used to enjoy. He has his valet to look after him when he gets back to port.

See story on page eight.

Cat Ran Away from—a Mouse

Tiggles the cat lay dreaming in front of the fire wondering what was for dinner. Then dinner walked into the room.

Tiggles saw a mouse coming across the carpet towards her. The mouse saw Tiggles, and stopped. Tiggles stared, the mouse stared. Tiggles licked her lips.

Then the mouse, instead of cowering away or seeking safety in flight, took a few steps forward. Tiggles, upset by this unusual conduct, retreated a foot or two. The mouse came on, and Tiggles, her hair on end and a wild look in her eyes, turned tail—and bolted.

Her owner, Miss Sarah Brodie, of Filey-avenue, Stamford Hill, London, N., said: "It was only a tiny mouse. I am afraid Tiggles is a coward."

TONIC EASTER RUSH

MERRY-AND-BRIGHT Britons, taking a holiday from the war, broke Easter records at some resorts yesterday.

London girls in beach pyjamas were among crowds which gave South Devon places their busiest Easter in fifteen years

Said one of the girls to the Daily Mirror:

"It's a tonic. More than ever I feel like telling Hitler to go to the deuce. And I can imagine nothing funnier than Lord Haw Haw's face if he could see how thoroughly our 'poor, dejected, starved people are enjoying themselves.'"

On the Broads, white sails filling in the breeze gave the real holiday look. Hire of yachts and motor-boats reached a record. Many of the Navy lads from East Coast ports spent a sailor's day off—sailing.

At Weston-super-Mare more than 200 people had to be turned away from one hotel. This year the town started special newspaper advertising to attract Easter holidaymakers and was delighted with the results.

All along the South Coast it was visiting day for thousands of newly-recruited soldiers. Wives and girl friends took the chance of seeing them.

1,400 Cars an Hour

Many parents travelled to see evacuated children in the West of England

While Bournemouth got most rail traffic, Brighton attracted the biggest proportion of the London motorists. Cars on this route averaged 1,400 an hour at the peak period. Car owners pooled their coupons and most cars had full loads.

A.A. officials reported that "from 15 to 20 per cent. of the motors were new small cars out on the road this Easter."

The number of bicycles was described as "hardly believable."

NEW HITLER SPEECH SOON

Hitler is to deliver a big political speech in the next few days, according to the Berlin correspondent of the Dutch newspaper Handelsblad.

Hitler is reliably reported to be spending Easter at his mountain home at Berchtesgaden, where it is said he is putting the finishing touches to his speech.

BRITAIN is forcing the pace in the battle with Germany for supremacy in the Scandinavian seas.

Another German merchant ship has been torpedoed off the Norwegian coast—the second in four days.

A third victim was also claimed yesterday. The crew of the German steamer Ostpreussen, bound for Gothenburg with a cargo of coke, took fright, and ran her aground off Skalderup, on the Danish coast.

The torpedoed steamer was the collier Edmund Hugo Stinnes carrying coal from Hamburg to Copenhagen.

As in the case of the German ship Heddernheim, torpedoed last Thursday in the Kattegat, all the crew of twenty-two was saved. Her captain is a prisoner in the submarine.

These two sinkings have alarmed the Germans, who did not know that a British submarine was operating on this vital route.

A report from Holstebro, Denmark, says that the Edmund Hugo Stinnes was stopped by two British submarines firing warning shots.

Norway Protests

More activities of British warships were revealed early today in a Norwegian communique which told of three incidents in the last four days when German freighters were challenged by our Navy.

Norway, alleging that her territorial waters were violated on at least two occasions, has ordered her Legation in London to lodge protests with the British Government.

According to an official statement by the Norwegian Admiralty yesterday a German trawler at Hustadviken, western Norway, reported on Thursday that she had been threatened by a British destroyer in Norwegian territorial waters.

On the same day a German cargo steamer was escorted by a Norwegian torpedo boat across Hustadviken when a British destroyer signalled and asked for the name of the German steamer.

"The Norwegian torpedo boat," the statement says, "obtained the withdrawal of the British destroyer from Norwegian territorial waters."

Wreck Sighted

The statement adds that last Friday a British destroyer tried to stop a German ship in Norwegian territorial waters near Obrestad, in south western Norway. This case was now being investigated by the Norwegian authorities.

The wreck of the steamer Edmund Hugo Stinnes was located yesterday about three miles off the Danish coast. A Danish inspection ship is making a survey of the exact position.

The crew of the Edmund Hugo Stinnes were given fifteen minutes to get away from the ship. Then they were able to reach the shore Two men were hurt in lowering the lifeboat and were taken to hospital.

The sinking of the Heddernheim in the Kattegat made a great impression on the neutrals.

(British United Press, Reuter, Associated Press.)

GERMANS NEED U-BOAT CREWS

GERMANY is making urgent appeals by radio for air and naval volunteers, holding out as an inducement advantages denied to soldiers.

According to German law, no man can be conscripted for U-boat service or the air force. Hence the appeal

It takes two years to train a submarine crew, and a crew requires a long rest after the nervous tension of a spell at sea in war conditions.

Germany has lost at least thirty submarines and their crews since the war began

Even though Germany is able to build craft to replace those lost, she is faced with the problem of manning them.

The appeal for the air force, says British United Press, asks for men from seventeen upwards.

AMERICA'S BEST DRESSED

British film star Anna Neagle is placed among the thirteen best dressed women in America, cables John Walters, Daily Mirror New York correspondent.

These thirteen, selected by a hundred of America's leading fashion designers, also include Katharine Hepburn and Mrs. James Cromwell.

WAR CLOSES A PUBLIC SCHOOL

AS the chapel bell rang at Weymouth College, Dorset, yesterday, the schoolboys filed into the chapel for the last time.

The war had taken its first toll of the public schools of Britain.

One hundred boys heard the Bishop of Salisbury preach at the closing assembly of the school, which had been in existence for seventy-seven years.

They heard him say that other schools would probably soon suffer the same fate as Weymouth College.

On Saturday they droned out Latin verbs and solved mathematical problems till noon Then they laid down their books.

Their headmaster, Mr. E. C. Moule told the Daily Mirror: "Thirty-five of the boys are forming a special house in Wellingborough School, Northants, under one of our masters, Mr. T. S. Nevill.

"Some are going to other schools. The college buildings are likely to be taken over by Dr. Barnardo's Homes.

NO LEAVE BOATS YESTERDAY

The War Office announced yesterday that no leave boats from the B.E.F. would arrive in England yesterday.

HITLER'S BALKAN GAMBLE

HITLER is gambling on a quick, bloodless victory in the Balkans where he has ordered German diplomats to start a war of nerves.

He plans to terrorise Rumania into agreeing to his demands for the devaluation of the lei, for the extra oil which he needs to fight the Allies, and for the extra wheat to feed his armies.

Threats of invasion are part of this terrorist campaign.

Hitler is pressing Hungary to allow German troops to march through that country to the Rumanian frontier.

German troops are reported to be massing on the Western Hungarian border.

Count Paul Teleki, the Hungarian Premier, is in Rome. Italian newspapers emphasise that the visit is for consultation only.

(Rome radio says that Italy is collaborating with Hungary on a plan to keep war from the Balkans.)

But in Hungary it is believed that Teleki is asking for help from Italy if Germany invades Hungary.

Italy is Hungary's oldest ally.

Meanwhile Rumanian troops are firmly entrenched on all frontiers.

Rumanian Trade Mission to London.—Page 4.

JOURNALIST EXPELLED

Mr. Maurice Lovell, Reuter's Bukarest correspondent, arrived in Budapest last night after being expelled from Rumania by order of the Government.

He was escorted to the frontier by armed guards.

The Rumanian Government took exception to a dispatch by Mr. Lovell alleging that Germany had submitted a virtual ultimatum to Rumania.—Associated Press.

DAILY MIRROR, Tuesday, March 26, 1940.

Daily Mirror

MAR 26

No. 11,324   ONE PENNY
Registered at the G.P.O. as a Newspaper.

ALLIES FIGHT IF RUSSIANS MARCH

—French Envoy

BRIDE RECEIVED THIS TELEGRAM AT CHURCH

STEPANEK CALLING!...

A MAN came to the microphone in the B.B.C. German broadcast at 10.30 last night and said: "Just as you, my listeners, are trying now to get London, and are possibly frightened in case you are overheard and denounced to the Gestapo, so, too, a few weeks ago in Berlin I was trying, sitting at my wireless set.

"You know me from the stage and from the cinema. I hope you remember me. My name is Karl Stepanek ..."

Stepanek was a very well-known actor on the German stage and screen.

He continued: "I am a Czech by origin, but I lived for some time in Berlin and worked in Berlin studios during the early part of the war.

Could Not Bear It

"Nobody forced me to leave Berlin. I am a so-called Aryan and nobody hindered my work. But I wanted to get away.

"I could not bear the atmosphere of Nazi Germany any longer."

Then Stepanek told his listeners of his impressions after he landed in Britain. He said that in Germany he was told by the lying Nazi propaganda that Great Britain was nearly defeated and was starving because of the U-boat blockade. He described life here as it is.

Stepanek did not say how he got out of Germany.

MAURETANIA REPORTED

The Mauretania, which left New York on Thursday, was expected at Cristobal, Panama Canal, Central America, at midnight and should pass through the canal today.

When the Queen Mary and the Mauretania left New York, it was surmised that they would be used as troopships for Australians and New Zealanders.

Nothing has been heard of the Queen Mary since she left.—Associated Press.

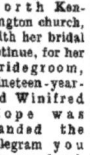

Waiting in a North Kensington church, with her bridal retinue, for her bridegroom, nineteen-year-old Winifred Hope was handed the telegram you see reproduced above.

And, unmarried, she took again her father's arm, and walked back to the door, to the bridal coach ... and home.

Bridegroom-to-be was Jack Lashbrook, whom you see in the small picture.

Her story is told, with other pictures, on page 11.

EGG SAVED A GIRL'S LIFE

A MOTHER'S sudden decision to buy an Easter egg and to turn back home with it before visiting a friend probably saved her daughter's life.

For when she arrived back with the egg she found the girl hanging by her ankles from a bedroom window, thirty feet above a greenhouse, and unable to help herself.

The mother, Mrs. Cook, of Corporation-road, Newport, Mon., went out to visit her friend, leaving her seventeen-year-old daughter Mabel in the house. She asked Mabel if she would clean the windows while she had gone.

On the way to her friend's house Mrs. Cook passed a shop window which had an inviting display of Easter eggs.

"Mabel is a very good girl, and I thought I would buy her one," Mrs. Cook told the *Daily Mirror*. "It was only a little sixpenny egg, but I thought I would take it back to Mabel

"Imagine my horror when I saw Mabel hanging by her ankles from the bedroom window. I was just in time to save her."

Mabel was little the worse.

"I must have stretched out too far," she said. "I lost my grip and just hung there, head downwards. I could feel my ankles slipping.

"Thank goodness my mother arrived back in time."

CRY MEANT BETRAYAL —HE DIED

From T. E. A. HEALY, "Daily Mirror" Correspondent with the French Forces.

R ATHER than warn the Germans of the presence of his raiding party, a French officer allowed himself to sink in an icy stream and drown without a cry for aid.

The officer - according to the French account he "proved himself by this act equal to the purest hero of ancient times"—was a member of a Colonial regiment. Waking and sleeping, they had been living a week with their fingers at the trigger.

Proved His Courage

A doctor in civil life, the hero had for many years carried out researches in Africa in tropical diseases. He came at war's command to serve his regiment on the Western Front.

Many times he proved his courage. When, on the night of his death, his Colonials planned a daring raid on German posts, they had to cross a flooded stream.

The officer requested the honour of being first to land on the enemy bank. He was entrusted with the task of discovering the best place for advance and retreat.

Finding a canoe he crossed, despite the violent current and the presence of German look-out men.

Dragged Down

On his way back the canoe sank. Undeterred, he plunged into the river and swam over, carrying a rope which he tethered to the German side as a guide for the raiding party.

Then he began his swim back to the French side. Exhausted by his efforts and the strong pull of the stream, he was drawn into a strong undercurrent.

A cry would have brought several men to his aid. But that cry would have given the alarm to German watchers. It was never given.

Instead, the heroic officer was drawn below the water to his death. Unconscious of the raiding party, the German sentries maintained their watch—in vain.

THE Allies will at once declare war on Russia if the Soviet moves against another European neutral, stated the French Ambassador to the United States, yesterday.

The Ambassador—Count Rene Saint-Quentin—declared in an interview at Boston: "If Russia attacks any other country we will not wait. We are ready. We will move against the Soviet at once." He said there would not be another Finland.

The Ambassador predicted increased military activity in the spring. But "not along the Western Front."

★

A Soviet guarantee to the South European States was discussed by Count Teleki, Hungarian Premier, at present in Rome, according to the Budapest newspaper, "Pester Lloyd," which usually speaks for the Hungarian Government.

★

Count Teleki had a long talk at the British Embassy before going to see Ciano, Italian Foreign Minister.

★

Ciano is believed to have assured Teleki that the Hitler-Duce talk left Italy's "wait and see" policy unchanged.

★

M. Reynaud, French Premier, called back his Rome Ambassador, broke his holiday to see the Italian Ambassador in Paris, and France's London envoy.

★

A contract with Rumanian oil companies for 200,000 tons of petrol has been secured by a company working for the French Government, it was revealed in Bukarest last night.

Yes, It Was Embarrassing!

No wonder Mrs. W. A. Ganderton is laughing. Starting her honeymoon at Ramsgate, she opened her travelling bag and found instead of her trousseau ....

ONE SHIRT (BOILED) FOR BRIDE

T HIS is what a London bride found in her bag when she arrived at her honeymoon hotel—

One boiled shirt;
A Homburg hat;
Pin-striped trousers;
A black jacket; and
A bank book.

The bride is Mrs. W. A. Ganderton, of The Roundway, Tottenham, N.

Borrowed Nightdress

And the clothes belonged to Mr. H. Pickles, of Ridgeside-avenue, Brighton.

"It was really rather embarrassing," she told the "Daily Mirror" at Ramsgate yesterday. "I could not go to bed in a boiled shirt. I borrowed a nightdress.

"We have not got my bag yet. Meanwhile, my only dress is the one I travelled in."

"At first," said Mr. Ganderton, "we could not understand what had happened, and then I realised I must have picked up the wrong bag when we left the motor-coach."

Mr. Pickles was returning from his mother-in-law's funeral at Bradford.

His Funeral Clothes

Going to unpack his funeral clothes, he found undies and all the luggage of a newly-married couple.

"I got a shock when I opened the bag," he said.

"My wife usually unpacks my things, but this time she stayed in Bradford and is coming on after me.

"I think the sooner we exchange cases the better, because I haven't much use for this one. I'd rather have my bankbook."

"Arriving from Bradford, I went from King's Cross Station to Charing Cross by bus. I put my bag beside the conductor.

"Mr. Ganderton must have got on afterwards and done the same.

"When he got off, he must have taken my bag by mistake."

Daily Mirror

DAILY MIRROR, Thursday, April 4, 1940.

No. 11,322 — ONE PENNY
Registered at the G.P.O. as a Newspaper.

CHURCHILL WAR LEADER IN NEW CABINET

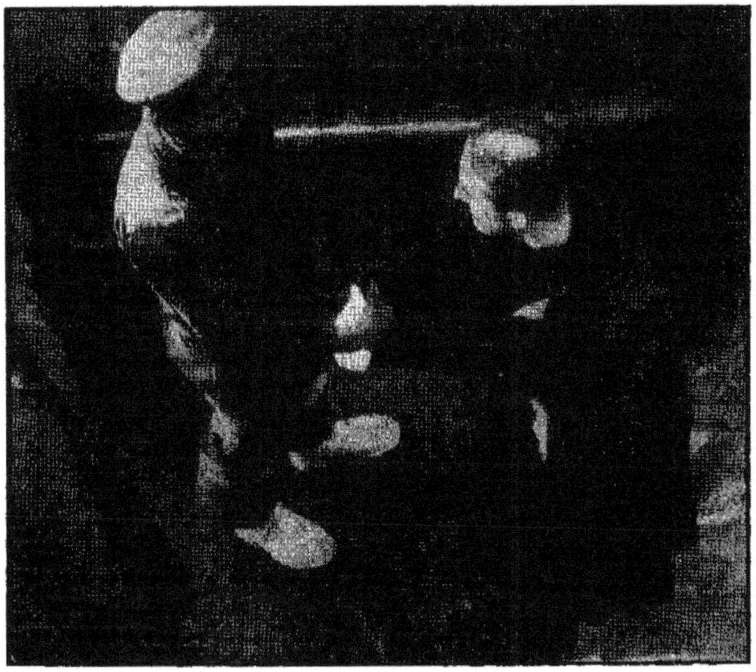

MR. WINSTON CHURCHILL is from today Britain's War Chief, the number one man of all our fighting forces.

As Mr. Chamberlain announced his Cabinet changes last night he revealed that Lord Chatfield, Defence Minister, has resigned; that his office is abolished and that Mr. Churchill will preside over the regular meetings of the Service Ministers.

These meetings, attended by the Ministers and their chiefs of staff, with Mr. Burgin, Minister of Supply, will deal with all problems of the war and make direct recommendations to the War Cabinet.

And Churchill, in the key position, becomes in fact a wartime Deputy Premier.

In the Cabinet changes Sir Samuel Hoare, Lord Privy Seal, aged sixty, becomes the new Air Minister in place of Sir Kingsley Wood, who takes Sir Samuel's old job.

The Food Boss

There is one big surprise. Lord Woolton, better known as Sir Frederick Marquis, chief of Lewis's, Ltd., becomes Food Minister.

Mr. W. S. Morrison, the former Minister of Food, goes to the comparatively unimportant job of Postmaster-General.

Other appointments are:
Mr. R. S. Hudson: Minister of Shipping.
Mr. H. Ramsbotham: Board of Education.
Earl De La Warr: First Commissioner of Works.
Major Tryon: Chancellor of the Duchy of Lancaster
Mr. Shakespeare: Secretary, Overseas Trade.
Sir Victor Warrender: Financial Secretary, Admiralty.
Sir Edward Grigg: Financial Secretary, War Office.

These changes are largely a reshuffle. Mr. Hudson takes on the job left open by the death of Sir John Gilmour, and Earl De La Warr accepts an unimportant post to make way for Mr. Ramsbotham at the Board of Education.

Mr. Chamberlain, writes the *Daily Mirror* Political Correspondent, has made his changes determined that there shall be no more complaints that the War Council is out of touch with Home and Service difficulties. Complete co-ordination has been his aim.

The new appointments have been submitted to the Opposition. Social-

Contd. on Back Page, Col. 4

Man with bandaged hand is a German wing commander. He's shaking hands with the skipper of a drifter which shot down his plane and then rescued the crew. **OTHER PICTURES ON BACK PAGE.**

AIR MURDER MEN SAVED BY VICTIMS

FIVE German airmen in a Heinkel bomber were shot down and then saved by a British fishing crew they tried to murder yesterday.

The fishermen were in a little Scarborough drifter. Bullets from their Lewis gun finished off a job a Spitfire fighter had started. The Heinkel flopped on the sea.

"We couldn't do anything but rescue the Germans," said one of the drifter men. "They looked so helpless clinging on to their sinking craft."

And the men who had fired burst after burst of machine-gun bullets a few minutes later were hauled to safety by their victims.

Only one precaution the fishermen had to take. Five armed Germans were enough to overpower them.

"So the airmen were warned that it would be their last moment if they came aboard with revolvers," said a drifter man.

One of the Nazis was a wing-commander.

The fishermen had captured the highest ranking officer so far taken in air operations.

When the drifter reached port, one of the crew said that the German wing commander confided that he

Contd. on Back Page, Col. 3

FELL 30 FEET —APOLOGISED

FIFTEEN minutes after he had crashed to what seemed certain death, a London office boy was back at his desk as usual yesterday.

He is fifteen-year-old Edmund Finn of Sangley-road, S.E.6.

Edmund crashed through a skylight, fell 26ft. on to a banister rail, rebounded on to a wall, fell another 10ft. and rolled down a dozen stairs.

He then wiped his slightly-cut hand and, after apologising for the mess, walked off as if nothing had happened.

Edmund said: "My only worry was who was going to pay for the glass, and my greatest relief was to hear that it was insured. I felt worse coming down than when I stopped."

He Will Feed Us

Lord Woolton becomes the new Minister for Food.

A GERMAN SOLDIER TELLS GERMANY

A Canadian soldier broadcast in German to Germany through the B.B.C. last night.

The soldier said he was born in Germany and left twelve years ago. "Like Hitler," he said, "I fought as a simple soldier in the German Army. I am convinced of another complete defeat for the German Army—unless Hitler and his gang are overthrown."

On Sunday, Monday,
Tuesday, Wednesday,
Thursday, Friday,
Saturday,
I see that smile
And whisper "I'll
Enjoy a glass of
that a day!"

'What a cheerful sight a Guinness is these days! You know you're going to enjoy your drink. You know it's going to do you good. During physical, mental or nervous strain, a Guinness a day is a magnificent natural tonic.

GUINNESS IS GOOD FOR YOU

DAILY MIRROR, Friday, April 5, 1940.

Daily Mirror

No. 11,333   ONE PENNY
Registered at the GPO as a Newspaper

Maid Will Be M'Lady Soon

RACE TO BUILD SHIPS

SERVANT GIRL TO MARRY A BARONET

BY A SPECIAL CORRESPONDENT

A SERVANT girl and a 38s-a-week farm labourer will go to the altar at Whitsuntide and leave the church as Sir John and Lady Fagge.

They will bear the name of a 300-year-old baronetcy.

The farm labourer, twenty-nine-year-old John William Frederick Fagge, has learned that he is inheriting the baronetcy through the death of his uncle, Sir John Harry Lee Fagge, of Massachusetts, U.S.A.

And the servant girl he will marry is Miss Ivy Friar, twenty-seven, of Church-lane, Newington, Kent.

Holding the solicitor's letter which told him the news, Mr. Fagge sat in his humble house in Whitstable-road, Faversham, Kent, last night and told the *Daily Mirror*:

"I nearly collapsed when I got this. I never saw my uncle. He never wrote to me."

"I Wouldn't Dream!"

"Both my parents are dead, and I'm the only Fagge left in the family. When I was a little boy my father used to tell me I might one day be a 'Sir.' I knew there was a baronetcy."

"But I forgot about all that. All my life I've had to get a living as a farm labourer."

"And I may go on being one. When I'm a baronet I'll still have to work."

"In fact I haven't had time to tell my employers about it all. Today I was in the hop fields. I'll be at work at 6.30 in the morning."

"But Ivy and I are going to marry at Whitsun. And then I will be a 'Sir' and she will be a 'Lady.' I have no idea if I'll inherit any money."

The future life of a baronet was washing up at the home of her employers, Mr and Mrs. B. H. Bishop, of Borden-lane, Sittingbourne, Kent, when a *Daily Mirror* representative went to see her.

This dark-haired and rosy-cheeked country girl said: "Yes, I'll use my title."

"But even when I'm a Lady I'll do my own housework.

"I would never dream of having any servants.

"John and I hope to have a nice house. But we wouldn't dream of having a motor-car."

Ivy, the eldest of a labourer's five children, will be a servant until she marries.

Mrs. Friar, Ivy's mother said "Whatever their title, they will always be just John and Ivy to me."

Miss Ivy Friar, maid to a family in Sittingbourne, Kent, with her fiance, Sir John Fagge, whom she is to marry shortly. Sir John is a farm labourer.

British Flying Ship Routs 6 Nazis: Story and Pictures Page 3

DEATH FOR RED PROPAGANDA

PERSONS found guilty of preparing, supplying or stocking anything that furthers Communist propaganda are liable to the death penalty under a decree submitted for the signature of President Lebrun, of France. The decree was framed at the last meeting of the Council of Ministers.

An official communique issued by the Ministry of the Interior announces the reinforcement of the police department responsible for the detection of Communist and Nazi activities.

The Government's decision to transfer concentration camps in Paris suburbs to North Africa is also announced in the communique.—Reuter

No. 1 SALESMAN OF DEATH

From JOHN WALTERS

NEW YORK, Thursday

DETAILS of a murder syndicate's Number One travelling salesman who guaranteed that he dispatched all his victims with "neatness and speed" astounded New York detectives who heard them today.

Assassin was Harry Strauss, popularly known in the gangster world as Pittsburg Phil who specialised in out-of-town murders on behalf of a syndicate that killed at least thirty men to order.

Pittsburg Phil's story was revealed by Abe Reles, the syndicate's vice-president, who is also in gaol.

Reles, known to fellow-criminals as Kid Twist, told how the syndicate fulfilled sixteen murder jobs outside New York.

Pittsburg Phil was appointed chief travelling killer said Reles, because he had a pleasing personality and dressed like a gentleman.

Another recommendation was that Phil enjoyed killing so much that his fee was low.

When the syndicate received an out-of-own order for a murder Phil would fill his revolver and board a for the victim's town.

There he would be met by persons who ordered the killing. After refreshments, they'd take him to the haunt where the victim was known to be.

Phil would shoot him dead, escape by car and catch a plane back to New York.

On these jaunts Phil would pose as a commercial traveller.

"Phil loved these trips," said Reles. "He got a tremendous kick out of pulling the trigger and seeing his man fall dead.

"He made a good impression everywhere he went."

MAURETANIA SIGHTED

Britain's 35,739-ton Atlantic liner Mauretania which left New York on March 21 for a secret destination, was sighted at Honolulu last night.

She is expected to call there to refuel, and the authorities are making preparations to receive her.—Reuter

BRITAIN is to produce ships by mass production in a new drive against the menace of the U-boats.

Within a few weeks every shipyard in the country will be building, working at full capacity on the type of vessel best suited to the particular yard—and completing them faster than ships can be sunk.

News of the great new shipbuilding plan is revealed by Mr William Westwood, secretary of the Shipwrights' Association, who says:

"Each yard will build one type of ship only, and that type will be the one it can build fastest and most economically."

The ships will be called emergency ships, will be built with the

Contd. on Back Page, Col. 5

Partners

A scheme for complete economic and military unity between Britain and France has been drawn up by experts from the two countries. The Supreme War Council will endorse these recommendations at its next meeting. The plan aims at establishing a partnership that will continue after the war. The Board of Trade last night issued notice of increased facilities for French imports.

Able Seaman ———— of H.M.S. ———— says

When I've only a minute for a stand-up meal it's

Fry's SANDWICH CHOCOLATE

2D AND 4D

DAILY MIRROR, Monday, April 8, 1940.

Daily Mirror

No. 11,335   ONE PENNY
Registered at the G.P.O. as a Newspaper.

APL 8

RAF GET 2 NAZIS —LOSE 2

AFTER the Germans claimed that their fighters had successfully intercepted twenty-four Vickers-Wellington bombers ninety miles north of the island of Sylt yesterday, the Air Ministry issued the following statement:—

"During a patrol over the North Sea by aircraft of the Royal Air Force this afternoon, enemy fighters were encountered and an engagement took place.

"One enemy aircraft was destroyed and at least one other is believed to have been damaged.

"Two of our aircraft failed to return."

The official German news agency had stated:—

"Twenty-four Wellington bombers were attacked by a swarm of German fighters about 150 kilometres (about ninety miles) north of the Island of Sylt this afternoon.

"Two British bombers were shot down, the others forced to retreat. There were no German losses."

5 Germans Down

Aerial warfare also flared up on the Western Front. Last night's French war communiqué stated:

"Very considerable activity in the air. Five enemy planes were brought down, one of them by the R.A.F."

The R.A.F. success was described by an announcement issued from the headquarters of the British Air Forces in France.

"This morning a fighter patrol of the Royal Air Force encountered a large formation of enemy fighter aircraft in the neighbourhood of Metz.

"The enemy formation attacked our patrol and, as a result of the numerous combats which were fought at a great height, one Messerschmitt 109 was shot down.

"All our aircraft returned safely."

Three air raid alarms were sounded in the Orkney Islands yesterday, but, so far as could be seen by civilians in the area, nothing transpired.

There were alarms lasting fifteen minutes each in the morning and afternoon.

SOVIET JAPAN DEADLOCK

Russo-Japanese trade negotiations in Moscow have reached a deadlock, according to a dispatch to Berlin.

Deadlock has also been reached, the dispatch asserts, in "all other open questions," such as the frontier demarcation between Manchukuo and Outer Mongolia and the fishery question. The deputation is returning to Japan.—Reuter.

STAR GAVE HER BLOOD
—but in Vain

Tears filled the beautiful big eyes of glamorous Jean Parker, right, when she learned yesterday studio-colleague Francis Heacock had died....

Jean, star of "The Barrier," "The Ghost Goes West" and many other films, was at work on the set when she heard that Heacock had suffered a fractured skull in a motor accident and was in urgent need of blood.

Immediately she forsook the camera, offered herself for a blood test—and discovered she was in the same category as the dying man.

Along with an actor of similar blood, Jean was rushed to hospital—and the transfusion took place ... but in spite of her heroic gesture, the effort was made in vain, as the man to whom she had given her blood had passed away.

NAZI SHADOWED BY A WARSHIP

A BRITISH warship is shadowing the German steamer Ankara, which is making a test-voyage through Yugoslav waters.

Ankara (4,766 tons) sailed from Dubrovnik for Trieste with 5,000 tons of bauxite.

The master, Captain Funk, hoped to outwit British warships in the Adriatic, but soon a British warship was reported to be following outside territorial waters.

24-Hour Limit

The Ankara may remain inside Yugoslav territorial waters for twenty-four hours, after which she must have permission from the Yugoslav authorities to extend the time limit.

Despite the reported presence of four British warships in the Adriatic, the Yugoslav harbour authorities on Saturday handed sailing papers to the Ankara requiring the ship to leave within three days.—Associated Press.

T.T.s ARE TO GET DRUNK

From JOHN WALTERS

NEW YORK, Sunday

GROUP temperance leaders in Oklahoma City delighted the populace today when they announced that on Wednesday they would get drunk on beer "in the interest of science and public morality."

Highlight of the teetotallers' noble experiment will be when they attempt to walk along a straight line.

They are breaking their temperance vows and gallantly risking hangovers to prove that beer sold in Oklahoma City is intoxicating and therefore should be banned.

BIG TRADE WAR TALK TODAY

BY OUR DIPLOMATIC CORRESPONDENT

TODAY LORD HALIFAX, BRITAIN'S FOREIGN SECRETARY, HAS THE FIRST OF HIS SECRET CONFERENCES WITH THE ENVOYS HE HAS SUMMONED HOME FROM THE BALKANS TO PLAN THE NEW ECONOMIC OFFENSIVE AGAINST GERMANY.

Eight Ambassadors and Ministers will take part in the talks. Each will explain what measures can be taken to cut off Germany's trade with the country where he represents Britain.

And each will be given precise instructions to defeat Hitler's pressure on south-east Europe.

Sir Hughe Knatchbull-Hugessen, British Ambassador to Turkey, arrived in London yesterday. The British Ministers to Greece and Hungary are already here, and three more — from Bulgaria, Rumania and Yugoslavia—arrive today.

German Threats

Sir William Seeds, Ambassador in Moscow, and Sir Percy Loraine, Ambassador in Rome, are home on leave, and will attend the conference.

By Thursday Mr. Chamberlain will know how much he can tell M.P.s when he addresses them that day behind the padlocked doors of the House of Commons.

Already Germany is threatening reprisals if the neutrals fall in with Britain's plan to tighten the blockade.

"Acquiescence in the blockade means helping the Allies," one Nazi spokesman said yesterday.

And Berlin saw this as a "decisive week-end" if Scandinavia did not make a stand against violation of her neutrality.

A wave of nervousness was evident in the Wilhelmstrasse, Berlin's Whitehall, as one conference followed another.

Late last night Sweden's Defence Staff announced "a stiffening of defence preparations because of present conditions." They did not disclose what these preparations are.

Norwegian seamen, angered by German attacks on Norwegian shipping, threatened yesterday to refuse to sign on German ships and trade union dockers may refuse to load German cargoes.

Norway Explains

And as the Germans torpedoed and sank another Norwegian ship, Professor Koht, Norway's Foreign Minister, explained that his country would be at war "if free shipping in Norwegian waters is interfered with to the advantage of a belligerent power."

But it was clear that Norway had little fear that the Allies would force her into war.

"After Mr. Chamberlain's and Mr. Churchill's recent speeches," Professor Koht said, "I dare to feel confident that Great Britain does not intend to violate international law or our neutrality."

He added: "The extent of Swedish ore exports to Germany via Narvik is exaggerated by many people. Much more ore is now going this way to Britain than to Germany."

HUN DEATH WATCH

AFTER torpedoing a Norwegian ship, the Navarra, the crew of a Hun submarine looked on as twelve seamen died.

The ship sank in two minutes.

Desperate men rushed to launch the lifeboats. One of the boats upset.

NOT A WATCHING GERMAN MOVED AS NEUTRAL SEAMEN FOUGHT FOR LIFE UNDER THEIR EYES.

The other lifeboat managed to save four only.

All the officers were among the twelve lost by explosion and drowning.

Then, leaving fourteen survivors to fend for themselves in an open boat miles from land in a heavy sea, the Germans sailed off.

Nine hours later the Navarra's survivors were saved by a Finnish ship.

Six weeks ago, Vice-Admiral Schniewidt, Chief of the German Naval Staff, promised Norway that her coal ships would not be attacked unless in convoy.

The Navarra, taking coal to Oslo, was not in convoy.

Neutral Norway has now lost fifty-five ships, totalling 220,000 tons, and 400 innocent seamen.

Children Hear

WEEK-END Atrocity No. 2: Two German bombers dived to machine-gun the lights of the Duncansby Head Lighthouse, John o' Groats.

The three keepers and their families, including six children, heard bullets whining past the dome.

No damage was done—except to the age-old law of men who sail the seas that a lighthouse, even in war, is sacred.

Little Target

ATROCITY No. 3: Does not take much telling

Belgian fishermen in three little boats went to sea on Saturday—unarmed, not even at war.

German warplanes roared down and pumped machine-gun bullets at the little boats.

No damage was done.

DAILY MIRROR, Tuesday, April 9, 1940.

Daily Mirror

No. 11,336 — ONE PENNY
Registered at the G.P.O. as a Newspaper.

4 NAZI SHIPS TORPEDOED OFF NORWAY: ONE TROOPSHIP

WARSHIP SINKS A U-BOAT

A BRITISH warship which engaged two U-boats in the North Sea sank one of them.

Norwegian steamers which arrived at Lillesand, in the Skagerrak, yesterday, were stated to have aboard fifty German and British survivors of the fight.

But the Norwegian Admiralty declared later that it had no confirmation of the landing of any British sailors.

One of the Norwegian ships which arrived at Lillesand had five bodies on her deck.

Norwegian steamers which arrived at Lillesand, in the Skagerrak, carried fifty German and British survivors.

Bodies Washed Ashore

The pilot said his vessel had a narrow escape during the fight between the warship and one of the U-boats.

Part of the side of the steamer was blown away by the concussion of the guns.

At several points along the Norwegian coast bodies have been washed ashore.

A single heavy explosion was heard four miles off Justøya Fjord, near Lillesand, after which several unidentified aeroplanes circled over the spot and flew off.

Later several more explosions were heard from the same direction, but further out to sea. What explosions they were it was impossible to tell from the land.—British United Press, Associated Press.

REMOVE THE MINES —Says Norway

ALTHOUGH Norway announced a sharp "protest" at the Allied laying of mines in her waters yesterday, it was learned officially in London last night that when the Norwegian Minister called on Lord Halifax in the afternoon he did not lodge a protest.

Norway, in her "protest," demanded the removal of the mines, which not

Contd. on Back Page, Col. 4

Scapa Raid— 3 Nazis Down

SCAPA Flow was raided last night for the fourth time. The German planes were driven off by British fighters and two are known to have been shot down. It is believed that a third met with the same fate.

This was revealed by the Air Ministry this morning.

Incendiary and high-explosive bombs were dropped. No damage was caused to warships or other ships.

A civilian was buried under debris by a high-explosive bomb, but was uninjured.

The roof of a farmhouse was damaged by fire high explosive bombs which fell near. No other damage to property was caused.

Residents of the Orkney Islands described the repelling of the raid as the most impressive spectacle they had ever seen.

"British fighter planes seemed thick as locusts," said one man, and the gunfire was at a safe distance, so that no splinters fell on the mainland."

Stromness Town Council was meeting when the alarm sounded. They decided to carry on discussing outstanding gas accounts.

In Kirkwall, Major John White, the head warden, was making a presentation to the retiring official of a meeting when the alarm was sounded. He went on with his speech and did not return to his post until he had completed the ceremony.

The official German News Agency made their usual claim that "several heavy warships" were hit.

TANKS, PLANES FOR A LANDING

A SURVIVOR of the German troopship Rio de Janeiro is reported from Oslo to have said that the ship had at least 500 people on board, and carried tanks, planes and troops for a landing.

The Rio de Janeiro is reported to have been on her way from Stettin to Bergen, Norway.

Many other German ships were with the Rio de Janeiro, but the convoy was dispersed by British warships, according to reports from Kristiansund.

The reports do not say what kind of ships the German vessels were.— British United Press.

PLANES DOWN IN NORWAY

A British plane made a forced landing at Kristiansund, it was reported last night, and the crew was interned. A German plane landed at Lyngstad nearby. The crew of two disappeared. —British United Press.

FOUR GERMAN SHIPS, ONE REPORTED TO BE CARRYING 300 NAZI TROOPS, WERE SUNK BY BRITISH SUBMARINES IN THE SKAGERRAK YESTERDAY, A FEW MILES OFF THE COAST OF NORWAY.

MORE THAN 400 MEN WERE DROWNED AND 150 BODIES AND EIGHTY DEAD HORSES HAVE BEEN WASHED OR BROUGHT ASHORE AT LILLESAND, ON THE SOUTH NORWEGIAN COAST. OF THE DROWNED 150 MEN WERE FROM THE TRANSPORT AND 200 FROM A SHIP WHICH HAD NOT BEEN IDENTIFIED. EARLY THIS MORNING 223 SURVIVORS HAD BEEN REPORTED.

The transport, the Hamburg steamer Rio de Janeiro (5,261 tons), was ordered to halt by a British submarine.

She refused. A torpedo struck her, and men threw themselves into the sea. A second torpedo was fired.

As it exploded, iron fragments struck a small Norwegian ship nearby and killed three men on board. These are believed to be Germans picked up from the sea.

Survivors in Uniform

A Norwegian destroyer picked up ninety-one survivors of the Rio de Janeiro and ten bodies and took them to Lillesand.

A second destroyer an hour later picked up forty-four more men, as well as nineteen bodies, and took them to Kristiansand.

Norwegian naval sources announced that thirty bodies had been recovered. The full number of survivors is not yet known.

Two hours before the sinking it had been reported that the German Fleet was out that 100 German warships were steaming into the Skagerrak towards Norway.

Then came the news of the sunken troopship. Was Germany attempting to land an army on Norway's shores?

If so, the landing force had been intercepted.

According to a Reuter message from Oslo all the survivors were young men in uniform with identification marks.

Submarines Get Two More

Two more German ships were sunk within three hours of the Rio de Janeiro. They were the Kreta (2,359 tons) and Posedonia (12,000 tons) described as tankers, but possibly also used as troop carriers.

Both were torpedoed by British submarines.

The captain of the Posedonia was

Contd. on Back Page, Col. 3

Where the war blew up yesterday—the area round the Norwegian coast.

At Lillesand, which you will find marked in the Skagerrak, bodies have been washed ashore. Off Arendal, close by, the troopship Rio de Janeiro was sunk. Three other German ships are said to have been torpedoed in the Skagerrak. The minefields laid by Britain are marked in the map—one shaded. Their purpose is made plain when it is noticed how they force shipping from the three-mile coast territorial water into the open ocean where they can be attacked.

ARMADA IS SIGHTED

A GERMAN armada of 125 ships, including a pocket battleship, heavy cruisers and destroyers, was sighted this morning off the Danish island of Lesoe, heading for Norway.

The German fleet had yesterday been reported on the move—see previous column—but no reports of its progress was received until hours after the successful British submarine action in the Skagerrak was known.

The German warships were believed to be making slow progress into the Skagerrak, apparently because they did not want to approach the Norwegian coast where all the lighthouses had been blacked out.

Included in the Armada is a large number of trawlers and coastguard ships, presumably for minelaying or minesweeping work.

DAILY MIRROR, Thursday, April 11, 1940.

Daily Mirror

No. 11,338 — ONE PENNY
Registered at the G.P.O. as a Newspaper.

APL 11

ALLIES IN 2 NORWAY PORTS

British Towns Gunned

German planes launched their first machine-gun attacks on British towns last night, when six raiders were brought down by British fighters and A.A. guns and three more are believed to have been shot down by fighters. This raid took place in the north of Scotland.

THE towns of Kirkwall and Stromness, in the Orkney Islands, were mercilessly machine-gunned by the raiders.

The enemy planes flew low over the houses, firing bursts from their guns.

Early today the only casualty known is a Service man on the island of Hoy, who has a bullet-wound in his foot.

The planes came over in four waves. Islanders witnessed thrilling dogfights in the moonlight, tracer bullets patterning the sky.

Six high explosive bombs fell on the island of Flotta, several on the island of Hoy, four in the sea near Long Hope village, and three on the island of South Ronaldshay.

Among the bombs which fell in the sea, one dropped near a ship in Scapa Flow.

There were altogether three raids on the north of Scotland.

The Admiralty, the Air Ministry and the Ministry of Home Security announced this morning that two Heinkel bombers were shot down in the first raid.

These were carrying out an attack upon a convoy, and when shot down fell in the Moray Firth. It is believed that a third enemy bomber was destroyed in the same engagement.

Later, the enemy attacked Scapa Flow. Air-raid warnings were sounded at 8.51 p.m. by way of precaution in the extreme north of Scotland, and the "Raiders passed" signal was given at about 10.30 p.m.

This raid was carried out by large numbers of enemy aircraft which attacked in successive waves of large and small formations.

The raid was abortive, and no

Contd. on Back Page, Col. 2

SURRENDER OSLO

THE British Fleet now command the entrance to Oslo, said Stockholm radio last night. They have given the Germans a time limit to surrender or be shelled.

The Germans, who had earlier ordered the stopping of all evacuation, at once told all Norwegians to get out of the city. This report was not confirmed in London.

TWO Allied forces last night landed on the Norwegian coast.

A Stockholm message said British troops have recaptured from the Germans the Norwegian ports of Bergen and Trondheim. The Germans denied that report, but it was confirmed by M. Hambro, Norwegian Premier and by British circles in Stockholm.

British warships yesterday burst through the German mine barrier across the Skagerrak and a fierce sea fight is in progress off the coast of Sweden. Four German cruisers and an unknown number of destroyers were sunk.

Nazi Cruiser Stranded in Fiord

German troopships steaming up the Kattegat, between Denmark and Sweden, were attacked and scattered by Allied ships near Marstrand.

At least two German transports were reported to be sunk. The others turned and ran for shelter.

A German fleet of ten or more warships fought all day against the still-firing Norwegian shore batteries and ships of the Allied Fleet.

Two German warships were sunk as the Allies attacked. A third, the cruiser Emden, was sunk at Horten, the port of Oslo, by the Norwegian cruiser-minelayer Olaf Tryggvarson, biggest and newest ship in the Norwegian Navy.

Stockholm radio last night flashed the news that a German warship was sunk by British action off Arendal, South Norway.

It also reported that a German cruiser had been stranded in a Norwegian fiord. The crew were taken off by a British ship. It is presumed that the German ship surrendered after being forced ashore.

British planes are engaged in the Kattegat fight. Loud firing was heard

Contd. on Back Page, Col. 4

BIG SEA FIGHT OFF SWEDEN

Losses

In sea fights off the coasts of Norway and Sweden reported German losses, compared with the Allies, are:—

ALLIES	GERMANY
2 Destroyers	6 Cruisers
	3 Destroyers
	3 Warships, size unknown
	9 Merchant ships (some transports)

In addition, three German destroyers were set on fire, one cruiser is believed sunk by British bombs, and a second cruiser is reported ashore.

The Germans claim that three British destroyers were sunk at Narvik. The Allies admit severe damage to one destroyer, slight damage to two cruisers and one destroyer, in addition to the two destroyers lost.

Narvik fighting—page 3.

NORWAY CLAIMS A SUCCESS

NORWAY, fighting on for her independence, claimed last night that her troops had been successful near Kongsvinger.

Fighting on a big scale is going on near Elverum, eighty miles north of Oslo.

After digging themselves in, Norwegian troops tenaciously resisted German attempts to break their line.

Several hundred Germans were killed when motorised units tried to advance.

According to the Stockholm radio, King Haakon of Denmark refused a request by Dr. Brauer, the German Ambassador at Oslo, that he should recognise the Quisling Government (the German puppet Ministry).

A statement issued in Berlin claims that German troops are now occupying Hamar.—British United Press, Reuter, Associated Press and Exchange.

Life is *brighter*— work is *lighter*— after Guinness

"I have been taking Guinness at lunch," writes a doctor, "and find a renewed vigour on resuming work throughout the day." "A tonic which gives you the necessary 'fillip' to carry on an exacting day's work," adds another.

Treat yourself to a cheerful, smiling Guinness at lunch. Guinness is good for you.

The above doctors' letters are quoted by special permission.

DAILY MIRROR, Saturday, April 13, 1940.

Daily Mirror

No. 11,940   ONE PENNY
Registered at the G.P.O. as a Newspaper.

Her Husband's a Hero

50 FACED 2,000

FIFTY men were seen to leave the British destroyer Hardy, wrecked and grounded after the fight in Narvik Fiord. They carried arms. On the hills above were at least 2,000 Germans. In the bay were German warships.

The British party vanished to form their own expeditionary force. Travellers arriving on the Swedish frontier yesterday reported that the fifty have now set up a British headquarters in a village down the Fiord. Already in the villages they are a legend.

FLEET WAITS

LARGE British forces were yesterday reported to be massing at Foldefiord, near Namsos, twenty-four miles to the north of Trondhiem, the West Norway port held by the Germans.

Two British battleships, four cruisers, four destroyers and a large number of planes are said to have arrived at the Fiord.

Two British destroyers are said to have attacked German warships in Trondhiem roadsteads. The Germans withdrew to hide in the deep bays of the fiord.

The Nazi fleet there is reported to be a pocket battleship and four other warships.

AIR BASE RAID

R.A.F. planes raiding the airfield at Stavanger, Norway, wrecked German fighter and bomber planes with machine-gun fire and killed many of the staff and aircraft personnel.

The raid was carried out by Wellington bombers of the Coastal Command, accompanied by long-range fighters.

The fighters arrived first. Their dives took the enemy by surprise and before the anti-aircraft defences could be brought into action bullets from the planes were spraying the hangars and aircraft out on the tarmac.

Three Junkers bombers were seriously damaged and, it is estimated, twenty of the ground staff were killed in the first attack.

The moment the attack finished and the British aircraft began to climb for a further offensive, intense machine-gun and anti-aircraft fire broke out.

Fire Broke Out

Half an hour later the Wellington bombers were on the job.

They swept down on Stavanger dropping heavy bombs.

Fierce but inaccurate anti-aircraft fire answered but again the bombers attacked, machine-gunning enemy machine-gun posts, anti-aircraft batteries, hangars and aircraft on the ground. A great fire broke out.

By this time many German fighter aircraft called from neighbouring

(Continued on Back Page)

SWEDEN: "WE WILL FIGHT IF—"

MENTION by the Swedish Premier in a broadcast last night of possible demands—obviously Nazi—to allow troops to pass through to Norway increased civilian tension.

"Once again our country experiences an hour of trial, which may be the most trying we have had for more than a century," said Hr. Hansson

"If war comes to our country we will fight to preserve our liberty.

"It is not compatible with strict neutrality to allow any belligerent Power to use Swedish territory for her enterprises. If such demands are made they must be rejected."

He said no demand of this nature had been made, and continued: "To maintain our neutrality means also that it is necessary, should the need arise, to defend it."

Lighthouses on the Swedish west coast between Haaloe and Tistlarna are to be blacked out at night. Partial or general black-out tests have taken place at Malmo, Scano and Gothenburg.

British United Press and Reuter.

R.A.F. LOSE 10 PLANES

THE R.A.F. lost ten aircraft in attacks on the German fleet, it was announced by the Air Ministry this morning. Four Messerschmitts were shot down and another two are believed to have been damaged.

The Air Ministry announced that throughout yesterday a series of strong formations of R.A.F. bombers searched Norwegian and Danish waters to locate and attack units of the German fleet returning to their home bases.

Warships Attacked

One formation penetrated into Kristiansand Fiord, attacked German warships and met with strong opposition.

Another formation, going north towards Stavanger, was met by a large enemy fighter force.

ITALIANS FOR ALBANIA

Twenty-five thousand Italian workmen have left Bari for Albania.—Exchange.

Proudest woman in the world yesterday was Mrs. Buzzard. You see her above with her brave husband when he arrived in London last night.

Commander A. W. Buzzard, of the destroyer Gurkha, continued to fire at German bombers until the sea was level with the deck of his sinking ship. At the end of this heroic action the Commander had to be dragged from his bridge.

Below, the gallant gentleman is mobbed by spectators who had waited at the station to give him the welcome of a hero. See other pictures of the Gurkha's crew on pages 3 and 10

IF IT'S CHOCOLATE THEN IT'S FOOD

There's a glass-and-a-half of fresh, full-cream milk in every ½ lb block of Cadbury's Milk Chocolate. It's the world's most delicious way of giving yourself quick energy.

CADBURYS
MILK CHOCOLATE
'feeds you on your feet'

DAILY MIRROR, Saturday, April 20, 1940.

Daily Mirror

APL 20

No. 11,346   ONE PENNY
Registered at the G.P.O. as a Newspaper.

Hitler 51 Today—Roosevelt Ready

Today it is fifty-one years since Mrs. Schickelgruber gave birth to the child Adolf Hitler. — Paris Radio.

Fears that the war may take a sudden turn for the worse (it has been suggested that Hitler's birthday will be the occasion) were expressed by President Roosevelt aboard the train which carried him from Washington to Warm Springs, Georgia, for a holiday.

"If another country is invaded I'll be right back," he told friends at the station.

He ordered the train to remain in readiness for his instant return to Washington, says British United Press.

ROME'S FATAL HOUR

MUSSOLINI hesitates on the brink of war. Reports from Rome last night strengthened the belief that he is about to give the word that will plunge Italy into the fight on the side of Germany.

"The Hour of Destiny" is the heading of a provocative article in "Popolo D'Italia," the newspaper Mussolini founded.

"A great people like ours," it states, "cannot look on like an outsider while events take place which will modify the map of the continent.

"A great people like ours cannot for ever consent to be watched over and controlled in its own house."

And in what reads like a direct incitement to war, the article goes on:

"There is no place in history for him who is without the love of danger. Nothing is created without something being destroyed. Life is generated in blood."

Across the Adriatic Yugoslavia struck at her traitors.

Dr. Milan Stoyadinovich, a former Prime Minister, was arrested. He is to be interned.

His brother Drahomir, a former member of Parliament was also arrested yesterday.

Treason Plot

As the arrests were made, Belgrade, the Yugoslav capital, revealed that in the search of the ex-Premier's house, papers found disclosed a plot to overthrow the Government at the same time as German troops marched in.

The arrest has ended this treason attempt, but Yugoslavia's position is tense.

A concentration of German troops on the Yugoslav frontier was followed yesterday by great activity among the Italian soldiers.

Hungary, too, is nervous and watchful. Ex-Premier Bela Imredy, chief Nazi sympathiser, was last night reported arrested.

In Rome last night anti-British propaganda continued with gathering force.

The Popolo di Roma reports a brilliant German victory at Narvik, with 2,300 British casualties. The German losses, this false report adds, were small.

SWIM FOR IT: HARDY LAST WORD

CAPTAIN Warburton-Lee, mortally wounded, gave his last order on board the destroyer Hardy, grounded on the shore of Narvik Fiord.

"Swim for it, boys," he said. "Every man for himself. Good luck." The boys swam through the ice-cold water to the shore 100 yards away.

They would not leave their captain. One of them swam with him to the beach.

"Is everyone all right?" he gasped, and died.

That story was told last night when sixty Hardy survivors arrived in London to be cheered by a welcoming British crowd and to be received by First Lord Winston Churchill (see page 9).

In all 130 survivors reached Britain. The London contingent, in a strange assortment of clothes —Norwegian jumpers, ski caps, women's clothing — told of the captain's dying heroism and their escapes on the hillside of the Norwegian fiord.

Petty-Officer E. Baggley, of Saint Jude Cottages, Plymouth, one of the sixty, told this story of the fiord fight:

"On that Tuesday night the pilot who had been guiding us into the fiord told our captain that the German forces were vastly superior.

"It must have been at this time that Captain Warburton-Lee sent his famous 'Shall we go in?' message to the Admiralty, because we were told shortly afterwards that we would be going into action at about 1.30 a.m."

In Blinding Snow

"We came into the fiord. There was a blinding snowstorm, and navigation was tricky. Visibility was no more than 200 yards.

"In fact, we came near to giving the whole game away—we saw two misty outlines and had half a mind to open fire. Had we done so, the Germans would have been warned of our presence, for those outlines were two huge rocks.

"At the mouth of Narvik harbour we sighted enemy ships and loosed torpedoes. Then our gunner officer fired a salvo straight across the bows of one of them.

"At this moment our torpedoes reached their mark. We saw the explosions and sparks were blown high in the air.

"Five of our torpedoes found their mark—another set fire to a jetty.

"The Germans thought it was an air raid, and opened fire with their pom-pom guns.

"Then they fired on us, and pink

Continued on Back Page

TWELVE PASSENGERS HURT IN TRAIN COLLISION

Twelve people had slight injuries when two passenger trains collided at Horsham (Sussex) last night.

Three of them were taken to hospital. They were: Mrs. O. Brown, of Ferndale-avenue, Chertsey (shock and neck injury); Mr. Hudson, of Parsonage-road, Horsham (dislocated shoulder); and Miss Rogers, of Stackbury-avenue, Chipstead, Surrey (face injury).

The line was not blocked, and there was no delay to other trains.

NORWAY CUT BY BRITISH TROOPS

BRITISH and Norwegian forces have united and established a defence line across Norway from Namsos, eighty miles north of Trondhiem, right to the Swedish border.

This is revealed by the Norwegian High Command. Stockholm radio announced last night.

Fighting is reported to be going on between British and German troops near Trondhiem; at Narvik, where the besieged Germans are now said to be in desperate straits; and at Elverum, seventy miles north-east of Oslo. The Norwegians are strongly entrenched there.

The clash between British and German troops in the vital Trondhiem area was reported from Stockholm.

The Germans were driven back. Many of the enemy were killed and wounded in the fight, which was described as the first between the Forces. It took place, says Stockholm, near Namsos, the railhead north of Trondhiem.

The Germans are understood to be evacuating Vaernes Aerodrome, near Trondhiem, which seems to have been rendered unusable by British bombing and heavy snowfalls.

The aerodrome has been so damaged that enemy planes attempting to land there have overturned.

While the Germans make frenzied preparations to meet an Allied attack in the Trondhiem sector, the landing of a strong British force at Molde, one hundred miles south-west of Trondhiem, is reported by the New York Journal, which attributes the statement to Mrs. Harriman, U.S. Minister to Norway.

H.M.S. Eclipse, Bombed, Returns Safely

The British destroyer Eclipse has been damaged by a bomb which burst near her, but has returned safely.

The attack, made some days ago, was announced last night in the following Admiralty communique:—

"As a result of a near miss during an enemy bombing attack some days ago, H.M.S. Eclipse was damaged but is now safely at her base."

The Eclipse is a destroyer of 1,375 tons, completed in 1934.

So far as is known there are no survivors from the British destroyer Hunter, which was sunk in the first attack on Narvik. There is a remote possibility that some of her crew may have reached the shore.

She was commanded by Lieut.-Commander L. de Villiers.

Germans Cut Off

It is also reported that more British troops are landing hourly at Stenkjer, sixty miles north of Trondhiem.

A new German landing is said to have been attempted near Bjorne Fiord, south of Bergen.

Forces concentrated at Rombaksjeg, near Narvik, and Bjornsfjell, three miles from the Swedish frontier, are now practically cut off from supplies by the British.

Narvik is encircled by Allied troops. says Columbia radio.

Heavy German bomber and transport planes have been taking food, munitions and supplies, as well as mountain artillery to the Germans there, according to a report from Luleau, Sweden. — Reuter, British United Press.

Still wearing the clothes he was given at Narvik, Lieutenant-Commander V. G. D. Mansell is seen here with his wife.

AVOID THE MISTAKE SOME MOTHERS MAKE EVERY SUMMER

IT is natural to think that because the winter is over children should be given a diet less rich in nourishment. Actually the very opposite is true.

MORE ENERGY HOURS

Long summer evenings almost double the hours during which children run about, play, and tire themselves. Children, and grown-ups too, burn far more energy during the long hot days of summer than they do in the short, cold days of winter.

THE PERFECT ENERGY-FOOD

Because it is so light, delicious, and nourishing, Cadbury's Bournville Cocoa is one of the finest means of replacing energy. Because it is so easily digestible it is exactly the kind of drink doctors recommend to promote truly restful and nerve-restoring sleep. Keep the children on Bournville throughout the summer—they love milk with it and it makes milk extra nourishing.

still 6d PER QTR. LB   11d PER HALF LB

CADBURY'S BOURNVILLE COCOA

A cup of cocoa is a cup of food

DAILY MIRROR, Monday, April 22, 1940.

Daily Mirror

APL 22

No. 11,347   ONE PENNY
Registered at the G.P.O. as a Newspaper.

OUR TANKS TAKE TOWN NEAR OSLO

—Stockholm Report

BRITISH AND FRENCH TROOPS, LED BY TANKS, YESTERDAY THREW THE GERMANS OUT OF HAMAR, SIXTY MILES NORTH OF OSLO, AND CAPTURED THE TOWN, ACCORDING TO UNCONFIRMED REPORTS FROM STOCKHOLM.

If that report is true it reveals a lightning stroke by the Allied Forces, a rapid advance to reinforce the Norwegian Army now resisting the Germans along a line from Hamar, on Lake Mjoessa, through Elverum to the Swedish frontier.

Germans Bomb Namsos

The landing places of the Allied troops have not yet been officially revealed, but a joint Admiralty and War Office communique last night said:

"There was considerable enemy air activity at Namsos during Saturday and many bombs were dropped. Extensive damage was caused to the town, but the only Allied loss was one British trawler sunk. There were no casualties to Allied troops."

The trawler was the Rutlandshire. The crew were saved.

Namsos is only fifty miles to the north of Trondhiem Fiord. Trondhiem itself, key town to the whole Norway coast, is being feverishly fortified by the German commander against the coming Allied attack.

In Stockholm it was reported that a British landing had been made at Andalsnes, 100 miles south of Trondhiem.

From there the British and French troops dashed by train and road to the outskirts of Hamar and were later reported to have made contact with the Norwegian Army.

It is presumed that the British units are either part of the force reported earlier to have been landed at Andalsnes, or at Laerdal, in the great Sogne fiord, eighty-five miles north-east of Bergen.

Laerdal, seventy-five miles up the fiord, is a position of great strategic importance with good road communications to Fagernes, terminus of a ninety miles railway from Oslo, and also to the important Oslo-Bergen railway.

Line Attacked

Andalsnes is the terminus of another railway to Oslo along the great valley of Gudbrandsdal, passing through Hamar.

The Germans have made repeated attempts to cut this line by seizing the junction of Dombass, fifty miles south-east of Andalsnes, with parachute troops.

Latest reports show that it was still controlled by Norwegian forces last night.

The British communique last night said:

"Operations in Norway are continuing. British troops are operating in conjunction with Norwegian forces."

Berlin confirmed the news of British troops at Andalsnes in a communique last night which said:

"British troop units that had been landed were effectively attacked by bombs at Andalsnes and suffered heavy losses of personnel and material."

The "heavy losses" are now known to be the usual German lies.

The Germans yesterday heavily bombed Lillehammer, north of Hamar, and the official German news agency last night claimed that their troops were in the town.

The Norwegians deny it.

An earlier dispatch from Norwegian headquarters said the Norwegian

Contd. on Back Page, Col. 3

WE BAG 8 ENEMY PLANES

FOUR Messerschmitts were shot down by the R.A.F. in France yesterday. No R.A.F. machines were lost in the fights.

This was announced by the Air Ministry last night. Four other German planes were shot down by the R.A.F. during the week-end—bringing the total bag to eight.

Two more (as reported on page 4) were destroyed by the French.

In addition to yesterday's bag of four, two other Messerschmitts are believed to have been destroyed.

Two of the enemy machines were lost when eight of our fighters attacked twelve Messerschmitts.

R.A.F. SMASH NAZI BASES

STRONG forces of R.A.F. planes struck heavy blows at Germany's transport of troops to Norway by three bombing raids on German air bases in Norway and Denmark during the week-end.

Great havoc was caused. Fires broke out. Hits were scored on hangars, runways and planes. Explosions were heard after bombs had burst. Bombs were dropped also on three seaplanes moored in a cove off Stavanger seaplane base.

All this was accomplished without the loss of one R.A.F. machine.

The raid on Aalborg aerodrome in Northern Denmark was the first onslaught against the Germans in Denmark. It took the enemy completely by surprise.

The pilot of one of our bombers said:

"My aircraft was the first of the formation to reach the aerodrome. The boundary lights were on, so were the obstruction lights on the buildings. A flare path was also lit up.

"While looking for a target we flew practically alongside a German transport aircraft. It was signalling, presumably asking for permission to land. My rear gunner immediately gave him something else to think about—we managed to get in a good burst of fire before the

Contd. on Back Page, Col. 4

★ **To Danes: Don't Fear British Bombers** ★

The B.B.C. appealed yesterday in Danish to the Danish people not to fear the British planes, as they would bomb only German air bases.

"Denmark is not forgotten by Britain, who is her friend, and Denmark will again be a free country," added the announcer.

BELISHA WED STORY DENIED

Asked about the report in a French newspaper that he had married Mlle. Jacqueline Delubac (above), a French actress, Mr. Hore-Belisha, former Secretary of State for War, said "Blah."

The French newspaper "Libarte" stated yesterday that they had married at Cannes.

Mlle. Delubac was the third wife of Sacha Guitry. Their marriage was dissolved on April 5 last year.

The report is denied by Mr. Goldman, with whom Mr. Hore-Belisha has been staying at Cannes.

Mr. Hore-Belisha's personal secretary told the "Daily Mirror" last night: "I know nothing about the rumours of Mr. Hore-Belisha's marriage."

GERMAN SHIP SUNK IN BALTIC

THE German merchant ship, Jurgen Fritzen (4,465 tons) sank yesterday near Landsort, in the Baltic south of Stockholm. Her crew of about thirty was saved.

The vessel was bound from Stettin to Stockholm with a cargo of coal.

Reports from Gothenburg, on the south-west coast of Sweden, suggest that a naval fight was in progress in the Skagerrak or Kattegat on Saturday night.

200 HELD IN NARVIK FREE

WHEN British destroyers made their first glorious attack on Narvik, the Germans were so surprised and bewildered that in their excitement they threw arms and ammunition into lifeboats in which they had placed British captives.

Two hundred of our merchant seamen, in British ships at Narvik when the Germans landed, escaped during the bombardment.

They made a twenty-five mile dash to freedom along a mountain road and were saved with the men of the Hardy, whom they met the day this destroyer ran aground.

Petty Officer Edward Baggley, of the Hardy, yesterday told the Daily Mirror their story.

The men had been bundled into a troopship which had just landed German soldiers. They were locked in the hold as prisoners, and the ship was about to sail for Germany.

"The first the British prisoners knew of the battle was when a ship alongside was blown up and splinters fell on the roofs of their cabins," he said.

"Hell Let Loose"

"Immediately the doors were unlocked and the German captain entered. He told them they could leave in ship's lifeboats. They were told to wait on the beach when the Germans would pick them up again.

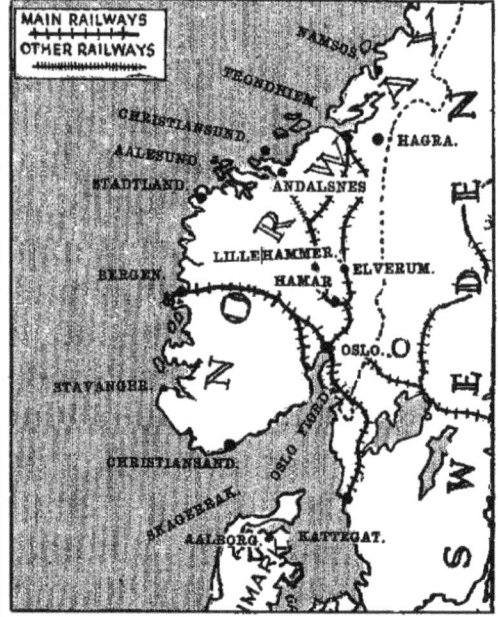

"The German crew hardly knew what to do. They threw arms into the lifeboats.

"The British rowed to the shore, 700 yards away, and made for the mountains. One man told me the harbour was like hell let loose. Bodies floated in the water and wreckage was strewn everywhere."

British troops have crossed Norway to reach the resisting Norwegian Army. Unconfirmed Stockholm reports say Allied troops with tanks and heavy guns, landed at Andalsnes, took the small railway line to Hamar which they recaptured from the Germans.

DAILY MIRROR, Tuesday, April 23, 1940.

Daily Mirror

APL 23

—No. 11,348 ONE PENNY
Registered at the G.P.O. as a Newspaper.

B.E.F SUCCESS IN NORWEGIAN FIGHTS

Duce Told "Keep Out"

BY A SPECIAL CORRESPONDENT

MUSSOLINI still hesitates to give Italy the word "War." And as he wavers strong influences are at work to persuade him to stay his hand.

The King of Italy, the Crown Prince, Count Grandi, General Badoglio and Marshal Balbo are among those who, in the past few days, have urged the Duce to keep out.

Mussolini's position is difficult. His friends say that he has been told plainly by Germany that she may decide "any day" to march into Yugoslavia.

Unless he marches, too, he will, therefore, miss his share of a part of this rich kingdom promised him by Hitler at their recent meeting in the Brenner Pass.

Count Ciano has for ten days been unable to accede to the requests for an interview made to him by the British Charge d'Affaires and the French Ambassador. Ciano's deputy has apologised and explained that Mussolini's son-in-law is suffering from a bad attack of influenza.

Reply Refused

There is says no possibility of putting the position as seen by the Allies before the highest authorities in power in Rome at the moment.

Disquieting news has reached Rome and Berlin about the country that holds the most important strategic position in South-Eastern Europe—Bulgaria.

King Boris's Government has refused to reply to a recently-made German request for assurances that British and French troops would be forbidden passage on their way to help Yugoslavia.

Yugoslavia is otherwise strategically cut off from any immediate Allied contact.

The Rome Press continues to threaten. "The day when Italy will come to a decision is rapidly approaching," says Il Tevere.

"Your Holy Duty"

A strong warning against spies, who were trying to make trouble in the Army, was issued yesterday by the Commandant of Belgrade, General Simovic.

Urging the people of Yugoslavia to exercise the utmost care in dealing with foreigners he said, "it is your holy duty to report to the office of the Commandant of Belgrade everything you see and hear which might endanger the nation's security."

YUGOSLAV PACT WITH REDS SOON

AGREEMENT in principle having been reached, the trade pact between Yugoslavia and Russia is likely to be signed within a fortnight, according to Jutro, a Slovene Opposition newspaper.

Immediately the agreement is signed, it adds, trade agencies are to be established in Belgrade and Moscow, and land and sea transport will be discussed.—Reuter.

Note in the north, on this map, Romsdale Fiord, where British troop landings are reported; Dombas, important rail junction where a U.S. attache has been killed; Trondhiem, reported threatened by Allied troops. Stavanger and Aalborg, German controlled aerodromes, have again been raided by the R.A.F.
Lillehammer and Hamar are other points in the news.

3 DEPUTY WAR CHIEFS

BY OUR POLITICAL CORRESPONDENT

TO lessen the strain on chief staff officers of intensified war, the Government has decided to duplicate key positions in the fighting services.

The following appointments have been made:—

Vice-Chief of the Naval Staff: Vice-Admiral Tom S. V. Phillips, aged fifty-two, at present Deputy-Chief of the Naval Staff.

Vice-Chief of the Imperial General Staff: General Sir John G. Dill, aged fifty-eight, at present Commanding the First Corps in France.

Vice-Chief of the Air Staff: Air Marshal R. E. C. Peirse, aged forty-eight, at present Deputy-Chief of the Air Staff.

Holders of these new posts will be members of the Board of Admiralty, Army Council and Air Council respectively, and will attend War Cabinet meetings at which their chiefs of staffs are unable to be present.

Air Ministry Also Strengthened

SINCE Sir Samuel Hoare became Air Minister in succession to Sir Kingsley Wood he, too, has been considering how to relieve the strain on the Ministry's organisation.

He has invited Sir Charles Craven, who has done invaluable work at the Admiralty, to work with Sir Wilfred Freeman, who is at present head of the production side. Both will serve on the Air Council.

CANADA'S PREMIER IN TALKS WITH ROOSEVELT

A talk which observers regard as highly significant in view of European developments will take place this week between Mr. Mackenzie King, Canada's Prime Minister, and President Roosevelt.

Mr. Mackenzie King is arriving today at Warm Springs, Georgia, and will stay until Thursday afternoon at the President's "Little White House" residence there.—Associated Press.

MARRIED 3 BROTHERS

WHEN a young man introduced his fiancee to his two brothers they said: "You've got the right girl. Just the one we'd have picked."

Neither thought that they, too, would woo and wed her. But they did.

The third brother, Mr. Louis Stockley, was wed in secret at Portsmouth a few days ago to his brothers' widow.

Not long after her marriage to Mr. Alfred Stockley, Mrs. Emily Stockley was left a widow.

That was about thirty-five years ago. Frank proposed, and she married her brother-in-law.

Always Happy

In 1913 he, too, died. The third brother, Louis, had not forgotten Emily—"the perfect wife," his family called her.

Though both in their sixties, they were married this month.

"We wanted to keep it secret," Mrs Stockley told the Daily Mirror last night at her new home in Fair Oak near Eastleigh, Hants.

"I don't see anything strange in marrying brothers, and all I can say is that I have always been happy as Mrs. Stockley."

"That's right," said Mr. Stockley. "It is just a family affair—that is what marriages are in this family—so we didn't tell anyone."

"There is nothing like keeping it in the family," the new bridegroom said.

"My brothers always admired Emily—she is a good wife—and even after all these years Louis remembered his words on her first wedding day.

"'You've got the right girl, the two brothers said. I don't know if either of them realised then that they too would marry her."

THE BRITISH ARMY IN NORWAY HAS ACHIEVED CONSIDERABLE SUCCESS AND IS GIVING VALUABLE SUPPORT TO THE NORWEGIAN FORCES.

That news was released by the War Office last night in a communique which said:—

"In our operations in support of the Norwegians our troops landing at many places have achieved considerable success in the face of great difficulties.

"They have gained touch with Norwegian forces, to whom they are giving all support in their power."

The landing places are still unnamed and no details are given of clashes with the Germans.

But from reports reaching Stockholm it is possible to piece together this picture of the fighting:

NARVIK.—The final Allied assault on Narvik began yesterday, according to a Norwegian military source in Stockholm.

After a warning by the dropping of leaflets telling civilians to hide in cellars or get into the mountains, the British force landed at Belsford, behind Narvik, and began their attack.

Retreat Cut Off

When the biggest German force moved to the north on the Tromsoe road to try to interfere with the Allied landing party, the Norwegians allowed them to advance about twenty-five miles to Gratangen before burning all big buildings and striking across the highway at Oesevatten, thus cutting off the possibility of the Germans retreating to Elvergaards Moen.

TRONDHIEM: The Allies are throwing an iron ring round Trondhiem to encircle the Germans in this key to the coast.

British troops have reached Stoeren, strategic railway junction thirty miles to the south.

North of the town they hold Namsos, now reported in ruins.

British air attacks on two emergency German air fields near Trondhiem.

Continued on Back Page

FAITH IN BOLD ALLIED THRUST

THE Allies' blow in Norway will be swift and hard.

Confidence in this was expressed last night by the Norwegian Minister in London, Mr. Colban, broadcasting in the B.B.C. Home Service.

"I know," he said, "that the Allied Governments have taken vigorous action for the battle to be fought on Norwegian soil.

"I trust, and I commit no indiscretion by saying that I have his Britannic Majesty's Government with me in this, that the action will be very strong and rapid. We all know that every day, every hour, now counts."

Sky Troops Land in Sweden

Military authorities in Norrbotten, Sweden's northernmost province, received word on Sunday from the frontier that a troop of men had been seen landing by parachute in Sweden, it was reported from Stockholm yesterday. Swedish ski patrols have been hunting for these troops, but no result of their search has yet been reported.—Reuter.

A.A. GUNS ROAR ON COAST

GERMAN aircraft approached the east and south-east coasts last night but were beaten off by pursuit planes and heavy anti-aircraft guns.

Searchlights swept the sky on the south-east coasts as heavy explosions were heard well out at sea. Gunflashes could be seen and shells burst at very high altitudes.

It is believed that enemy aircraft flew over one East Coast town three times.

A Nazi plane was caught in the beams of a searchlight, and there was heavy firing from the anti-aircraft batteries all around.

The plane made off to sea in a south-easterly direction.

Ten minutes later the batteries again opened fire as plane engines were heard.

Twenty minutes after that there was more heavy firing.

No air raid warning was given and no bombs were dropped.

Shrapnel in Streets

A resident of the town said that the planes made off as the barrage crept dangerously close to them.

In another town a mile or so away a raider was seen just after 10 p.m. flying at a great height. Within a few minutes a second raider was seen.

An eye witness said that the fire of the ground gunners was splendid, and that many shells could be seen bursting very close to the planes, which flew out to sea.

An official of an hotel said: "Firing went on for nearly an hour and a half after the first guns were heard."

Another spectator said that shrapnel fell in the streets, but no damage was done.

Aircraft stated to be travelling towards the coast brought the anti-aircraft defences into action near another East Coast town.

When Very lights dropped the gunfire ceased.

SHIPS' COLLISION BLOCKS MOUTH OF THE DANUBE

The mouth of the Danube was blocked yesterday owing to a collision between a Greek ship and an Italian one.

Both grounded in the main channel leading from the river to the Black Sea.—British United Press.

DAILY MIRROR, Wednesday, April 24, 1940.

Daily Mirror

No. 11,349 — ONE PENNY
Registered at the G.P.O. as a Newspaper.

APL 24

VICTORY BUDGET TAXES ALL SALES

BRITISH IN 200-YD. GUN WAR

BRITISH and German troops, 200 yards apart on the Trondhiem front, were reported last night to be blazing away at each other with machine-guns.

This fighting is taking place at Steinkjaer, the little town on the fiord north of Trondhiem, where the Norwegians have built a "Mannerheim Line."

The Allies, fighting also on at least three other fronts, are approximately equal to the strength of the Germans at Trondhiem.

Despite constant air raids by the Germans, it is claimed that no damage has been done to the British defence positions, although headquarters have had to be moved twice.

The ra ty with which the German aircraft found the British headquarters makes our troops suspect a well-developed spy system.

"North of Trondhiem," says a British War Office statement, "our troops have been counter-attacked and a sharp engagement has ensued."

Fighting is also reported to be in progress south of Trondhiem—at Melhus, only twelve miles from the town itself.

Allied troops are said to have arrived at this point from the Romsdal Fiord by the railway from Andalsnes via Dombaas and Stoeren.

This line is under British and Norwegian control in spite of bombing by German aircraft and enemy attempts to cut it by means of parachute troops.

Advance Continued

Further south, fierce fighting is reported in the heart of Norway for what is known as the "gateway" to Oslo—the strategic high road and railway line linking Lillehammer at the bottom of the Gudbrandsdal valley to Hamar and Oslo.

Although Germans claim to be still in possession of Lillehammer, the latest reports received in Stockholm indicate that British and Norwegian troops have continued their advance from there to Moelv, thirty miles to the south.

The Germans claim to have captured Canadian troops near Lillehammer.

But it was stated in London that no Canadian units are fighting in Norway, although individual Canadians may be there with the B.E.F.

The Norwegian High Command states: "Our troops made an advance at Valdres and took 100 prisoners."
— *Reuter, British United Press and Associated Press.*

NARVIK CONSUL SHOT REPORT

WHAT has happened to the British Consul at Narvik? No communication has been received in London from him since hostilities in Norway began.

An American seaman, interviewed by the Stockholm newspaper "Dagens Nyheter," declares that the Consul was shot by the Germans the day they entered the town.

The seaman, Patrick King, claims that he was in Narvik when the Germans entered, and that four German soldiers, with fixed bayonets, entered the Seamen's Home and asked whether there were any Englishmen there.

The British Consul was discovered, he said, and after brief questioning was executed.

Nothing is known in London of this report.—*British United Press.*

SIR JOHN SIMON, introducing his Pay-for-Victory Budget in the House of Commons last night, gave Britain a new tax—the Purchase Tax, by which everybody in the land will pay his share of the war cost.

Everything you buy, except food, drink and services like gas and electricity, will be taxed.

Certain articles on which heavy duties are already charged, like petrol and tobacco, will not be included.

The tax will be paid when the retailer buys from the wholesaler or manufacturer.

Letters Will Cost 2½d. a Stamp

HERE are the chief tax increases announced by Sir John Simon in his two hours nine minutes Budget speech in the House of Commons last night:—

INCOME TAX
Increase from 7s. to 7s. 6d. as announced in the Emergency Budget. Allowances reduced. Earned income relief, now one-fifth, reduced to one-sixth; marriage allowance down from £180 to £170, children's allowance reduced from £60 to £50.

BEER
Penny a pint more.

WHISKY
Increase of 1s. 9d. to 16s. a bottle.

TOBACCO
Duty up by 3d. an ounce.

SURTAX
To be payable on £1,500 next year.

TELEGRAMS
Threepence more on greetings or ordinary priority messages or night telegraph letter.

TELEPHONES
Rates up 15 per cent. The 1s. night calls up to 1s. 2d.

POSTAGE
Letters to be 2½d.; postcards to be 2d.; 1d. more for letters in Imperial post; foreign postage up by ½d. No change in rates for correspondence to Forces overseas. Change begins on May 1.

MATCHES
Duty doubled. Box of fifty, now 1d., to cost 1½d. Booklets of twenty, now ½d., to be thirty for 1d.

It is probable that the wholesaler will put an Excise stamp on the goods sold, but the public will not have to buy stamped goods.

The new tax has two objects. The first, of course, is to raise more money for Britain's war chest. The second is to check luxury spending.

The amount of the tax or the date when it will begin are not yet known. Sir John Simon knows that it cannot be operated at once.

Before End of Year

A register of wholesalers will have to be compiled; long discussions must take place before the amount of the tax can be determined.

And, since many manufacturers sell direct to the public or have their own retail organisations, the new Purchase Tax law is likely to be complicated.

Certainly Sir John Simon doesn't expect the new tax to yield him much money immediately.

"If the preliminary arrangements are carried through successfully," he said, "I hope to get something from it before the end of the year."

The new tax is Sir John's big hope of paying for the war as it is being won. All his Budget blows are heavy but none so heavy as many people expected. Britain is prepared to pay for victory.

One part of the Budget is directed against Stock Exchange speculation and profiteering.

Dividends Limited

Dividends of public companies are to be limited. No company will be allowed to pay more dividend during the war than it paid in any one of the three years before the war.

Those companies who have not been able to pay dividends will now be restricted to a distribution of 4 per cent.

The issue of bonus shares during the war will be prohibited—a rule that will stop companies paying dividend at the old rate on watered capital.

Another form of tax evasion is doomed—the one-man company.

"No sort of tolerance will be shown," Sir John said, "to citizens who seek to escape their proper share of taxation."

(Speech begins on page 2.)

Cigarettes 8½d. for Ten Today

Tobacco prices go up today, whisky on Friday and beer on Monday.

This was announced last night after the Budget tax increases were known.

The Imperial Tobacco combine stated last night:

"Since many retailers are short of stock, the following increase in their retail prices are authorised to take effect as from tomorrow—April 24—pending the issue of new price lists:—

"Tobacco will cost 3d. an ounce more. Cigarettes now costing 5d. for ten will be 6d., those costing 7d. will be 8½d."

The prices of whisky at 16s. a bottle and gin and rum at 15s. 6d. a bottle were recommended to come into operation on Friday.

The increased taxes on beer, tobacco, letters and phone calls will mean 1s. 7d. a week to the pocket of the average man—if he buys at his old rate.

He buys two and a half pints of beer a week, smokes seventy cigarettes, posts five letters and makes seven phone calls a week.

PLAN TO SHIP U.S. TROOPS

AMERICA'S War Department has perfected plans for the transportation of United States troops from New York Harbour to Europe or elsewhere.

This disclosure was made by Mr. George Randall, head of the general committee of port traffic of the Association of American Railways, at a hearing of the Interstate Commerce Commission in New York yesterday.

Mr. Randall said that plans had been perfected for the "possible transportation of troops."

The subject was dropped quickly because it had no direct bearing on the matter under discussion.

Remarking that it was the confidential property of the War Department, Mr. Randall afterwards refused to amplify his statement.—*Associated Press.*

PEASANT DIET PLEA FOR WAR

A RETURN to the eighteenth century English "peasant's diet" of wholemeal bread, vegetables, milk, cheese and potatoes, was suggested last night by Dr. J. C. Drummond, scientific adviser to the Ministry of Food, as the basis for the nation's future food plans.

He was opening "The Nation's Larder" series of talks at the Royal Institution, London.

Nutrition experts, said Dr. Drummond, had played a great part in planning the war for Germany, and if Germany could maintain her supplies she would not be beaten on the nutritional front.

There was a good deal of evidence that the German people were not getting that diet. The winter had ruined potatoes and made vegetables scarce.

TALK WITH ROOSEVELT

President Roosevelt and Mr. Mackenzie King, Canadian Prime Minister, conferred at Warm Springs, Georgia, yesterday on Canadian-American relations.—*Associated Press.*

DAILY MIRROR, Friday, May 3, 1940.

Daily Mirror

MAY 3

No. 11,357 — ONE PENNY
Registered at the G.P.O. as a Newspaper.

TEN DAYS, SAYS ROME: NAVY WATCH

"A BRITISH and French battle fleet, with cruisers and ancillary craft, is already in the eastern basin of the Mediterranean on its way to Alexandria," Mr. Chamberlain announced in the House of Commons last night.

So much of the German Navy has been destroyed in the Norwegian adventure that the Allies have been able to send back to the Mediterranean warships needed for a time in the North Sea.

So the ships of two great Navies wait for Mussolini to move.

In Rome, Mr. William Phillips, U.S. Ambassador, making his second visit in two days to the Duce, is reported to have been told "ITALY WILL MAKE NO WAR MOVE WITHIN THE NEXT TEN DAYS AT LEAST."

Mr. Phillips saw both Mussolini and his son-in-law, Ciano. He was assured, according to Rome reports, that Italy has no designs on Yugoslavia and plans no war move—for the present.

It is believed that Mr. Phillips explained to the Duce that if Italy goes to war no American ships will trade with her—a vital factor to a nation that depends so largely as Italy on imports of raw materials.

The impression in Rome is that after ten days Italy's non-belligerent attitude may suddenly change, but that her decision still depends on the turn of events.

Tension Revived

Fascist officials explain that Germany wants to see a neutral Yugoslavia remaining a source of supplies, and that Italy will adhere to this policy.

But the news that the Allied battle fleets were moving eastward in the Mediterranean revived tension in Rome last night.

In Egypt new precautions were taken. Army and police leave was cancelled. All strategic centres were heavily guarded. A Bill providing the death penalty for spies and traitors was presented to Parliament.

After conferring with the British Ambassador and defence chiefs, the Egyptian Premier declared that the situation was serious, but that there was no occasion for immediate alarm.

In Washington President Roosevelt and the Italian Ambassador had a conference. The State Department later announced that they did not think Italy was about to enter the war—yet.

Man Arrested in Crowd to See King

A few moments before the King and Queen arrived back in London from their tour last night, police officers mingling in the crowd of several hundreds outside Euston Station arrested a man who had been seen carrying something in his hand.

The man, aged about twenty-five, offered no resistance, and after being searched in a room at the railway station, was taken to Clerkenwell police station. He will appear at Clerkenwell Police Court today charged with being in possession of an offensive weapon.

Few people in the crowd knew of the incident. The man was driven away in a police car immediately after the King and Queen had left the station.

WHY ALLIES CAME OUT

"ALTHOUGH it has not been possible to capture Trondheim, I am satisfied that the balance of the advantage lies with the Allied Forces."

That was Mr. Chamberlain's judgment on the Norway situation when he revealed in the House of Commons last night that British troops in Central Norway have been withdrawn.

"We have withdrawn the whole of our forces from Andalsnes," the Premier added, "under the very noses of the German planes without, so far as I am aware, losing one man in this operation."

He explained, what had already become apparent, that the British troops were faced with the great difficulty of fighting without aeroplane support, that the existing aerodromes were in enemy hands and our fighting aircraft could not operate.

Nevertheless, "our troops fought with gallantry and determination and inflicted heavy losses on the enemy."

Mr. Chamberlain said our losses
Continued on Back Page

A WISE MOVE SAYS AMERICA

MR. CHAMBERLAIN'S announcement of the British withdrawal from Andalsnes was felt to be inevitable in American military circles because of the start Germany obtained.

For some time past the opinion has been expressed in these quarters that the German-Norwegian campaign was in the nature of a decoy.

The refusal of the British to fall into this trap, despite the adverse effect such a decision might have on public opinion, is held to be wise.

In Washington, Reuter adds, it has been rumoured that Hitler's Scandinavian adventure was a prelude to two new moves—an Italian attack in the Mediterranean and a German raid on England through Holland.

A Swedish Foreign Office official commented: "The effect on Sweden will be terrific. It means that Sweden must come more and more under German influence."

Typical Swiss comment was: "You British are always too slow."

HIS DIVE SAVED THE GUN

FOR diving over a barricade to retrieve the only gun left to repel a German attack, Sergeant William Adlam, of the Gloucestershire Regiment, received the immediate reward by Lord Gort of the Military Medal, and becomes the first Territorial to be decorated in the war.

On the night of April 4 Sergeant Adlam, who belongs to a Territorial Battalion of the Gloucestershire Regiment, was acting as platoon sergeant in a forward position. A raiding party of Germans attacked his post, which was under considerable pressure.

Gunner Wounded

A Bren gunner of the British post was wounded and the gun fell over the barricade. It was the only weapon holding the barricade, and Sergeant Adlam at once saw the danger of the post being rushed from that side if the gun was not brought back into action.

In spite of heavy fire and without consideration of the danger, Sergeant Adlam recovered the gun and opened fire on the enemy. He was under fire again later the same night and gave assistance to a patrol.

In the announcement of the award it is stated that the general bearing of Sergeant Adlam during the action, which lasted over eight hours, and on subsequent occasions when on patrol, has been the best possible example for the men.—Exchange.

FRENCH SUBMARINE SINKS A U-BOAT

A FRENCH submarine has torpedoed and sunk a U-boat in the North Sea.

The French communique last night also revealed that a French destroyer had been seriously damaged and one patrol ship sunk by a mine.

These French naval losses are understood to have taken place in a North Sea fight within the past forty-eight hours.—Reuter and Associated Press.

Major-General B. C. T. Paget, D.S.O., M.C.

36 OF HUNTER CREW FOUND

TWO officers and thirty-four ratings from H.M.S. Hunter, which was sunk in the first battle at Narvik on April 10, are among 127 British seamen now in Northern Sweden, it was reliably learned in Stockholm yesterday.

Nearly all the seamen are in a school at Jorn.

The officers are First-Lieutenant H. A. Menteth and Engineer-Lieutenant A. G. Reid. Menteth was wounded and taken to hospital at Skelleftea, near Jorn.

There is no news in Stockholm, however, of another thirty-three seamen whom the Germans, on the same day as the others crossed the Swedish border, told the Swedish authorities would cross in a few hours' time.

The seamen are to be interned for the time being until their status is decided. Those proved to be from warships will be interned for the duration of the war.—British United Press.

WAR CHIEFS SPEAK

For the first time since the war the Premier and the three Service Ministers — Mr. Winston Churchill, Sir Samuel Hoare and Mr. Oliver Stanley — will on Tuesday and Wednesday make personal statements in the House of Commons on the Norwegian operations.

A Hero of Two Wars

Fifty-three-year-old Major-General Bernard Charles Tolver Paget, D.S.O., M.C., the man to whose "determination and skilful dispositions," the Premier said yesterday, we owe the fact that our forces were withdrawn from Andalsnes without loss, is a hero of the last war.

He served in France and Belgium and received a wound that has left his left arm practically useless.

This does not prevent him from having the energy of a man half his age, and playing most games with tremendous keenness.

During the war he was mentioned four times in dispatches, three times decorated, and promoted.

From 1926 to 1929 he was an instructor at the Staff College, Camberley, and after commanding a brigade in India, he was brought home to succeed Lord Gort as Commandant of the College in 1938.

There is a portrait of General Paget in the Royal Academy this year. It is by Mr. Kenneth Green, who stated that he found the General an excellent sitter and a delightful, warm-hearted personality with a strong sense of humour.

The perfect emergency ration

2d and 4d

Fry's Sandwich Chocolate

DAILY MIRROR, Wednesday, May 8, 1940.

Daily Mirror

No. 11,861 — ONE PENNY
Registered at the G.P.O. as a Newspaper.

WHO HELD BACK NAVY? ADMIRAL HERO ASKS

DUTCH END ALL LEAVE

HOLLAND last night took the most extreme precautions against the threat of German attack that she has so far thought necessary.

All leave for the Army, Navy and Air Force was cancelled, and the men told to report for duty immediately.

Two classes of marines—those of 1927 and 1928—were recalled. These men are specially concerned with coastguard duties.

The Inspector-General of Shipping has forbidden ships to enter certain areas from next Saturday evening to Monday morning. The areas concerned are the Meuse-Waal Canal, and River Meuse above Grave and the Juliana Canal.

Leave has also been cancelled for workers in the war industry, and the men in the anti-aircraft and searchlight sections.

All outgoing international telephone calls and teleprinter communications from Holland were suspended last night. No reason was given.

Bombing Threats

An offer of a house in America for the Dutch royal family if Holland is invaded has been refused by Princess Juliana on behalf of Queen Wilhelmina and herself.

"Our place is here, whether or not danger threatens. We will never desert," she said.

Yesterday's German newspapers speak in huge headlines of the "great decisions that are in sight." They speak of fresh British "designs" against the neutrals.

The Nazi Press also seemed to hint last night at the possibility of air raids on shipyards in Great Britain—perhaps with the deliberate intention of making British flesh creep.

BERLIN TALKS OF NEW MOVE

BERLIN political circles were talking last night of "preventive counter-action."

"It has now been proved beyond question," neutral correspondents were told, "that the Allies plan further to extend the war front and to involve even more neutrals in the hostilities."

Renewed anxiety over the general situation in Europe was reflected in reports reaching Paris from various sources last night.

Mr. Chamberlain's reference to Sweden—considered in Paris as a veiled warning—coupled with the news of leave cancellations in Holland and the unfounded story of a telephone conversation between M. Reynaud and Mr. Chamberlain, were all noted.—Reuter.

GOEBBELS BULLIES AGAIN

Goebbels declared yesterday Germany will no longer tolerate publication in neutral newspapers of reports of acts of cruelty by German troops.

It was added naively, says Exchange: "As the German Government has prohibited such acts, all messages giving such reports must be lies."

In Name of God, Go, Premier Told

"In the name of God, go!" Mr. L. S. Amery, Conservative ex-Cabinet Minister, said that to the Government in Parliament last night.

He was quoting what Cromwell said to the Long Parliament in 1653 after it had been in power for thirteen years:

"You have sat too long here for any good you are doing.

"Depart, I say. Let us have done with you. IN THE NAME OF GOD, GO!"

The Long Parliament went.

Peers in Revolt

THERE is a revolt against Mr. Chamberlain in the House of Lords, writes the "Daily Mirror" political correspondent.

The Government are alarmed about the probable trend of today's war debate in the Upper House. Influential Tory peers—Lord Salisbury is one of them—will be bitterly critical.

As a result it is expected that a Carlton Club Tory meeting will be immediately called. The Government will then be warned that unless they adopt a far more virile and resolute war policy they cannot count on Tory support.

DIVE ON AFRIDI

THE British destroyer Afridi was sunk by a German plane which, flying against the sun, swooped down nearly to her funnel tops before releasing the fatal bomb.

This was revealed by an Associated Press correspondent who landed at a Northern port yesterday.

He says that on May 3 the convoy was bombed by thirteen Nazi planes. He was on board the flagship convoying warships, and saw the whole fight.

Also on board the flagship were the British headquarters staff and the commander of the French Alpine Chasseurs, General Audet.

The whole party narrowly escaped death when a heavy bomb fell only fifty yards on the portside of the side and a hail of incendiary bombs came down around it.

The French destroyer Bison was struck and sank after the wounded and survivors had been taken on board another ship.

Soon afterwards the attacking air squadrons reassembled and dived on the Afridi. She was hit and began to list badly, and the survivors were transferred to accompanying ships.

After these rescues Nazi bombers reappeared and swooped down in a perfect sunspot almost to her funnel tops, losing the fatal bomb.

Going Back a Bit

Chairman at the South-Eastern Conscientious Objectors' Tribunal yesterday: To what Church do you belong?
Applicant: Anglo-Saxon.

HELP IS PLANNED, SAYS NORSE KING

KING HAAKON OF NORWAY, in a proclamation to his people from "somewhere in Norway," declared yesterday:—

"In Northern Norway we still occupy strong positions, and from which this may succeed, with the help which is now being planned, in re-conquering the rest of the country.

"It is the enemy's superiority, both in numbers and technically, both on the ground and especially in the air, which has forced us to retreat.

"We have reason to believe this will soon be changed."

It was not war but murder and arson which the Germans were practising in Norway, said King Haakon. But the morale of the people remained unshaken.

"Even if the burdens are heavy and sorrow and privation strike our homes, do not lose courage," said King Haakon.

CAN'T LET GERMANY WIN

Immediately after an interview with Roosevelt in Washington yesterday, Mr. James W. Gerard, a former U.S. Ambassador to Germany, said: "We can't afford to allow the Germans to win."

Mr. Gerard emphasised he was expressing his personal opinion.—British United Press.

Conservative M.P.s moved into open revolt against the Government in the Norway debate in the House of Commons last night.

Mr. Amery told the Cabinet: "Get out; Go." Earl Winterton suggested an inquiry to discover the persons responsible. Admiral Sir Roger Keyes, in a dramatic speech, revealed that he had offered to lead the attack on Trondheim, had been told that such a move was not necessary.

HEAVY salvos of criticism were fired at the Government last night by Sir Roger Keyes, hero of Zeebrugge, when in Parliament he bitterly attacked the mishandling of the Norway campaign.

"The capture of Trondheim," he said, "was essential, imperative, vital."

Norwegian officers had come to him begging him to help their efforts for a frontal attack. He had urged the Admiralty to go in, he had offered to organise and lead the attack.

When at last he was able to express his views at the Admiralty that there was no difficulty in going into Trondheim, but it was not considered necessary as the Army was making good progress and the situation in the Mediterranean made it undesirable to risk ships.

"It astounds me that the Naval Staff would not realise the attack on the port of Namsos was doomed to failure if German ships were left in command of Trondheim Fiord.

"The German naval forces there were only two destroyers which could have been eliminated with little risk."

"I Foresaw Another Gallipoli"

He told the Admiralty that if the Italian bluster worried them about ships, some of our old ships could have been used in Norway without affecting the strength of the Fleet.

"When I realised how badly things were going I foresaw another Gallipoli."

Sir Roger declared that whoever was at fault it was not the officers and men.

He was wearing the uniform of an Admiral of the Fleet" because "I speak for some officers and men of the fighting, sea-going Navy who are very unhappy."

Our General, advancing from Steinkjer to Trondheim, he said, expected British ships to support him—not two German destroyers, who fired on his flank, landed troops behind his advance forces and captured or destroyed them.

If we had only used our Fleet courageously, the Germans by now would have been in a very dangerous position and eventually would have been decisively defeated.

Sir Roger spoke not as a politician, but as a sailor. He hesitated over his words, but when they came they were blunt and devastating.

Throughout his speech, Mr. Winston Churchill sat with bowed head. For him, Sir Roger expressed his admiration.

"I look to him to help to win the war. I hope that he will accept my view, which, after all, is based on experience, precedent and achievement.

"I do beg him to steel his heart

Continued on Back Page

New Low for the £

First American reaction to Mr. Chamberlain's speech came when free sterling fell on Wall Street to 3.38 dollars—the lowest level touched in the war. Before the market closed sterling had dropped still further to 3.37¼.

"Special Drene Shampoo is 'tops' with me"
says
LILLI PALMER
Now starring in "Ladies into Action" at the Lyric Theatre, London.

"I GOT a new thrill the very first time my hair was shampooed with Special Drene... it leaves hair so radiantly lovely and so very easy to set in any style right after shampooing. My hairdresser recommends Special Drene for every type of hair... it is so quick and simple to use. I like the best of everything, and when it comes to shampooing my choice is Special Drene every time."

GLAMOROUS HAIR CAN BE YOURS TOO... WHEN YOU USE

SPECIAL **drene** SHAMPOO

6d., 1/6 & 2/6

DAILY MIRROR, Tuesday, May 14, 1940.

Daily Mirror
MAY 14

No. 11,366 — ONE PENNY
Registered at the G.P.O. as a Newspaper.

BATTLE OF 2,000 TANKS RAGING

Dutch Govt. Flees

THE Dutch Government has been transferred "elsewhere" in order to give it greater freedom of action, a proclamation broadcast by the Amsterdam Radio from General Winkelman, Commander-in-Chief of the Dutch forces, stated last night.

Queen Wilhelmina in London

WITH a Service type gas mask slung over her back and wearing a plain black coat and skirt, Queen Wilhelmina of the Netherlands, brought to England in a British warship, was welcomed at Liverpool-street Station last night by the King. He shook hands with her and kissed her on both cheeks.

But the first to greet her was Princess Juliana, who with Prince Bernhard and the two baby princesses, had reached London in the morning.

Police cleared a way for the royal car, which drove straight to Buckingham Palace, where the Dutch Queen stayed the night. Her daughter and son-in-law, after a short stay at the Palace, returned to their temporary home in Eaton-square, S.W.

The King and Queen afterwards left for Dorset.

Germans Bombed Juliana's Ship

IT was learned last night that bombs dropped round the British ship which brought Princess Juliana and her family to England just as they were about to board her at The Hague.

A Dutch ship standing by was heavily bombed and machine-gunned by German airmen, who apparently believed the royal family to be aboard her.

Amid the roar of gunfire the Prince and Princess were hurried up the gangway. The baby Princess was carried in her gas-proof cot by an officer.

A sailor told the "Daily Mirror": "Bombs dropped near us as we lay off The Hague waiting to pick up the Prince and Princess. A ship near us was nearly sunk. It looked as though the Nazis thought the royal party were aboard her.

"For some time it was murder. But when we got clear we had a steady journey. Princess Juliana wept a little."

Princess Juliana Arrives—Page 8.

FIFTEEN hundred to 2,000 French and German tanks were fighting in one Belgian sector last night—the greatest battle yet between mechanised troops.

British tanks were also in action as the Allied advance forces fought to delay fierce German thrusts through the gap in the Albert Canal defences and the Belgian Ardennes.

These attacks were an attempt to prevent the Allied forces linking up with the Belgians and the Dutch. They were part of an offensive on a 250-mile front stretching from Holland to the Moselle.

Last night, Paris said French, Belgian and Dutch advance troops were falling back on strategic positions in face of savage onslaughts. The enemy flung in more and more forces as the day went on.

The Allied tanks, fighting delaying actions, put up a brilliant show with superior material.

Late last night it was stated that at any moment the Germans might clash with the main forces of the B.E.F.

Advanced mechanised units had been in contact with the enemy for some hours.

Plan Counter-Attack

Reconnaissance planes gave the British headquarters a "picture" of the enemy movements.

And early today staff officers were working out times and positions for a counter-attack.

A Belgian officer, passing through the British lines on the way back from the battle zone, said:

"The Germans have spared nothing in human life to make yard by yard progress. We have had to give ground and some of our troops are falling back at this moment."

Tanks Hit Hard

Last night's official French war communique stated:

"German troops today continued their mass attacks in both Holland and Belgium. In Holland they made some advance, especially on the lower reaches of the Meuse.

"In Belgium, in the region of Saint Troud, French counter-attacks, led mainly by tanks, inflicted heavy losses on the enemy.

"The Germans made a particularly important effort in the Belgian Ardennes, where they achieved some progress.

"Our light mechanised units, having fulfilled their delaying action, fell back on the Meuse, which the enemy had reached at one point.

"The enemy exerted strong pressure on Longwy (in front of the Maginot Line). His attacks were repulsed, as were those la unched east of the Moselle and in the region of the Saar.

"Fifteen enemy aircraft were shot
Continued on Back Page

FAKED CALL-UP ON B.B.C.

SOMEONE telephoned to the B.B.C. last night asking them to broadcast an announcement ordering the call-up of R.A.F. reservists.

The B.B.C. thought the message came from the Air Ministry. So they broadcast it.

Three hours later they had to broadcast an admission that the call-up notice was false.

The Air Ministry denied all knowledge of it.

Air Force reservists were not required.

The authorities tried to trace the telephone call, and inquiries were still in progress at midnight.

"We received verbal instructions over the telephone in the first place which we understand emanated from the Air Ministry," said a B.B.C. official. "We gave the announcement at 7.15 p.m. and took the first opportunity to issue a correction.

"It was not till ten o'clock. Of course, we regret the delay in the cancellation, but as soon as the Air Ministry got into touch with us we took the first chance of putting it out.

"We are still examining the possibility of the message being the result of a pure misunderstanding."

An Air Ministry official said: "All we can say is that the original message did not emanate from the Air Ministry."

HANDS IN POCKETS ARE FORBIDDEN

DUTCH police, continuing their drive against Holland's Fifth Column, yesterday announced that people are forbidden to walk about the streets with their hands in their pockets.

Groups of more than three civilians have been banned.

ALLIES SMASH RAILWAYS

French artillery and Allied air bombs yesterday shattered part of the Istein railway tunnel under Germany's "Gibraltar of the Rhine," closing a section of this vital military railway incorporated in the Siegfried Line, to military traffic.

Railway traffic between Freiburg in Breisgau (Germany) and Basle (Switzerland) has been stopped by the Germans owing to the shelling of trains by French artillery, Beromunster radio reported last night.

T.U.C. Strong Man Is Labour Minister

Mr. Ernest Bevin is Britain's new Minister of Labour. He is one of the strongest and most able Trade Union leaders in the history of the movement.

He started as a farm worker, got a job with a Bristol restaurant firm, drove a milk float, then became an official of the Dockers' Union and earned the title of The Dockers' K.C. as advocate for the men at a dockers' court of inquiry in 1921.

As general secretary of the Transport and General Workers' Union, he has played an important role. He was chairman and president of the T.U.C. in 1937.

A big man in figure as well as in Trade Union affairs, he has a dominant personality, stands no nonsense.

AND NOW HE SAYS . . .

Mr. Ernest Bevin

I'LL ASK ALL TO WORK LIKE HELL

MR. ERNEST BEVIN, speaking as Labour Minister for the first time, said at Bournemouth last night:

"I hope the War Cabinet will not allow vested interests, profits or anything else, to stand in the way of maximum production.

"If this is the policy of the Government, I will ask my people to work like hell to save the lives of our lads.

"I have heard a lot of talk about equal sacrifices. The working classes are generous to a fault, but it is not by mucking about with pennies of their wages that you get the best out of the workers.

"It is the belief that the worker is getting a square deal, and not merely giving profit to the employer, that will enable the work to win the war and get back to a decent peace. In that spirit the Labour Party has undertaken to go into the Government.

Promise to Unions

"I can promise the trades union group that I will not let them rust. There must be in the workshops, among shop stewards and others, a feeling that they are part of the Government. Then they will stick it through to the end.

"If trade union conditions have to be relaxed we shall take steps to see that everything was restored at the end.

"The position is critical and violent, and will require tremendous energy.

"When I said 'yes' this afternoon to the Prime Minister, I wished I was ten years younger. Strikes are difficult and hard and involve suffering. This struggle represents death, and it represents the blotting out of the finest strata of the manhood of the nation."

EGYPT BEGINS EVACUATION

EGYPT last night began the evacuation of the civil populations of all the strategic western desert towns along the Egyptian-Libyan frontier.

The Military Governor ordered the immediate abandonment of homes in three important centres, Mersa Matrum, Sidi Barrani and Sollum.

The evacuation was decided on in view of a possible Italian war move.

Government sources declared that the Mediterranean situation was "slightly reassuring," but emphasised that Egypt must constantly be "exceptionally cautious and vigilant."—Associated Press.

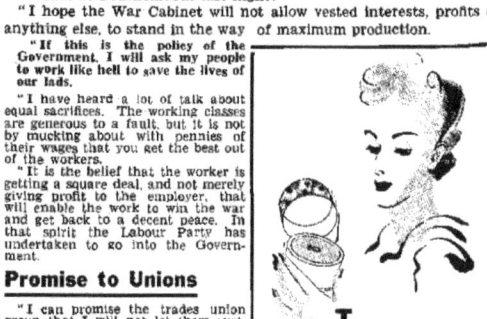

There's more in face powder— than meets the eye

"DOES this powder contain any materials which swell when moistened?"

Why is this question so important? Because it is impossible to prevent tiny grains of powder from getting into your pores, where they become moist. If these grains swell, they force open your pores, and leave them permanently enlarged.

Coty "Air Spun" powder contains no materials which swell when moistened, it cannot cause enlarged pores.

Two very lovely shades

Have you tried *Gitane* or *Brumes*, two of the loveliest "Air Spun" shades? "Air Spun" costs only 1/3, or 2/3 for the economy size box containing twice as much powder. From all good shops, or the Coty Salon, 2 New Bond Street, W.1.

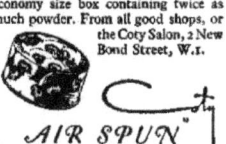

AIR SPUN
The face powder that stays on

Daily Mirror

DAILY MIRROR, Saturday, May 18, 1940.

No. 11,370 — ONE PENNY
Registered at the G.P.O. as a Newspaper.

MAY 18

CONQUER OR DIE ORDER BY GAMELIN

GENERAL GAMELIN gave this order to the soldiers of France last night:—

"THE FATE OF OUR COUNTRY AND THAT OF OUR ALLIES, THE DESTINIES OF THE WORLD, DEPEND ON THE BATTLE NOW IN PROGRESS.

"BRITISH, BELGIAN, POLISH SOLDIERS AND FOREIGN VOLUNTEERS ARE FIGHTING AT OUR SIDE, AND THE ROYAL AIR FORCE IS FIGHTING TO THE DEATH, LIKE OURS.

"ANY SOLDIER WHO CANNOT ADVANCE SHOULD ALLOW HIMSELF TO BE KILLED RATHER THAN ABANDON THE LITTLE SPOT OF NATIVE SOIL WHICH WAS ENTRUSTED TO HIM.

"AS ALWAYS IN GRAVE HOURS OF OUR HISTORY, THE ORDER TODAY IS 'CONQUER OR DIE.' WE MUST CONQUER."

Enemy Loses 1,000 Planes

Germany has lost more than 1,000 planes since she invaded the Low Countries on May 10.

THIS estimate, given by the Air Ministry last night, is based on a careful study of all sources of information.

To this figure must be added the enemy's losses in Poland and Norway.

Yesterday's German High Command communique gave the losses of Allied aircraft as 1,462.

"It is thought that the High Command must have published their own losses in error," comments the Air Ministry. "Allied losses are, in fact, only a small fraction of the German claims."

But it adds this warning:—

"In spite of these heavy inroads into the fighting strength of the German Air Force, it must be understood that their reserves are considerable, and that they are, for a time at least, able to sustain their effort."

Bombed on March

More heavy attacks by the R.A.F on troop columns and lines of communication inside Germany are revealed by the Air Ministry, which states:—

"Bombers again raided military objectives in Western Germany. Many objectives sustained direct hits in these operations, in which none of our aircraft was lost.

"Simultaneously a force of medium bombers made sustained attacks on enemy transport and petrol reserves in the woods round Sedan.

"During yesterday enemy thrusts in the valley of the Meuse were fiercely and successfully attacked. Pontoon bridges were blown up, roads blocked and troops on the march bombed and machine-gunned.

"The enemy were hampered and harassed at key points, and mechanised units received heavy casualties.

Another squadron of Blenheims, supporting the French Army, bombed a key position at Gembloux. They encountered a large formation of enemy fighters and intense ground fire. Eleven of them did not return.

The Navy's Great Holland Feat:
Full Story: Page 8

Premier Sees King
The Prime Minister, Mr. Churchill, was received in audience by the King at Buckingham Palace at 10.30 last night.

SECRET NEW NAZI TANK

A NEW heavy tank, not previously seen on the battlefield, has been used by the Germans in their attack from the Ardennes and Luxembourg.

The new mechanised unit is much more heavily armoured than those used in the Polish campaign.

The French tanks, however have proved to be more than a match for the new German weapon.

It is doubtful whether the Germans have large reserves of this type, which contributed to the surprise element in the enemy offensive.

Delayed-action bombs, which in some cases have exploded a fortnight after they were dropped, have also been used by the Germans in attacks on several French aerodromes.—Reuter.

Successes on the Belgian battlefront are claimed by the Germans.

In a communique issued last night they stated that German troops had marched to the south and north of Louvain into Brussels, the capital city, nd Malines.

They also claim to have reached Antwerp's fortifications.

HUNS IN BRUSSELS

AS Gamelin made this call to French troops battling to stem the break-through on the Sedan sector, the British troops in Flanders were withdrawn to positions west of Brussels.

A communique stated:

"Certain readjustments of the front having become necessary, the B.E.F. was withdrawn to positions west of Brussels. This readjustment was carried out without interference.

"There is no question of any collapse or break through in this sector, as suggested by the German communique."

A German High Command communique claimed that their troops had marched into Brussels after breaking Allied resistance south of Louvain.

The enemy also claimed to have broken through north of Louvain to occupy Malines. They said that troops thrusting from the north had pushed up to the fringes of the fortress of Antwerp.

The Berlin radio said the next defence line for the B.E.F. in Belgium was Antwerp—Ghent—Lille.

The Germans made new violent efforts to increase the depth of the

Contd. on Back Page, Col. 4

RICH MUST EAT SIMPLER FOOD

THE rich must eat simpler food, and hotels and restaurants must stop serving luxury meals.

This statement was made in Edinburgh yesterday by Mr. Robert Boothby, Parliamentary Secretary to the Ministry of Food.

"Two criticisms were being made against the Ministry of Food, said Mr. Boothby.

One was that there was still too much luxury consumption of food by the well-to-do in this country, especially in hotels and restaurants.

"I agree," he said, "I think it must be cut down. No one can afford luxuries of any kind in this country today. Everything must go into the production and importation of essential necessities for the conduct of the war."

Price Problem

The second criticism was more formidable. He was asked what was the use of recommending foods which were beyond the purse of many poorer people.

"This raises the problem of price," said Mr. Boothby.

"We are fully aware of this problem, and of its urgency, and it will be given serious consideration by the Government."

Mr. Boothby mentioned the foods which he considered to be the basis of a perfect diet.

These were milk, oatmeal, potatoes, vegetables and fruit, "with an occasional herring when you can get it."

TROOPS GUARDING B.B.C.

Broadcasting House is being guarded day and night by troops. Soldiers were on duty there yesterday for the first time.

THEY ARE GREAT

FROM T. E. A. HEALY
Our Correspondent with the French Army

RIGHT now the French Army carries civilisation.

And in this hour I want it to be known that never in the seven months I have been with the French Army have I seen what was realised, but not evident. No puerile optimism. Just stern appraisal of what depends on them. And grim, unspoken determination to do it.

I have seen them come from an inferno in which everything that the Germans had was thrown against them from land and from air. And never have I seen a trace of weakness or defeatism.

Never have I been more impressed with the quality of the officers and men of the French Army. And never more proud to be associated with them as your representative.

They move up into battle. I have heard no word of complaint.

DON'T
PUT YOUR CHILDREN AT THIS DISADVANTAGE

IT is natural to think that because the winter is over children should be given a diet less rich in nourishment. Many mothers make this mistake every summer. In consequence their children start the winter, with its ills and trying weather, at a disadvantage, because they have become run down during the summer.

SUMMER TAKES MORE OUT OF THEM

The long warm days of summer take far more out of children, and grown-ups too, than the short cold days of winter. There are longer hours of daylight in which to burn up energy and the hot weather is more tiring. Unless the extra energy burned up is replaced health will suffer.

THE PERFECT ENERGY-FOOD

Because it is so light, delicious, and nourishing, Cadbury's Bournville Cocoa is one of the finest means of replacing energy. Because it is so easily digestible it is exactly the kind of drink doctors recommend to promote truly restful and nerve-restoring sleep. Keep the children on Bournville throughout the summer — they love milk with it and it makes milk extra nourishing.

Still **6d** PER QTR. LB
11d PER HALF LB

CADBURY'S BOURNVILLE COCOA
A cup of cocoa is a cup of food

DAILY MIRROR, Tuesday, May 21, 1940.

Daily Mirror

MAY 21

No. 11,372   ONE PENNY
Registered at the G.P.O. as a Newspaper.

11 PLANES ATTACK 111 —BAG 11

ELEVEN Hurricanes, sighting a hundred and eleven enemy aircraft, attacked them and shot down eleven, eight of which were fighters.

Four of our machines returned. The German planes—ninety bombers and twenty-one Messerschmitt 110's—did not drop a single bomb.

This latest feat of the R.A.F. was announced by the Air Ministry last night.

One young pilot in this battle, which was fought on Sunday during patrols over Holland and Belgium, took on four H.E. 111s one after the other and destroyed three of them.

Reports so far received confirm that thirty enemy aircraft were destroyed by the R.A.F. on Sunday and many others heavily damaged.

Victories against such odds are not won without loss. Fourteen of our fighters are missing.

An important bridge in the war zone survived eight efforts to bomb it to destruction.

Then the pilots and crews of four British bombers presented themselves to their commanding officer, and the senior pilot said: "Sir, can we have your permission to finish it?"

The squadron leader replied: "Do it." The four bombers took off; and none returned. But the bridge was destroyed.

Fighter patrols of one R.A.F. group alone brought down over fifty Heinkels, Dorniers, Junkers and Messerschmitts during Saturday and Sunday with less than half that number of casualties to themselves.

Saw 34 Crash

They watched thirty-four of their enemies crash and knew that their bullets had put the other sixteen out of action.

Bomber aircraft of the R.A.F. maintained their pressure on enemy lines of communication on Sunday night.

Oil refineries in North-West Germany were also successfully attacked.

South of Brussels operations were carried out against railway stations and bridges.

The railway bridge at Roux sustained a direct hit.

Damage was done to rolling stock and the permanent way.

Troop and tank concentrations were attacked in the Aisne sector. Near Sedan a lorry park was set on fire.

From these operations, involving a large number of R.A.F. bombers, only two have failed to return in spite of intense enemy anti-aircraft fire.

FORCES TOLD OF GERMAN LOSSES

GERMAN troops are getting their first taste of dive-bombing attacks, their planes are suffering losses three times as great as they are inflicting, and their newspapers are commenting ruefully on the accuracy of British artillery, British troops were told last night in a bulletin from G.H.Q. broadcast by the B.B.C.

They were told that while they had been saying that lightning war "never strikes in the same place twice," headquarters had been preparing plans to meet the Blitzkrieg successfully.

This was Hitler's last hope.

RAF Pilot Stole a Ride—on Nazi Tank

A British pilot, shot down over enemy territory, coolly got unsuspecting Germans to give him a lift back to his own lines.

Before the plane crashed he took to his parachute. Landing near an advancing column of tanks he ran across and jumped on to the nearest one.

Only then did he realise where he was. The tanks were not French—but German!

He decided to keep his grandstand seat, and trust that in his flying kit any Germans seeing him there would not recognise him.

It worked. He got a free ride at the enemy's expense, staying on the tank until he reached a place where he could jump off and strike across country back to the Allied lines.

"This incident is typical of the bravery and initiative that characterise the pilots of the Royal Air Force," said Captain H. H. Balfour, Under-Secretary of State for Air, when he told the story in a broadcast last night.

Mrs. Thorn shows her husband how she escaped from Belgium. Mrs. Thorn is the woman who . . .

MILKED COW AMID BULLETS

WHILE German planes zoomed overhead machine-gunning a Belgian train crammed with refugees, a woman jumped out to milk a cow in a nearby field to get milk for three babies.

Bullets spattered round her as she calmly filled several empty beer bottles with milk, then clutching them in her arms, she ran back to the train.

She was Mrs. Renee Thorn, Belgian wife of Mr. Arthur Thorn, retired sea captain, of Dovercourt, Essex. After travelling for a week without sleep and with practically nothing to eat, she has arrived home.

"Our train took twenty-four hours from Antwerp to Ypres," she told the *Daily Mirror*. "Normally the journey takes an hour. All the time we were machine-gunned and several people were killed and wounded."

"The babies had to be fed. I suppose I was lucky not to have been killed while milking the cow."

While she was in Ostend the Germans bombed and sank the boat she was to have boarded. It was already packed with refugees.

"I saw the boat sinking," she said. "Of the people on board about 350 were killed or injured."

Police in Firearm Swoop

THOUSANDS of firearms—guns, rifles and revolvers—were "rounded up" by the police yesterday, and are now safe from parachutists or fifth columnists.

Police vans yesterday called at the shops of gunsmiths, sports outfitters, pawnbrokers and secondhand dealers and took away their stocks of arms.

The biggest drive was in London, but Birmingham, Glasgow, Edinburgh, Bristol and other big cities also yielded up large supplies of arms and ammunition.

From two shops near Liverpool-street, E.C., a full vanload of revolvers was collected.

Some were old single-action Colts, others the snub-nosed five-shooter issued to the British Army forty years ago. From other dealers came Service rifles, some adapted for sporting and competition shooting.

Terrific Power

"We were shown 'Authority to collect,' and soon afterwards police arrived with a van," a member of the staff of a famous gunmakers in the West End told the "Daily Mirror." "They took everything which would fire ball ammunition from .22 upwards.

"Some of the rifles are very expensive sporting weapons with terrific hitting power and extremely accurate sighting."

The arms were taken to police stations, where they were classified. Hundreds of thousands of rounds of ammunition were also collected

Aliens' Arms Ban

The Home Secretary yesterday made an order which forbids aliens to possess firearms, ammunition or explosives without a special permit from the police.

The order applies to aliens of all nationalities throughout the United Kingdom.

The firearms covered by the prohibition include shotguns, except air guns, air rifles and air pistols.

Any firearms, ammunition or explosives at present in the possession of aliens must be surrendered.

Interruption in Anglo-French Telephones

Telephonic communication between Great Britain and France was interrupted last evening and had not been fully resumed late last night.

GERMANS THRUST AT CHANNEL

GERMAN armoured forces were swinging north-west last night in an attempt to thrust a wedge between the main French armies and the Allied troops in Belgium.

The British and Belgian armies fell back to ward off the threat to the Channel ports as the French fiercely resisted the enemy advance across the plains of North France.

German spearhead was five mechanised divisions—with 60,000 men. Most of the punching power was concentrated on a thirty-mile sector between Le Cateau and La Fere—where the enemy claim to have reached the west bank of the canal running from the River Oise to the Sambre—and in the St. Quentin sector.

The German High Command claimed that on the left flank of their bulge into France they had captured the citadel of Laon.

But north of Laon the French sent their tanks into a counter-attack and a German mechanised column was destroyed.

And in his drive north-west Hitler is taking the risk of a threat from the B.E.F. to the German right flank.

Paris radio said early today that British forces withdrawn from Belgium aided French units in another Allied counter-attack at St. Quentin.

General Weygand is regrouping swarms of his infantry around the St. Quentin area.

There is violent fighting along the flanks of the German bulge. In many places the opposing light advance elements are operating behind each other's lines.

Allied Push

The French repulsed attempts to extend the pocket to the south of Rethel. German forces, which crossed the Aisne were thrown back.

A French War Ministry spokesman said the Germans had pushed further towards the Channel, taking St. Quentin, and were advancing on Peronne, which was "perhaps held by light advance units."

Fighting also raged around Caudry, ten miles south-east of Cambrai, but the French hold Cambrai and La Fere.

A French counter-attack is being made from La Fere.

The German military commentator, who was less triumphant in tone, stated over Deutschlandsender:

"As we expected, the Allies started their counter-attacks in a north-east direction with the aim of relieving their armies in Belgium. Other surprises are possible, too, but we are ready."

Columns Pounded

The official French communique stated:

"The German thrust is still very strong in the region north and west of Saint Quentin.

"New enemy attacks have been repulsed in the Montmedy region. There is nothing of importance on the rest of the front.

"There was great activity of our aviation in the course of the day.

"Numerous reconnaissances prepared the engagement of bombing formations on armoured enemy units.

"Heavy bombing was carried out on the columns, retarding their progress and inflicting severe losses on them."

A Paris military source said early today that the most encouraging development was the discovery that the main German forces are unable to follow up their mechanised units so effectively.
Associated Press, Reuter British United Press.

At Front After 8 Weeks

"In our infantry columns at the Western Front soldiers are marching who have undergone a training of only eight weeks," a spokesman of the German High Command stated in a broadcast yesterday.—Reuter.

Enlarged pores can be avoided

How you can foretell the future of your skin

DOES your face powder contain ingredients that swell? Just imagine what happens if it does. Sometimes tiny grains of powder get into pores — especially nose pores — which are larger than others. If these grains swell when moistened by the skin, the pores are forced open and permanently enlarged.

This can't ever happen with Coty "Air Spun" powder. "Air Spun" is guaranteed to contain no materials that swell — no orris root or artificial adhesives either.

Ask to see the full range of "Air Spun" shades next time you buy powder. Make a special point of seeing *Miblonde* and *Gitane.* "Air Spun" costs only 1/3 a box. Large size 2/3, contains twice as much powder.

Coty
AIR SPUN
THE POWDER THAT STAYS ON

Daily Mirror

Wednesday, May 22, 1940.
MAY 22
No. 11,373 — ONE PENNY
Registered at the G.P.O. as a Newspaper.

AMIENS BURNS AS B.E.F. FIGHT FOR PORTS

Aircraft: 7 Day Week, Nights Too

An urgent appeal to aircraft workers to work week-ends and also to work night and day, was made by Lord Beaverbrook, Minister of Aircraft Production, last night.

The appeal stated:—

"All employees of aircraft factories, aero-engine works, factories making component parts for aeroplanes, and plants engaged on sub-contracts for the air programme, are invited to work on Saturday and Sunday, May 25 and 26, and also on Saturday and Sunday, June 1 and 2.

"Keep calm," said the management. "We were only waiting to sort out the most highly-skilled men. Tonight you go full steam ahead. Tomorrow, bring mattresses with you!"

The men grinned delightedly. There was no argument about money.

Workers of at least one factory had not waited for Lord Beaverbrook's appeal.

They sent a deputation to the management complaining that they were not being asked to work long enough or at high pressure. "We want to get on with the war," they said, grimly.

"They are asked to work by night and by day, full overtime for the present.

"Any firm unable to follow this advice for any reason should send me a telegram explaining the difficulties, and I will do what I can to smooth them out."

THE B.E.F. early today faced up to the battle for the Channel ports following the enemy thrust to separate them from the main French forces.

German advance forces reached Amiens and Arras yesterday, and last night both towns were in flames after incendiary bomb attacks.

Paris radio officially announced this morning that Abbeville is not occupied by the Germans.

The capture of Arras was partly due to the German Air Force. It bombed the station, set houses on fire and co-operated in the street fighting between the German and British forces which went on night and day for over twenty-four hours.

In bright moonlight the battle for Arras went on from house to house, street corner to street corner, with hand-grenades, tanks, machine-guns and every other weapon thrown into the struggle.

The enemy claimed to have isolated Anglo-Belgian forces by reaching Abbeville at the mouth of the Somme. But this claim was based on the extreme limits of raiding motor-cycle units and other light forces.

The thrust was supported by every trick of total warfare, including hundreds of parachutists and organised fire campaign from the air.

The French War Office spokesman said early today that only 3,000 to 4,000 Germans pierced the Allied line to take Amiens and Arras.

"The front is confused, with the French still holding Cambrai, east of Arras, and behind the German advanced positions," he declared.

"Battle is engaged between the British and German forces.

"On the rest of the front the

BOMBS RAIN ON GERMAN TROOPS

FIGHTING brilliantly against odds, the R.A.F. is striking again and again at German lines of communication and mechanised columns, beating off attacks by enemy fighters and inflicting many times its own losses.

"Today our bomber and fighter aircraft have been continuously engaged in operations over the confused fighting fronts in Belgium and Northern France," the Air Ministry announced last night.

German troops, moving once again over the battlefield of Arras, Bapaume, St. Quentin and Cambrai, were subjected to repeated attacks by R.A.F. planes through Monday night and the early hours of yesterday.

In the light of an almost full moon the distinctive features of the countryside, familiar twenty-three years ago to young pilots of another generation, were easily discerned, and only in two instances did the raiders have any difficulty in locating their target.

Tanks, armoured cars, troop transports and other reinforcements were vigorously attacked.

Near a village off one of the main roads leading to Cambrai, a section of Blenheim bombers located and attacked a mile-long procession of motor transport.

Nearer to Cambrai, another section of Blenheim aircraft attacked motorised units protected by pom-poms and light guns on mobile platforms. Cross-roads and important railway lines in the district of Bapaume were also bombed and temporarily made unusable.

Attacks by other Wellington aircraft were also successful.

Outside Le Cateau two hits were made on a stationary train which was about to move off.

Wellington aircraft concentrated mainly on a triangular area between Cambrai, St. Quentin and Hirson.

Roads and railways were searched and troops and transports on the move, and troop concentrations taking cover in copses and forests were bombed and machine-gunned.

One aircraft spotted troops in the forest of Nouvion and dropped bombs. Within a few minutes a raging fire spread over a wide area.

3 FACTS BY DUFF COOPER

THREE facts about the fighting can be definitely stated, Mr. Duff Cooper, Minister of Information, said in a broadcast last night.

They are:—

1: The present objective of the enemy is the Channel ports, from which he hopes to launch war upon this island.

2: Small parts of his mechanised troops have succeeded in eluding their opponents in advancing great distances and coming near to their objective.

3: The armies of England and France are undefeated.

"In enormously superior numbers they occupy the battlefield, and the counter-attack when it comes should prove formidable," Mr. Duff Cooper said.

The news, he said, was grave.

"But there is no cause for serious alarm still less for panic.

"Through the successful employ-

Contd. on Back Page, Col. 2

PARIS DENIES GENERAL CAPTURED

PARIS radio this morning officially denied that General Giraud and the staff of the French 9th Army had been captured.

Earlier a Paris spokesman acknowledged that some members of the general staff had been taken prisoner, but one report said General Giraud escaped in a tank.

For the German drive towards the Channel coast, Hitler has appointed General Walter von Reichenau, above, to command the Eighth Army.

'Battle Not Yet Decisive'—Reichenau

General von Reichenau, whose Army faces the British and Belgians, told neutral journalists last night that the fighting so far had only been in preliminary encounters.

"Thus far we have only been in the preliminary encounters to the decisive battle," he said, speaking at his headquarters outside Brussels.

"We have won the first tricks, but we have yet to meet the enemy's main body," he added.

The British and the Belgians, he said, had two army corps in front of him.—British United Press.

IRONSIDE AT THE PALACE

The Prime Minister and General Sir Edmund Ironside, Chief of the Imperial General Staff, were received in audience by the King at Buckingham Palace last night.

Fill In Your Identity Card Now

The space on the right-hand inside page of your identity card, marked, "Do nothing with this part until you are told," must now be filled in with your signature and address. Do it at once.

And from now on everybody should carry his or her identity card properly filled up and be ready to show it if asked.

These instructions were issued last night in a Ministry of Home Security bulletin.

French troops are on positions chosen by the High Command.

"Despite the grave situation, the issue must be awaited with confidence."

Hitler's big thrusts are now swinging to the B.E.F. front. He has appointed General von Reichenau, commanding his Eighth Army, to handle operations against the Anglo-Belgian Armies.

The British troops, in good heart, are resisting in chosen positions and hitting back at every opportunity.

"They are fighting like hell," said an officer.

Against waves of armoured cars

Contd. on Back Page, Col. 4

4 Night Raids on Coast

ANTI-PARACHUTE troops were on duty at an East Kent town last night when the first air raid warning for months was sounded.

In a second raid off the south-east coast a German plane released a salvo of bombs which exploded on the water with a great roar.

Heavy gunfire, including bursts of machine-guns, were heard in East Kent.

Pursuit planes went up and searchlights were active everywhere.

People who were in the streets went quietly to the nearest shelters. At local cinemas audiences preferred to sit quietly until the end of the show.

In the South-East Coast raid where no alarm was sounded, naval patrol boats opened fire on an enemy plane, but no hits were recorded.

The raider finally made off.

Another air-raid off the South-East coast last night began at 10.35. The all-clear signal was given at 11.40.

The raid started with heavy gunfire and continuous bursts of machine-gun fire. The raiders were evidently trying to machine-gun shipping off the coast.

No damage reported.

Early this morning anti-aircraft batteries at an East Coast town opened fire on unidentified aircraft. No air-raid alarm was given. Searchlights swept the sky. No bombs were dropped.

The night air activity followed an afternoon of intense firing.

The first heavy salvos were heard at 1.50. Others, much heavier and more prolonged, followed at 2.30.

ROYAL DUKE WOUNDED

THE Duke of Gloucester has been slightly wounded while on duty in France, it was revealed last night.

For three successive nights the Duke, who is serving with the rank of Major-General, was in areas which were heavily bombed.

During one of these attacks he received cuts caused by the result of bomb explosions, and both his hands were badly bruised.

Despite his wounds, the Duke, who as announced from Buckingham Palace, has returned "on urgent duty from France and is expected to return to G.H.Q. at an early date," yesterday visited the Mansion House to hear of the progress of the Red Cross and St. John Fund for the sick and wounded in the war. He was accompanied by the Duchess.

The Duke, who is forty, has been Chief Liaison Officer, British Field Force, since a few days after the outbreak of war.

Duchess of Gloucester Loses Kinsmen.—Page 8.

Daily Mirror

MAY 24

No. 11,375 — ONE PENNY
Registered at the G.P.O. as a Newspaper.

DAILY MIRROR, Friday, May 24, 1940

Arms for the Police

Steps have been taken to increase the arms available for the police, Sir John Anderson, Minister of Home Security, told Parliament yesterday.

There was no intention of turning the police into a combatant force, he said, but it was desirable that many of them should be armed.

The men issued with rifles are all ex-Servicemen and all are expert shots. The officer on right was seen yesterday checking a civilian's identity card.

MOSLEY ARRESTED: M.P. HELD IN GAOL

SIR OSWALD MOSLEY and eight of his Fascist lieutenants were yesterday arrested in a lightning round-up ordered by the Home Secretary under the defence regulations.

Others taken into custody, but not in connection with the arrests of the Fascists, were Captain A. A. Ramsay, Conservative M.P. for Peebles, described as "president of the Right Club" (who is now in Brixton Prison), and Mr. John Beckett, secretary of the British People's Party.

Leading Fascists arrested were:—
A. Raven Thomson, editor of the Fascist paper "Action."
M. Francis-Hawkins, director-general of the British Union.
F. E. Burdett, Captain U. A. Hicks, C. F. Watts, H. McKechnie, G. Bruning and Mrs. Dacre-Fox.

The Duke of Devonshire stated in the House of Lords last night that a considerable number of people of British nationality had been arrested.

Five thousand male enemy aliens had been interned.

"This has wrecked the possibility of fifth columnist aid in an east coast invasion," he said.

Viscount Elibank urged the Government to investigate the personnel of the B.B.C., which, he said, would be the first institution to be taken over by a German invading force.

Lord Elibank added: "I know at least one individual in the B.B.C. in London who certainly should not occupy the position he does. He is married to a German lady whose brother is fighting against us."

A statement issued by the Home Office last night declared:

"Under New Powers"

"Under new powers conferred by the amended regulations, the Home Secretary made orders last night for the detention of a number of the leading Fascists.

"In a statement in the House of Commons today Sir John Anderson made it clear that this action had been taken not on account of any opinion held or expressed by the British Union of Fascists, nor on account of their propagandist activities, but because of the danger that the organisation might be used in the execu-

Contd. on Back Page, Col. 4

Sir Oswald Mosley, leader of the British Union of Fascists, who was arrested by police officers last night.

25 NAZI PLANES OVER CHANNEL

TWENTY-FIVE aeroplanes, believed to have been enemy machines, were seen over the Channel flying from an easterly direction, a short time before an air-raid alarm was given on the South-East Coast early last night.

This was the second raid alarm in Kent within forty-eight hours.

The planes were noticed to turn towards the French coast, however, and just after they were met by an intense anti-aircraft fire from shore batteries.

One observer, who was on the cliffs saw a machine go hurtling down into the sea, where it sent up a column of water.

The all-clear was sounded after about forty-five minutes.

Back to Play

Cinema programmes continued as usual, and very few people left to seek shelter.

Children playing games in public parks went to shelter as soon as the sirens sounded, but they came back to resume their interrupted games afterwards.

Thirty R.A.F. fighters were seen over this side of the Channel during the time the alarm was on.

BEAT TANKS WITH PICKS

PICKS and shovels and a parcel of British labourers proved too much for a couple of German tanks on the Western Front.

The tanks had arrived at a small village near Arras in search of petrol.

Their drivers pulled up at a filling station, not noticing a number of members of the Auxiliary Military Pioneer Corps.

And that is how these tanks came "unpicked."

The Pioneers, who had been working on the road, rushed up and attacked the tanks with their pick-axes, sledge-hammers, shovels and whatever else they could lay their hands on.

The tanks' guns could not be brought to bear on them, and it was not long before these lads had put the caterpillar tracks out of order.

The tank crews could not face the labourers either—and are now the first pick-axe-pacified Huns in captivity.

B.E.F. IN BOULOGNE NIGHT BATTLE

BRITISH and French troops last night fought desperately at Boulogne and Abbeville against German advance units threatening to cut completely the communications between the main Allied Armies.

To relieve enemy pressure in the battle for the Channel ports—Calais, twenty-two miles from Dover, is also menaced—the French made counter attacks in the south of the salient, along the Somme front.

Their advance forces reached the suburbs of Amiens, said the French war communique. Bitter street fighting went on early today.

Magnificent work by the R.A.F. is cutting down the number of enemy advance units getting through for spearhead attacks, and isolating some of them. Supply lines are being cut.

But the problem still facing the Allied forces is that not one of six Channel ports, of paramount importance for feeding and maintaining the B.E.F., is free from the threat of attack by German spearhead detachments.

That is the situation caused by the break through to the Channel. This is the position on the other fronts:—

A powerful Allied force holds a solid, continuous and organised front from the North Sea to Bapaume—along the Scheldt to Valenciennes, skirting Cambrai and extending to Arras and the region south of Arras.

In the south—from the Channel to the Rhine—there is a line of French positions along the Somme, the Aisne, the Meuse and the Maginot Line.

Mr. Churchill Tells

Mr. Churchill, telling the House of Commons of the new German thrust, said:

"The German armoured forces, which made their way through the breach in the French Army, have penetrated into the rear of the Allied Army in Belgium and are attempting to derange their communications.

"Abbeville is in enemy hands, and heavy fighting is proceeding around and in Boulogne.

"It is too early yet to say what the result of this coastal fighting may be, but it evidently carries with it serious implications.

"Meanwhile, General Weygand, who is in supreme command, is conducting operations involving all the Allied Armies with a view to

Contd. on Back Page, Col. 5

FRIENDS WITH SOVIET AIM

"We are taking immediate steps to improve our relations with Russia," stated Mr. R. A. Butler (Under-Secretary to the Foreign Office) in a written reply in the House of Commons last night.

Sub Leader ———— stationed at ———— says

When I've only a minute for a stand-up meal it's

Fry's SANDWICH CHOCOLATE

2ᴅ AND 4ᴅ

Daily Mirror

DAILY MIRROR, Monday, May 27, 1940.

No. 11,377   ONE PENNY
Registered at the G.P.O. as a Newspaper.

IRONSIDE IS HOME DEFENCE CHIEF

Register Children at Once

Registration for the evacuation from towns on the English east and south-east coasts, announced last night, will be opened immediately and should be completed by one o'clock on Wednesday afternoon.

Parents should register their children at the school they usually attend.

Children who have not been registered will not be evacuated.

S.E. Coast Children Are To Be Moved

THE Government have decided that since Holland and parts of Belgium and Northern France are now in enemy occupation, the following towns on the east and south-east coast of England are to be declared evacuation areas:—

Great Yarmouth.
Lowestoft, Felixstowe.
Harwich, Clacton.
Frinton and Walton.
Southend, Margate.
Ramsgate, Broadstairs.
Sandwich, Dover.
Deal and Folkestone.

Arrangements are being made for children whose parents wish them to go, to be sent from these areas to safer districts in the Midlands and Wales.

THE defence of Britain has been placed in the hands of General Sir Edmund Ironside.

He leaves his post as Chief of the Imperial General Staff to become Commander-in-Chief, Home Defences.

General Sir John Dill takes General Ironside's place as Chief of the General Staff. He was previously vice-Chief.

To make way for General Ironside, Sir Walter M. St. G. Kirke retires from the post of Commander-in-Chief, Home Forces.

The War Office announced the changes. They have been made to meet the situation caused by the German break through and the threat of an attack on Britain.

The Government have placed in the hands of one soldier, General Ironside, the control of all measures against invasion by sea or air.

Sir Edmund's command at home can be compared with the role of Lord Gort in the field.

His appointment does not mean that big changes in the present plans such as the formation of the Local Defence Volunteers are certain.

But as Commander-in-Chief he will review the whole situation.

The Berlin Radio said last night: "General Ironside's new appointment proves that the people of London are beginning to understand what a grave turn the war has taken for Britain."

General Ironside is now technically subordinate to Sir John Dill, fifty-eight-year-old Ulsterman, who was a staff officer in the last war.

The new appointments follow quickly the sweeping changes in the French High Command. But it is pointed out that all the British officers concerned possess the full confidence of the War Cabinet.

Chief in a Month

Sir Edmund Ironside stands over 6ft. 4in. He was a Major-General at thirty-nine, and he is now sixty.

It was when Lord Gort became Commander-in-Chief of British Field Forces on the outbreak of war that he was made Chief of the Imperial General Staff.

Sir John Dill becomes Chief of the Imperial General Staff within a month of being brought back from the field to help direct Britain's war strategy.

He was General Officer Commanding-in-Chief, Aldershot Command, when war broke out. Then he was appointed to command the First Army Corps of the British Expeditionary Force, but last month he was brought back to England to be Vice-Chief of the Imperial General Staff.

"That Devil Dill"

When Sir John was commanding British forces in Palestine, the Syrian bandit, Fawzi Kawkaji, offered £500 for the capture "of the British devil Dill, dead or alive."

Sir Walter Kirke, who is sixty-two, was one of the builders of the modern Territorial Army.

Last night he issued this special order to the men he has led:

"On handing over command, I desire to express to all ranks my thanks for their never-failing support and my confidence in their ability to meet all dangers in the spirit which British soldiers have ever displayed in the hour of trial.

"Under the inspiring leadership of my successor you will, I know, play your part in the struggle for liberty with the utmost courage and determination.

"Good-bye and good luck."

REYNAUD VISITS LONDON

M. Reynaud, the French Premier, visited London yesterday to confer with Mr. Churchill and other War Cabinet members. He was back in Paris last night.—Reuter.

General Sir Edmund Ironside, now Commander-in-Chief of Home Defences.

General Sir John Dill, new Chief of the Imperial General Staff.

General Sir Walter Kirke, who now retires on retired pay.

CALAIS IS HELD: NAVY SHELLS ENEMY

Britain Works and Prays

Britain gave a magnificent response yesterday to the calls of her King and her leaders to make Sunday a day of prayer and toil for victory.

The stained-glass windows of the little parish church at a South-East coast rattled ceaselessly throughout a special service to mark the "Day of National Prayer."

As the ...-robed Mayor read the lessons the thunder of the guns on the battlefields in France echoed through the church. At times drowning his words.

Now and then low-flying bombing planes roared out across the Channel overhead. It was a memorable service—a service of prayer in the shadow of battle.

As the bewigged macebearer led the civic procession from the church along the cliff-top promenade, clouds which had hovered over the Channel all morning cleared suddenly.

The French coast, with dense clouds of smoke pouring from fires in the Calais district, could be seen with the naked eye.

The Mayor halted for a second and faced the sea. Then he raised his right hand in salute.

✦ ✦ ✦

Empire Prays, story and pictures, pages 8 and 9; Sunday starts Victory Work Push story and pictures, page 3.

BRITISH and French troops last night held Calais and Dunkirk. The French official communique stated that Boulogne had been taken by the Germans after fierce street fighting. But Paris reported that Allied forces still hold the town's citadel.

German shock troops attacking on the outskirts of Boulogne were smashed by shells from British warships firing over the town.

The battle for Calais is still south of the town. British soldiers fought magnificently with the French to repulse every enemy attack yesterday.

The German High Command, however, claimed last night that Calais had fallen after hard fighting, and that the advance had continued to Gravelines, half way from Calais to Dunkirk.

The Calais claim was later completely denied in London.

Early today the German News Agency followed up with a statement that Lens and Bethune, north of Arras, had been occupied.

The French War Office spokesman declared that the enemy had failed to gain any new ground in the last forty-eight hours.

"Stubborn Allied resistance has halted—at least temporarily—the German advance toward the Channel," he said.

"Enemy Mown Down"

The French communique stated:

"In a violent struggle on the Somme we have made further progress.

"On the northern front the enemy, who in the last few days had accumulated considerable forces in the region of Boulogne, has succeeded in taking possession of the town after a fierce struggle in the streets.

"In the latest engagements between the Aisne and the Meuse, it is confirmed, particularly by information

Continued on Back Page

PREPARE!— ROOSEVELT

PRESIDENT ROOSEVELT told the U.S.A. this morning to prepare for the "approaching storm." He was broadcasting an appeal for the Red Cross.

He stressed the "futility, the impossibility" of the idea of isolation.

"Obviously a defence policy based on that is merely to invite future attack," he said.

"To those who had closed their eyes for isolationist reasons, and to those who would not admit the possibility of the 'approaching storm'—to all of these the past two weeks meant the shattering of many illusions.

"They have lost the illusion that we are remote and isolated, and therefore secure against dangers from which no other land is free," the President said.

"In some quarters with this rude awakening has come fear bordering on panic.

"I have not shared those illusions. We are now more realistic, but let us not be calamity howlers and discount our strength."

Start on Sunday

This evacuation will start by special trains, on Sunday next, June 2.

Arrangements are also being made for a similar evacuation of schoolchildren on June 2 from Chatham, Gillingham, Rochester and Sheerness, which have already been made evacuation areas.

The local authorities concerned are now making arrangements to register school children for evacuation.

It is vitally important that parents living in these areas should register their children without delay, otherwise they will not be evacuated.

Parents Warned

Mr. Malcolm MacDonald, the Minister of Health, emphasised this point in a broadcast last night.

He pointed out that, while there is no question of compulsory evacuation, parents should co-operate for the safety of their children.

"Only children who are registered will be taken. Those who are not registered will be left behind," he added. "If you do not register your children you may speedily rue it."

Mr. MacDonald said the new evacuation areas were confined to the stretch of coast nearest the territory in enemy occupation.

"If there had been sufficient reason to make a similar change over any wider area of the country the Government would have made it," he continued.

Detailed arrangements for the reception of the children are being worked out. It is expected that the reception areas will be in the counties of Hereford, Nottinghamshire, Shropshire, Staffordshire, Warwickshire, Worcestershire, Derbyshire, Gloucestershire, Glamorganshire and Monmouthshire.

Those who leave will go with parties of their schoolfellows. They will be accompanied by their teachers, who will look after them in their new places of residence.

A.R.P. TELEPHONE WIRES CUT

When Ipswich (Suffolk) air raid wardens went on duty last night they found their telephones out of action. The wires had been cut. Police are investigating.

...Wednesday, May 29, 1940.

Daily Mirror

MAY 29

No. 11,379   ONE PENNY
Registered at the G.P.O. as a Newspaper.

LEOPOLD: STORMY SCENE

KING LEOPOLD told his Ministers of his treacherous intention at a stormy meeting in his chateau at five o'clock on Saturday morning.

They rejected his proposal to surrender and walked out, M. Spaak, Belgian Foreign Minister, revealed in Paris yesterday

This now makes significant the visit to London on Sunday of M. Pierlot, the Belgian Prime Minister, and four of his colleagues, including General Denis, Defence Minister.

The same day it was separately announced that M. Reynaud, French Premier, was in London to confer with Mr. Churchill and other members of the War Cabinet.

On Monday, it was stated in Paris yesterday, the Belgian Cabinet notified Leopold of its rejection of his capitulation plan.

The Belgian Army ceased to resist at 4 a.m. yesterday.

M. Spaak revealed yesterday that Leopold put forward his proposal to four Cabinet Ministers at the Chateau Wyondal, near Thourout, twelve miles south-west of Bruges.

Disowned by Country

Leopold said he intended to remain at the chateau whatever happened, and would ask the Germans for permission to live at a Belgian castle near the coast.

The four Ministers, before walking out, told him they would fight on, said M. Spaak.

Yesterday Leopold was disowned by his country, and last night the Belgian Government was preparing to bring charges against the King and to form a provisional Government.

The Belgian Senate and Chamber of Deputies in Paris approved the Cabinet's action in disowning the King.

"The action of one man does not commit an entire nation," the Belgian Premier stated in a broadcast from Paris. "The Belgian Army will be reorganised in France. It will fight on."

Belgians in Paris echoed their Government's accusation of their King's treachery by crying, "The King is dead. Long live Belgium."

At a big demonstration attended by M. Pierlot and members of his Government before the statue of

(Cont. on Back Page, Col. 5)

Castle for Traitor King

King Leopold of the Belgians will be placed in a Belgian castle until a final decision is made on his future, said the Hamburg announcer in English last night.

War Holidays: Statement is Likely Today

A statement may be issued today by the Minister of Labour on the question of holidays this year, Sir Walter Citrine, General Secretary of the T.U.C., stated last night.

Sir Walter's statement refers to the need for a continuous drive for increased production and output of munitions, and the effect of holidays in the important factory centres, especially in the North, where the wakes are an important feature of the life of the workers.

Complicated questions may arise as to rates of pay and other matters under agreement between employers and the Trade Unions.

The magnificent withdrawal from Boulogne had its heroines as well as its heroes. . . . For the women of this country are not afraid to face danger. . . . As nurses and ambulance drivers and as members of the Auxiliary Services they are playing their part.

This picture, taken from a War Office official film, shows women ambulance drivers getting ready to embark for England. (Another picture on the back page.)

OUR HEAVY BOMBERS RAID 6 GERMAN TOWNS

R.A.F. bombers, doing their utmost to relieve enemy pressure, have bombed military objectives behind the lines, again and again.

On Monday night heavy bombers attacked objectives at Dusseldorf, Duisberg, Dortmund, Hamburg, Bremen and Cologne.

Our medium bombers have repeatedly attacked road and rail communications in areas immediately behind the German armies.

From all operations thirteen of our planes failed to return, while twenty-two of the enemy were destroyed or damaged

BIG U.S. DEFENCE MOVE

President Roosevelt announced last night that a special National Defence Commission is to be formed, composed of seven prominent citizens, to supervise the defence programme.

GREAT R.A.F. ATTACK TO HELP B.E.F.

AS the unbroken and undefeated B.E.F. fought a grim retreat in North France and Flanders last night, the greater part of the Allied Air Forces launched a tremendous offensive to help them.

Curtains of bombs were dropped in front of the German forces who stabbed toward Dunkirk at the flank which was left uncovered by the surrender of the Belgian Army by King Leopold.

Late last night the French military spokesman said Dunkirk was still in Allied hands.

"It will be necessary to do our utmost to withdraw our Army from the positions it now occupies," said Mr. Duff Cooper in a broadcast to the nation last night.

Earlier, the Prime Minister told the House of Commons that it must prepare itself for "hard and heavy tidings."

Leopold surrendered his army—about 300,000 men—as it was fighting bravely and inflicting terrific losses on the enemy.

This strong resistance on the left flank of the B.E.F. collapsed without warning, with Leopold's capitulation leaving the British no time to plan its front.

Did Not Falter

The result was that the Germans were able to deliver an immediate threat westward from the River Lys against the triangle which the British and French troops are defending.

But against attacks from east, south and west, the Allied defence did not falter for a moment.

While fighting off the German attacks, the Allied troops manoeuvred to present a front to the dangers threatening from east, south and west.

Then the R.A.F. and the French Air Force sent up every available plane to help the soldiers.

On the attacking Germans the airmen poured bombs and machine-gun bullets.

South of the break-through, along the Somme front, the French began an important movement which early today was developing favourably in face of enemy resistance.

"Our Somme positions are unshakable," said the Paris radio

Last night's French war communique stated:—

"The decision taken by the King

(Cont. on Back Page, Col. 2)

HUGE LOSSES, GERMANS TOLD

GERMANS were warned on their radio last night to prepare for news of huge German losses. "Losses corresponding to the bitter resistance of the Allied armies," was the phrase.

In Austria alone there are 60,000 wounded in hospital, according to a B.B.C. German broadcast.

The German officer commanding the attack on Boulogne admitted in a radio interview yesterday that his forces were so badly mauled that reinforcements had to be sent before the town could be taken.

Flower of Germany

"Germans, do you want to know France's answer to the capitulation of the King of the Belgians?" asked the announcer in the French news broadcast in German last night.

"Then think of Verdun," he continued. "The territorial gains of your army mean nothing. In 1918 the German advance was the prelude to the German defeat.

"The flower of Germany's manhood lies dead on the battlefield of Northern France, and your best material has been destroyed.

"But our troops are intact and we have enormous resources of raw materials. Above all, behind our armies stand a united nation and a united Empire."—Reuter.

NEW MINISTRY'S LUXURY BAN

A MINISTER for National Economy, with the special duty of urging self-sacrifice throughout the country, will shortly be appointed, writes the *Daily Mirror* Political Correspondent.

The Ministry's job will be to persuade the public to avoid buying luxuries.

The Department will, I understand, have powers to prohibit the sale of certain types of luxury goods.

In making purchases, the public will be asked to buy only those things which they immediately need, and those must be British or Empire.

WE WON'T BOMB NAZI WOMEN

Mr. Attlee announced in the House yesterday that we would not bomb and machine-gun the German wounded, or women and children, as the Germans have done to the Allies.

"The British Government," he said, "hold themselves free to take such action as they consider appropriate, but it is not their intention to exact retribution from the wounded or from women and children."

K·L·G
Sparking
PLUGS

The margin between Governmental

demands for K.L.G. plugs and our

maximum output is small delays

in fulfilling private orders are

sometimes unavoidable when they

occur — we beg your indulgence.

CORNITE

5/-

JUST AS GOOD FOR *your* CAR

DAILY MIRROR, Thursday, May 30, 1940.

Daily Mirror

MAY 30

No. 11,380 ONE PENNY
Registered at the G.P.O. as a Newspaper.

B.E.F. BATTLE ON AS NAVY COVER DUNKIRK

OUR HEARTS WITH YOU...

The King to His Troops

"The hearts of every one of us at home are with you and your magnificent troops in this hour of peril," states the King in a message to Viscount Gort, Commander-in-Chief of the British Expeditionary Force. This is the message:—

All your countrymen have been following with pride and admiration the courageous resistance of the British Expeditionary Force during the continuous fighting of the last fortnight.

Placed by circumstances outside their control in a position of extreme difficulty, they are displaying a gallantry that has never been surpassed in the annals of the British Army. The hearts of everyone of us at home are with you and your magnificent troops in this hour of peril.

Lord Gort has replied:—

The Commander-in-Chief, with humble duty, begs leave on behalf of all ranks of the B.E.F. to thank your Majesty for your message.

May I assure your Majesty that the Army is doing all in its power to live up to its proud tradition and is immensely encouraged at this critical moment by your Majesty's words."

THE B.E.F. AND THEIR FRENCH COMRADES WERE DESPERATELY ATTEMPTING TO CUT THEIR WAY TO THE CHANNEL COAST THROUGH GERMAN FORCES, LAST NIGHT.

While French troops commanded by General Prioux made a determined thrust to open the road to the coast, British forces at some points succeeded in getting through the enemy lines. At other places they stubbornly defended the way of retreat.

Behind the main Allied forces heroic detachments fought a rearguard action in the streets of Lille, and French "suicide squads" held out on the flanks of the path to the sea.

At the coast, Allied naval forces, under France's Admiral Abrial, held open the rescue port for the troops—Dunkirk, and its fortified area.

A big French fleet lay off the coast raining shells on the German forces attempting to bar the retreating Allied troops from the port.

Despite enemy air attacks and the thrust along the coast, a steady stream of arms and supplies is going into Dunkirk from a large number of ships.

Supreme Courage

French marines and British naval engineers went ashore and transformed Dunkirk into an armed camp.

German bombing squadrons, trying to smash the communications to the port, were themselves smashed by British and French planes.

Along the coast, at Calais, British and French units still held out in a part of the town.

The French military spokesman said last night that the main British and French forces were backing towards Dunkirk while their rearguard fought a delaying action against the attacking Germans.

The rearguard action in Lille was a street battle.

With supreme courage, the soldiers covering the retreat of their comrades desperately disputed every foot of the way.

The Germans flung big forces across the road to the sea at Cassel, northwest of Lille.

Through these concentrations the French Army, commanded by General Prioux, desperately tried to cut a way through.

It was to help this effort that the French Navy's big guns opened up on enemy troops.

Some Belgian troops are reported
Contd. on Back Page Col. 5

INVADERS MAY LAND TO DIE

Cripps To Be Made Ambassador

SIR STAFFORD CRIPPS will go to Moscow as the fully-accredited British Ambassador, writes the *Daily Mirror* Political Correspondent.

This was learned in London last night as the Russian radio was saying that the Soviet Government would not accept Sir Stafford or any other envoy unless he came as Ambassador.

Moscow radio quoting Tass, the official Russian news agency, said: Various conflicting reports have appeared in connection with the trip of Sir Stafford Cripps to Moscow. Tass is authorised to state the truth as follows:—

"In answer to a suggestion from the British Government to appoint in Moscow an envoy extraordinary in the person of Sir Stafford Cripps, the Foreign Commissar has directed the Soviet Ambassador to London to inform the British Government that the Soviet Government cannot accept Sir Stafford Cripps or any other special envoy from Moscow.

ready in Athens

"If the British Government really desires to conduct trade negotiations and not merely to confine itself to talking about some non-existent turn in Anglo-Russian relations it could do so through Sir William Seeds (the Ambassador) or any other person holding the position of ambassador if Sir William Seeds is to be replaced."

Last night Sir Stafford was already on his way to Russia.

Earlier, Mr. R. A. Butler, Foreign Under-Secretary, stated in the House of Commons that he hoped to make a statement soon on Sir Stafford's mission.

Sir William Seeds, who succeeded Lord Chilston, went as Ambassador to Moscow in January, 1939. He came home "on indefinite leave" last January.

THOUSANDS of German invaders may land in Britain—but they will die.

Mr. Harold Nicolson, Parliamentary Secretary to the Ministry of Information, said in an Empire broadcast yesterday.

"It may well be that by the employment of methods which did not exist in previous wars they may be able to land in Great Britain some thousands of their troops.

"Yet do not imagine that a virile and unbending race of forty-five million people will for long allow some thousands of the enemy to remain upon our shores, or that these forces could maintain themselves for long against the overwhelming power of our fleets.

"The whole country will rise as a man to resist such invasion, and whatever confusion or destruction may momentarily occur, the ultimate issue is beyond doubt."

Hate by B.E.F.

Speaking of the Allies' difficult position in Flanders:—

"I do not think we shall hear much more after this battle of those legends which were spread by enemy propagandists to the effect that the British Empire had grown old and tired and that in some way the tough fibre of our ancestors had been softened by years of security, prosperity and peace.

The Germans had brought against the young men of the B.E.F. the most terrific apparatus of terror which had ever been devised by the ingenuity of man, and they now learned that the soldiers of the Empire know no fear.

"But they have learnt anger," Mr. Nicolson added.

"We are a gentle-hearted race and it takes much to rouse us to rage, but I am told by those who have returned from Flanders that a mood of fierce moral indignation was roused in our soldiers by witnessing the methods which the Germans had employed."

Refugee Horrors

Most dreadful of all, he said, was the deliberate manner in which the Germans had exploited the fear and terror of the civilian population in order to confuse and dismay the fighting forces.

Roads were blocked by streams of refugees and upon these hapless old men, women and children the German bombers have dived from the air
Cont. on Back Page, Col. 3

PRIVATE BAGS 2 NAZI PLANES

A YOUNG French soldier has shot down two Nazi planes with a Lewis gun.

His column was moving up to the front when they were attacked by the planes. The young private lay at the roadside and with a deadly burst shot down the first raider.

Shortly afterwards another plane skimmed across. Once again the soldier's gun blazed away and this machine too hurtled to its doom.

The courage of French tank crews who hurled their machines time and again against superior numbers of the enemy was also told in London last night.

In one action in which 110 German tanks took part the French put seventy out of action although they were themselves inferior in number. In another attack two French tanks threw off fourteen German machines and destroyed seven of them.

During the Aisne battle a company of tanks annihilated a whole German company without loss of a single machine.

Mr. Cordell Hull, United States Secretary of State, last night ruled that Americans may now fly bombers to Canada, whence many are being flown to Europe. This action means the speeding-up of delivery of U.S. warplanes for the Allies.

Planes from America already fighting in France—story on back page.

Good for STRENGTH

You've had something more than a drink when you've had a GUINNESS

DAILY MIRROR, Saturday, June 1, 1940.

Daily Mirror

JUNE 1

No. 11,382 — ONE PENNY
Registered at the G.P.O. as a Newspaper.

B.E.F. REARGUARD MEN ARRIVING BACK

BRITISH soldiers who were fighting a desperate Flanders rearguard action yesterday morning were among the thousands of B.E.F. men arriving in England last night.

They had been in action for days almost without rest. Some of them had battled back to the coast from near the Luxemburg border.

Over in the Flanders hills, British and French outposts still battled on to hold open the path to the coast and gain more precious hours for the withdrawals.

Early today the French military spokesman said the number of Allied troops evacuated had reached "important proportions."

Small boats were still ferrying "Gort's Unbreakables" and their French comrades from open beaches to vessels waiting at sea.

Allied warships and airmen fought on to protect them.

Planes of the Fleet Air Arm dived to drop bomb salvoes on crowded German troops and ammunition trucks on the Nieuport road.

The attack on Dunkirk by the main German forces is now held up by the flood waters released by Allied

Continued on Back Page

R.A.F. Drop Water for Defenders

R.A.F. squadrons have dropped water, ammunition and hand grenades to the heroic garrison of Allied troops and Marines in Calais, it was revealed last night.

Late at night orders were received at an air field in the South of England.

Water was taken first. Each aircraft was loaded with two cylindrical containers, each containing ten gallons, which were fitted into the bomb rack. They were fitted with parachutes that open automatically.

As dawn was breaking two sorties each of ten aircraft left with the water. In twenty minutes they were approaching Calais. The town was in flames.

The leading planes met light anti-aircraft fire, but those that followed encountered heavy fire. One was lost, and most of those behind the leaders were hit several times. As they passed over the citadel, the pilots came down to as low as 50ft. to make sure

GORT STAYS TILL LAST

From BERNARD GRAY
"Daily Mirror" War Correspondent

BRITISH officers from the War Office stood on the quayside of a south-east port yesterday scanning the khaki-clad crowd on the decks of every ship that came in from the rescue of the B.E.F.

They were looking for Lord Gort, the Commander-in-Chief, and although the search had gone on all day it was still unsuccessful when I left last night.

Lord Gort stays with the last of his Unbreakables in the B.E.F., and has apparently decided not to leave till the last boat.

For a fortnight the Nazi radio liars have been telling us that this V.C. hero of the last war, one of the bravest men the Army has ever known, is back in England.

Only Thought Is for His Men

I met men stepping off destroyers yesterday who told an entirely different story. Only a few hours before, Lord Gort, still smiling, had been with them, passing from one group of weary men to another, cheering them up.

"He never mentioned himself," one man told me. "He seemed concerned entirely about us. He told us we'd still win the war; that although the Nazis had given us a bad time they would get it all back."

One high officer who landed said he did not know where Gort's headquarters are.

"He is roughing it with his men," he added. "He's been shelled and bombed just as much as the rest.

"We who know him are convinced he will not return till the last. Unless, of course, he received a direct War Office order to come back."

Lord Gort won his V.C. for an exploit in 1918. Leading his men across the Canal du Nord under severe artillery and machine-gun fire, he continued directing when he was wounded.

Wounded again by a shell, he was placed on a stretcher, but despite enormous loss of blood got up and carried on the fight.

HITLER MEETS ITALIAN ENVOY

HITLER received the Italian Ambassador, Signor Dino Alfieri, at his headquarters behind the Western Front yesterday.

Ribbentrop, the Nazi Foreign Minister, was present.

While this Axis meeting was taking place, it was learned that the Italian Government has broken off the negotiations with Britain over the contraband control, and that Italian journalists are hurrying out of France.—Reuter and Exchange.

General Prioux, who commands the French rearguard.

General, the Viscount Gort, V.C., D.S.O., Commander-in-Chief, the British Field Forces.

How Summer warns MOTHERS

ANY mother can see that children are far more tired at the end of long hot summer days than they are after the shorter, colder ones of winter. This is nature's plain warning that they are burning up more energy, and that every care must be taken to see that the extra energy taken out is put back again by their food. Otherwise there is a real danger that they may become run down, and arrive at the beginning of winter in a poor state to resist its ills.

NOURISHMENT IN WARM WEATHER

Many mothers honestly think they are doing the best thing for their children's health by giving them a diet less rich in nourishment.

It is true that children's appetites are sometimes jaded, but do not be misled. They need more nourishment, not less.

NOURISHING AND TEMPTING

Cadbury's Bournville Cocoa offers the perfect solution to the difficulty of finding nourishing but tempting foods. It has a high energy value, is light and easily digestible, and — *very important* — is so delicious that children actually look forward to it eagerly.

Make Bournville Cocoa a summer standby — and remember these two special values —

1 It makes milk — itself one of the finest energy foods — into a glorious chocolatey drink.

2 At bedtime it is exactly the kind of drink doctors advise for a night of sound, energy-restoring sleep.

Still **6d** PER QTR. LB
11d PER HALF LB

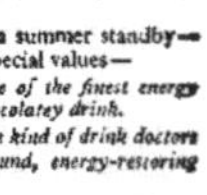

CADBURY'S BOURNVILLE COCOA
A cup of cocoa is a cup of food

DAILY MIRROR, Monday, June 3, 1940.

Daily Mirror

JUNE 3

No. 11,383 — ONE PENNY
Registered at the G.P.O. as a Newspaper.

NAVY FIGHTS TO SAVE THE LAST THOUSANDS

THE Allied Navies are ready for the final, critical task at Dunkirk—the rescue of the last thousands of the British and French rearguard men, who for days have held up the enemy assaults.

More than four-fifths of the B.E.F., and tens of thousands of Frenchmen, have been saved, said Mr. Anthony Eden, Britain's War Minister, over the radio last night.

But as he spoke, the difficulties facing the remainder of the Allied troops, and the men fighting for them, were growing.

With so many fewer men, the work of defence became heavier. Enemy air attacks inside Dunkirk's defence ring were intensified. Big German guns began to register on the beaches.

But the small craft acting as "ferries" coolly went on bringing the troops from the storm of shells and bombs. The men are now being shipped with their arms and baggage in definite units.

To the soldiers waiting on open beaches for the rescue boats, aeroplanes dropped food, water and medicines. The fiery sand, lifting and swirling round them in the coast winds, is adding thirst to their ordeal.

But as they wait, they are still Gort's Unbreakables.

Men who arrived back in England yesterday said the Allied defence ring ran in an arc five miles from Dunkirk. Two-thirds of the arc is barred by hawks.

Yet, in his attempt to crush the last resistance and stop the evacuation, Hitler ordered infantry to attack across the floods yesterday.

Die in Floods

The German soldiers waded up to their waists in reckless attacks which withered under fierce Allied machine-gun fire.

Dead and wounded alike disappeared beneath the flood water as the bullets tore gaps in the enemy ranks.

Last night's French communique, telling the story of the great Allied rearguard action, declared:—

"This retreat, accomplished by troops attacked from all sides, deprived of all rest for twenty days, and suddenly left uncovered on their left by the surrender of Leopold, will remain a heroic example of tenacity.

"The enemy's territorial gains have been offset by immense losses of human life and material. The German force was sorely tried. Our Armies, whose morale is higher than ever, are ready to face fresh engagements."

Hitler's Somme Threat

At Calais heroic Allied troops still hold the Citadel. Once more they got food and water supplies from aeroplanes yesterday.

Paris radio said last night that the Germans were obviously preparing a new attack on the "French front," where material and troops were being massed.

One of the Somme sectors was visited by M. Reynaud, the French Prime Minister, and Marshal Petain. Later they declared: "The morale of the troops has never been higher."

M. Reynaud congratulated the Command on the new defence plans.

Foreign messages: British United Press, Associated Press, Reuter.

HOW LITTLE SHIPS RESCUED THE B.E.F.

By EWART BROOKES

"Daily Mirror" Staff Reporter, who went to Dunkirk on one of the rescue ships

FOR seventeen hours we have been pulling aboard members of the B.E.F., just some of the many thousands at Dunkirk.

I was one of the volunteer crew of a motor yacht which left a south-east coast port. We were the Harry Tate navy.

Open motor-boats, slick varnished motor-cruisers, hard-bitten tarred fishing boats, Thames barges and the "shilling trip around the lightship" pleasure boat of the peace-time beach.

Everything that would move and float.

"Holiday Cruise"

It looked like a holiday cruise as we set course. Then we closed up to the Flanders coast.

My skipper, a grey-haired London doctor with two sons somewhere in the B.E.F., never lost his quizzical smile.

When the coast-line was only a grey smudge, above us was heard a deep drone. Bellowing German machines flew low over the bigger ships off the coast, ships we were to load from our trailing string of small boats.

"Close in, put your small boats ashore, fill them up and take them

Continued on Back Page

DAY'S BAG OF 149 NAZI PLANES

ALL records have been broken by the R.A.F. in the last twenty-four hours. During that time they brought down nearly 100 German planes," said the Paris radio commentator yesterday.

One authorised French source gives the total German losses of planes on Saturday as 149.

R.A.F. fighters had a big share in this. They set up for themselves a day's record figure—78 German bombers and fighters destroyed or severely damaged.

That was the total toll taken over the Dunkirk beaches between dawn and 7 p.m. on Saturday, says an Air Ministry bulletin issued last night.

"Huge formations of Nazi bombers, escorted by fighters, came out and attempted to sink the ships. But when they attempted to bomb, our fighters attacked and drove them off.

"Many Junkers, Heinkels, Dorniers and Messerschmitts soon crashed into the sea after their bombs."

Thirty-seven Enemy Planes a Day —page 14.

Unarmed—Got His Plane

Although he had no ammunition left, a fighter pilot brought down an enemy bomber by getting on to his tail and worrying him so much by a series of stunts that he made a fatal error in turning and crashed.

Sailing home to dear old England"... that is what the men of the B.E.F. sang as they left the hell of Dunkirk behind them... Boats of all descriptions—paddle steamers, motor launches, rowing boats—were pressed into this magnificent ferry service. Some, like the one in this picture, were towed home... and every one of them was crammed with men of the Allied armies.

(Other pictures on pages 3, 8, 9 and 16.)

DUKE DIES IN ACTION

THE Duke of Northumberland has been killed in action while serving with his regiment, the Grenadier Guards, in the retreat to Dunkirk.

This was learned yesterday when his flag, the Blue Lion Rampant, floated at half-mast on the keep of Alnwick Castle, a message having been received from the Duchess of Northumberland by the Duke's commissioner.

The Duke would have been twenty-eight next month. He was a bachelor. He was the eleventh Duke to have died in battle since 1297. None was killed in the last war.

Henry George Alan Percy, ninth Duke of Northumberland, succeeded his father in 1930. He is succeeded by his brother, Lord Hugh Algernon Percy, aged twenty-six, who is serving with the Army.

The Duke of Northumberland

QUEEN MARY TOOK COMMAND

QUEEN MARY yesterday visited the battle-stained men of her own regiment billeted in a West Country village on their return from Belgium—and she took a shirt and a pair of socks for each of the 135 men.

On Friday a message reached the village where the Queen is staying that troops from the B.E.F. were arriving that night a few miles away and would need shirts.

Queen Mary took command.

"Her dear practical mind saw at once that there would not be enough shirts to go round," said one of the people living nearby. "She went herself to Bath to buy shirts and material for making them and they were busy sewing all yesterday up at the big house."

How the men cheered her as she walked into the drive of the empty house where they are billeted.

"Darned Hard"

As she walked round, smiling at each man, she asked the C.O.: "Did you have a hard time?"

"Darned hard, your Majesty," was the reply his men heard him give.

As she walked out to her car, Queen Mary found that the whole village had turned out to cheer her. Already they have collected £39 in twenty-four hours for her regiment.

Queen Mary then drove to another village a few miles away, where 400 men from different B.E.F. units were drawn up in the main street to greet her.

"She walked right along between our double ranks," said a sergeant, "and never missed smiling at any of us. We thought it was wonderful of her."

Men in a factory have collected £250 for their unexpected guests.

DAILY MIRROR, Wednesday, June 5, 1940.

Daily Mirror

JUNE 5

No 11,385 — ONE PENNY
Registered at the G.P.O. as a Newspaper.

WE NEVER SURRENDER

DUNKIRK —LAST MEN GO

UNDER the bullets of German machine-guns, the last of the Allied forces defending Dunkirk were embarked yesterday, it was officially announced last night.

Admiral Abrial, the French commander of the forces who have been defending Dunkirk while the embarkation operations were proceeding, was the last to leave the town, said the French radio commentator.

The evacuation ended at seven o'clock yesterday morning, it was stated.

And already some of the soldiers rescued from Flanders have taken their place in the defence line, stretching from the Somme to the Rhine, against which the next great German offensive is almost immediately expected.

The last two Britons to reach England from Dunkirk landed yesterday with a crowd of French troops—Corporal C. Huntington, of Shirebrook, Nottingham, and Private J. Cowlam, of Hull, both of the East Yorks regiment. They were picked up by a French fishing boat.

Last night's French official communique stated:—

"The embarkation from Dunkirk was completed today in conformity with the prearranged plan."

"Until the last moment, first in the suburbs and then in the town itself from house to house, the rearguard put up a heroic resistance.

Port Now Useless

"The enemy constantly reinforced, ceaselessly continued his assaults and was ceaselessly counter-attacked. The last embarkation took place under the fire of German machine-guns.

"This implacable defence and the success of these difficult and vast operations under the orders of Admiral Abrial and General Falgade have had a definite influence on the development of the struggle.

"Admiral Abrial declares that the work accomplished by the British was magnificent."

An earlier French communique had stated that the port of Dunkirk had been made useless.

The French Navy, it was added, had lost in the Dunkirk operations seven destroyers—Jaguar, Chacal, Adroit, Bourrasque, Foudroyante, Ouragan and Sirocco—and the supply ship Niger.

"Most of the crews of our lost naval vessels were saved."

NEW CHARGE—SPREAD HAW-HAW RUMOUR

A charge of being responsible for a rumour that he had heard from a German broadcast by Lord Haw-Haw that the Nazis were going to attack a Mansfield school is being brought today against a man at Mansfield.

This was stated yesterday by Mr. J. L. Nicol, Regional Information Officer, at the inaugural meeting at Nottingham of the North Midland Regional Advisory Committee, which will function under the jurisdiction of the Ministry of Information.

This will be the first case of its kind under the new regulations.

"**E**VEN if large tracts of Europe fall into the grip of the Gestapo and all the odious apparatus of Nazi rule, we shall not flag or fail. We shall go on to the end, and shall fight in France, on the oceans and in the air. We shall defend our island, whatever the cost, and shall fight on the beaches and landing grounds, in the fields and streets. We shall never surrender.

"Even if—which I do not for a moment believe—this island or a large part of it were subjugated, our Empire abroad, armed and guarded by the British Fleet, would carry on the struggle until, in God's good time, the New World, with all its force and men, set forth to the liberation and rescue of the old world."

IRONSIDES FOR HOME DEFENCE

SMALL bodies of highly mobile and strongly-armed troops—to be called "Ironsides"—are being organised for home defence by General Sir Edmund Ironside, Commander-in-Chief, Home Forces. There will be many hundreds of these formed from the Regular Army.

The War Office, announcing this last night, says that Sir Edmund has sent to each "Ironside" a copy of the following saying by Oliver Cromwell:—

"Your danger is as you have seen! and truly I am sorry it is so great. But I wish it to cause no despondency, as truly I think it will not: for we are British. It's no longer disputing, but act instantly all you can."

The name Ironside, first given to Cromwell himself by Prince Rupert after the battle of Marston Moor, 1644, was later given to the troopers of his cavalry — those "God-fearing men," raised and trained by him in an iron discipline.

It traditionally implies great bravery, strength or endurance.

400,000 Local Defence Volunteers

Lord Croft, Under-Secretary for War, stated in the House of Lords last night that 400,000 had volunteered for the L.D.V.

"It is no mere outlet of patriotic emotion that we are endeavouring to recruit," he said, "but a fighting force which may be at grips with the enemy next week or even to-morrow."

"That is the attitude the War Office takes towards these forces. The response has been absolutely magnificent. I doubt whether it has been equalled in any part of the world."

Lord Strabolgi said that besides making open spaces unusable for the landing of invading planes we should do the same with large spaces of water.

Lord Breadalbane suggested that each local area should have a lorry armoured against splinters and bullets and armed with a couple of guns.

254 DEAD IN PARIS RAID

Death-roll in Monday's Paris air raid was 254, of whom 195 were civilians and fifty-nine soldiers, says the Paris War Ministry. It adds: 652 were wounded—545 civilians, 107 soldiers.

Twenty-five of the German bombers which took part in the raid were brought down.

MILITARY objectives in Munich, Frankfort-on-Main and the Ruhr were bombed by Allied warplanes as a reprisal for Monday's raid on Paris, the official Havas Agency announced last night.

A Berlin report yesterday stated that a "suburb of Munich" was bombed by an Allied plane, and eight people were killed. One bomb, it was stated hit a factory, causing much damage.

R.A.F. fighters maintained offensive patrols throughout Monday and early yesterday in the Dunkirk area.

In Germany refineries, oil tanks, supply depots and marshalling yards in the Ruhr Valley, Rhenish Prussia and in the neighbourhood of Frankfort were among the important military objectives attacked.

Factories which were hit included one of the most important motor works in Germany. Many fires and explosions were caused.

At Mouheim several attacks were made on a munitions works. Hundreds of incendiary bombs were released.

Paris Bombs Picture—page 3.

THAT proclamation of the unbreakable Allied will to fight on for freedom was made by Mr. Winston Churchill in his speech to the House of Commons yesterday — the greatest speech ever made by a Prime Minister of Britain.

Standing as the staunch embodiment of that will to fight, he declared:

"I have myself full confidence that if all do their duty, and if nothing is neglected, and the best arrangements made—as they are being made—we shall prove ourselves once again able to defend our island home.

"We shall ride out the storms of war and outlive the menace of tyranny, if necessary for years."

A roar of cheers answered his superb, stark confidence.

"The British Empire and the French Republic, linked together in their cause and in their need, will defend to the death their native soil, aiding each other like good comrades to the utmost of their strength," said Mr. Churchill.

These were other vital points in the Prime Minister's speech (the full report of which starts on page 3):—

WE MUST EXPECT ANOTHER BLOW ALMOST IMMEDIATELY —EITHER AT FRANCE OR OURSELVES.

✦ ✦ ✦

We shall not be content with a defensive war. We shall build up the B.E.F. once again.

✦ ✦ ✦

Meantime we must bring Britain's defences to the height of efficiency

✦ ✦ ✦

From Flanders 335,000 British and French soldiers were evacuated. Our casualties were 30,000 dead, wounded and missing. The enemy's casualties were far heavier.

✦ ✦ ✦

But thankfulness at the escape of the B.E.F. must not blind us to the fact that what happened in North France and in Belgium was a colossal military disaster.

✦ ✦ ✦

We lost 1,000 guns, and all the transport and armoured vehicles.

✦ ✦ ✦

Yet in the record-breaking arms effort, now on, that loss should be made up in months.

The Noble Story of Calais

Given an hour to surrender, 4,000 British and French troops, ordered to hold Calais to the end, spurned the demand to give in and kept the German hordes at bay for four days.

Then silence fell on the port. Thirty unwounded survivors were taken off by the Navy.

This noble story of the heroic defence of Calais is told on page 3.

Pictures of the Evacuation: Pages 8 & 9

FRY'S retain pre-war prices

LORD WOOLTON'S APPEAL FOR SOLDIERS' WIVES

Lord Woolton, Minister of Food has appealed to manufacturers to produce goods 'within the reach of the wives of serving soldiers.'

Fry's Cocoa is still at the pre-war price—6d. per quarter pound —*and the quality is unchanged.* There is no more economic food-drink than Fry's Cocoa.

The price and quality of Fry's Four-in-one and Fry's Chocolate Spread also remains unchanged.

FRY'S COCOA 6d. per ¼ lb.
FRY'S FOUR-IN-ONE 6d. per ¼ lb.
FRY'S CHOCOLATE SPREAD 6d. per carton

Issued by J. S. FRY & SONS LTD. SOMERDALE, BRISTOL

DAILY MIRROR, Friday, June 14, 1940.

Daily Mirror
JUNE 14

No. 11,393   ONE PENNY
Registered at the G.P.O. as a Newspaper.

BRITISH VOW TO FRANCE

A SOLEMN assurance that Great Britain would continue to give France the utmost aid in her power, was sent by the British Government to the French Government early today.

The British Government reiterated its resolve to continue the struggle at all costs "in France, in this island, upon the oceans and in the air wherever it may lead us."

The assurance concluded with a significant sentence referring to the dawn of the day when civilisation is freed from the nightmare of Nazidom.

"It may dawn sooner than we now have the right to expect."

"In this solemn hour for the British and French nations and for the cause of freedom and democracy to which they have vowed themselves," the message said, "his Majesty's

Contd. on Back Page, Col. 4

REYNAUD'S FINAL CALL TO U.S.

PAUL REYNAUD, PRIME MINISTER OF FRANCE, BROADCASTING TO THE WORLD LAST NIGHT, SAID HE HAD MADE A LAST APPEAL FOR HELP TO THE UNITED STATES.

"Clouds of planes must come from the other side of the Atlantic in order to crush the power which is crushing Europe," he declared. "It is no time for half-hearted measures. The struggle is now for France's very life."

But he also said: "France will never give in. Our race will never allow itself to be overrun by an invasion. Our resurrection will come."

The speech (reported on the back page) caused a stir in Washington.

A copy was rushed to President Roosevelt at the White House, where the official comment was: "Everything is being done that possibly can be done."

And as the French Army, unbroken, fought on against German armoured columns pouring over the Seine and driving through a twenty-mile gap over the Marne, Reynaud told the civilised world it was now the time to repay the heroism of the soldiers of France.

"France has the right to say to the other democracies: 'It is your turn now,'" he declared.

Britain was already acting—and swiftly. It was stated in London that every available British soldier, and all possible arms and equipment, were being rushed over the Channel to aid the French Army.

Massive and immediate British support was promised at the recent meeting of British and French leaders.

Before he spoke, his Government announced that Paris had been declared an open city, with no military objectives. The capital's military forces were withdrawn.

Then the French Cabinet was called by President Lebrun. The meeting ended just after 9 p.m. and a communique revealed that it was Reynaud's broadcast that the Ministers discussed.

The French war communique was issued while the world still awaited Reynaud's words.

It said: "On both sides of Paris,

Contd. on Back Page, Col. 1

"Paris Surrenders" Radio Fake

A German radio station last night broadcast a fake message in French to hoax the world into believing that Paris had surrendered.

It had been announced that M. Reynaud would make an important statement at 10.30.

Just before that time Paris radio went off the air. So did Toulouse.

Suddenly on the Toulouse wavelength an announcer read the following bulletin:—

"The German High Command today delivered an ultimatum to the city of Paris, stating that the city would be bombed unless it surrendered. Faced with this threat the Military Governor of Paris has decided to surrender."

Almost immediately Toulouse broke in, but the fake announcer could be heard adding, "This is the voice of the people."

French stations are now jamming the broadcasts of the "voice of the people."

TRIPS TO EAST COAST BANNED

A TWENTY-MILE-DEEP strip of the East Coast from the Wash to Sussex and all the South-East Coast from Whitstable to the Romney area is out of bounds for pleasure trips by road or rail.

The chief seaside resorts affected are Hunstanton, Sheringham, Cromer, Yarmouth, Lowestoft, Felixstowe, Dovercourt Bay, Frinton, Clacton-on-Sea, Southend, and inland towns such as Canterbury, Colchester, Ipswich and Norwich.

No Cheap Tickets

The Ministry of Home Security, making this announcement last night, says

"It is not desired to interfere with journeys into these areas for business or other important reasons, but the influx of persons on pleasure trips, or making visits which are not urgent, is strongly deprecated."

"This applies to journeys by rail or road, and steps are being taken to curtail travel facilities to these areas, including cheap day tickets by rail.

"The Minister of Home Security is confident that the good sense of the public will be sufficient without other measures to ensure compliance with this request which is made in the public interest."

TURK-NAZI TRADE PACT

TURKEY has signed a new trade agreement with Germany, it was announced in Ankara last night.

At the same time as the agreement was announced messages were being flashed all over the world indicating that Turkey was preparing to fulfil her obligations to the Allies.

According to a Reuter message from Ankara, Turkish peasants, the men to be called up under the latest order were leaving their homes.

The new trade pact has not surprised authoritative circles in London, where it is said to be "of no political significance."

The Germans speak of twenty-one million Turkish pounds as being the amount involved. This is a mere £4,000,000 sterling.

Children Will Go Abroad

British children will soon be evacuated to safety in the Dominions or the United States if their parents are willing.

FREE passages will be available for those who cannot afford to pay. Miss Horsbrugh, Parliamentary Secretary, stated in Parliament last night that she hoped plans would be announced in a few days.

Major Braithwaite (C., Buckrose) told of thousands of offers, coupled with millions of dollars received from the United States, to take children from Britain.

Parents Shirking

The result of the two days' registration of children for evacuation which closed last night is very disappointing in Chatham, Rochester and Gillingham.

About 645 children have been registered, leaving about 6,000 still in the towns.

The numbers registered were: GILLINGHAM, 361; CHATHAM, 174; ROCHESTER, 110.

Yet these towns constitute one of the most vulnerable areas outside London in the south of England.

Fewer than one-eighth of the schoolchildren left in Great Yarmouth have been registered for the new evacuation. More than 2,000 children will remain in the town.

(Don't run from home: page 3.)

Found at Dunkirk..

...this picture of a bonny boy and, written on the back, the message reproduced below. It was found among a pile of wrecked kitbags on the quay by Mr. A. J. Lusty, Old Contemptible, and manager of a Dunkirk hotel.

He has sent them to us with the message: "If you can find to whom they belong, give them back with the compliments of one of the last Britons to leave the remains of Dunkirk."

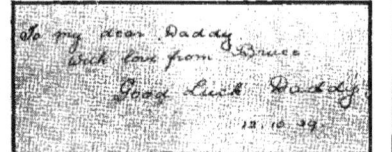

You Needn't Listen

to enemy broadcasts in English giving names of British fighting men alleged to be prisoners of war.

These announcements are made to get an audience for enemy propaganda. Relatives of missing men do not need to allow their anxiety to be exploited.

Such German broadcasts are noted and checked in Britain. The names will be published in the *Daily Mirror*.

Provided the enemy information is detailed enough, next-of-kin will at once be told by a Government service.

Anti Haw Haw League—page 2.

"I'm all for Special Drene Shampoo— always!"

SAYS

POLLY WARD

Glamorous Star of Stage

I WAS thrilled to find how truly radiant my hair became after a Special Drene shampoo. Another thing I like about Special Drene Shampoo is that no special rinses are necessary. And my hair is so easy to set in a smart hair style right after the shampoo. Special Drene is wonderful!"

GLAMOROUS HAIR CAN BE YOURS TOO... WHEN YOU USE

SPECIAL **drene** SHAMPOO

6d., 1/6 & 2/6

DAILY MIRROR, Saturday, June 15, 1940.

Daily Mirror

No. 11,894 — ONE PENNY
Registered at the G.P.O. as a Newspaper.

JUNE 15

The Spirit That Has Never Lost a War

These are some of the men who left a South of England port yesterday, with a new British Army for France. With them went guns, motorised units, new equipment . . . AND THE SPIRIT YOU SEE IN THIS PICTURE: THE SPIRIT THAT HAS NEVER FAILED TO CARRY BRITISH TROOPS TO VICTORY. (Story and other pictures on pages 6 and 7.)

FRENCH HOLD ON, REPULSE ATTACK

K.C.B. FOR DUNKIRK ADMIRAL ABRIAL

BRITAIN has awarded the K.C.B. to Admiral Abrial, of the French Navy, for his heroic work during the withdrawal of the Allied troops from Dunkirk.

Three French Generals were also honoured.

An Honorary Knight Commandership of the Order of the Bath is conferred upon General Georges Maurice Jean Blanchard, an Honorary Knight Commandership of the Order of the British Empire upon General Benoit Leon de Fornel de la Laurencie, in recognition of their distinguished services in Belgium and Northern France, and an Honorary Companionship of the Order of the Bath upon General de Brigade Marie-Emile Bethouart, in recognition of distinguished service in Norway.

WEYGAND'S men, dourly holding on as thousands of British soldiers poured into France to help them, smashed a violent enemy assault on the Maginot Line last night, and even counter-attacked in other sectors.

At certain points the German pressure slackened.

This news was given in the French war communique. It was the answer to earlier enemy claims that the Allied resistance had collapsed along the whole front when the French line was withdrawn behind Paris, now occupied by the Germans.

"The French Army is fighting magnificently, holding out against overwhelming odds," said a high Air Force officer after he had flown over the lines.

"There is no need for unwarranted panic."

The Germans are attempting to crush France before effective help can be given.

The assault on the Maginot Line, designed to break the "hinge" linking up with Weygand's mobile forces, was announced as the third phase in the great offensive.

Enemy advance forces are now at least twenty miles south of Paris on both the east and west of the capital.

On the east, they are near Romilly-sur-Seine, seventy-five miles from

Contd. on Back Page, Col. 4

B.B.C. SCRAP BOW BELLS BECAUSE OF ALARM PLAN

Since church bells must not be rung except as a warning of enemy landings from the air, Bow bells, the B.B.C. interval signal, is faded out. The "tick-tock" signal will be used instead.

Within twenty-four hours of the introduction of the order banning church bells, William Metcalfe, aged eighteen, baker's labourer, was remanded at Bradford Police Court yesterday charged with ringing the bells of St. Peter's Church, Laisterdyke, Bradford.

WARNS OF NAZI PEACE TRICK

HITLER, now his troops have entered Paris the day before he said they would, may open a peace offensive within the next few days.

Mr. Harold Nicolson, Parliamentary Secretary to the Ministry of Information, warned Britain of that at Leicester last night. He went on:—

"Hitler will assure the peoples of France and Britain that he has no desire to subjugate their countries, but that all he desires is their complete disarmament.

"He will say to us that we may keep our Empire—apart from such colonies as he may desire for himself—but that we must abandon our free, democratic institutions and accept a Government nominated from Berlin and at the same time surrender our fleet to Germany and Italy.

Bitter Blow but—

"The moment that he obtains our fleet he would sweep upon London, and from there would slowly, carefully and thoroughly stamp out the liberties of our countries and reduce our working people to the level of slaves.

"The capture of Paris, is, of course, a great triumph for Hitler personally, and a bitter blow to France and her Allies.

"We must always remember that Paris means more to the ordinary French person than even London means to us.

"Although they have captured

Contd. on Back Page, Col. 3

IF IT'S CHOCOLATE THEN IT'S FOOD

There's a glass-and-a-half of full-cream milk in every ½ lb. block of Cadbury's Milk Chocolate. It's the world's most delicious way of giving yourself quick energy.

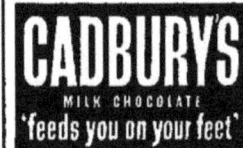

CADBURY'S MILK CHOCOLATE
'feeds you on your feet'

DAILY MIRROR, Monday, June 17, 1940.

Daily Mirror

JUNE 17

No. 11,395   ONE PENNY
Registered at the G.P.O. as a Newspaper.

FRENCH CABINET SHOCKS: PETAIN PREMIER

★ British Children Are Welcome—U.S.

Thousands of American families would welcome English children into their homes for the duration of the war, writes John Walters, our New York correspondent.

Mr. William Osborne, chairman of the U.S. Children's Aid Society, said last night that an enormous number of Americans would be delighted to care for and feed English children without charge.

British officials in New York and other American cities have already received many inquiries from Americans anxious to help and who would look after the children.

B.E.F. FIGHTING IN NORMANDY

The War Office announced last night: "Operations in which the B.E.F. are engaged in conjunction with the French Armies continue in Normandy. Details of the fighting are not at present available.

GERMAN motorised columns last night reached a point eighteen miles north of Dijon—more than 180 miles south-east of Paris.

The Germans' chief effort is now directed towards turning the flank of the Maginot Line, a part of the garrison of which has been withdrawn. It is stated that they are flinging into this effort 150 divisions.

Last night's official French war communique said:

"The Germans reached Melun and Fontainebleau in the South-East of Paris. Local attacks continue in the Aigle sector.

"German motorised columns reached a point eighteen miles north of Dijon.

"The movement of the French Army in Alsace and Lorraine is proceeding according to orders."

ITALIANS LOSE 4 SUBMARINES

FOUR Italian submarines have been sunk in action, it was announced last night.

An official announcement giving the sinking by an Italian submarine of the British cruiser Calypso, said it occurred during a recent engagement with enemy submarines.

The British scored direct hits on two submarines which were set on fire.

According to the Swiss wireless Allied naval units have sunk the Italian steamer Fortunata (4,786 tons) off Teneriffe, Canary Islands.

Ship Scuttled

The Italian ship Marzocco (5,106 tons) is believed to have been scuttled off the East Scottish coast.

Thirty-one members of the crew were landed at a British port and taken in charge by the military.

The fishing boat Hope noticed two ship's lifeboats a few miles off the coast. She drew alongside and discovered that the crews were Italian.

A rope was thrown and the Italians made fast. Both boats were then taken in tow.

"Violent fighting," says Italy.—*k page.*

MARSHAL PETAIN, EIGHTY-FOUR-YEAR-OLD HERO OF VERDUN IN THE LAST WAR, BECAME PRIME MINISTER OF FRANCE AT MIDNIGHT LAST NIGHT IN THE GRAVEST HOUR IN HER HISTORY.

The veteran chose General Weygand as his Vice-Premier. And Admiral Abrial, the hero of Dunkirk, also entered the Government.

In all, the new Government contains four Army leaders and two Admirals.

Paul Reynaud's Cabinet was dismissed after it had met three times. The second meeting was to consider whether America's reply to France's call for aid would permit her to continue the struggle in her own territory.

AT THE THIRD, CALLED BY PRESIDENT LEBRUN AT 10 P.M., A MESSAGE FROM MR. WINSTON CHURCHILL WAS BEFORE REYNAUD'S MINISTERS.

In London was issued an authoritative statement (given fully in column five) declaring that in any event Britain would fight on for victory.

And Sir Ronald Campbell, the British Ambassador to France, with Brigadier General Spears, the liaison officer between the British and French forces, saw Reynaud during the day.

Reynaud himself did not receive a post in the new Cabinet.

In addition to Marshal Petain and General Weygand, these were the appointments:—

Minister for War: General Coulson.
Minister of Air: General Pujeot.
Minister of Marine: Admiral Darlan; Minister of Justice: M. Laval.

A post for Admiral Abrial has not yet been selected. M. Paul Boncour, an ex-Premier, is also expected to be in the Government.

Marshal Henri Philippe Petain was appointed Ambassador to Spain last year, but was recalled by Reynaud to become Vice-Premier in his Cabinet reconstruction on May 18.

He assumed command at Verdun in 1916, was Commander-in-Chief of the French on the Western Front in 1917, and at the signing of the Armistice in the railway coach in the Forest of Compiègne, he was attached to Marshal Foch.

In 1918, Petain was appointed Marshal of France.

Admiral Abrial was made a K.C.B. this month by Britain in recognition of his work in the Dunkirk evacuation.

France's new Premier, eighty-four-year-old Marshal Petain.

Attack Failed

The French, he continued, are having a difficult time, as they are forced back on to strategical retreat tactics.

The Germans, attacking in the Rheims area, are spreading out fanwise south of Troyes and towards Chaumont.

Two days ago, he said, the Germans launched a big frontal attack against the Maginot Line in the Saar area. This was a complete failure, and was repulsed with tremendous losses for the Germans.

The Germans attacked on Saturday in the Neuf Brisach area. The move was more or less a failure, though the Germans managed to establish a bridgehead, and some small units were able to cross there.

"Units of the French Air Force have continued their energetic action on the whole battlefield," said a communiqué.

Contd. on Back Page, Col. 2

CHAMBERLAIN SEES KING

Mr. Neville Chamberlain, the Lord President of the Council, had an audience of the King at Buckingham Palace last night.

SOVIET, NAZI BORDER MOVE

WITH Lithuania completely occupied by half a million Red troops, the official Soviet agency announced last night that Russia had sent an ultimatum to Latvia and Estonia, Lithuania's neighbours in the Baltic. This means that all three countries, which could form German bases for attack on the Soviet Union, will be occupied.

A Moscow communique said that Russia had data to prove that Latvia had never cancelled a military alliance directed against the U.S.S.R. with Estonia, "but extended it by drawing also Lithuania into an alliance and attempts also to draw in Finland."

The communique added that this alliance was "profoundly dangerous and menacing to the security of frontiers."

"Common Defence"

A Berlin report said that the Estonian Government had resigned after informing Russia that its demands had been accepted.

With thousands more troops, with powerful air forces still streaming over the Lithuanian border, Germany made a quick counter move.

German troops are now occupying the Finnmark region of Norway, and are establishing military headquarters at Kirkenes.

A Stockholm message says that the deposed Lithuanian President, M. Smetona, is reported to have arrived in Germany with members of his Cabinet.

General Skucas, Lithuanian Minister of the Interior and the Chief of Police have been sent to prison.

Addressing the Lithuanian people yesterday, M. Merkys, the acting President, emphasised that the arrival of fresh Soviet forces was necessary for the common defence. Lithuania is on the border of East Prussia. The Soviet Government has bases in this country. After accusing the Lithuanian Government of encouraging fifth column elements, who kidnapped Red soldiers, Moscow obtained a reconstruction of the Lithuanian Government.

It's Up to US

The final issue of the war depends on the strength and morale of the people of this country, said Mr. H. B. Lees-Smith, M.P. for Keighley, Yorkshire, on Saturday night.

The responsibility rested on the plain man and woman, because the whole Continent of Europe was leaning on us, and the New World was looking to us to hold the fort till the vast resources of the Dominions and the United States could come to our aid.

WE GO ON TO VICTORY

GREAT BRITAIN'S resolve, now more than ever, is to fight on for victory. Said an authoritative London statement last night:

"At a time like the present, it is natural that there should be baseless and ill-informed rumours of peace proposals and peace negotiations.

"It cannot be too clearly and definitely stated that Great Britain is firmly and resolutely determined to continue the struggle until victory has been won.

"Even if France's resistance on land were seriously weakened, she still has the most powerful navy in Europe after the British Navy, and this great Allied Fleet is fully capable of enforcing the blockade which has become ever more effective as a result of Italy's entry into the war.

"Germany has used up her resources on a reckless scale in the present offensive, and though these reserves may not yet be exhausted, unless she can defeat the British Empire and its Allies within a few months her chance of defeating them at all will have vanished.

"The tremendous resources of the British and French Empires, together with those which the United States have placed at the disposal of the Allies, will play a weightier part with each week that passes.

"And, as week succeeds week, the man power of Britain takes its place in the struggle with ever-increasing momentum.

"In the last five weeks more men have been called up than in any corresponding period in our history, and the figure already attained is

Contd. on Back Page, Col. 1

DAILY MIRROR, Wednesday, June 19, 1940.

Daily Mirror
JUNE 19

No. 11,397   ONE PENNY
Registered at the G.P.O. as a Newspaper.

LEADERSHIP, GIVE US LEADERSHIP

1,750,000 MEN FOR DEFENCE

Strength of the defence forces now in Britain, Mr. Churchill stated, are:
- 1,250,000 Regular soldiers.
- 500,000 Local Defence Volunteers.
- The Dominion Armies.

Report of Mr. Churchill's speech begins on page 2.

DICTATORS FIX TERMS

HITLER and Mussolini, in a four-hour meeting at Munich last night, decided their terms for an armistice with France. The terms, which were not disclosed, were sent to Bordeaux.

It was reported in Rome that the Dictators ordered their armies to take positions for a final attack on France if their terms should be refused. Earlier, Berlin declared the terms would be unconditional surrender—or "destruction of the French system."

For two and a half hours the Dictators conferred alone. Then they called in Von Ribbentrop and Ciano, their Foreign Ministers, and their Chiefs of Staff. Both Hitler and Mussolini left Munich when the talks ended.

The French made a peace approach to Italy yesterday through the Papal Nuncio.

FIGHT ON—PETAIN

MARSHAL PETAIN last night ordered all French and Allied combatants on land, sea and air to keep on fighting.

He said armistice negotiations had not even begun, and warned the Allied soldiers that German forces were using the white flag to take important points without fighting. The French military spokesman said the Germans now had full possession of all France north of the Loire, except part of Brittany.

Four French armies were still fighting a desperate retreat, and inflicting severe losses on the enemy. The First French Army along the Seine had withdrawn to a line running east from the Gulf of St Malo on the north-west coast.

Tunnel Blown Up

The French communique (see page 2) admitted that enemy advance guards were in Cherbourg. The German thrust toward the Swiss frontier threatens the left rear of the French Army of the Alps.

And there were indications that the French were regrouping their forces on a new line with an east wing based on the Jura Mountains —which cover the southern end of the Maginot Line.

French troops blew up the four-mile railway tunnel under Gold Mountain, in the Jura, through which famous expresses travelled in peace-time. The eastern mouth of the tunnel lies on the Swiss side of the mountain.

Refugees Barred

Petain's Government took action against the refugee problem which as hampered resistance.

Civilians in the war zone were told to stay at home and leave the roads clear for the army.

All French towns of over 20,000 inhabitants were declared open towns, to provide shelter from battle and bombardment.

The commander of the powerful nch forces in Syria, General Mittauser has issued a proclamation the fight continues on land sea air

The Premier leaving Downing-street for the House.

" THE battle of France is over. I expect that the battle of Britain is about to begin."

Thus, Mr. Churchill in the House of Commons yesterday, and now there can be no illusions in anybody's mind about the ordeal before us.

Mr. Churchill spared the feelings neither of the politicians who have failed us, nor of the public who must face the dangers to come.

" Hitler," he said, " knows he will have to break us in this island or lose the war."

He explained that the Navy makes a mass invasion impossible, but that " the Navy have never pretended to be able to prevent raids by 5,000 or 10,000 men thrown ashore at several points on some dark night."

He went on to " the great question of invasion from the air, and the impending struggle between the British and German Air Force."

Our Air Force could deal with any air invasion " until our Air Force has been definitely overpowered."

We must expect enemy bombers now. There may be raids by parachute troops and attempted descents by air-borne soldiers. They would get a warm welcome

"But," he went on, "the great question is—Can we break Hitler's air weapon?"

He paused, and there was a deep regret for the past in his voice as he added. " It is a very great pity we have not got an Air Force at least equal to that of the most powerful enemy." In his broadcast speech last night he added a further comment on this "We were promised that five years ago" he said

R.A.F. Hope of Improvement

His next words were a tribute to the gallantry of the R.A.F. who at Dunkirk undoubtedly beat the German Air Force, inflicting a loss of three or four to one.

" We hope," he said amid cheers, " to improve on that rate."

In his other glance at the past Mr. Churchill said:—" There are many who wish to hold an inquest on the conduct of the Governments and of the Parliaments during the years that led up to this catastrophe

"They seek to indict those who are responsible for the guidance of our affairs. This also would be a foolish and pernicious process There are too many in it"

"There are too many in it." That makes tragic reading, Mr. Churchill. It tells a tale of deception and cowardice.
But you ask us to forget the past, and we respect you.
Therefore, until the future becomes the past, we leave it at that.

Having dealt with the politicians of the past, Mr. Churchill turned to the people of the present.

He did not underrate the ordeal before us, but believed that our countrymen and women would prove capable of standing up to it.

" Much will depend on themselves. Every man and woman will have the chance to show the finest qualities of our race, and render the highest service to the cause, and all will be helped to remember ' He nothing common did or mean upon that memorable scene.' "

You need not worry about the men and women of Britain, Mr. Churchill.
The common people of the land have the courage.
Give them arms and give them leadership and they will not fail as they have been failed.
BUT ABOVE ALL GIVE THEM—

LEADERSHIP

BOMBS ON THAMES TOWNS

ENEMY aircraft over the Thames Estuary last night dropped high explosive and incendiary bombs. They also fired machine-guns.

Air-raid warnings were sounded in six counties, and in East Anglia villagers cheered as they saw a Nazi bomber shot down in flames.

A British fighter engaged the bomber, which was caught in the beam of a searchlight, and shot it down.

An explosion obviously caused by a bomb, shook one town on the Thames Estuary.

A plane was heard overhead, and searchlights tried to locate it. People ran to air-raid shelters.

Several explosions were heard. Half an hour later people returned to their homes, but three more explosions occurred

Heavy Fire

At another point near the Thames Estuary air-raid sirens were sounded, and the sky was streaked with searchlight beams. There was intense A.A. fire. No bombs were dropped.

Enemy planes flying at a great height were seen to be firing their guns.

The raid on the Thames Estuary was seen by many people travelling on late trains from London to East Kent towns.

They could see searchlights playing in the skyline, and had a dis-

Continued on Back Page

U.S. TO GO CONSCRIPT

PRESIDENT Roosevelt announced in Washington yesterday that some form of compulsory Government service for men and women of all classes would be proposed soon.

The proposal, he said, was being studied and might be sent to Congress by him within the next three to six weeks.

Compulsory service would be military only in its broadest terms. It would probably represent about one year's training for all young Americans, women as well as men.

Technical Training

Training would include combat duties, as well as duties behind the lines, such as communications, technical, aircraft and mechanical work.

He envisaged technical training for work of industrial production necessary to support a fighting army.

The President emphasised that compulsory training did not necessarily mean boys were to be trained solely to be infantrymen, pilots and other fighting personnel, but training in all skilled technical jobs

Mr. Oliver Simmonds, M.P. for Duddeston, Birmingham, who has returned to London after having flown to New York and back in three weeks —his visit was concerned with aircraft production—said yesterday that of many Americans whose views he valued, not one believed America would stay out of the war.

Prevailing opinion appeared to be that the United States would not declare war earlier than one month or later than six months hence

Daily Mirror

DAILY MIRROR, Monday, June 24, 1940.

No. 11,401 — ONE PENNY
Registered at the G.P.O. as a Newspaper.

JUNE 24

PETAIN YIELDS FRANCE—LEADER HERE TO FIGHT ON

AFTER depriving him of his rank, the Bordeaux Government announced last night that General de Gaulle, who broadcast from London a "Fight on" appeal to Frenchmen, would be court-martialled.

"He will be charged with refusing to return to his post and addressing an appeal to French soldiers from foreign territory," it was stated.

General de Gaulle, Under-Secretary for War in M. Reynaud's Government, who is under fifty, came to London when the French military situation became critical to confer with the British Staff. Rapid developments prevented his return before the fall of the Reynaud Government.

General de Gaulle's appeal—Page Seven.

GERMAN ATTACK IS REPULSED

WHILE the Bordeaux Government were discussing handing over their country to Hitler, French troops smashed a German attack on Fort de l'Ecluse, the "Gibraltar of the Rhone."

FIGHTING SAVAGELY, THEY ALSO DROVE THE GERMANS OUT OF THE MOUNTAIN TOWN OF BELLEGARDE.

The Germans captured Bellegarde early on Saturday after an attack by artillery, dive-bombers and fighter planes.

French troops dynamited the railway south of Bellegarde to prevent an attack from the north along the Rhone.

The reorganised French Army of the Jura and the Alps, reinforced by Maginot units, held German motorised units south and east of Lyons and drove back advanced columns north-west of Grenoble with heavy losses.

A French radio commentator stated that the French were not only fighting fiercely, but had even launched counter-attacks.

At All Points

The Eastern Army, fighting in square formation, was maintaining close contact with the South-Eastern Army facing the Italians.

This force had completely stopped Italian attempts to advance.

Yesterday's French war communique stated:—

"Italian attacks in the Alps continue. We repulsed them at all points."

The German High Command claimed that 500,000 French soldiers had surrendered in Lorraine.

"Only a few sections of the Maginot Line are still resisting," said the Nazi communique.

BALLOONS GOT TWO BOMBERS

DURING last week's air raids two bombers were brought down by our balloon barrage in addition to enemy losses already reported, says last night's A Ministry communique.

R.A.F. aircraft delivered a daylight attack on the enemy occupied aerodrome at Merville, to the west of Lille.

Despite heavy anti-aircraft fire a series of shallow dive attacks was made on hangars, as well as on aircraft on the landing ground.

Fighters patrolling over France shot down one Messerschmitt 110, and it is considered that six other enemy aircraft were probably destroyed. One of our fighters is missing.

WINDSORS AT MADRID

The Duke and Duchess of Windsor, with their suite, arrived at Madrid from Barcelona last night.

Sir Samuel Hoare, British Ambassador, called on the Duke of Windsor shortly after his arrival in Madrid.

24 POINTS OF DISHONOUR...

THE TERMS

THESE are Germany's armistice terms which have been accepted by the French Government:—

1.—Immediate cessation of hostilities. French troops already surrounded to lay down arms.

2.—For security of German interests, territory north and west of following line to be occupied: Geneva-Dole, Chalon-sur-Saone, Paray le Monial, Moulins Bourges, Vierzon, thence to twenty kilometres east of Tours, thence south parallel to Angouleme railway to Mont de Marsan and St. Jean de Pied de Port. The areas not yet occupied in this territory to be occupied immediately on conclusion of the present convention.

[The territory to be occupied is nearly two-thirds of France, including all the north and its industrial areas, all the north-west and all the west coast.]

"After Hostilities"

3.—In occupied area Germany to have all rights of occupying power, excluding local administration. The French Government to afford all necessary facilities. Germany will reduce to a minimum occupation of western coast after cessation of hostilities with Great Britain. French Government to be free to choose for itself the seat of Government in non-occupied territory or even to transfer it to Paris if desired. In the latter event Germany will allow the necessary facilities for administration from Paris of both occupied and non-occupied territory

4 French naval, military and air forces to be demobilised and disarmed within a period to be decided with the exception of troops necessary for maintaining order. Size and armament of the latter to be decided by Germany and Italy respectively French armed forces in occupied territory to be brought back into unoccupied territory and demobilised. These troops will previously have laid down their arms and material at places where they are at the moment of the armistice.

5 As a guarantee, Germany may demand surrender in good condition of all artillery, tanks, anti-tank weapons, service aircraft, infantry armament, tractors and munitions in territory not to be occupied. Germany will decide the extent of these deliveries

6 All arms and war material remaining in unoccupied territory which are not left for use of French authorised forces to be put in store under German or Italian control. Manufacturers of new war material in non-occupied territory to stop immediately

7 Land and coast defences with armaments, etc in occupied territory to be handed over in good condition. All plans of fortifications, particulars of mines, barrages, etc, to be handed over

8 French Fleet, except that part left free for safeguard of French interests in the colonial empire, shall be collected in ports to be specified, demobilised and disarmed under German or Italian control. German Government solemnly declares that it has no intention of using for its own purposes during the war the French Fleet stationed in ports under German control, except those units necessary for coast surveillance and minesweeping Except for that part (to be determined) of the Fleet destined for

Contd. on Back Page, Col. 2

PETAIN REPLY TO CHURCHILL

MARSHAL PETAIN, Premier in the Bordeaux Government, trying to justify his surrender, last night declared his "sorrowful amazement" at Mr. Churchill's "grief-and-amazement" statement.

Broadcasting, Petain said: "He is competent to judge the affairs of his own country, but is not competent to judge those of France—much less of French honour. Our flag is intact."

In an apparent reference to the British Government's appeal to Frenchmen to rally behind it, Petain said:

"No one can divide France while she suffers. Mr. Churchill must know that our faith in ourselves has not wavered."

At the end of the speech the Marseillaise was played twice.

The Armistice terms were not included in the radio news bulletin (says Associated Press).

DESPITE THE "TOTAL SURRENDER" ARMISTICE TO BE ACCEPTED BY THE PETAIN GOVERNMENT, FRANCE'S STRUGGLE IS TO BE CONTINUED BY A FRENCH NATION COMMITTEE TO BE FORMED IN LONDON IN AGREEMENT WITH THE BRITISH GOVERNMENT.

This was announced in a broadcast last night by General de Gaulle, who was military chief in the Reynaud Cabinet, and who is rallying French resistance. "On the soil of France herself," he declared, "there is no longer an independent Government capable of upholding the interests of France

Earlier, it was reported in Cairo that the French forces in Syria would not lay down their arms. General Mittelhauser, Commander of this Army, had announced this resolve, and the Governor-General of Syria broadcast his agreement.

There is a spirit of resistance in the French colonies. Britain would give them all the help necessary for continuing the fight.

Base for Attack

The terms accepted by Petain make nearly two-thirds of France, including all the northern provinces and all the west coast, a huge base for attacks on Britain.

They involve the "recall" and internment of the French Navy, the disarming and demobilisation of the Army, and the surrender of all France's armaments, material resources, naval bases and communications for the enemy's use.

These are terms for an armistice only. When France is helpless Hitler could impose much harsher conditions for peace, including big territorial demands.

Furthermore, Mussolini has still to take his share.

The German terms do not come into effect until six hours after an armistice agreement with Italy.

Last night the Italian terms were handed to the French representatives in a villa outside Rome. Mussolini was not present, and Ciano led his representatives.

The Petain Government met for two hours in Bordeaux.

This was the speech broadcast by General de Gaulle from London.

"The armistice accepted by the Bordeaux Government is a capitulation.

"This capitulation was signed before all means of resistance had been exhausted. It delivers into the hands of the enemy, who will

Contd. on Back Page, Col. 3

K·L·G Sparking PLUGS

The margin between Governmental demands for K.L.G. plugs and our maximum output is small: delays in fulfilling private orders are sometimes unavoidable, when they occur—we beg your indulgence.

CORDITE — JUST AS GOOD FOR *your* CAR — 5/-

K.L.G. SPARKING PLUGS LTD. PUTNEY VALE, LONDON, S.W.15

Daily Mirror

Tuesday, June 25, 1940.

No. 11,402 — ONE PENNY
Registered at the G.P.O. as a Newspaper.

PETAIN GIVES IN TO ITALY, TOO

FRANCE'S second humiliation was completed last night with the signing of an armistice with Italy.

The German and Italian High Commands ordered their troops to stop fighting at 12.35 this morning (British Summer Time). This, in accordance with Hitler's terms, was six hours after he had been told that the Franco-Italian agreement was signed.

The Petain Government met three times at Bordeaux yesterday to consider the demands Mussolini was able to make only fourteen days after he declared war.

The only reports on these demands came from Zurich, Switzerland. They said that the Italian dictator wanted strong military positions at Djibouti, Tunis, Algiers and Morocco—and part of France's Mediterranean Fleet.

In the evening, Petain and his Ministers bowed to the Italian dictator. They telephoned their delegates in Italy and ordered them to sign the terms.

At 6.15 General Huntzinger signed for France, Marshal Badoglio, Chief of the Italian General Staff, for Italy. Twenty minutes later the Germans were told.

"War at End"

The official German News Agency announced: "The Franco-German armistice is now valid. The German High Command has in consequence ordered the cessation of hostilities from 1.35 a.m. tomorrow (12.35 a.m B.S.T.).

"The war in the West is at an end." Petain's Cabinet meets this morning to examine a final agreement between the three Powers. When this is ratified, the text will be made public.

The people of France will then be confronted with a situation in which tragic concessions have been signed, sealed—and delivered.

Details of the terms will be published simultaneously in France, Italy and Germany, but not until tomorrow.

A commission will lay down the conditions for carrying them out.

The seat of the Government, at present at Bordeaux, will probably be transferred to a town in the centre of France.

Ten Days of Jubilation

Hitler has ordered flags to be hoisted throughout Germany for ten days—ten days of jubilation to celebrate the victory which has cost him thousands and thousands of German dead.

The Fuehrer's message was "Ours is the most glorious victory of all time.

"In all humility we thank God for His protection. I hereby order the flags to be hoisted all over Germany for ten days and church bells to ring for seven days."

Bremen and Hamburg radio stations went off the air at 11.4 last night during the reading of Hitler's proclamation. The R.A.F. were over.

France's Day of National Mourning

The Bordeaux Government has decided that today shall be observed as a Day of National Mourning. There will be a funeral service for the war in Bordeaux Cathedral. Petain will be present. But last night the French people still did not know the full reasons for mourning. Petain had not yet told them Hitler's terms.

Bombs on South: Warning in London

LONDON had its first air raid warning since last September early today.

Warnings were sounded over a wide area in the south, and bombs were dropped in one south-east district.

In South-West England several bombs were reported dropped, but no details were available whether there were any casualties.

Gunfire met the raiders.

Two Over Wales

Shortly after midnight in the south-west, the throb of a plane engine could be heard, apparently flying very high. It was going in a north-westerly direction, but returned. The throb could be heard for some time.

Soon afterwards there was the sound of anti-aircraft fire.

In Wales two planes were seen. No bombs were dropped.

FRENCH AFRICA WILL FIGHT ON

A "fight on" proclamation was issued last night by General Nogues, Commander-in-Chief of the French forces in North Africa. It was broadcast by Morocco Radio. General Nogues's order reads:

"In spite of the signing of the Armistice, I have ordered the forces under my command to continue fighting. I therefore order as follows:—
(1) Everybody must stay where he is.
(2) All my orders have to be obeyed.
(3) The integrity of North Africa is guaranteed by your discipline."

General de Gaulle, in London, yesterday said, "I have reason to believe that the French Fleet will not surrender."

General de Gaulle, formerly Reynaud's military adviser, whose court-martial has been ordered by the Bordeaux Government because of his "Fight on" broadcast, added:

"From the information I have received, I am convinced that all parts of the French Empire will go on fighting."

He revealed that he was in telegraphic communication with General Nogues, Commander of the French forces in Morocco; General Mittelhauser, French Commander-in-Chief in Syria; and General Catoux, in charge in Indo-China.

BRITISH SINK SEVENTH ITALIAN SUBMARINE

British naval forces have destroyed another Italian submarine east of Suez, the Admiralty states.

This is the seventh Italian submarine known to have been sunk since Italy declared war on June 10.

MUDDLE

Muddle and red tape are still hindering Britain's fight. Every day, somewhere, there are glaring examples. And every day, in this newspaper, I will expose one of them—with your help. If you know an instance of the muddling which helps Hitler, let me know.

To ram home the point, I will send the facts in full to the Minister of the Government Department concerned. We shall see which of Whitehall's Mandarins really puts Britain's interests above bureaucratic red tape.

Below I give the first story in this war on muddle—BILL GREIG.

IN a Midland aircraft factory there is a lathe not working this morning.

It should be. Desperately the nation needs its output. It would be, had the works not been clogged with Red Tape.

Trained to use this lathe was Geoffrey Smedley, and a mighty fine worker he was. He was fourteen last April, when he left school to enter the factory. With a few weeks' training he could equal a man at the job.

Then someone found that Geoffrey, though of age to leave school, had broken a technical rule by departing from his books before the end of a term.

Geoffrey was ordered back to school. His employers wrote to the Air Ministry protesting that:

It would be extremely difficult to train another boy at short notice, and that the formality of completing a school term, admirable as it may be in peace-time, is not the most important thing today.

Did the Air Ministry say: "To hell with this, we need planes"? No.

They merely replied that they would take "appropriate action."

This terrific effort resulted in a letter saying that the Ministers of Labour and Agriculture had been consulted, and that the boy must return to school. The finish to this letter showed the genius of the Muddlers. It read:

Thus Section 138 of the Education Act, 1921, which requires school attendance of a public elementary school child until the end of the term in which he becomes fourteen, holds good.

"Is there a Minister in this country who really realises that old England is up against it?" an official of Geoffrey's firm asks me. I wond too.

I do m than wonder, I say openly the people who put that lathe into idleness by enforcing a technical point of law are helping Hitler. Their petty pride, their pompous satisfaction with their own little power paves the way for the Nazi hordes.

There are others like them. They should and must be exposed. Give me the facts and we can do so together.

MORE COAST CHILDREN TO GO

All registered schoolchildren in Portsmouth, Southampton and Gosport are to be evacuated, the Ministry of Health announced yesterday.

About 9,000 children will be moved on Thursday and Friday to areas in Surrey, Hants, Dorset, Wilts and Somerset.

THREE MORE AREAS OF ESSEX PROHIBITED

Three more Essex areas—the urban districts of Hornchurch, Brentwood and Thurrock, and the rural district of Ongar—have been declared prohibited areas for holidays and recreation.

This was announced last night under the Defence Regulations.

HAND LOTION IN THE OFFICE

WHATEVER your job in an office —whether you are the telephone operator or the Staff Supervisor — you'll find your hands are constantly grubby. You can't help it — even the most luxurious office seems to affect hands that way. But constant washing does make hands rough and red, and to prevent this happening it's a good idea to keep a bottle of Coty Hand Lotion in your desk. Use it regularly every time you wash.

NON-STICKY
Coty Hand Lotion is absorbed by the skin the minute you put it on, so that there's no chance of your hands sticking to typewriter keys and carbon paper.

IT'S PERFUMED, TOO
Coty Hand Lotion not only soothes, softens and whitens hands but actually perfumes them. It's a beauty product as well as a salve. You can get it in many of the famous Coty perfumes at 2/6 a bottle.

From all the best perfumery and beauty counters, or the Coty Salon, 2 New Bond Street, London, W.1.

Coty HAND LOTION

MIRROR, Saturday, June 29, 1940.

Daily Mirror

JUNE 29

No. 11,406 ONE PENNY
Registered at the G.P.O. as a Newspaper.

29 Die in Channel Islands Bombing

GERMAN warplanes bombed the Channel Islands last night, killing twenty-nine people. They swept down and machine-gunned civilians, including helpless people in an ambulance.

Twenty-three of the victims were killed in Guernsey, where thirty-six people were seriously wounded and many others slightly injured.

At least six people died in Jersey, and several were wounded.

Women were among the dead.

Only two hours after the attack it was officially announced that the Islands had been demilitarised and made an open area.

Ninety thousand people had been rushed by air and sea from Jersey and Guernsey to the mainland in one of the swiftest evacuations of the war. Twenty-two thousand people were left.

Ambulance Riddled

Then, last night, Junker bombers roared over the islands and loosed their bombs.

They swept low to machine-gun civilians.

An ambulance taking three of the wounded to hospital was riddled with bullets.

The driver was hit, but the three wounded people inside escaped further injury.

So badly damaged was the ambulance that the wounded, including the driver, had to be transferred to another vehicle.

The Government decided to evacuate the islands in view of the fact that German forces were in occupied France only thirty miles away

Some by Plane

The garrisons were withdrawn with all their equipment. Everything of value which might be seized by German raiding parties was removed. Practically all of the remaining potato crop was lifted, acres and acres of tomato plants were stripped, and many of the famous herds of Jersey and Guernsey cattle shipped over to England.

German planes circled overhead as the trek of the 90,000 people began. Only last night did the Government allow the Press to reveal the story.

The children went first. Then mothers and babies. And for all men up to forty evacuation was compulsory. Some of the older people stayed behind.

Many people walked out of their homes at two minutes' notice, leaving....

Continued on Back Page

FAMILIES TO GET ORDER TO MOVE

THE Government has now made plans for the compulsory evacuation of most of the civilians in certain areas threatened with invasion.

If the Army declares it necessary for defence, civilians will get orders to go at short notice.

The orders will apply mainly to women and children, who will be moved out by rail in family parties.

These evacuations may be on a big scale.

Last night the Ministry of Health, in a circular, advised authorities in reception, neutral and evacuation areas to make adequate billeting arrangements.

It may be necessary to evacuate children to areas which are not first choice for safety, but which are safer than the home district.

Meantime, the movement of children from evacuation areas will continue to be on a voluntary basis. But the evacuation plans for an emergency have been completely revised.

The Ministry of Health circular was sent to both the reception and evacuation area authorities for London and Portsmouth groups, Medway towns and Sheerness.

Still Registering

Plans and railway time-tables now provide for:—

Evacuation of registered schoolchildren from each evacuation area. The Government will decide whether and when the order should be given for individual areas. As before, these local schemes can be put into operation separately or in groups.

A further evacuation, if necessary, of those schoolchildren remaining whose parents then want them to go. This movement is being planned in several sections. Registration will remain open in all evacuation areas till further notice.

In Greater London, the Medway towns, Southampton, Portsmouth and Gosport, where the registered children have already been evacuated, registration will also continue and small parties of children will be sent out as they are registered.

The circular discloses that though the plan for further evacuation of schoolchildren announced in February provided for the removal of 560,000 schoolchildren, the total registered was fewer than 240,000.

The effect of the recasting of the transport and other plans is to provide first for the evacuation of registered children from particular areas as this becomes necessary, and to have transport plans ready for a subsequent evacuation.

Plans for the first evacuation provide only for the totals at present registered.

Save Children's Lives

These plans will be prepared in detail, but there can be no guarantee that conditions will enable them to be fully operated.

In any case, parents can speed-up the arrangements if they say in advance whether they want their children to be moved. Registration will therefore remain open.

"In directing any measures of evacuation which are found necessary either for military reasons or in the interest of the safety of children, the Minister is anxious to reduce to a minimum the inconvenience and hardship which may arise," the circular adds.

"It is only the stern necessity of national interest which calls for such decisions, and he is confident that he can rely on the co-operation of the local authorities in the measures necessary for the effective conduct of the war and the preservation of the lives of children."

The Ministry announced that payment has been authorised of travelling expenses and a billeting allowance at the rate of 3s. and 2s. a week to mothers with children under five in evacuable areas who can go to relatives or friends in reception areas.

CHEAPER NEW POTATOES

From tomorrow the maximum retail price of home grown and Channel Islands new potatoes will drop from 3½ to 3d. per lb., and from the following Sunday there will be a further reduction to 2½d. per lb.

Red Tape is more important than lives to the Muddlers who are hindering Britain's war effort.

Preservation of human life has been one of the greatest cares of the Government, but its aim is being frustrated by hundreds of petty officials who find in a regulation something more sacred than the life of a man, woman or child.

Day by day the evidence against the Muddlers grows. It is now a damning and terrible indictment. I shall continue to expose them with the help of every fact you can give me. More than that, every possible fact will be sent to the Minister concerned. It is in their power to rout the Muddlers. — BILL GREIG.

MUDDLE

HERE is a case where Red Tape has won a great victory over life.

In Castle-street, Christchurch, are shops and houses with small backyards. Many families live there, but the yards provide no room for shelters when the bombs fall.

Mr. S. J. Watson lives at the Cranley Hotel, Castle-street. No Anderson type shelter was issued to him, so he bought one. He felt that he need not worry about a place in which to put it for, in common with other shops, his yard has an exit to the Castle ruins.

These ruins consist of two old walls on top of a mound of earth about 30ft. high and 200 yards in circumference. The mound in itself is ideal for breaking the force of bomb blast.

As a formality, Mr Watson wrote to the air raid precautions authorities seeking permission to put his shelter in the castle ground. Here is the reply:

"I have to inform you that your letter of June 19 was placed before the Civil Defence Committee.

"I have been instructed to explain to you that the castle ruins have been scheduled as an ancient monument, and that it is not the property of the Council. It is only leased to them, and furthermore the large number of restrictive covenants attached thereto present any such work being contemplated.

"I trust you will appreciate the position."

This letter is signed by Victor B. S. Smith, as sub-controller of the Bournemouth - Poole - Christchurch area. I can tell Mr. Smith that Mr. Watson does not appreciate the position. Neither will any other sane minded person in the country.

That the right of an ancient monument to be protected from possible danger should be considered greater than the right of a British subject to protect his life is beyond the comprehension of the ordinary man.

This correspondence will most certainly go to the Minister of Home Security. I hope he acts quickly.

IN Southampton there have been many applications for shelters which it has not yet been possible to fulfil. In Regent's Park-road are people with gardens which to erect them who are, too anxious to get them. They cannot.

In the same road are several empty houses with Anderson shelters in their gardens. Permission was sought for the transfer of these. The answer was "No." Empty the houses might be, empty the shelters might be when the bombs fall, but once down the shelters must remain.

If the sirens sound tonight there will be six or seven people crowded dangerously in some of the shelters in Regent's Park-road. Red Tape will have sealed the entrances to the others.

TO SURVEY MAN POWER

SIR WILLIAM BEVERIDGE, the economist and sociologist, has been appointed Britain's manpower surveyor by Mr. Ernest Bevin, the Minister of Labour and National Service.

His office is that of Commissioner to survey the available resources of manpower of all kinds—including men, women and young persons, now employed or out of work. He will report suggestions on how these resources can be utilised fully for national purposes.

Mr. A. Reeder, Deputy Director of Statistics in the Ministry, will act as secretary to the survey.

Sir William is sixty-one. He was director of the London School of Economics from 1919 to 1937. Since then he has been master of University College, Oxford, his own University, where he had a brilliant career. His first Government post was Director of Labour Exchanges at the Board of Trade, 1909.

RAIDERS OVER

ENEMY aircraft were over the east coast and Wales during the night. Bombs fell in Wales, and there was a heavy explosion in the south-east.

Searchlights went into action when a plane believed to be German flew over a south-eastern area and continued inland for some time. Later the throb of more engines was heard.

CALAIS BOMBED?

Terrific reports of bomb explosions were heard continuously at a south-east coast town last night, coming from the direction of Calais.

Some of the distant explosions were so heavy that they rattled windows and doors.

It was obvious that heavy bombarding of some sort was in progress.

IF IT'S CHOCOLATE THEN IT'S FOOD

Bournville bucks you up — gives you an instant supply of energy when you're feeling low. This famous plain chocolate — containing sunshine Vitamin D, iron and other minerals — is also abundantly rich in carbohydrates, for quick, immediately available energy. Look for the famous red packet.

CADBURY'S Bournville

PLAIN FLAVOUR CHOCOLATE

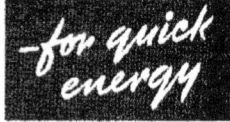

for quick energy

DAILY MIRROR, Monday, July 8, 1940.

Daily Mirror

No. 11,413 ONE PENNY
Registered at the G.P.O. as a Newspaper.

JULY 8

FRENCH PLANES IN GIB. RAID

FRENCH BOMBERS HAVE BEEN USED TO ATTACK BRITISH WARSHIPS. PETAIN IS TAKING WAR ORDERS FROM HITLER.

A communique issued by the Navy Ministry of the Petain Government yesterday declared that two squadrons of French machines took part in an air raid on British warships at Gibraltar along with German and Italian squadrons.

Later the French Havas Agency reported that Petain had "forbidden" British warships or planes to come within twenty miles of the French coast, and had threatened attack on any vessel or machine which entered the banned zone.

And Rome radio reported from Madrid that by order of the Germans, France's Spanish frontier was closed on Saturday night.

The French aeroplanes which attacked Gibraltar were being disarmed under Hitler's armistice conditions, but were rearmed.

Said Petain's Navy Ministry: "British vessels which took part in the cowardly attack at Oran (on the French Fleet) were raided. At least one large British vessel was hit."

In Gibraltar it was stated that the raid did no damage and caused no casualties.

Enemy planes were over Gibraltar again yesterday, but were driven off by anti-aircraft guns before they dropped any bombs.

Not only are French warplanes being rearmed for attacks against the British, but Hitler and Mussolini have ordered that France's naval bases must be kept on a war footing.

Safe from Hitler

The section of the French Fleet at Alexandria is now safe from falling into enemy hands.

It has been demobilised—without any friction between the British and French naval men.

French officers and sailors who want to fight on against Germany and Italy will get "fullest facilities" from Britain, including pay.

The others will be taken back to France.

Reuter, British United Press, Associated Press.

HITLER AND CIANO MEET

COUNT Ciano, Italian Foreign Minister, arrived in Berlin at 11.15 a.m yesterday and was received by Hitler at 12.30.

They went into conference at once. The offensive against England was discussed between Ciano and Hitler, according to the Rome correspondent of the Swiss paper Basler Nachrichten.

Ireland, the correspondent adds, is naturally the first act in an attack against England, and this point was discussed.

"Tomorrow," says the Italian Stefani news agency, "the Duce's envoy will visit the western battlefield to convey the salute of allied Italy to the victorious German armies."—Reuter.

The greatest of all hindrances to the war effort lies in our Civil Service, with its antiquated methods, its cumbersome routine, and its complete inability to cope with anything new.

The rank and file are not to blame. They are the bitterest critics of their own work. With the knowledge they possess they place the blame on the shoulders of the little group of men at the top, headed by that champion of safety-first methods, Sir Horace Wilson.

My war on the Red Tape Muddlers has brought me closely in touch with the Civil Service. Everywhere I hear criticism of Sir Horace Wilson as the man to whom a filing cabinet is a shrine and red tape the incense he burns before it. Change or departure from precedent is unthinkable to him. High Civil Servants told me of meetings with him, of attempts to speed the vital work. The result—smiling politeness but nothing done.

Even a European war, it seems, cannot be allowed to interfere with the dignity of the Civil Service. Sir Horace, friend and confidant of Chamberlain, the man whose favourite phrase is "Think it over" sees no need for change.

I ask any business man how long he would tolerate the methods below—how many months they would take to bring him to the bankruptcy court?

BILL GREIG.

Muddle

THE whole tradition of work in the Civil Service is based on the phrase, "Check, check again, and then get somebody else to check."

That this system of divided responsibility must inevitably lead to two, if not three, people doing the work which in any commercial house would be done by one is ignored.

I went to a Labour Exchange to watch at work the system which authority lays down for paying a man unemployment benefit. Here is what happened:—

The amount of benefit due was calculated by one clerk on a pay sheet. Separately another clerk made a similar calculation on a coupon.

The man was the handed the coupon. He took it to a third clerk who examined the amount and called it out to a fourth clerk, who now had the sheet prepared by the first clerk. The fourth clerk paid out.

The coupons were then sent to the Ministry of Labour (now decentralised by divisions all over the country) for the whole process to be subjected to a further check. Four men had already been involved in the payment of just over £1, yet the whole matter had to be gone into again!

It is admitted that the method is ridiculous. But no one official dare take the responsibility of ordering a change. The burden must again be divided. The Minister has given managers permission to reduce the routine work, but the responsibility in every case must be theirs. The result that few take the risk.

No Civil Servant has the power to ignore anything, no matter how trivial.

Anybody, for instance, is free to write to a Government Department. Thousands of letters come every day from every type of person, cranks and lunatics alike. All have to be filed, registered and passed on.

Members of the Service whose job it is to read these letters have to go on minuting and commenting. They asked to be given reasonable discretion to throw away the obviously useless or insane letters, but this has been refused. The number engaged in this work is colossal.

The reason is that at any time a crank or a lunatic may go to his M.P. and say, "I have written to the Ministry and nothing has been done." In case the M.P. desires to raise the matter there must be a complete record.

Nowhere is the system of divided responsibility seen more clearly than in the accounting department. Payments are so slow that contractors are daily forced to ask for advances to allow them to carry on vital work. This means the setting up of a second department to try to counteract the effects of excessive caution in the first!

I was told of a case where two men working in adjoining rooms daily posted to each other correspondence on trivial matters which business men would have decided on the telephone in a few minutes. The necessity for a "record" for the all-important filing cabinet made this impossible.

Sir Horace Wilson could change all that. He refuses. Those under him complain that when high posts are vacant there is no hope for any but the "safe" man.

So, day by day, the Civil Service grows in size. Every inch it adds to its girth blocks the war effort.

And the only man who can do anything continues to worship at the foot of a filing cabinet.

Submarine Hits 5 Nazi Ships

A BRITISH submarine which attacked two enemy convoys hit five supply ships with torpedoes.

After the first attack, the rest of the convoy fled in disorder.

News of this success was given in an Admiralty communique last night. It stated:—

H.M. submarine Snapper (Lieutenant W. D. A. King, D.S.O.) sighted a convoy of supply ships escorted by an armed trawler and aircraft.

Scattered Convoy

"The Snapper attacked and hit two ships with torpedoes. The remnants of the convoy scattered and made in disorder for the shelter of a fiord

"Later the Snapper sighted a large convoy escorted by armed trawlers and aircraft. A successful attack was carried out and three ships were hit with torpedoes."

Lieutenant W. D. A. King was awarded the D.S.O. after sinking at least four German ships during the Norwegian campaign.

The Snapper belongs to the Shark class of submarine, many of which have already done excellent work in the war

Lieutenant W. D. A. King, commander of the Snapper.

FAKED S.O.S. ROUSES U.S.A.

By JOHN WALTERS

NEW YORK, Sunday.

WHEN the Mackay radio station in New York picked up a fake SOS message tonight saying that the U.S. destroyer Barry had been torpedoed by a Nazi U-boat off Spain—

The American Navy planned Atlantic mobilisation;

President Roosevelt stopped an important conference and rushed from the room to plan action;

The nation's broadcasting programme was disrupted, and

The giant liner Manhattan was sent off her course.

The S O S was the most sensational radio hoax yet played on America

Shortly after the message was picked up the U.S. Navy Department announced that it was in touch with the vessel, which was not in distress.

The Navy Department added that the Barry was safely anchored in a neutral port but declined to say where.

Angry Washington officials are trying to find where the message originated.

When the S O S was received U.S. broadcasting programmes were halted so that the nation could be told of developments.

Some Washington officials hint that the hoax may have been played by agents of a foreign Power.

G-men have been asked to investigate the origin of the false report.

It was learned from operators of the Mackay Radio that some doubts as to the authenticity of the message existed.

AN URGENT REQUEST

TO SMOKERS.

EMPTY CIGARETTE AND TOBACCO CARTONS, CARDBOARD BOXES AND TINS.

Please hand these to your Tobacconist. By doing so you will help your Country

THIS ADVERTISEMENT IS ISSUED BY THE IMPERIAL TOBACCO COMPANY (OF GREAT BRITAIN & IRELAND) LTD.

Daily Mirror

DAILY MIRROR, Tuesday, July 9, 1940.

No. 11,414 — ONE PENNY
Registered at the G.P.O. as a Newspaper.

2oz. TEA RATION FROM TODAY

TEA is rationed from today at 2oz. a week for each person, whether an adult or a child.

In a fortnight's time margarine will be rationed in association with butter and cooking fats.

Luxury feeding at hotels and restaurants has been stopped. You can have a fresh fish course or a meat course. But you cannot have both.

There will be no more icing on cakes. And "general confectionery" will be cut down.

THESE measures to force common sense and care in the nation's feeding were announced last night. Lord Woolton, the Food Minister, stressed the reasons.

BRITAIN is now alone against the enemy. She must face a long siege.

Every conceivable effort will be made to bring us to our knees. There will be a ruthless submarine campaign—plus air bombing.

"THE time has come when people must no longer ask themselves How much can we afford to eat? but How much may we eat assuming that everybody has the same rations? said the Food Minister.

TO deal with those who will not co-operate an Order which will make it a criminal offence to waste food is being considered.

WE are bringing into the country every ounce of food we can get," said Lord Woolton.

"But in the last fortnight the position has materially altered. To quote the words of a Lancashire friend: 'England has now got through to the final.'"

COMMON-SENSE about bread is recommended by the Bakers' and Confectioners' Advisory Committee. They suggest that the present forty-five different sizes of loaves should be reduced to four—one-piece tin, one-piece Coburg (a round loaf), one-piece sandwich and a Vienna loaf.

Lord Woolton explains the new rationing: Page 3

DESTROYER TORPEDOED

AN official Admiralty communique last night announced that the destroyer Whirlwind had been hit by a torpedo and subsequently sunk.

Survivors were rescued by another of H.M. ships before the Whirlwind sank.

Next of kin of casualties have been informed.

The Whirlwind was completed nine months before the end of the last war and was fitted for war purposes as a minelayer.

The commander of the Whirlwind in recent months, Lieutenant-Commander J. M. Rodgers, was mentioned in dispatches for work achieved by his ship in December, 1939.

S.E. COAST BAN ON CARS

Private cars and motor-cycles are forbidden five miles from the South-East Coast. That new order was announced yesterday.

Drivers of cars required for essential purposes can obtained a police permit.

Muddle on the East Coast.—Back page.

TODAY'S STORY OF THE BIG MUDDLE IS TOLD ON PAGE THREE

Unarmed and single-handed she disarmed a German airman—Mrs. E. M. Cardwell.

UNARMED SHE CAUGHT A GERMAN AIRMAN

A GERMAN airman landing by parachute was captured yesterday by an unarmed woman.

When Mrs. E. M. Cardwell, wife of a North-East farmer, was sorting papers in her sitting-room, a groom rushed in to say that paratroops were descending nearby.

"I sent him off to his cottage about a mile away for his shot-gun," Mrs. Cardwell told the *Daily Mirror*. "Then I went to the phone to tell the police—but the phone was not working.

"I sent off the other man on his bicycle to get the police, and a few moments afterwards when I was alone I saw a German land in a field just over the front garden hedge."

Mrs. Cardwell at first thought she would get one of her husband's guns.

"But on second thoughts I decided that the German might be a better shot than I, so I went outside without a gun," she said.

Surrendered

"When I got to the front door and saw a big hulking German in full kit just landing with a parachute trailing behind him, I could hardly believe my eyes. I shouted to him, 'How dare you come here? Put up your hands at once.'

"I signed what I wanted him to do.

"As he pulled himself together he smiled at me and put up one arm. He was bleeding from one leg and looked half terrified. Pointing over the fields he indicated a column of smoke apparently rising from his burning plane.

"By this time he had reached the lawn and was coming towards me. Stand still, you, I shouted.

"Then I stamped my foot and blazed at him again: 'Put up your hands. It is no use trying to shoot.

Contd. on Back Page, Col. 3

"DON'T WANT A GESTAPO HERE"

PROTESTS against a "Gestapo in Britain" were made at Surbiton Town Council meeting last night.

Councillor E. Dowson asked the Mayor if he would consider forming an espionage army or corps, the object of which would be that nobody should trust each other and that it would be a means of bringing traitors to book.

Protesting against the proposal, Councillor H. G. Reynolds, a local magistrate, said we did not want anything like a Gestapo in this country.

The Mayor said he did not think a "Gestapo" had been suggested, and he would bring the matter before the Emergency Committee.

L.D.V.s Pass the Million

THE nine divisions of the B.E.F. which were brought back from Dunkirk, have been reorganised and brought up to full strength, and are now at the disposal of the Commander-in-Chief for the Battle of Britain.

Local Defence Volunteers now number 1,060,000, and soldiers of the divisions at home are at full strength.

Side-by-side with the strongest British Army of all time are aligned thousands of Empire and foreign troops.

And new recruits are being drafted in at the rate of 7,000 a day.

At the same time the creation of further new battalions is now going on at full speed.

By training a new industrial army for the skilled tasks of arms production and by "up-grading" lesser skilled workers, the Ministry of Labour has accomplished the remarkable feat of putting back into munitions work from the unemployed more men than the Fighting Forces have taken out.

Arming Rapidly

The arming of the L.D.V.s is being rapidly carried out, and during the last few weeks great strides have been made in the task of making Britain impregnable.

Britain's readiness to meet any threat is best expressed in the words of the high authority who gave the details last night.

"The Army is in excellent heart," he said. "It is confident of its ability to attack and destroy the enemy, should he attempt to set foot on this island.

The position in industry was explained yesterday in the following terms: The Minister of Labour decided today to ask for skilled workers not at present engaged in work of vital national importance to register at once at his labour exchange so that when the nation's machine - tool capacity has been fully mobilised the maximum use of it to work can be made.

There is no impending conscription of labour, as has wrongfully been stated. The Minister hopes and believes that he can go through the war without having to use to the full the drastic powers with which he is invested.

With grouping of docks it is confidently believed the enemy will not be able to succeed in blockading this country or stop our work of production.

The Minister hopes to publish in a few days an Order regulating wages and arbitration.

L.D.V. Officers Will Wear Shoulder Bars

Local Defence Volunteer officers are to have their rank made clear by shoulder bars similar in style to those worn by the Royal Air Force officers.

According to an Army Council Instruction, Zone Commanders will wear five bars, Area Commanders four bars, Officer Commanding a company three bars, Adjutant two bars, and Platoon Commander one.

ACTION AGAINST FRENCH WARSHIP

"Successful action" against the most recently completed French capital ship Richelieu (35,000 tons) was taken by the British Navy early yesterday, it was learned in London this morning.

OPERATIONS to prevent units of French Fleet from falling into enemy hands continued.

Fuller particulars are expected to be available today.

Launched in January, 1939, the Richelieu was the first of four ships of her class. Her speed exceeded 30 knots, and her armament included four 15in. guns and fifteen 6in. quickfiring guns. Other ships of her class still incomplete are the Jean Bart, Clemenceau and Gascoyne.

The cost of the Richelieu was first estimated at £5,000,000, but later became much higher.

Filled with troops, the French auxiliary cruiser Esterel has left Aruka, Netherlands West Indies, in an attempt to break through the British blockade to Martinique (says the *Daily Mirror* New York correspondent).

Messages from Aruka told how French troops stationed there since May 12 poured into the Esterel with full equipment.

The situation at Martinique, the French island in the West Indies, according to reports received in Washington, has become more and more tense.

Five American destroyers are rushing toward Martinique to look after United States nationals.

British ships are said to be preparing to move into Martinique unless French warships there are scuttled or surrendered.

Among the vessels is the aircraft

Contd. on Back Page, Col. 2

Daily Mirror — Friday, July 12, 1940

No. 11,417 — ONE PENNY
Registered at the G.P.O. as a Newspaper.

BY ORDER

For the defence of Britain sweeping powers over your home were announced last night. There is to be a local rent and debts "holiday" for people ordered out of defence areas.

RENT, DEBT "HOLIDAY"

HOUSEHOLDERS ordered to leave defence areas will not be required to pay rent, mortgages, rates, water, gas, electricity and telephone charges for their locked-up homes.

There will be a "holiday" too for hire purchase payments.

Relief will be granted to people whose businesses have been affected.

These measures were announced by a new Order last night. They apply only to people who have been compulsorily evacuated.

The regulations apply to any premises which are unoccupied at the date when the area is declared an evacuation area, or which subsequently become unoccupied.

Your Furniture

The Order says that these sums are not recoverable during the period of the evacuation.

Rent, rates, sums secured or charged on the premises, sums payable periodically for any right enjoyed in connection with the premises, sums payable for water, gas, electricity or telephone services.

Premises taken over by any Government Department are held to be unoccupied.

No premises will be held to be occupied merely because furniture or other goods remain ———

Hire Purchase

The Order states that no sum will be recoverable during the evacuation period under any contract for hire or hire-purchase of goods by

1. Anyone who uses the goods solely for the purpose of a business, and has ceased to carry on the business.
2. Anyone who has ceased to live in the area.

These reliefs will not apply to rent or money payable under a contract entered into after the date of the regulations, nor for the hire or hire-purchase payments unless the goods, or some part of them, were in the area at the beginning of the evacuation.

A Court can remove or modify the reliefs granted by the Order if it is satisfied that a person who has unoccupied premises has at any time lived in the area since the beginning of the evacuation period.

It may also do so if the person liable, or anyone else with his consent, has been enjoying a substantial benefit from the premises or goods.

The Regional Commissioner can appoint persons to take any measures for the preservation or removal of ——— in an evacuation area.

PAID HOLIDAYS RIGHT STANDS

Workers who are covered by the Holidays With Pay Act may have to wait till next spring before they get their holiday to which they are entitled this year.

The season within which workers must be allowed a holiday with pay is prolonged till March 31, 1941, to meet cases in which owing to the emergency, it has not been practicable for an employer to give the holiday at the normal time.

Cases where, by reason of the emergency, a whole week cannot be given at one time, the worker may be given his holiday in not more than two spells. One of those spells must, however, normally precede or follow the worker's weekly rest day.

"Subject to these changes," stated the Ministry of Labour yesterday, "the rights given to workers by the statutory holiday directions remain in full force and effect."

YOUR HOME AS A FORT

YOU can be ordered to make your home into a fort against enemy attack by an Order in Council issued under the Defence Regulations.

The Home Secretary can direct occupiers of premises "to carry out measures for hindering hostile attack."

You can be ordered to clear rooms, such as lofts, to prevent the spread of fires caused by incendiary bombs.

When an order to clear rooms is not obeyed, an authorised person had to "use force" to get it carried out.

The Home Secretary is given powers to ban or regulate the use of any vehicle on the roads.

New powers to prevent work being interrupted by trade disputes are given to the Minister of Labour (Mr. Ernest E).

Strikes and lock-outs can be banned.

Tribunals can be set up to settle trade disputes. Terms must not be less favourable than the recognised terms and conditions, and employers will be ordered to carry them out.

Power to refer disputes to the Industrial Court will not be affected.

Departures from rules or customs regarding any job may be recorded.

The Home Secretary now has power to discharge and release on licence prisoners, and convicts.

Full story of raids on back page.

R.A.F. BAG 27

IN other ——— of hectic air fights yesterday, the Royal Air Force destroyed twenty-seven German aircraft — twenty-two round the coasts of this country and five at Boulogne.

While raiding planes could be heard overhead, people on the south-east coast last night watched what looked across the Channel like a gigantic fireworks display in the vicinity of Boulogne. Sounds of heavy explosions drifted across the sea at frequent intervals.

German searchlights pierced the sky over a thirty-mile stretch of the French coast. Then vivid flashes of tracers and anti-aircraft shells stabbed the darkness.

No such spectacle had been seen from the south-east coast since the beginning of the war.

Of the twenty-two planes shot down off the British coast, three were accounted for by anti-aircraft guns, eighteen by fighters and one by a Coastal Command plane.

Many others were so severely damaged that it is unlikely they reached their bases.

Our total losses were four fighters, and it is already known that the pilots of two of them are safe.

The twenty-two planes shot down off our shores were among strong forces of bombers, escorted by fighters.

Contd. on Back Page, Col. 1

EVACUATION POSTPONED

The scheme for evacuating children to the Dominions is being postponed.

There will be an announcement in the House of Commons next week to this effect, and that if it comes into operation later it will be much modified.

Shipping difficulties and possible dangers are among the reasons for ———

MR. JOHN LAING, head of contracting firm John Laing and Son, Ltd., is QUITE certain of the outcome of this war....

So confident that he's made arrangements for the letting of a "highest class office building" in Westminster, S.W.

ONLY THE BUILDING HASN'T BEEN BUILT YET.

In fact, before they CAN build it, they've got to pull down the building occupying the site at the moment—the old Westminster Hospital, no. a Services Club under the Y.M.C.A.

Mr. Laing has put the sign you see above outside the building, and advises would-be tenants to apply to the agents.

"And," he said last night, "I've got other big schemes in hand."

A NEW WAR DIET FOR YOU — But There May Be More Beer

SOON you may have to live in health, work and fight on a diet very much different than at present.

It won't be very palatable until we get used to it.

But there will be plenty of beer with which to wash it down if Mr. R. A. Hudson, Minister of Agriculture, has his way.

M.P.s cheered him when he told them last night.

"The House will be relieved to know that I have put in a plea that the diet should be supplemented by adequate supplies of beer."

I am told writes our Political Correspondent, that a scientific diet scheme is being worked out whereby the public will be advised to

Eat more beans, vegetables and potatoes,
Eat less meat
Eat bread made of potato flour.

Farmers Sacked if—

Mr. Hudson warned farmers that Britain must be able to grow enough food to keep the population in good health in case our present import policy was seriously imperilled.

There was plenty of food in the country—but we might not always be so fortunate.

"We must insure ourselves against the possibility of our capacity to import being imperilled by enemy action," he said.

"Tens of millions of people in Europe will soon face the danger of starvation. Many millions may well perish.

"British agriculture with modern methods, modern machinery, modern science and the necessary labour and drive can and will play a large part in saving the people of this island from suffering a similar fate."

He stated that he proposed to introduce a Bill shortly to enable com———

Contd. on Back Page, Col. 3

U.S. PLAN TO GET BRITISH BASES

A RECOMMENDATION that the U.S. should acquire and fortify Fleet and air bases in the British territories of Nova Scotia and Bermuda with a view to strengthening their Atlantic defences is made by the House of Representatives Military Sub-Committee.

The defences, it is added, are "deplorably weak."

Nova Scotia is a province of Canada on the Atlantic seaboard.

The Bermudas are a group of about 300 small islands in the Atlantic, about fifteen of which are inhabited 580 miles from the US.

RED FLEET IN BALTIC

Extensive manoeuvres in the Baltic Sea, lasting three days, have just been completed by the Soviet Baltic Fleet, according to Moscow Radio. Battleships, cruisers, destroyers, high-speed boats, submarines and aircraft took part.—British United Press.

WAR BUDGET IN AUGUST

THE Emergency War Budget is expected to be introduced in the first week of August, writes the *Daily Mirror* Political Correspondent.

The tremendous speed-up of armament production must be paid for.

Income tax, now 7s. 6d. in the £, will be increased. The super tax will also be raised.

Luxury buying will be rendered impossible.

A form of compulsory saving may be introduced.

DOMVILE'S SON DETAINED

Compton Domvile, Admiral Sir Barry Domvile's twenty-two-year-old son, has been detained under the Defence Regulations by police of the Special Branch, who went to his home in Roehampton Vale.

Both Sir Barry, who was chairman of The Link, a pro-Nazi organisation, and Lady Domvile, are detained.

DAILY MIRROR, Saturday, July 13, 1940.

Daily Mirror

JULY 13

No. 11,418 — ONE PENNY
Registered at the G.P.O. as a Newspaper

Water for Shelter Cost 5s.

water which he estimated would be used in mixing the cement.

The householder is Mr. H. S. Gates, an insurance clerk, of Mutton-Way, Potters Bar. He earns just over £5 a week, which means that he is not entitled to a free Anderson shelter.

The material he bought to make his own shelter was unloaded outside his gate and there seen by an inspector from the Barnet District Gas and Water Company.

The inspector called at the house and left a form which told Mr. Gates that he must pay for the water.

The estimated charge is five or six shillings.

Mrs. Gates told the *Daily Mirror*: "I am furious. We pay 3s. 1d. a quarter water rate and now it seems that we must pay more than half a quarter extra.

To Use Bath Water

"I have decided to save all the water from baths and on washing day. In this way I hope to be able to avoid paying the extra.

"It is an imposition. We are doing only what the Government advises in building a shelter. I have a schoolboy son and as an invalid mother to think of and I want them to be safe."

The cost of this home-built shelter will be about £6.

In this district there are stated to be more than 400 people entitled to Anderson shelters who have not yet received them.

Mr. J. F. Hazeldine, general manager of the Barnet District Gas and Water Company, told the *Daily Mirror*: "It is customary to charge for water used for purposes other than domestic. We charge a minimum of 5s."

BOMBER SINKS YACHT—1 KILLED

The patrol yacht *Warrior II* (Captain A. E. Johnston, R.N.) has been sunk by an enemy bomber in the English Channel.

"One rating was killed," the Admiralty stated last night, "and his next-of-kin has been informed. The remainder of the crew have been landed safely."

U.S. WILL SEND EQUIPMENT FOR DUTCH TROOPS HERE

All Dutchmen in Great Britain, between the ages of twenty and thirty-five, who had to register for military service, will shortly be called up for training, it was stated yesterday in well-informed Dutch circles. Calling up notices will be issued in the first week of August.

The Dutch authorities have ordered the most modern military equipment from America.

The Dutch troops will wear British battle-dress with an orange line and the word "Netherlands" on the sleeve. This is to prevent the confusion that might be caused by uniforms not familiar to the public.

Some of the remains of a Heinkel III bomber which finished its career on a south coast beach. Thanks to the R.A.F.!

A WATER company inspector saw air raid shelter materials lying outside a house.

He promptly handed in a demand for payment for the

ICING BAN DATE FIXED

MAKING of iced cakes, cream buns, eclairs and similar confectionery is banned after August 5.

The date was announced last night by the Ministry of Food. It will be an offence to place sugar on the exterior of any cake, biscuit, bun, pastry, scone, bread, roll or similar article, after baking.

Glucose and fondant are included in the term "sugar," but not chocolate.

These banned goods, made before August 5, may be sold up to September 2.

This order does not ban the use on cakes of jam, jelly or lemon and other fruit curd. But it does ban butter cream, marshmallow, chocolate fondant, almond paste, and marzipan.

Chipolata Sausages

Up Penny a Pound

PRICES of chipolata and cocktail sausages may be increased by a penny a pound from Monday. The same order says that in future pork sausages must comprise at least 90 per cent. of pork meat.

Maximum wholesale price of Grade "C" beef sausages will be 5½d. per lb. Kosher sausages retail prices will be: Grade "C," 10d. per lb.; Grade "B," 1s. 2d. per lb.; Grade "A," 1s. 4d. per lb.

TWINS BORN IN A.R.P. POST

When Mrs. Alice L. Sabine, aged forty-two, of Bowles-road, Camberwell, S.E., was rescued from a fire-endangered house at midnight, she took refuge in a neighbour's house.

She had to leave there as the flames were spreading, and went to an A.R.P. post two streets away. In the office of the A.R.P. post she gave birth to twins, a boy and a girl.

Children to Stay in England

IN view of the fate of the *Arandora Star*, the Government cannot take the responsibility of sending shiploads of children from the country without convoy.

Therefore the Government scheme for evacuating children to the Dominions and America is postponed.

There is ample shipping available—but owing to the great demands made on the Admiralty, there are not sufficient naval vessels left free to convoy the children's ships.

Americans in England have cabled asking that U.S. ships be sent to take the children overseas.

But meanwhile children sent over the Atlantic outside of the Government scheme go at their parents' risk, or at the risk of voluntary associations which arranged the transport.

This situation was revealed by the Ministry of Information.

It raises once more a vital question about the French Fleet.

The *Arandora Star*, taking enemy aliens to Canada, was torpedoed by a German submarine.

The Germans intend to intensify submarine action.

And the question is: Where are France's submarines?

Mr. Churchill has failed in his speeches to account for the total of these craft.

So has Mr. A. V. Alexander, the First Lord.

Now Mr. Chamberlain is to make a statement—on Tuesday—about the sea evacuation.

Will HE answer the question: Where are the French submarines?

RAF STRIKE BACK IN STORM

THE R.A.F., while fighting brilliantly in defence of Britain, are defying summer hail and snowstorms to keep up their offensive against targets in Germany.

Eleven enemy raiders were brought down yesterday, making seventy-one in three days.

And as these new defence successes were announced last night, details of the latest R.A.F. night attacks on enemy targets were also revealed.

Roaring through storms of rain, hail and snow, our bombers struck deep into Germany.

Munition works at Ludwigshaven and near Cologne were bombed by the light of parachute flares. Blast furnaces at Siegburg, fourteen miles from Cologne, were attacked with heavy-calibre bombs.

At Mutterstadt a low-level attack on a large factory produced big explosions and a blaze.

Just after midnight a bomber raided the docks at Bremen. Buildings were hit and a large fire started.

Two-Hour Attack

The plane had part of one airscrew shot off by A.A. fire, but finished the job—and got back.

Another night raider, penetrating 300 miles into enemy territory, successfully attacked a large factory building on the fringe of Strasbourg, in southern Germany.

Salvos of bombs straddled the target and after two large warehouses had been hit the raider's crew watched a continuous series of explosions.

When these R.A.F. men were sixty miles away on the homeward course they could still see a huge blaze.

For two hours, waves of our bombers attacked the Rotterdam airport with high explosive bombs. More than a hundred bombs were dropped on the air base at Texel.

These big and widespread blows at Germany cost three British planes. The Germans themselves lost eleven.

Continued on Back Page

SAW FIGHT JOINED IN

AN Anson reconnaissance aircraft of the Coastal Command, on convoy duty, spotted a fight between some Spitfires and German bombers yesterday, joined in and brought a bomber down.

The Anson, a hundred miles an hour slower than the Spitfires, fastened on to a German bomber, twisted and turned and nearly collided with it, and eventually sent it crashing down into the sea.

While escorting a convoy the Anson pilot sighted three Heinkel 111's preparing to attack the bombers, and at 6,000ft. he found six more Heinkels. Then the Spitfires appeared. The Heinkels, pursued by the British fighters, sped past the Anson, which, however, was able to get on the tail of one of the bombers.

"I did not like the idea of this Heinkel getting away," the pilot said afterwards.

Relief if Home is Left Voluntarily

Even if you voluntarily evacuate your home in a defence area, you will still be entitled to a rent and debt "holiday," writes the *Daily Mirror*'s Political correspondent.

Voluntary evacuees will be on the same footing as those ordered to leave. Hundreds of householders in coastal districts are affected.

The concession does not apply to people who leave homes situated outside the defence zones.

CADBURY'S PRICES

The prices of the three following lines have been slightly increased.

New prices are:—

MILK CHOCOLATE
4 oz 4½d · 8 oz 9d

MILK BRAZIL NUT
4 oz 5½d · 8 oz 11d

MILK TRAY ASSORTMENT
6½d per qtr. (loose)
1 lb box 2/4 ½ lb box 1/2
¼ lb box 7d

Lines and packings not mentioned in this list remain unchanged in price

e.g. All 2d Blocks, Bournville Chocolate, Whole Nut, and Fruit and Nut Chocolates, Filled Blocks, Roses and Vogue Assortments, Bournville Cocoa, Bourn-vita and Chocolate Biscuits.

All Cadbury's prices are based on careful costings and will only be changed as costs demand.

Cadbury Bros. Ld

DAILY MIRROR, Friday, July 19, 1940.

Daily Mirror

No. 11,433   ONE PENNY
Registered at the G.P.O. as a Newspaper.

PLANS TO BEAT WINTER WITH New Loaf, Sugar and Tea

BRITAIN has food plans to beat the war strain of the winter.

Rations of tea, sugar and even fats are likely to be increased for the cold, dark months.

A new "fortified" bread will revolutionise and increase nutrition. The energy-producing Vitamin B 1, plus calcium, to provide stamina and build bone in children, is to be introduced into white flour.

Meat supplies at reasonable prices will be kept up—"because people like meat, it makes them happy."

There will be more communal feeding. There is to be a survey of factories to find out where it is needed.

Announcing this in the House of Commons last evening, Mr. Robert Boothby, Parliamentary Secretary to the Ministry of Food, said:—

"We are going to fortify white flour with vitamin B1, and a small quantity of calcium salt will be introduced into the loaf.

"It will be some months before there is a sufficient supply of bone to fortify the entire bread supply.

"When that time arrives the public will be given the choice of fortified white bread, or high extraction wholemeal bread at the same price, and each consumer will be free to buy the kind of bread he wishes.

Definite Hope

"This is an unprecedented and revolutionary step.

"It will attract world wide attention and, in conjunction with the milk scheme, lay the foundations of a nutrition policy which will not only have a beneficial effect on the health of our people, but be hailed by scientists all over the world as a great advance on anything hitherto achieved in this field."

He held out this definite hope.

"If, as we confidently expect, the enemy's threatened attack in the next two or three months is defeated, our supply position should enable us to increase the distribution of tea and sugar, and, perhaps, even of fats, during the winter months."

Dearer Potatoes

But he said that the country's switch to greater home production had meant rising costs.

The public must be prepared to face increases in the price of potatoes, milk, eggs and home-produced beef and mutton.

Mr. Boothby said we now had enough cereal feeding stuffs to last several months "even in the unfortunate and unexpected event of heavy losses at sea."

Mr. Banfield asked the Minister to reconsider the restriction of sugar icing for bride cakes. "It's a serious matter for some of these girls getting married," he said.

An appeal to increase the tea ration was made by Mr. Rhys Davies.

Mr. Boothby said he knew the tea ration pressed hardly upon many classes. "I wish the general public to bear it with fortitude for the next few critical weeks. Then we hope to increase it before the winter begins," he added.

SECRET DEBATE FOR LORDS

The House of Lords will hold a secret session next Wednesday. The debate will be on foreign affairs.

Miss Hannah (Nona) Rees, who has married Sir J. P. F. Mansel, Bart., was at one time a maid at the baronet's home.

GIRLS FOR R.A.F.

WOMEN, aged from eighteen to thirty-five, "able to work under pressure without getting rattled," are wanted as radio operators by the R.A.F.

Pay is 1s. 4d. a day while under training, and 2s. 2d. a day when trained.

Though the women radio operators will not have to fly, they will release large numbers of R.A.F. radio operators for other duties.

"We want women of education and intelligence," an Air Ministry official told the *Daily Mirror*. "They need not be experienced because we shall train them.

"The main qualification sought is that applicants shall be coolheaded and able to carry on with their work in all circumstances.

"There are already some women radio operators in the R.A.F. We need more. Good sight is essential."

TO RULE DISPUTES

A statement on the constitution of the new national tribunal to be set up by the Minister of Labour to deal with disputes on wages, hours and conditions in wartime is likely to be issued tonight.

Any disputes and applications for wage increases which are still outstanding will have to be referred to arbitration, and decisions given by the proposed national arbitration tribunal will be binding on the employers and the unions and the workmen.

Nazis 'Invade' Spain

The Germans are now "invading" Spain.

Americans who arrived home from Europe yesterday said uniformed Nazis had trickled into nearly every part of Spain.

German military officers and soldiers were over-running Barcelona and crowding the hotels in Bilbao, where the influx of Germans is said to be so great that "Americans were forced to live in boarding-houses or sleep on board ship."—Reuter.

BARONET WEDS MAID

THE wedding of a baronet to a girl who worked as a barmaid at his sister's public house, and was afterwards a maid at his manor, was revealed yesterday.

The bridegroom was Sir John Philip Ferdinand Mansel, Bart., of Maesycrugiau Manor, Carmarthenshire, Wales, and the bride Miss Hannah (Nona) Rees, twenty, a farmer's daughter.

The bride was a barmaid at the Beehive Inn, Pencader, when Sir John met her. The Beehive is kept by his sister, who married eight years ago Mr. David Jones, an omnibus proprietor and greyhound owner.

Lady Mansel was at the Beehive Inn last night.

It is understood that Sir John, who is twenty-nine, is joining the Army this week as a private.

Parents' Blessing

Mr. D. Rees, a brother of the bride, who works for a local bus company, told the *Daily Mirror*:—

"My sister was employed at the manor until about twelve months ago. Then she left and has been living at home with my people."

Miss Maggie Rees said: "My mother and father approved of the marriage and gave Sir John and my sister their blessing."

The bridegroom is the elder son of the late Sir Courtenay Mansel, and the bride is the daughter of Mr. and Mrs. Ben Rees, of Cwmhuplyn, Pencader. Mr. Rees is a district councillor

Bridal Party of Four

Mr. Rees opposed Lady Mansel in a County Council election some years ago.

The bridal party consisted of four people. The bride had as bridesmaid her sister, Miss Mattie Rees, and the bridegroom was accompanied by Mr. Samuel Rees, of Market House Hotel, Carmarthen, who was best man.

After the ceremony Sir John and Lady Mansel left for Cardigan for their honeymoon.

In addition to property at Maesycrugiau, Sir John owns considerable property in Swansea, including the Manselton estate.

CONSCRIPT DOCTORS

DOCTORS may be ordered to perform any services specified by the Minister of Labour and National Service as necessary to secure adequate medical staff for hospitals or other public purposes, it was announced last night.

For the present directions will normally be given only to doctors within the first two years after their first qualification.

It is expected that essential posts will be staffed in most cases on a voluntary basis and that only in a small number of cases will compulsory powers have to be exercised.

STAY, SAYS PREMIER

MR. CHURCHILL told the House of Commons yesterday that he did not think the military situation required "anything in the nature of a large-scale exodus from this country."

He also said such an exodus was most undesirable.

His views are apparently not shared by some of his Ministers. They sent their own children over the Atlantic.

One of these Ministers, the *Daily Mirror* learned yesterday, is Mr. Richard Law, Financial Secretary to the War Office, who has evacuated his two sons to America.

His American-born wife has gone with the children "to see them settled in her mother's home; after which she will return," it is stated.

The Prime Minister said that the Government would make sure that in the use made of offers of hospitality from the Dominions and the U.S.A. the rich would secure no advantage—"if advantage there be"—over the poor.

Any further emigration that might
Contd. on Back Page, Col. 2

'Special Drene Shampoo is first with me every time!'
says
JEAN GILLIE
Rising young Star of Screen and Stage.

"I find that a shampoo with Special Drene fills my hair with glorious highlights and fresh loveliness. It's a very thrifty glamour-aid, too—very little for an abundant lather—no special rinses. Also, my hairdresser says Drene makes waves last longer. I shall always insist on Special Drene Shampoo"

GLAMOROUS HAIR CAN BE YOURS TOO ... WHEN YOU USE

SPECIAL
drene
SHAMPOO
6d., 1/6 & 2/6

Daily Mirror

JULY 20

No. 11,424 — ONE PENNY
Registered at the G.P.O. as a Newspaper.

Lieutenant-General Sir Alan Brooke with Mr. Winston Churchill during an inspection of Southern Command defences. Another picture of Mr. Churchill's tour in middle pages.

DUNKIRK FIGHTER NEW C-IN-C

HITLER SAYS SUBMIT

HITLER gave Britain an ultimatum last night. "Talk peace or I destroy you." As he piled threat on threat he called it his final appeal to reason.

He made not a single concrete proposal. He spoke to Britain in the way he has spoken to every country he planned to make a Nazi vassal—as a reasonable man of peace.

Despite the war aims announced by his Press and other Nazi leaders, he declared he had never desired the destruction of the British Empire. He said he was still sad that he had not reached an agreement with Britain.

"There are no grounds for the prolongation of the war," he said. Then he proceeded to threaten.

"British statesmen probably have no real conception of what it will mean once the German offensive begins in earnest against the British Isles.

"What is coming will visit the British people, not Churchill, who will probably go to Canada. He may think the outcome will be the annihilation of Germany, but it will be the destruction of a great world Empire."

Preparing the way for a threat of air attack, he used the claim, repeatedly refuted, that the R.A.F. was bombing German civilians.

"Thus far," he said, "I have hardly answered this bombardment. But when my answer comes, it will be terrible for millions of people."

"My Conscience..."

Then he spoke "as a victor appealing for common sense."

"In this hour I consider it my duty to relieve my conscience and to direct my last appeal to England," he said. "This time, I think, I shall be believed, as I am not the defeated who is begging.

"Churchill could, of course, cry to the world that again I am afraid. Anyway, I have relieved my conscience towards the things which are to come."

He declared: "This war can end only with the destruction of England or Germany. I know it will be England."

He opened a ninety-six minute speech to the Reichstag — where Hess sat in a place of honour — by going over all the old arguments about the hardships of the Versailles Treaty.

He argued that he had never been the aggressor. Despite the seizure of Czechoslovakia and the attack on

Contd. on Back Page, Col. 2

EVACUEES ARE STRANDED NOW

Mr. F. C. Blair, Canadian Director of Immigration, revealed yesterday that several hundred persons, including some children with adults from Britain, were stranded in Canada because friends and relatives who had invited them were falling in their obligations.

These friends had not realised their financial responsibilities as money could not be imported.

A liner arrived yesterday with more than 150 British children. — Reuter.

—LAUNCHES BIG AIR ATTACK

MORE than 150 German planes — bombers and Messerschmitts — were fought off by British fighters on the South-East Coast yesterday in Hitler's biggest air raid on Britain.

Four German bombers and seven fighters were brought down. Five British fighters are missing.

The first big battle took place about noon, when nearly seventy German raiders attempted to bomb a convoy.

Sighting a formation of about twenty Messerschmitt 109 fighters the British pilots each singled out a Nazi machine and attacked. Two of the Messerschmitt 109s were shot down, one diving into the sea in flames.

The third Messerschmitt 109 was hit by one Hurricane pilot and then attacked by another Hurricane, which fired several hundred rounds of machine-gun bullets into it at close range.

In the second action, which took place during the afternoon, more than fifty German bombers and fighters attempted to raid a south coast harbour. Six patrolling Hurricanes split up to engage the enemy.

Three, however, were immediately attacked by twelve Messerschmitts and the three other Hurricane pilots counter-attacked.

A sergeant-pilot, diving after a Messerschmitt, found himself in the middle of a formation of about ten Junkers 87 dive-bombers, but he shot one down.

Three Spitfires chased two other Messerschmitts. Their reports state: "Fired three two-seconds bursts. Enemy went down."

Two Spitfire pilots saw twelve Messerschmitts at 13,000ft. In spite of the fact that they were outnumbered six to one, the Spitfire pilots dived to attack.

One chased his Messerschmitt down to 3,000ft., but had to break off the engagement when another Messerschmitt 109 got on his tail.

Turning about, the British pilot attacked the newcomer head on, and the Messerschmitt was set on fire.

As the opposing fighter smashed by each other, their wing tips touched. The Spitfire pilot felt his machine shudder, and is confident that the Messerschmitt crashed into the sea.

A German plane which appeared over a South-West England village yesterday afternoon dropped ten bombs, one of which damaged a council school.

We Answer: 'To Hell...'

LAST night Britain sent her reply to Hitler through the B.B.C. in German.

Said the announcer: "Well, Herr Hitler, in your marvellous speech you have appealed to our feelings in order to stop the war against you. Is it the first time that you have put forward such a proposal? We recall all your assurances, from the one you made at Munich to the last pledge over Holland and Belgium, and we really cannot take you seriously.

"To hell with all your lies. We reject your appeal from our own will, and because of our responsibility towards the world."

BRITAIN has a new Commander-in-Chief, Home Forces — a man who has had "front line" experience in Flanders and France against Hitler's war machine.

He is Lieutenant-General Sir Alan Brooke — who is given the rank of acting General — a tank and gun expert who led the Second Corps of the B.E.F. He succeeds General Sir Edmund Ironside as chief of the nation's defence.

General Ironside is appointed Field Marshal. He remains on the active list, and will be available for consultation or command.

General Gort, who was Commander-in-Chief of the B.E.F., is now made Inspector-General of the Forces for Training.

To the post vacated by General Brooke — that of General Officer Commanding-in-Chief, Southern Command — is promoted another officer who has had first-hand experience of Hitler's forces.

57 Next Week

This is Lieutenant-General C. J. E. Auchinleck, who commanded the Allied forces in the Narvik fighting. General Brooke will be fifty-seven next Tuesday.

His appointment means that it is now considered essential to place the command of the Home Forces in the hands of a man who has had first hand experience in France and Belgium in this war.

He was in the Dunkirk rearguard fighting while commanding the Second Army Corps with the B.E.F., and he was knighted for the work he performed in this brilliant military feat.

General Brooke is regarded as the Army's greatest expert on gunnery and mechanised warfare.

"The Wizard"

He has earned the nickname of "Wizard."

During the last war he invented the "barrage map," which came into common use for directing artillery fire.

In recent years he has been commandant of the School of Artillery, Inspector of Artillery, Director of Military Training, and Commandant of the Mobile Division.

In July, 1938, he was appointed to command the Anti-Aircraft Corps. He had to prepare to meet the autumn crisis with a comparatively small force, not sufficiently supplied with guns and searchlights.

Sir Alan was mentioned in dispatches five times during the last war and awarded the D.S.O. and bar, and Belgian Croix de Guerre.

Sir Alan is one of the Northern Ireland family of "Fighting Brookes."

Northern Ireland has now pro-

Contd. on Back Page, Col. 1

ADMIRAL ABRIAL FREED

The French Admiral Abrial, hero of the Dunkirk evacuation, has been freed by the Germans at the request of the French Government, and appointed Governor-General of Algeria in succession to M. Lebeau, it was announced last night, says Associated Press.

RED WAR GAMES

RUSSIAN submarines will take part in exercises in the Pacific according to an announcement by the Commissariat of Navy, broadcast from Moscow last night.

The exercises will extend to all the shores and rivers of the Soviet Union.

The Red Fleet will also take part in the manoeuvres which will begin on Russia's navy day, July 28, and will be "the nearest fleet to real war." Landings and defence against landings will be made in the Baltic, where air units will attempt attacks.

THIS SUMMER ERROR SETS CHILDREN BACK

SUMMER ought to be the time when children are building up their resistance to the ills of next winter. Unfortunately, because of a natural error, they frequently arrive at the beginning of winter much less fit than they should be.

Some mothers think that in warm weather it is wise to make the children's diet far less rich in nourishment. Actually the very opposite is true.

MORE NOURISHMENT — NOT LESS

Long summer days take far more out of children than those cold days of which so much is spent indoors during winter. Unless the extra energy burnt up is replaced by extra nourishment in food, their health is bound to suffer.

NOURISHING AND DELICIOUS

In summer, children often cannot face heavy food. So Bournville Cocoa, light, packed with energy and *delicious*, is a boon to harassed mothers. It is nourishing by itself. Its delightful flavour makes such a splendid food as milk — about which some children are difficult — into an eagerly sought-for treat. Make Bournville your summer stand-by.

Remember, as a bed-time drink Bournville is exactly the kind that doctors advise because it is so easy to digest. Try some to-night yourself.

Still **6d** PER QTR. LB
11½ PER HALF LB

CADBURY'S BOURNVILLE COCOA
A cup of cocoa is a cup of food

Daily Mirror

DAILY MIRROR, Wednesday, July 24, 1940

No. 11,427 — ONE PENNY
Registered at the G.P.O. as a Newspaper.

HOW YOUR TAX WILL BE STOPPED OFF PAY

I WON'T—MINISTER TO M.P.s

SIR JOHN ANDERSON, Minister for Home Security, refused in Parliament last night to promise discussion of every amendment which might be made concerning civil Courts under the Emergency Powers (Defence) No. 2 Bill.

"I cannot and I will not," he said.

"It would be absurd, he said, to give an assurance so absolutely rigid and formal as that.

"If assurances such as he had given were not to be accepted in the spirit in which they were given, it was going to be very difficult to give any assurance at all.

Put Him In His Place

Mr. A. Bevan (Ebbw Vale) moved amendments with the object of ensuring that the Home Secretary should embody all that he wanted in the first set of regulations to be made under the Bill.

If the Home Secretary desired to issue more regulations he should come to the House for power to do so.

The House at the earliest possible moment should reassume its power over the Home Secretary in regard to the Bill.

The Home Secretary had no right on account of recent events to ask the House to give him these powers in perpetuity.

Mr. Silverman (Nelson and Colne) said the Government was asking the House to give by blank cheque power over the life and liberty of every citizen by executive action without limitation or review of any kind.

The Home Secretary, replying to Mr. Shinwell, said that if he undertook to discuss a body of regulations with members of the House and if, as a result of discussion, certain understandings were arrived at, he would not regard it as honourable subsequently to make regulations involving departure from those understandings without further consultation.

The amendments were withdrawn.

"Enemy Action"

Earlier, Sir John had stated that "enemy action" under the Bill means not only invasion, but exceptionally heavy aerial bombardment which might bring about turmoil and confusion.

He moved the first of six amendments of a declaratory character designed to give effect to a promise he made during the second reading that words would be inserted to make it clear that the Government's intention was that there should be set up, if necessary under the civil law, courts of a special but not of a military character.

The amendment was agreed to.

PREMIER SEES KING

The King received the Prime Minister in audience at Buckingham Palace last night. Mr. Churchill remained with the King for about half-an-hour. The King also received Air Chief Marshal Sir Cyril Newall, Chief of the Air Staff.

Pointing to the place where she saw a German plane crash is fifteen-year-old Betty Brown, daughter of a south-east coast farmer. With her is Mr. Westwood. Together they ran to the plane and disarmed the Nazi airmen.

Betty Brown is the girl whose story is told on page 6.

DALADIER TO BE TRIED

THE responsibility of M. Daladier, former French Premier, and three members of his Cabinet for the declaration of war against Germany is to be considered by the courts, it was announced by the Petain Government last night.

The three Ministers indicted with him are M. Yvon Delbos, former Foreign Minister, M. Campinchi, ex-Minister for the Navy, and M. Mandel, ex-Minister for Colonies.

M. Daladier arrived at Marseilles yesterday from French Morocco with a number of French Deputies. They were ordered not to leave the city.

Three other ex-Ministers and a member of the Chamber of Deputies are also to be tried by court-martial on charges of abandoning their posts. They had been mobilised, and are stated to have left Bordeaux on June 24 for Casablanca without authority. They will be tried as military deserters.

The Petain Cabinet has also approved a decree for the withdrawal of French citizenship and confiscation of property of all Frenchmen who left France between May 10 and June 30 "without valid reason."—Associated Press and British United Press.

INCOME TAX

Standard rate raised to 8s. 6d. in £.
Smaller rate of 3s. 9d. on first £165 of taxable income raised to 5s.

SURTAX

Rate starts at 2s. on incomes over £2,000, which means that out of every £ over £2,000 the State will get 10s. 6d.
On every £ over £20,000 the State takes 18s.

BEER

Extra 1d. a pint.

TOBACCO

Extra 2s. a lb. This means another ½d. on a packet of ten cigarettes, and 1½d. an ounce on all tobaccos.

ENTERTAINMENT

Prices of seats go up on October 6.
CINEMAS.—The rise in the price of seats "will not be alarming," it was stated last night. Many "sixpennies" will have to go.
THEATRES.— Increases will be graded according to districts. A London West End manager said it might be possible to retain the 1s. 6d. gallery seat.

LUXURIES, ETC.

Twenty-four per cent. on retail prices of :
Cosmetics, toilet preparations, furs, jewellery, haberdashery, furniture, real silk articles, lace, china and porcelain, cut glass ware, fancy goods.
Twelve per cent. on retail prices of :
Clothing and boots and shoes (not children's), medicine and drugs (except exempt kinds), newspapers, periodicals, books, certain household goods such as saucepans and "hollowware" generally.
NO TAX ON: Fuel, electricity, gas, water, etc., children's clothing and boots and shoes.

WHAT YOU'LL PAY

THIS is what you will have to pay in income tax under the new rate, compared with the present charge.

SINGLE PERSONS

Earned Income £	Present charge £ s.	New charge £ s.
200	12 10	16 13
250	20 6	27 1
300	28 2	37 10
400	56 11	78 5
500	87 16	105 14
600	119 1	142 1
1,000	244 5	282 15

MARRIED COUPLES—No children

£	£ s.	£ s.
225	2 5	4 7
250	7 3	9 11
300	15 0	20 0
400	30 12	40 16
500	61 11	75 19
600	92 16	111 7
700	124 1	146 15
800	155 6	182 4
1,000	217 16	253 0

MARRIED COUPLES—One child

Earned Income £	Present charge £ s.	New charge £ s.
300	5 12	7 10
350	13 8	17 18
400	21 5	28 6
500	43 16	54 14
600	74 1	90 2
700	105 6	125 10
800	136 11	160 19
1,000	199 1	231 15

MARRIED COUPLES—Two children

£	£ s.	£ s.
350	4 1	5 8
400	11 17	15 16
500	27 10	36 13
600	55 6	68 17
700	86 11	104 5
800	117 16	139 14
1,000	180 6	210 10

MARRIED COUPLES—Three children

£	£ s.	£ s.
400	2 10	3 6
500	18 2	24 3
600	35 11	47 12
700	67 16	83 6
800	99 1	118 19
1,000	161 11	189 5

TO gear up Britain's war effort still further, your income is cut and your spending controlled by the new War Budget introduced yesterday.

You pay more income tax—standard rate is raised to 8s. 6d.—and more for tobacco, beer and amusements.

But the Government removed one big worry for millions by making it compulsory to deduct income tax from wages and salaries before they are paid out. This applies to everybody, from mechanics to company directors.

This is how the system will work:—

You will fill in your assessment form as usual. Then the tax authorities will tell your employer how much you have to pay.

The employer will deduct this sum in equal instalments from your wages —weekly or monthly—and pay it to the authorities.

No Secrets Disclosed

No secrets will be disclosed to your employer. If you have other sources of income he will not be told about them.

Nor will any family details be revealed.

The new method will probably start in January.

The new taxation will raise an extra £239,000,000 toward the cost of the war—£57,000,000 a week at the moment.

The Chancellor, Sir Kingsley Wood, said that extra taxation had to be laid on all classes.

And although the old Purchase Tax had been dropped, the war effort demanded a brake on personal spending.

This was to be done partly by a higher income tax, and partly by graded taxes on luxuries and other goods.

The Chancellor said that this Budget was only an interim one both for direct and indirect taxation.

The *Daily Mirror* political correspondent states: I learn that another Budget is expected before December. Income tax is likely to go up to 9s. 6d. or 10s. within the next twelve months.

Chancellor's Speech: Page 11.

SOLDIERS LEFT OUT

Regret that no concession had been made to soldiers in the matter of postage and the tobacco duty was expressed during the Budget debate by Mr. Lipson (Ind., Cheltenham).

If nothing was done, the Chancellor would be faced with an overwhelming demand for an increase in soldiers' pay, he said.

Insomnia

Genasprin soothes QUICKLY —time it!

'Genasprin' gives you deep sleep quickly. It is pure. It disintegrates in a second. It cannot upset your digestion or your heart. Doctors recommend it.

Sold only by qualified chemists.
3d., 6d., 1/3, 2/- and 3/6.

At every time of strain or pain 'GENASPRIN' sees you through

DAILY MIRROR, Friday, July 26, 1940.

Daily Mirror

JULY 26

No. 11,429 — ONE PENNY
Registered at the G.P.O. as a Newspaper.

KISSED BY NAZI FLYER

A GERMAN airman of eighteen landed by parachute last night—and kissed a maid's hand.

This is how it happened....

The raid was over a south-wester district. The maid, Mavis Young, nineteen, was sheltering in a dug-out when she remembered that she had left a gas-iron on. Ignoring machine-gun fire and explosions, she left the shelter to turn off the iron. Then the airman landed almost beside her.

He was one of a bomber crew of four. One was killed and the others taken prisoner.

Mrs. le Bailly, wife of Major R. F. le Bailly, said: "I had told Mavis and her brother Roy, the gardener's boy, that they had better go into the shelter and then I went indoors to tell my husband.

"As I came out I saw the airman come down almost on the sundial, outside the dining-room window.

"The maid and the boy followed me as I approached the airman.

"He was shaken. He was only about eighteen, and a good-looking boy.

"My maid and the gardener's boy helped to prop him up against the wall, and I sent the maid for some whisky.

"She brought it and gave it to the airman. He could not drink at first, but Mavis put her hand behind his head and forced the whisky down his throat.

"He said 'Thank you,' and took hold of her hand and kissed it.

"He really was very grateful.

"Mr. Weston, the schoolmaster—the school is opposite us—took charge of him. I telephoned the police and told them what had happened.

"Mavis belongs to the district. She is nineteen, and a very sensible girl. She was not unduly excited at the experience."

Captain F. E. B. Guise, platoon commander in the Home Guard, said he and his men saw the bomber coming down with the starboard engine shot away.

Four men leaped from the plane. The parachutes of three opened. The fourth, however, dropped like a stone. His body was found later.

One of the airmen, said Captain Guise, came down in a field near a bridge, and was arrested by one of the Home Guard.

The airman was very shaky, and

Contd. on Back Page, Col. 1

★ ★ ★

20 Enemy Planes Down

Twenty enemy aircraft—eleven bombers and nine fighters—were brought down yesterday by R.A.F. fighters in a series of battles off our shores, it was announced by the Air Ministry this morning.

In the day's operations five of our fighters were lost, but the pilots of two of these are known to be safe.

An Admiralty communique, issued late last night, announced that H.M. trawlers Kingston Galena (Skipper S. Jackson, R.N.R.) and Rodino (Temporary Skipper J. C. Winning, R.N.R.) have been lost as the result of enemy air attack.

A SEAMAN, thrown into the water when the Lancastria went down, found himself near a soldier who was still wearing his tin hat, and the following "conversation" followed:

Soldier: Can you swim, mate?
Sailor: No, can you?
"No. (Brief pause.) What shall I do with my tin hat?"
"Get rid of it."
"How?"
"Hang it up."

GERMANS SANK SHIP, PROMISED SAFE PASSAGE

THE French ship Meknes, taking 1,300 French naval officers and men home from Britain, was sunk without warning by a German torpedo boat, although a safe passage had been guaranteed by the Germans.

At least 300 men lost their lives. British warships and planes rescued about 1,000 survivors.

And Berlin last night accused Britain of sinking the Meknes "to make propaganda against Germany." They declared they knew nothing about the sinking.

The Meknes had the French colours painted on both sides, and when she was torpedoed was fully lit, with a searchlight trained on the French ensign.

2 Women on Board

The survivors, including two women and a girl of five, were landed at a south coast port yesterday.

An officer said: "We were first machine-gunned by coastal motor-boats, and then a torpedo hit the ship. There was an explosion which killed several men outright. The ship went down in five to ten minutes.

"There was barely time to get the boats into the water, and hundreds jumped overboard and afterwards clung to the rafts."

An ambulance worker, who gave first aid to the injured told the "Daily Mirror": "Many of these Frenchmen are so enraged against the Germans that they no longer desire to be repatriated.

"One man said: 'I wanted to go home to see my people, but now I shall wait until after the war and I have helped this country to beat these murderers.'"

Mr. Alexander, First Lord of the Admiralty, said in the House of Commons yesterday that the French Government had been informed of our intentions to repatriate these men in French ships.

Mr. Davidson (Lab. Maryhill), addressing the Lord Privy Seal, asked: "Will every step be taken to see that the French people are fully informed of this outrage?"

"Certainly," replied Mr. Attlee.

SOLDIERS SANG AS BOMBED LINER SANK

BY A SPECIAL CORRESPONDENT

STRUGGLING for foothold on the side of a 16,000-ton British troopship as she lay half-capsized after a bomb attack, scores of veterans of the Auxiliary Military Pioneer Corps—the "Thin Red Line"—laughed in the face of death and went down with the ship, a song on their lips.

Smiling as he watched them stood an immaculate British officer, coolly smoking a cigarette. He could not swim. He went down with them.

As enemy planes circled over the sinking vessel, a soldier with a Bren gun blazed away at them from the tilting deck until he was waist deep in water. He was swept away by the sea.

This valour was shown in the loss of the Lancastria, famous old Cunarder, sunk at anchor off St. Nazaire, in the Bay of Biscay, after taking aboard B.E.F. men, and women and child refugees from France.

Crammed in the liner were 5,000 troops and refugees, plus a crew of 300. There are 2,823 people missing, it was stated last night, the first time the full story was revealed.

Some of those missing may have been able to reach the shore.

Eight enemy bombers attacked the liner, and some survivors believe the planes were Italian.

At first they missed.

Machine-Gunned Them

The soldiers were so tightly packed that they could not move. But they jeered at the enemy airmen.

But the machines came back and a salvo hit the Lancastria.

She listed heavily, making it difficult to get the boats launched. Then she capsized and sank half an hour after being hit.

The discipline aboard the ship during that half-hour was perfect.

The soldiers pressed back to form an alleyway for the women and children to reach the boats.

Then came the order: "Every man for himself."

One of the crew said: "The sea was almost a solid mass of men clinging together life flies, covered with thick oil.

"There were women and children struggling for their lives, too.

"Yet those aeroplanes roared down and machine-gunned the people in the water.

"Some of the airmen seemed to be taking photographs of the terrible scene.

"Badly wounded men were floating in their life-jackets. Many of these life-jackets became empty."

"A Grand Lad"

A company sergeant-major of the Auxiliary Military Pioneer Corps told me:—

"I gave the order to man the hosepipes, for smoke was coming up the hatch. It was impossible to obey, because the troops were jammed so tight in the alleyways.

"Just then the ship gave a sudden lurch to port till she was listing at an angle of 45 degrees. We were thrown off our feet.

"From the bridge came the order: 'Every man for himself,' and I chucked hatchboards over the side to act as rafts when we got into the water. By this time the ship was

Contd. on Back Page, Col. 2

WHY?

THE first news of the sinking of the Lancastria was published in America.

It came to the British public in cables from New York.

The British Government, forced at last into the open, allowed these cables to pass the Censor, and later—sixteen hours later!—issued a statement of their own.

For this final burst of speed we are grateful, but had the story not appeared in the American Press you would still be without an official account; you would still be hearing and repeating and embellishing the rumours so many of you have already heard.

Why this official secrecy, this censorship, this suppression of news known to the 2,477 survivors? For even the secrecy ex-

WHY?

perts in the Government will admit that the survivors knew the Lancastria had been sunk.

All 2,477 of them.

And their relatives and friends knew, and whispered it around.

And their relatives and friends spread the story in an ever-widening circle of whispered exaggeration that became wilder as it grew.

The Daily Mirror, in common with other newspapers, knew of the tragedy when it happened, but the knowledge was useless. It was stopped.

Was the suppression part of the Government's deliberate and dangerous campaign of secrecy that the Prime Minister has now, thank God, thrown over?

The public can take all the news, be it good or bad—want to take it, will insist on taking.

We hope this latest exposure will scotch for ever this mania for keeping the public in the dark.

If it does not, then the public will want to know

WHY?

KING TAKES SHELTER ON NAVAL TOUR

THE King spent ten minutes in an underground shelter yesterday during an air raid when he was making a naval tour of the south coast.

He had just finished an inspection of new recruits to the Navy at a big barracks when the raid started. The men marched off to their shelters and cheered the King as he drove slowly past them in his car to a shelter. Within a few minutes of the end of the raid the King was inspecting a factory.

'Special Drene Shampoo keeps my hair sparkling'

SAYS

JEAN COLIN

Fascinating Star of Stage and Screen.

MISS Colin goes on to say — "It's really quite miraculous how easy my hair is to set right after a shampoo with Special Drene. Moreover, no other shampoo gives my hair such thrilling, dazzling beauty. All my friends agree — Drene gives that really glamorous hair."

GLAMOROUS HAIR CAN BE YOURS TOO ... WHEN YOU USE

SPECIAL

drene

SHAMPOO

6d., 1/6 & 2/6

Daily Mirror

No. 11,430 — ONE PENNY
Registered at the G.P.O. as a Newspaper.

DAILY MIRROR, Saturday, July 27, 1940.

SEA BLITZ NEW NAZI ATTACK

THE Germans have launched a new form of sea attack.

Dive bombers are being sent into action against convoys in the English Channel to prepare the way for surface raids by motor torpedo boats.

The "spearhead assault" tactics developed in Flanders and France—with dive bombers blasting the way for tank attacks—is being adapted for a "blitz" (lightning) war at sea.

Exactly the same aeroplanes are being used, the Stuka dive-bombers.

The new sea tactics, it was revealed last night, were introduced in Thursday's raid on a British convoy in the Channel.

Stuka bombers raided the ships, then nine motor torpedo boats sped to the attack.

The enemy were routed, but not before some loss to us. The dive-bombers sank five small coasters.

Then the R.A.F. went into action, and the majority of the twenty-eight enemy planes shot down on Thursday were machines which took part in the convoy raid.

As the enemy motor torpedo boats came into attack the convoy they were sighted by two British destroyers. Immediately the raiding craft turned away, put out a smoke screen and fled.

The destroyers, with two of our own motor torpedo boats racing alongside as "escort," steamed through the smoke, their guns firing toward the enemy craft.

Then twenty Stuka bombers dived out of low clouds to attack the destroyers.

Defied Bombers

The warships manoeuvred rapidly away from each other to dodge a hail of bombs and threw out thick smoke screens. Their anti-aircraft guns drove off the aeroplanes.

They again sped in pursuit of the enemy torpedo boats—and were once more attacked by German bombers.

Water spouted hundreds of feet high beside the destroyers. Time and again watchers on the shore saw the ships' bows appear from behind a huge screen of spray. Both destroyers steamed on.

Then Spitfires swept up to fight off the enemy planes.

Both destroyers were damaged, and in one of them, the Boreas, commanded by Lieutenant-Commander M. W. Tomkinson, there were casualties.

But both ships were steaming along normally after giving up the chase.

An Admiralty communiqué last night said that the convoy which was attacked consisted of twenty-one small coasters, escorted by Navy trawlers.

Two successive waves each of thirty enemy aircraft took part in the air attack. The five vessels sunk had a total tonnage of 5,104. The five damaged—one was beached—had a total tonnage of 5,133.

This answered the German claims that eleven ships totalling 43,000 tons were sunk and further vessels totalling 12,000 tons severely damaged.

SPAIN IN SOON—ITALY

An Italian report that Spain will soon enter the war on the side of the Axis Powers was broadcast yesterday by an American radio system.

SLEEPS WITH 30,000 WASPS

DENNIS FOSS, twenty-four, of Bilford-avenue, Worcester, never feels lonely in the night. He sleeps with 30,000 wasps in his bedroom.

While spring cleaning this year his mother found a small round-shaped "something" on the ceiling of her son's bedroom. She was going to knock it off with her broom when she saw wasps buzzing in and out.

The "something" was a wasps' nest.

Dennis begged his mother not to destroy it, and the wasps, undisturbed, carried on with their building.

Their home now measures 15 inches across.

Dennis told his mother that he liked the wasps for company. He liked to wake up in the morning and watch them at work before he had to do the same.

And since discovering the nest three months ago, neither he nor his mother has suffered one wasp sting.

Keeps Windows Open

Dennis keeps his bedroom windows open night and day to allow the wasps to fly in and out. Newspapers protect the walls.

Mr. T. Bradford, an expert beekeeper, of Castlemorton, near Malvern, considers this nest inside a bedroom quite the most remarkable thing he has seen in twenty-seven years' study of bees and wasps.

He assures Mrs. Foss that the wasps will not abuse her hospitality so long as she does not interfere with them.

He estimates that the nest houses at least 30,000 wasps.

They will not disperse, he says, until November.

GAOL SHIP FOR 200 I.R.A. MEN

The Ulster Government is to intern 200 members of the I.R.A. on a ship anchored some distance from land under heavy Army guard.

The engines and inside structure of the ship will be removed, and cells will be erected in long tiers. There will be deck games.

The purchase of a ship has become necessary because the Government cannot find accommodation for the internees.

During the troubles in 1922 Ulster adopted a similar plan.

FRANCE: COLONIES QUERY

The French Government announced in Vichy yesterday that it has requested the United States to explain its attitude to the French possessions in the West Indies, especially in the event of an attack by a non-American power.—British United Press.

TELL THE TRUTH

"The Government need have no fear in trusting the people or that the morale of the nation will be lowered by knowledge of the truth.

"Our morale would be upset if we became aware that the Government were not telling us the truth or that they were suppressing important facts.

"The truth, no matter how unpalatable, will stiffen the backs of 99 out of every 100 people."

—Lord Harewood at Hull yesterday.

Now It's Not Such a Muddle

Three weeks ago I revealed the astonishing situation which was causing a bottleneck in the scrap and steel industry. Mr. Morrison, the Minister of Supply, has acted quickly. He has issued new instructions, and taken steps to deal with possible abuses in the future. Thank you, Mr. Morrison, for cutting out the Red Tape and getting facts for yourself. That is the way to get things done.—Bill Greig.

DEAR Bill Greig,—

The revelations made by the "Daily Mirror" regarding the iron and steel scrap muddle have had definite results.

On Wednesday representatives of the Independent Scrap Iron, Steel and Metal Merchants Association were invited to discuss the position with Mr. Herbert Morrison, the Minister of Supply. As a result at least the dangerous effect of monopoly of sale granted to the National Federation has been partly shattered.

In the past, as you revealed, only members of this Federation were able to sell to the steelworks, and every ton of scrap went through their books, whether collected by one of their members or not.

THIS WAS ONE OF THE CAUSES OF A "BOTTLENECK" WHICH CAUSED GREAT ALARM IN THE INDUSTRY.

Mr. Morrison gave the independent merchants a guarantee that in future they will receive the full price, and no "rake off" will be allowed. He continued:—

"I shall watch this position carefully and see that no bottleneck does arise, that the Federation really can control its members and that it is in a position to prevent any abuses or attempts at speculation.

"If I find any breach of this guarantee I shall have no hesitation in taking away the licence of the firm—no matter how big it is."

Mr. Morrison also told us that he would "tolerate no obstacle, either commercial or technical, to the free flow of scrap."

♦ ♦ ♦

The position, therefore, is greatly improved. More than 3,000 merchants in this country can now get the full price for their scrap, which was previously only obtained by the 300 members of the Federation—often in respect of metal they never saw or handled.

For this change we can thank the Daily Mirror. Before its disclosure it was impossible for merchants even to get an hearing at the Ministry. Immediately your article appeared, bringing the facts to the notice of the Minister, it was obvious that a change had taken place. Conferences were arranged, and Mr. Morrison proved only too anxious to straighten out the Muddle.

The courageous way in which you dealt with this has had its reward. There are still anomalies, and we still have grievances, but from the national view point you have done great service.—Wm. C. Parker, Vice-President, Independent Scrap Iron, Steel and Metal Merchants' Association.

4,000,000th Man Today

One of the men registering today with the 1906 class will be the four millionth to register since conscription began last year.

The numbers registering on July 6, 13 and 20 brought the total to 3,800,000. More than 300,000 will register today.

Included in the registration will be those who have reached the age of twenty since June 22.

Three more classes—the 1905, 1904 and part of the 1903—have yet to sign up under the last Royal Proclamation. No dates for these have been fixed.

The times of today's registration, according to the initial letters of surnames, are: A to B, 12.30—1 p.m.; C to E, 1—3; F to J, 2—3; K to O, 3—4; P to S, 4—5; T to Z, 5—6 p.m.

Ships Bombed Off Ulster

German aircraft has attacked shipping off the coast of Northern Ireland.

Flashes from anti-aircraft guns could be seen by watchers.

Heavy gunfire was heard from the shore.

British fighters reached the spot and one German plane is reported to have been shot down.

The attack lasted some time.

IF IT'S CHOCOLATE THEN IT'S FOOD

Cadbury's BOURNVILLE

PLAIN FLAVOUR CHOCOLATE

for quick energy

★

Bournville bucks you up — gives you an instant supply of energy when you're feeling low. This famous plain chocolate — containing sunshine Vitamin D, iron and other minerals — is also abundantly rich in carbohydrates, for quick, immediately available energy. Look for the famous red packet.

Daily Mirror

No. 11,433 — ONE PENNY
Registered at the G.P.O. as a Newspaper.

JULY 31

ARMY MEN GET VC

Captain Killed 17 Nazis

Boxer Won Last Fight

THE Army's first Victoria Crosses of this war have been won by Lieutenant (now Captain) Harald Marcus Ervine-Andrews, of the East Lancs Regiment, and the late Lance-Corporal Harry Nicholls, of the Grenadier Guards.

The captain, it was announced last night, climbed on top of a straw-roofed barn and—with a rifle and a Bren gun—fought enemy forces trying to reach Dunkirk during the evacuation.

Mortar-bombs crashed through the roof. But he held on, and killed seventeen Germans with the rifle and many more with the Bren.

Lance-Corporal Nicholls, who has since been killed in action, picked up a Bren gun and, firing from the hip as he ran, silenced three machine-guns. Four times wounded, he fought on till the enemy fell back.

He Loved a Scrap

Nicholls, twenty-five years old, ex-Army boxing champion, loved a scrap. The odds didn't matter to him (writes a *Daily Mirror* correspondent).

When Nick was in the boxing ring, the crowds knew they were going to see a real fight. Six feet tall, massively shouldered, Nicholls could hand out punishment—and take it.

Two years ago Nicholls smiled happily as he ducked under the ropes into the ring, to oppose a champion, a man who had beaten him many times before, who knew his every move.

The match was an item in a friendly annual competition. There was nothing great at stake—just the scrap.

In the first second the champion's left whipped out. Blood streamed from a deep gash above Nicholls's eye. He fought on half-blind. A grin on his face.

Wounded Four Times

At the end of the round, his seconds treated his eye. It was badly wounded. The seconds threw in the towel. Nicholls pleaded to be allowed to fight on. They wouldn't let him.

Now Nick is dead. He gave his life for his country in another fight. It was no friendly, no seconds to stop him going on, despite his wounds. Here is the official story of his last scrap:

"On May 21 Lance-Corporal Nicholls was commanding a section in the right-forward platoon of his company when the company was ordered to counter-attack.

"At the very start of the advance he was wounded in the arm by shrapnel, but continued to lead his section forward; as the company came over a small ridge the enemy opened heavy machine-gun fire at close range.

"Lance-Corporal Nicholls, realising the danger to the company, immediately seized a Bren gun and dashed forward towards the machine-guns firing from the hip. He succeeded in silencing first one machine-gun, and then two other machine-guns, in spite of being again seriously wounded.

"Lance-Corporal Nicholls then went on up to a higher piece of ground and engaged the German infantry massed behind, causing many casualties, and continuing to fire until he had no more ammunition left.

"He was wounded at least four times, but absolutely refused to give in. There is no doubt that his gallant action was instrumental in enabling his company to reach its

Contd. on Back Page, Col. 1

M.P.s HUSH IT UP

IGNORING a plea by Earl Winterton that secret [...] fair to Press and [...] ve Dr. Goebbels a chance [...] ead "wicked lies," the of Commons last night debated by 200 votes to 109—to [...] reign affairs in secret.

[...]el Wedgwood, too, declared [...] Government must not take [...]age of its vast majority to prevent public expression of criticism in [...]use any more than they could Press.

"It would be unfortunate," declared Colonel Wedgwood, "if the [...] se abdicated its duty of public [...] icism in favour of the newspapers."

[...]eeches of both M.P.s were interrupted by cries of "Divide."

The Premier had left the question [...] Secret session or public debate—to the free vote of the House.

ay What They Felt

Mr. Churchill recalled that last [...] ek the Government were led to believe that it was the wish of the House that the debate on foreign [...] airs should take place in secret.

"Thus members of all parties could say what they really felt about foreign countries without any danger of adding to the number of those countries with which we are at present at war," he said amid laughter.

The Government made arrangements for the secret session, but it appeared that some newspapers preferred that the debate should take place in public. Mr. Churchill went on:—

"We are assured that secrecy is undemocratic, especially in time of war, and that it would be wrong for M.P.s to have privileges in matters of information not enjoyed by the whole mass of the nation, and that the Government should take [...] nation and the enemy fully into [...] confidence, and let the whole world see plainly exactly how and where they stand in relation to all other countries at the present critical juncture.

Embarrassing

"The Government was now in the embarrassing position of a servant receiving contradictory orders from those whom it is their only desire to serve.

The Government had therefore found a means of giving the House an opportunity of expressing whether they should have a secret or public session, and he had also arranged that his preliminary debate could itself take place under conditions of the best publicity.

The Premier therefore moved "that remainder of this day's sitting be rest session and that strangers be

td. on Back Page, Col. 3

..THQUAKES KILL 300

ree hundred were killed and hundreds more injured in violent earthquakes in the central plateau of Anatolia, Turkey, yesterday.

[...] ve villages were destroyed, says

Lance-Corporal Harry Nicholls, one of the new V.C.s, photographed with [h]is wife and eight-month-old baby shortly before his death in May.

18, SAVED RAID VICTIMS

WHILE bombs were falling on a town in Kent, eighteen-year-old Donald Louis Jones—youngest air raid warden in his centre—coolly crawled under tons of wreckage to rescue two trapped civilians.

He knew that at any moment he might be crushed to death, but he did not hesitate.

He reached the two victims and found they were pinned down by two heavy joists which had fallen from the floor above.

There he stayed for four hours, protecting with his body the heads and faces of the trapped people from debris dislodged during the rescue operations. All that time Warden Jones knew that the heavy building material above them might collapse.

Throughout those four hours he constantly encouraged the two victims and gave directions to the rescue party.

Last night it was announced that the youth's heroism has earned him the O.B.E. Medal (Civil Division). He is the first air-raid warden to be so honoured.

"It was mainly owing to his courage and endurance that the victims were eventually released," states the *London Gazette*.

Jones, who is a troop leader in the Boy Scouts, was at work last night at an aircraft factory where he is apprenticed—turning out bombers for the R.A.F.

So secret is the work that no one could visit him to tell him what had happened.

His widowed mother, Mrs. Freda Jones, told the *Daily Mirror* last night: "He came home after the raid and told me practically nothing about it. But I found out that they had to scrape the [...] him and bath him before [...] could even recognise him. He [...]s made A.R.P. work his hobby, and as a part-time warden he is, of course, unpaid."

U.S. TO TAKE FRENCH ISLE

From JOHN WALTERS

NEW YORK, Tuesday.

THE United States are preparing to send an armed naval expeditionary force into the Caribbean Sea to occupy on behalf of all the American Republics the possessions of France, it was reported here tonight from Washington sources.

The start of the expedition only awaits ratification by delegates at the Pan-American conference at Havana.

It is understood that the move is timed for late August or early September. Ratification of the scheme by the South American nations is regarded in Washington as almost certain.

The move would mean the demilitarisation of French naval craft at the French Island of Martinique, including the aircraft carrier Bearn, on which are 100 American planes.

American forces would be assisted by Cuban, Brazilian and Argentine warships. According to the plan, the force would include three battleships, five heavy cruisers, one aircraft carrier, thirty-seven destroyers and 2,500 marines.

The aeroplanes on the Bearn, it is believed, could be brought back to the United States and resold to England.

Awarded the V.C. Captain Harald Marcus Ervine-Andrews

DAILY MIRROR, Thursday, August 1, 1940.

Daily Mirror

AUG. 1

No. 11,434 ONE PENNY
Registered at the G.P.O. as a Newspaper.

WARSHIPS CHASE SEA RAIDER

RAF BAG 240 IN JULY

At least 240 German planes were destroyed by the R.A.F. and our ground defences in July. More than 600 Nazi air officers and men have been killed or captured.

THESE Air Ministry figures, given last night, relate only to planes known for certain to be destroyed—but many others were accounted for.

The R.A.F. carried on day and night raids. Objectives in Northern France, Holland, Norway and Belgium, as well as Germany, were attacked on Tuesday with the loss of only one plane.

Two Sea Gladiator aircraft of the Fleet Air Arm intercepted three Italian Savoia 79 aircraft in the Mediterranean and shot down one of the Italian machines in flames says last night's message.

A second was badly hit and it is unlikely that this machine regained its base.

One of our Sea Gladiators made a forced landing in the sea. The pilot was picked up unhurt.

In R.A.F.'s most recent raids damage done to sidings at Ostend, to dispersed aircraft on the aerodrome at Querqueville, near Cherbourg, and to hangars and other aircraft at St. Ingiepert, Boulogne.

A dive attack was made on the Querqueville Aerodrome through a heavy barrage of anti-aircraft fire and bombs were dropped from a low level

DEFENCE PLAN IS ATTACK

MANY of Britain's road blocks are to be cleared out of the way so that our troops can take the offensive in case of an attempted invasion.

The defence situation it was stated last night, has changed. Two months ago there were comparatively few trained troops left in the country. Road blocks at points where troop-carrying planes might land became an essential precaution.

Now we have sufficient well-trained, well-equipped troops, who will attack enemy forces trying to get a foothold in Britain, and not merely man barricades.

Hence, many road blocks which would hinder quick movement and shock tactics of our soldiers are to go. And many will be reduced.

Churchill Sees Coastal Defence

"I don't know whether Hitler has missed the bus, but he won't have such a comfortable journey as he might have had a few months ago," said Mr. Churchill yesterday during a surprise visit to north-east coastal defences and to a shipyard.

Crowds cheered the Premier on his tour.

There were many examples of camouflage along the stretch of coast and the Prime Minister was interested in them all. One observer said: "If Mr. Churchill's smiles were a measure of his satisfaction, he was indeed satisfied."

At the shipyard, where he spent an hour, the workers gathered round while he spoke to them.

The country, he said, urgently needed the craft they were building. He thanked them for the great effort they were making to speed up output.

BRITISH warships were last night chasing the German raider which was damaged in a fight with H.M. armed merchant cruiser Alcantara in the South Atlantic.

The raider, reported to be a fast French merchantman seized and converted by the Germans, escaped from the Alcantara after a shot had reduced the British ship's speed.

Later, British warships were in hot pursuit of the German vessel off the Brazilian coast, stated Associated Press from Buenos Aires.

It was suggested that the warships might include Sir Henry Harwood's squadron, which smashed the Graf Spee.

The 22,181-ton Alcantara, in peacetime a Royal Mail cruise liner, mounts four guns on each broadside. She is commanded by Captain J. G. P. Ingham, R.N., who was awarded the D.S.O. for bravery in the battle of Jutland.

An Admiralty communique stated that although the enemy raider escaped destruction by the merchant cruiser's guns, she sustained damage affecting her fighting efficiency.

"Immediately on sighting the raider the Alcantara engaged," said the communique.

"On being hit the enemy at once turned away, making use of smoke floats, but she was chased by the Alcantara until a shot reduced the latter's speed, thus enabling the raider to escape.

"The damage sustained by H.M.S. Alcantara is slight. The British casualties amounted to two killed and seven wounded. The next of kin are being informed."

It was reported that a German shell hit the Alcantara's boiler-room She headed for Rio.

First news of the raider's activities came on July 19 with the arrival of forty-one survivors at St. Barthelmy, West Indies, from the British merchant ships King John and Davisian, which had been sunk

He Was at Jutland

The commander of the Alcantara, Captain Ingham, was recalled to the Navy after having been on the retired list for eighteen years. He is sixty-one.

He was in command of H.M.S. Warrior at Jutland.

His wife told the Daily Mirror last night: "I know my husband will be disappointed that the German raider got away—but he will have been glad to have got a shot at it."

Captain Ingham, whose home is at Kensington, has two children, Neville and Eleanor. Neville, who is twenty-one, has a commission in the Army.

The Admiralty also announced last night the sinking of an Italian tanker during a plane v. warship encounter in the Mediterranean.

A communique said that the Greek tanker Hermione, under charter to the Italian Government and carrying 300 tons of petrol and 200 tons of lubricating oil for the Italian forces in the Dodecanese Isles, was intercepted in the Aegean Sea by the British Naval Forces.

A heavy Italian air attack developed and the Hermione was sunk by our gunfire. We had no casualties

YOU MAY NOW DRILL, BUT—

THE thousands of civilians who cannot get into the Home Guard are to be given the chance to become fit by military training in their spare time.

A legal ban on drilling by civilians has been lifted to allow towns to organise training. The only condition is that no firearms are to be used in drilling.

The plan was announced last night it was pointed out that in many districts there are no vacancies for the Home Guard — which is 1,250,000 strong—and recruiting has stopped.

Many local authorities appealed for permission to provide facilities for the thousands of civilians of all ages who are still looking for an opportunity to train for an emergency.

These include men anxious to get fit before they are called up.

The big obstacle was a series of laws aimed to prevent "unlawful assembly" and "unlawful drilling."

But the Secretary for War has now given general authority for drilling either with "tokens" representing arms—such as walking-sticks and broomsticks—or without arms at all.

The Army will co-operate. But it cannot guarantee to send along its own instructors, who are too busy.

Local authorities who cannot provide a training ground can apply for the aid of the Central Council of Physical Training.

This Council has already arranged for drill or football grounds all over the country.

BRITISH DESTROYER SUNK BY AIR ATTACK

An Admiralty communique issued just before midnight said "The destroyer H.M.S. Delight (Commander M. Fogg-Elliot, D.S.O. R.N.) sustained damage as a result of enemy air attack and subsequently sank
The loss of life was small."

The British liner Alcantara, now armed for defence. She met the German raider which has been menacing British shipping in the South Pacific, put her to flight, and chased her until a shot slowed her down, and the runaway raider got away.

HER JOB IS TO CHOOSE CHILDREN FOR OVERSEAS

Miss Beryl M. Power is to be in charge of choosing children for the Children's Overseas Resettlement Board. Her official title will be Director of Selection. She is forty-eight.

Miss Power, who was appointed Assistant Secretary of the Ministry of Labour last year, has been loaned to the Board it was announced yesterday.

She was the first woman to reach the rank of Assistant Secretary of the Ministry—only one step from the distinction of being the first woman permanent secretary of a great Government department.

DUCHESS OF WINDSOR: PLASTIC OPERATION

A "plastic" operation on the Duchess of Windsor is to be performed by Dr. Daniel Shorell, ear, nose and throat specialist, in the Wickersham Hospital, New York (writes John Walters, Daily Mirror New York correspondent).

Dr. Shorell has specialised in plastic surgery Early this month he lifted the face of the 70-year-old actress, Edna Wallace Hopper.

Newspapers describing the operation said the transformation of the actress was miraculous, and Shorell made her look twenty-five years younger. Wealthy New York society women have had their faces lifted by Dr Shorell.

Friends of the Duchess said they believe the operation will be on the Duchess's nose, or for the removal of moles from the face.

The Duke and Duchess of Windsor appear in the liner's passenger list as "Captain and Mrs. Wood," says Reuter

FLEET SAILS FROM GIBRALTAR

Madrid radio said last night that the British Fleet sailed from Gibraltar yesterday and was manoeuvring in the Straits. It was believed that it would soon head for the Mediterranean

Five submarines led the file followed by four destroyers, one aircraft carrier and three capital ships, the announcer said —Associated Press

Good when you're TIRED

You've had something more than a drink when you've had a GUINNESS

DAILY MIRROR, Tuesday, August 6, 1940.

Daily Mirror

AUG. 6

No. 11,438
ONE PENNY
Registered at the G.P.O. as a Newspaper.

WHY HITLER HAS WAITED SO LONG

Unfit in H.G. to Go

HITLER has delayed mass air raids on Britain in order to pile up the resources of his Air Force and train hundreds of extra air crews for an attempt at a knock-out blow.

Probably the Germans are not quite ready. But when their air blitzkrieg comes, we may expect not fifty or a hundred machines in an attack, but hundreds.

To set against this is the fact that British air production is now running neck and neck with that of the Nazis. Although it must be remembered that we have a big leeway to make up, our production rate has by no means reached its peak.

This authoritative view was given last night. And here is a summary of the situation both as regards the German Air Force and the R.A.F.

Goering spoke quite fairly when he said recently that his airmen have as yet done little more than conduct reconnaissances over England.

"Tough" Airmen

These operations make small demands on his bomber strength. Goering is using them to train more "front line" crews.

But the airmen he is using at present are not mere youths. Their average age is twenty-six.

Nor is their morale poor. Those captured are tough, truculent, and worthy representatives of their service.

When they dodge away in day raids it is probably under orders—to conserve machines.

This is our air defence situation.

We have many more fighters. We have more reserves, and more experienced pilots than ever before.

Hitler's bombers will meet a tremendous R.A.F. opposition. And our pilots have been much better at keeping the enemy from his objectives than he has been against our own attacks

Remember This

But this must be remembered:

Neither the Germans nor ourselves have yet solved successfully the problem of intercepting bombers at night. In any raid, a number of planes are sure to get through the defences.

In the intensified raiding which must be expected, our fighters cannot cover the whole of the sky

Their absence from any particular point where the enemy drop their bombs does not mean the R.A.F. are doing nothing. They will be doing a great deal very effectively, but it will not often be apparent.

Our fighters operate over specified defence zones.

It is now seven weeks since Hitler started fairly extensive night bombing over this country, using anything from fifty to a hundred machines against widespread objectives.

In those seven weeks the confirmed German air losses totalled 307 machines. We do not know how many others did not get back home. Our own losses were 172.

The German night bombing has been far from effective.

But it is believed that the incessant

Continued on Back Page

HITLER IN CONFERENCE

Hitler returned to Berlin on Sunday and conferred with Von Ribbentrop, Goering and Von Brauchitsch.—Associated Press.

Invasion Men Train in Baltic

There is evidence that German preparations for an attempt to invade Britain are being made not only in Dutch and Belgian harbours, but in secret and distant areas of the Baltic, where the Norway invaders were trained.

Light troop-carrying craft could be brought to the North Sea either by the Kiel Canal or by the sea route—in favourable weather.

These movements would take a few days, and the R.A.F.'s patrols believe they would spot them in time.

The Germans are said to be planning to use towed gliders. The R.A.F. have themselves proved that this is feasible. Gliders would probably be used to carry stores or parachutists, not ordinary troops.

There seems to be no doubt that the Germans are putting long-range guns on France's northern coast.

U.S. SABOTAGE PLOT

THE Chief of America's G-Men, Mr. Hoover, disclosed yesterday that acts of sabotage against Roosevelt's National Defence Programme had been unearthed.

Agents have been placing emery dust in aeroplane engines and destructive metal in the motive power of naval vessels, Hoover told the national conference of Federal and State law enforcement officials.

Subversive agencies, he added, had conducted schools for teaching the "most terrible means of creating destruction.

"Incendiary bombs have been designed no larger than a cigar which will create disaster," he said.

"Plans to place chemicals in boilers with the idea of creating wholesale destruction have been discovered.

"We find every one of these heinous things has been done and is being done by persons shielded by innocent but subversive forces."—Associated Press.

At Los Angeles yesterday the District Attorney, Mr. Buron Fitts, said that he had "a startling amount of evidence" pointing towards a plot to assassinate prominent Americans and to overthrow the United States Government by violence.

The evidence will be presented to a county grand jury today, Mr. Fitts said, and two men had already been arrested.

Roosevelt Warns

Mr. Fitts said that the evidence to be given to the grand jury would describe the influencing of prominent Hollywood film personages to Communist ends and a programme to "capture" and "ultimately destroy" trade unions

He said that the grand jury would be told the story of a meeting in Hollywood at which it was decided that when the present American Government is overthrown Mr. Henry Ford and other prominent industrialists would be given the chance "to join the party" or be shot.

President Roosevelt urged unity between the Federal and State Governments in strengthening national defence and uncovering subversive activities, in a message to the Federal-State Conference on Law Enforcement Problems.

"We must be vigilant, always on our guard and swift to act," President Roosevelt wrote. "But we must also be wise, cool-headed, and not express our activities in the cruel stupidities of the Vigilante.

"That is where the fifth columns form the line."

The meeting is designed to promote closer co-operation in guarding against spies, saboteurs and fifth columns

GREEK PLOTTERS FAIL

A plot to overthrow the regime of General Metaxas, which yesterday celebrated its fourth anniversary, was revealed yesterday by the inspired newspaper, *Kathimerini*.

The newspaper said that the conspirators had been banished.—Associated Press.

60,431 MORE LACK JOBS

THERE were 60,431 more unemployed in Britain between June 17 and July 15, it was announced yesterday. The increase is mainly among women and juveniles.

The total of workless does not include the number absorbed into Government training centres, otherwise the July figure would have been 66,225, instead of 60,431.

This increase is the first effect of the Government's policy of reducing home consumption and also of the loss of coal exports to France

Coal Exports Hit

The total of workless was 827,266 as against 766,835 on June 17, 1940—the lowest total recorded since the extension of unemployment insurance in 1920—and against a total of 1,256,424 on July 10, 1939, or a reduction of 429,158 during the last twelve months

The biggest increase in unemployment among men was in the coal mining industry, where the increase during the month was 25,990. This is largely accounted for by the collapse of France and the practical disappearance of the export trade to Europe.

Nevertheless, there were 45,000 more people employed in the coal industry on July 15 than there were at the corresponding period of last year.

The other industries which contributed to the increased unemployment were textiles, clothing, boot and shoe, leather and furniture.

These are the industries, the home consumption of whose products is being restricted with a view to concentration on the export trade.

In the London division there was an increase of 20,200 in the unemployed, a large proportion of whom were in the clothing trades.

EVACUEE BOY, 15, MISSING IN U.S.

Fifteen-year-old Michael Murray, British boy evacuee who vanished from New York, left a note saying he was going to join the Army in Canada.

Above you see Michael and below (left) his mother, with whom he travelled to New York.

"Plenty of guts and commonsense. Can look after himself better than most grown-ups," a relative, Mr. P. G. U. Pope, of East Burnham, near Slough, said of Michael last night. "He's a good kid and could get along with anyone. He's adventurous and widely-travelled . . . possesses any amount of pluck.

"He was educated in Austria and Italy and can speak German and Italian fluently."

Michael, who helped his mother in Red Cross work in France, protested strongly against having to leave the danger zone. He tried to join the British Army several times, but was rejected as too young.

Unfit in H.G. to Go

ALL members of the Home Guard, whatever their keenness and experience, who are not completely fit, are to be weeded out.

A survey is to be made to make certain that every man has the endurance needed in case of invasion.

All ranks are concerned in this revision, whether local commanders or rankers.

Neither past experience in the Services, social position, nor any consideration except that of suitable physical fitness will affect decisions

It is likely that the places of older retired officers in senior positions will be taken by men who have had more recent service with the Forces.

Many retired officers are in the Home Guard ranks, as well as men who have served in two or three wars. But age alone will not be a bar. Many men at sixty are physically fit.

Steps are being taken to see that the Home Guard is receiving the right kind of military training.

EIRE BANS A CARDINAL

PASSAGES in Cardinal Hinsley's religious broadcast on Sunday to the Forces and to America were suppressed by the Eireann censor for yesterday's Eire Press.

Though this censorship has no hard-and-fast rule concerning the Cardinal's speeches—he is Archbishop of Westminster—it has previously taken action on his war pronouncements.

A member of the editorial staff of an Eire newspaper said last night:—

"Reports of Cardinal Hinsley's broadcast urging 'that every Christian knight of the British cause should wear a cross under his tunic' was banned.

"I cannot understand the ban, since the speech was broadcast for all to hear who cared to listen. To my knowledge nothing of it appeared in two Eireann morning papers."

Cardinal Hinsley was attacked by the German Press yesterday, says British United Press. The *Zwolf-Uhr-Blatt* says:—

"Perhaps Hinsley wants a salary increase. For him, the destruction of the German people is a good cause.

"Hinsley is a bailiff of the plutocratic system."

GERMAN NIGHT RAIDS

Enemy aircraft crossed the south-east coast last night flying very high. Searchlights were active and bombs were reported dropped.

Planes believed German were also over a north-east coastal town.

In the Midlands souvenir hunters searched for the remains of 100 incendiary bombs rained on cornland.

TOBACCO FOR TROOPS— STATEMENT TODAY?

When the Finance Bill comes before the House of Commons today for its second reading, the Chancellor, Sir Kingsley Wood, may announce the scheme for giving soldiers and airmen, in common with sailors, a duty-free ration of tobacco.

DAILY MIRROR, Saturday, August 10, 1940.

Daily Mirror

AUG. 10

No. 11,442   ONE PENNY
Registered at the G.P.O. as a Newspaper.

WAR JOB CALL-UP OF ENGINEERS

HUNDREDS of thousands of engineers not yet on war work must register at employment exchanges this month ready to be transferred to arms jobs as soon as they are needed.

Registration will take place from Monday, August 19, to Friday, August 23, and the Government hopes to secure 300,000 names. Failure to register and neglect by an employer to give the required information is an offence.

All skilled men over twenty-one in the engineering and allied trades, and all men under sixty-five who, since January, 1929, have worked twelve months in any of the specified trades, must register. Exceptions are made in the case of men already engaged wholly on Government work and in certain specified industries.

Exemption applies to men in shipbuilding or ship repairing (including marine engineering where carried on in a shipyard or ship-repairing establishment) and men engaged on the manufacture of iron, steel, brass, copper, zinc, lead, tin, aluminium or other non-ferrous metals, main railway companies and the London Passenger Transport Board.

This is the first time compulsory registration of people in industry has been ordered with a view to placing the men in occupations in which there is a shortage of skilled labour.

In the industries selected for registration there are fully a million men employed. Quite 80 per cent. are engaged on some form of Government work.

Still More Wanted

That does not mean, however that only 20 per cent. will register, as many of the men are not fully occupied on Government work.

"However many men we get under this scheme," said an official of the Ministry, "we will want a great many more.

"We could place from 20,000 to 30,000 men tomorrow if we had them. New factories are coming along and in a few weeks' time we will require another 50,000 men, and after that another 50,000."

The registration is called for under the Industrial Registration Order, issued by the Minister of Labour last night.

Men whose surnames begin with the letters A to E register on Monday, August 19; F to J on Tuesday, August 20; K to O on Wednesday, August 21; P to S on Thursday, August 22; and T to Z on Friday, August 23.

Full list of the affected trades is on back page.

ONLY FOUR LOAF SHAPES

From August 26 onward housewives will have only four types of loaf to choose from, instead of, at present, forty-five.

The four standard shapes will be the tin, ovenbottom, sandwich, and what is known in Scotland as a Batch loaf.

In addition, bakers will be permitted to sell a Vienna loaf of 8oz. and rolls not exceeding 2oz.

16 WARPLANES GIFT BY M.P.

A MILLIONAIRE M.P., father of eight children, has given Britain sixteen Hurricanes and Spitfires—cost £100,000—to replace the losses sustained by the R.A.F. in Thursday's rout of the Nazis over the English Channel.

The M.P., Mr. Willard Garfield Weston, forty-one-year-old biscuit manufacturer, who sits for Macclesfield, Cheshire, hit upon the idea of his gift while he was reading the heroic story of the R.A.F.'s Channel victory, in which sixty German planes were brought down and Britain lost sixteen machines.

Yesterday he telephoned the Ministry of Aircraft Production, and said a cheque for £100,000 was on its way round—"to buy sixteen Hurricanes or Spitfires we lost in yesterday's battle."

And last night, in the oak-panelled lounge of his house at Marlow, Bucks, Mr. Weston told the *Daily Mirror*:

"I've only one regret. All the money in the world can't buy back the lives of those R.A.F. pilots.

"What fellows! While England has men like them to guard her from the air, there's no need for any worry about this war."

"I hope people won't get me wrong. I'm a wealthy man and I've given this money as a private expression of gratitude and of admiration of a set of heroes.

"As I read of that battle over the ticker-tape in the House of Commons I was thrilled through and through. It sure was swell.

"I know no money could mitigate the sorrow of relatives of those pilots who willingly sacrificed their lives. I'm a family man—I'm proud to say I've eight young children—and I know family life and its value.

Next Best Thing

"I'd gladly give every penny to restore those boys to their folk. But I can't. The next best thing is to replace their machines.

[Of the pilots of the sixteen lost planes, thirteen are missing. Two of the other three were wounded.]

"We Canadians appreciate this country," he continued. "England has done a lot for me; there's nothing I wouldn't do for her.

All our boys in this country feel the same. I hear a lot from them. Every Canadian soldier or airman in this land has a standing welcome to my home. They come whenever they please—just roll in, and have a good time. "I know many of their home-folk. A lot come from Toronto my home town. I know their mothers and fathers.

"And I know something about war. I went through the last two years of the last lot—just as a private. I wasn't good enough for stripes."

Mrs. Weston told the *Daily Mirror*: "My husband is a terribly busy man, doing his bit for the war effort in an industrial capacity and I know he would gladly sacrifice every penny he has to give back life to the dead pilots. Willard Garfield Weston came from Toronto to England seven years ago to "make a better and cheaper biscuit." In five years he was a millionaire.

The £100,000-cheque-for-warplanes man—Mr. W. Garfield Weston, M.P., with his wife and eight children. He's made himself a millionaire.... "When you have a lot of children you've got to get busy and do something about it!" he once said.

FAITH STRONGER THAN A BOMB

The Waterfall family who live in a cottage in the West Country put not all their faith in A.R.P. Every day they have family prayers... and outside their home is a printed verse proclaiming their faith. It comes from Psalm 5, verse 11—"Let all those that put their trust in Thee rejoice because Thou defendest them."

A BOMB FELL NEARBY ON THURSDAY NIGHT. NONE OF THE FAMILY OF SIX—NOR EVEN ONE OF THEIR LIVESTOCK—WAS INJURED. ALTHOUGH DOORS AND WINDOWS BLEW IN AND CEILINGS CRASHED DOWN.

..The house next door was wrecked. Luckily there was no one at home.

Bride's Roses Will Bear Mother's Name

When Miss Eve Uprichard walks to the altar at St. Edmund the King Church, Kingsdown, Kent, today, for her marriage to Mr. Mansergh Wellband, she will carry a bouquet of Betty Uprichard roses.

These roses, of a beautiful salmon pink colour, were developed in 1921 by a Northern Ireland grower, Mr. Alexander Dickson, who named them after Miss Uprichard's mother, Mrs. Betty Uprichard. Since then the rose has won numerous prizes. The roses the bride will carry were grown in the garden of her home—Oaklands, Kingsdown, Kent.

THE ARMY IS IN LOVE...

"I WAS very much impressed while having to read the men's letters by the way every man seemed to be in love with his wife. I think that speaks volumes for the home life of England."

That view of the modern British soldier was given yesterday by Father Burroughs, a Catholic chaplain, who did censor work while at a hospital in France.

Other views on the Army of today given by Northern Command chaplains, are:—

Rev. T. B. S. Thompson, Deputy-Assistant Chaplain-General to the Command: "There is much more of religious sense among the men than in the last war.... Also, look at the colossal amount of tea consumed new instead of beer."

Another chaplain: "I don't think there has ever been a finer set of men in the British Army

WINDSORS' SHIP MAILS TAKEN
—Say U.S. Owners

When the American liner Excalibur called at the British island of Bermuda to land the Duke and Duchess of Windsor, 132 bags of mail were removed from the vessel, according to officials of the American Export Line, owners of the Excalibur.

Officials of the Line are indignant, as the ship called at Bermuda only to allow the Windsors to disembark.

"This is the reward we get for helping them out," one official said, according to Associated Press.

IF IT'S CHOCOLATE THEN IT'S FOOD

CADBURY'S

BOURNVILLE

PLAIN FLAVOUR

CHOCOLATE

for quick energy

★

Bournville bucks you up — gives you an instant supply of energy when you're feeling low. This famous plain chocolate — containing sunshine Vitamin D, iron and other minerals — is also abundantly rich in carbohydrates, for quick, immediately available energy. Look for the famous red packet.

MIRROR, Monday, August 12, 1940.

Daily Mirror

No. 11,443 — ONE PENNY
Registered at the G.P.O. as a Newspaper.

AUG. 12

60 FALL TO R.A.F. AND GUNS

Last of a Raider

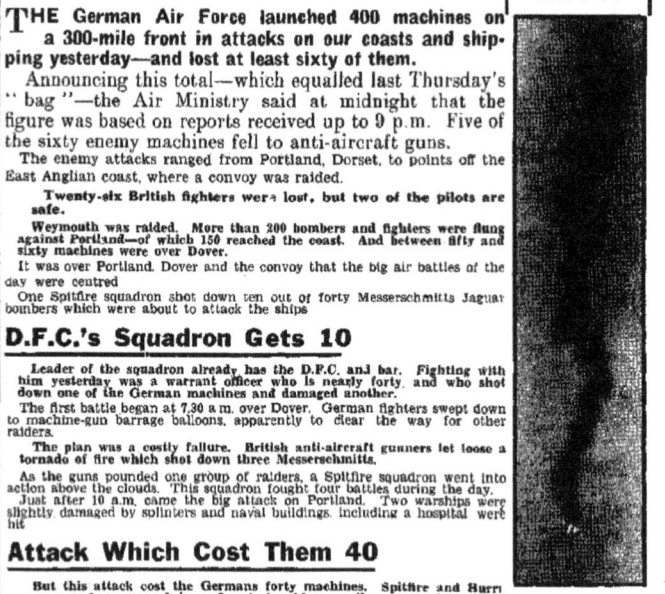

THE German Air Force launched 400 machines on a 300-mile front in attacks on our coasts and shipping yesterday—and lost at least sixty of them.

Announcing this total—which equalled last Thursday's "bag"—the Air Ministry said at midnight that the figure was based on reports received up to 9 p.m. Five of the sixty enemy machines fell to anti-aircraft guns.

The enemy attacks ranged from Portland, Dorset, to points off the East Anglian coast, where a convoy was raided.

Twenty-six British fighters were lost, but two of the pilots are safe.

Weymouth was raided. More than 200 bombers and fighters were flung against Portland—of which 150 reached the coast. And between fifty and sixty machines were over Dover.

It was over Portland, Dover and the convoy that the big air battles of the day were centred.

One Spitfire squadron shot down ten out of forty Messerschmitts Jaguar bombers which were about to attack the ships.

D.F.C.'s Squadron Gets 10

Leader of the squadron already has the D.F.C. and bar. Fighting with him yesterday was a warrant officer who is nearly forty, and who shot down one of the German machines and damaged another.

The first battle began at 7.30 a.m. over Dover. German fighters swept down to machine-gun barrage balloons, apparently to clear the way for other raiders.

The plan was a costly failure. British anti-aircraft gunners let loose a tornado of fire which shot down three Messerschmitts.

As the guns pounded one group of raiders, a Spitfire squadron went into action above the clouds. This squadron fought four battles during the day.

Just after 10 a.m. came the big attack on Portland. Two warships were slightly damaged by splinters and naval buildings, including a hospital were hit.

Attack Which Cost Them 40

But this attack cost the Germans forty machines. Spitfire and Hurricane squadrons roared in and out, breaking up the enemy formations, zooming and diving and picking off machines in a long series of dog fights.

One auxiliary squadron shot down ten Messerschmitts. And a regular squadron which destroyed twenty-one German raiders last Thursday added another five to their bag.

The Portland anti-aircraft gunners claimed two of the raiders.

Just as the Portland combats finished, another battle developed further east from Dover, round to the North Foreland. The Spitfire squadron which had begun the day's fighting now went into action for the fourth time. They met thirty Messerschmitt 109s dodging in and out of the clouds 4,000ft. up.

Four of the Spitfires chased all thirty Messerschmitts through the clouds, bringing down two of them.

Only an hour before, the same Spitfire squadron had been ordered to patrol over a convoy off the East Anglian coast. There they found forty Messerschmitt 110 Jaguar bombers about to attack the ships.

Stripped to Waist

Luckily the Spitfires saw the enemy before they themselves were sighted. The Jaguars were taken by surprise. Too late they tried to form a protective circle. Ten of them were sent down into the sea.

In the evening, two German bombers were destroyed off the east coast.

Superb shooting by British anti-aircraft gunners—who were stripped to the waist in the sunshine—was a feature of the day's action.

A *Daily Mirror* reporter who saw some of it said: "It made one's heart sing to see the way the guns plastered the sky with metal.

"I saw one shell burst right under an enemy fighter. Instantly

Contd. on Back Page, Col. 5

Caught in the middle of our anti-aircraft barrage—which German airmen have said "is Hell"—the German plane in the above picture was trying vainly to escape when the camera caught it. You can see the shells bursting round it.

TROOPSHIP HIT: 740 SAFE

WHEN the British transport Mohamed Ali El-Kebir (7,527 tons) was torpedoed and sunk by a U-boat in a night attack in the Atlantic, 740 survivors were landed out of a total of 860 troops and naval ratings on board.

This was announced by the Admiralty last night.

The survivors were rescued by another ship and landed at a Scottish port.

The transport liner sank in about two hours. Most of the 120 missing men were soldiers who were in their bunks as the torpedo struck. Heavy seas were running, making difficult the work of lowering and getting away the lifeboats.

Some soldiers who jumped overboard when the transport began to list were drowned in the rough sea.

Until well on into the morning the rescue vessel was picking up men clinging to rafts and wreckage.

Ignored Own Safety

Mr. William Olley, canteen manager on the liner, gave help to many of the wounded.

"The ship's doctor and the military doctor," he said, "showed magnificent devotion to duty in attending to the injured regardless of their own safety. Because of the heavy seas we had a hard time getting the stretcher cases on to the lifeboats, but somehow it was done.

"Before I got away with the injured in the last boat Captain Thom-

Contd. on Back Page, Col. 1

One of our balloons coming down in flames during the German attacks on the barrage.

GHOST IN GOLOSHES IS LAID BY B.B.C.

WITH proper ceremonial the B.B.C. laid the Ghost in Goloshes last night, and never again, in the home programme at least, will his soft measured footsteps be heard.

In his place will be heard the clear, rather thin tones of three chords—b, b, c—repeated slowly and deliberately with something of the diffidence of a beginner at practice.

Many Suggestions

The programme that introduced the new signal and farewelled the old gave samples of the many suggestions that have been made—the surge of waves on the shore, fanfares, birdsong, the mooing of cows and bleating of sheep, drum and trumpet, hammer on anvil.

All had their faults, and the new signal is chosen because it is direct and unobtrusive.

Cabinet's Thanks to the R.A.F.

The Prime Minister has sent the following message to the Secretary for Air:—

"The War Cabinet would be glad if you would convey to the fighter squadrons of the R.A.F. engaged in Thursday's brilliant action their admiration of the skill and prowess which they displayed, and congratulate them on the defeat and heavy losses inflicted on the far more numerous enemy."

In this action the R.A.F. brought down sixty German planes which attacked a convoy.

CAROL'S ENVOY IN MOSCOW

The Moscow radio announced last night that M. Grigore Gafencu, the new Rumanian Minister to Moscow, had arrived in the Soviet capital yesterday.—Associated Press.

NEW PROTECTED AREAS

The Home Secretary has made a further Aliens (Protected Areas) Order, naming the counties of Cornwall and Devon and most of Somerset as protected areas.

The order also extends protected areas in Bucks and Northants and comes into effect from Thursday next.

This German plane, shot down in flames by one of our fighters, became entangled with a barrage balloon. The picture shows balloon and plane ablaze coming down together.

89 BRITISH DOWN—NAZIS

TO whip up the enthusiasm of the Germans for the exploits of Goering's air force, the Nazis staged a running commentary on the raids on Britain yesterday.

Every few minutes the announcer came on the air to describe some fresh success and make some new fantastic claim of British losses. By late last night they claimed that eighty-nine of our planes were down.

This is the sort of thing that was put over.

4.20 p.m.—"The British naval port of Portland has been subjected to air attack by German bomber units.

5.10 p.m.—"An air attack on a convoy is now in progress in the Channel. Seventy merchant ships, accompanied by fourteen warships, have been attacked by German divebombers and bomber squadrons."

5.15 p.m.—"In the naval harbour of Portland the walls of the quay have collapsed. Wrecks and burning ships litter the water."

Later the radio announced that seventeen German planes were missing.—Reuter.

DAILY MIRROR, Tuesday, August 13, 1940.

Daily Mirror

AUG. 13

No. 11,444 ONE PENNY
Registered at the G.P.O. as a Newspaper.

NAZIS RAID NAVAL PORT
39 DOWN

GOERING again launched all-day air attacks over the Channel yesterday. It was estimated that at one time nearly 500 enemy aircraft were in action in mass raid — greatest total since war began.

Fiercest raid was on Portsmouth and the dockyard, and bombs landed on several R.A.F. aerodromes.

But again Goering's squadrons were slashed by R.A.F. fighters and anti-aircraft guns. Man after man baled out from wrecked German machines.

And last night the Air Ministry announced: "In to-day's air engagements round our coasts, the total of enemy aircraft so far known to have been destroyed is thirty-nine. Nine of our aircraft are missing."

Early this morning it was announced that, in addition to the thirty-nine thus recorded, "it is probable, but not yet confirmed, that many more were destroyed."

Spitfire and Hurricane pilots got thirty-two of the Nazi bombers and fighters already confirmed.

And anti-aircraft gunners had their best day since the south coast raids began—they shot down seven bombers.

For the first time Lewis gunners of a searchlight company in England saw their bullets hit and bring to earth a raider. A Junkers 87 was diving over them towards its objective. The Lewis gunners waited to open fire until it was very close, then saw it continue its dive—to destruction.

Bomber Exploded

Light anti-aircraft gunners in the Portsmouth area brought three Junkers 87 down in flames. Crews of heavier guns watched their shells bursting round German bombers so high that they looked like specks. A few seconds later raiders crashed to earth.

White parachutes of German airmen were seen among the shell bursts. One battery got a direct hit. The bomber exploded and two complete machine-guns from it fell to earth.

The German attacks on important military objectives — Portsmouth and the Kent and Sussex coasts—secured very minor results.

Other raiders made a big attack on the Isle of Wight. They hit houses and a church.

At night a force of about seventy German bombers and fighters raided a south-east coast town. But once more little damage was done. Many bombs fell in open country and others in the sea.

At midnight raids were still going

Continued on Back Page

He Just Dropped in to Lunch

"Where am I?" was the first question a British pilot asked as he climbed out of the cockpit after making a skilful forced landing with his shot-riddled plane after the Portland battle on Sunday.

Members of the Home Guard who ran to his aid told him the name of the village close by.

"Oh, I've got an uncle living there," he said, "I'll drop in to lunch." And he did.

10,000 Join Revolt

TEN thousand Albanian tribesmen were reported last night to be in revolt against their Italian conquerors. Fierce fighting is going on in the north.

Meanwhile, Rome has turned its propaganda guns against Greece, accusing her of "aggression, oppression, barbarity and persecution," and of giving Britain refuelling bases for warships and planes.

Rome said, too, that Albania was quiet, but a Belgrade message stated that already 400 Italian soldiers had been killed by the tribesmen.

Three Italian warships with troops aboard were said to have arrived at Durazzo, the Albanian port.

The leader of the Kut Veles tribe has told the Italian authorities that he will oppose the order requisitioning food, cattle and mobilisation for the Italian Army.

Censor Intervenes

Rome radio announcer said it was well known that there were dreams in Greece of a greater Greece by the occupation of Albania.

"It is Britain that has been supporting this idea," the Fascist announcer continued, "and that is why the Greek Government allowed Britain to establish 200 oil bases in Greece from which the British Fleet is now being refuelled."

The British United Press correspondent in Athens was cut off by the censor when he was reporting that demands by Italy for the cession of a strip of Greek territory opposite the Island of Corfu were expected in Athens.

Italy would send a note of protest to Greece regarding the assassination of Daut Hoggia, who advocated the return of Ciamura annexed to Greece in 1913, to Albania.

(*British United Press and Associated Press.*)

"WOMEN C.O.s" TO BE SACKED

THE resolution passed last month by York City Council to end the employment of conscientious objectors, was intended to apply to women as well as men, it was stated at last night's meeting of the Council.

A motion that the resolution be rescinded was defeated by twenty-eight votes to twenty.

Alderman W. H. Birch said he thought it "loathsome" for any official to have to "sniff out" objectors. "I would like to know how this differs from the Gestapo," he said.

The Town Clerk, Mr. T. C. Benfield, said that already one person had received notice. Another who was to get notice had resigned.

The Admiralty, the Air Ministry and the Ministry of Home Security issued this communique last night:

"The enemy bombing attacks which began over the Kent coast this morning were later extended to the Isle of Wight and Portsmouth, where large forces were employed.

"An attack on H.M. Dockyard met with little success.

"Some bombs were dropped on the outskirts of the dockyard area, setting fire to a store, and causing minor damage to a jetty. Two small harbour service craft were damaged, and subsequently sank.

"In other parts of Portsmouth a railway station was hit and a number of buildings, including a brewery, were set on fire.

"Casualties were caused, including some deaths, but they were not numerous having regard to the large number of bombs dropped.

"In the Isle of Wight, a church and some houses were damaged and a few people were injured.

"Later reports have also been received of the attacks on the coasts of Kent and Sussex. Bombs were dropped at a number of points and slight damage was caused to several R.A.F. aerodromes. Some houses and other civil property were also hit.

"Casualties in this area were very light, although several cases of fatal injuries have been reported. The enemy have been heavily engaged at all points by our defences, which have again inflicted severe losses with few casualties to themselves."

INVASION DOOMED

A SECRET envoy sent to Britain last month by President Roosevelt to investigate the British war effort, has reported that an invasion of Britain is doomed to failure, says the *New York Post*.

This special emissary, Colonel William J. Donovan, is one of the foremost American military experts. He was a noted United States Army leader in the last war.

According to the *New York Post* he has conveyed to his immediate chief, Colonel Franklin Knox, U.S. Navy Secretary, a highly optimistic report on Britain's prospects.

Fighting Morale

He is convinced, says the newspaper, quoted by the British United Press, that an invasion is doomed to failure, and that Germany's numerical air superiority is offset by the superior quality of British planes and the greater fighting morale and doggedness of the British.

Colonel Donovan was instructed before he set out on his special mission, to see everybody and to look into everything.

He was received by the King and conferred with Mr. Churchill, Mr. Eden, Mr. A. V. Alexander, Mr. Herbert Morrison and Mr. Ernest Bevin. He inspected our defences and was terrifically impressed with the optimism expressed by soldiers, sailors, airmen and munition workers.

SUNDAY'S RECORD BAG, 65

The five enemy planes, it was announced last night, were shot down by anti-aircraft fire of H.M. ships on Sunday were not included in the figure of sixty confirmed as having been destroyed during the day.

The total bag of enemy aircraft was sixty-five—a new record. The ships were H.M.S. Windsor and H.M. trawler Edwardian.

What Captured Nazi Pilots Say

"This is what comes of coming to England," said the pilot of a Messerschmitt 109 which was shot down in a cornfield on the south-east coast to the sergeant who captured him.

And the picture below shows what does come to German planes that come to England.

AIRMEN from other German machines which crashed yesterday paid tributes to the R.A.F.

A pilot who spoke English and was said to have been educated at Oxford, expressed admiration for the fine work of the pilot in the pursuing plane. He added that if the R.A.F. kept up its present activity in Germany "the war would soon be over."

Another German pilot was having wounds dressed when he said:

"Those Spitfires are very good. This is my heaven. I am out of it."

Pilot of a Heinkel 111 bomber brought down by a Hurricane exclaimed:

"A shell got the port engine, a shell got the middle engine, a million marks gone."

One of the Nazi airmen who landed by parachute spoke in broken English to the man who captured him. What he said sounded like: "No more fighting—English too good."

EPIDEMICS IN FRANCE

SPECIAL measures taken by the Swiss authorities in the Porrentruy region revealed yesterday that the whole area of the Maiche Plateau in occupied France has been stricken by epidemics of smallpox, diphtheria, typhoid and paratyphoid.

The Prefecture of Porrentruy has advised the population to boil all foods from France, and not to eat raw fruit or greens of French origin, says Associated Press.

LINDY'S VIEWS 'SHOCK' WIFE

MRS. LINDBERGH is "pained and shocked" by her husband's pro-Nazi views, according to a close friend of the family, cables the *Daily Mirror* New York correspondent.

She has joined her mother, Mrs. Morrow, in expressing to him her dislike of his public outbursts opposing aid to the Allies, and she may shortly make a statement publicly identifying herself with the Allied cause.

Daily Mirror

DAILY MIRROR, Wednesday, August 14, 1940.

No. 11,445 — ONE PENNY
Registered at the G.P.O. as a Newspaper.

Enemy Losses

HERE are totals of Nazi raiders shot down by the R.A.F. and the guns in 3 Days:

Sunday . 66
Monday . 62
Tuesday . 69
Total 197

In those three days the R.A.F. lost forty-six.

YESTERDAY'S TOTAL 69

SIXTY-NINE GERMAN AIR RAIDERS WERE SHOT OUT OF THE SKY BY R.A.F. FIGHTERS AND OUR ANTI-AIRCRAFT GUNS YESTERDAY.

It was a record. It was our answer to the Germans as their air attacks reached a new high pitch with a fierce raid on Southampton.

Twenty-nine of the smashed raiders were shot down in two hours of terrific air fighting.

At one time German machines were toppling out of the sky at the rate of about one a minute.

Eleven British fighters are missing, but five of the pilots are safe.

The Germans destroyed were thirty-two bombers, twenty-three fighter-bombers and fourteen fighters.

Five hundred German planes came in three waves for the Southampton area and the Kentish coast.

His Gunsight

Patrols of Spitfires and Hurricanes went into the attack. The anti-aircraft gunners opened up and got three, bringing the two-day gun "bag" to ten.

In the Southampton area alone the fighters destroyed twenty-two of the enemy. Nine were Junker dive bombers brought down in the space of minutes by a single Spitfire squadron.

This squadron also got four fighters. The day before it shot down seven. And by last night it had lost not a single pilot or machine.

It was in the same engagement that A.A. gunners scored a direct hit on an enemy plane and saw it crash into the sea after pieces of wreckage had fallen on the gun sight.

Air combats went on hour after hour. A patrol of Hurricanes met in all nearly forty Dorniers. The pilots took the chance to bring their total of successes since Sunday to thirty.

The Germans bombed Southampton, the Isle of Wight, Berkshire and Wiltshire, attacked aerodromes in the

Contd. on Back Page, Col. 1

GIRL, 9, PLEADS TO U.S.

From JOHN WALTERS
NEW YORK, Tuesday.

NINE-YEAR-OLD London evacuee Josephine Allfrey (pictured above with her brother) is to appear before the solemn United States Senate Foreign Relations Committee in Washington to plead for American ships to be sent to Britain to evacuate children.

Making her dramatic appearance as a "typical British child," blonde, blue-eyed Josephine will stand before the committee hand in hand with Mrs. Harold Pulsifer, in whose Maine home she is being looked after for the duration of the war.

Mrs. Pulsifer, who is chief of the organisation urging that "Mercy Ships" be sent to Britain, hopes the sight of beautiful Josephine will so touch the hearts of the committee members that they will urge amendment of the Neutrality Law.

Self-Possessed

The committee includes rigid Isolationists who have so far bitterly opposed the "Mercy Ships" scheme.

Josephine's father is Mr. Robert E. Allfrey, an aeroplane designer, her mother an ambulance driver.

Her home is in Parkview-court, Fulham High-street, Fulham, S.W.

"She won't let shyness interfere with her mission—she's too sincere and genuine in her desire to see other English children taken to safety like herself," her mother told the *Daily Mirror* last night. "I took Phina and her five-year-old brother Philip over to America in the autumn."

TORPEDO BOATS IN ACTION

A BRITISH motor torpedo boat dashed between two enemy light warships and fought them with hand grenades and machine-gun fire yesterday.

This attack at point-blank range was too much for the enemy. Their return fire was ineffective.

Some of our torpedo-boats were travelling at thirty knots when they spotted the two enemy ships 100 yards away.

One of our little ships, thinking the nearest enemy was an E-boat, decided to ram her.

But she was much larger, and her attacker was damaged about the bows.

Then the second British ship dashed between the enemy.

Then a third of our torpedo boats, said the Admiralty last night, passed beyond the enemy ships.

She sighted two larger vessels and attacked at close range with machine-gun fire.

Running Fights

Later, one of our ships had two running fights with an E-boat.

Not long afterwards our ships were attacked by a German plane from a height of 500ft.

We opened hot and accurate fire.

We had no casualties, and none of our ships suffered damage except the one which rammed the enemy. She, too, returned safely.

A German High Command communique, quoted by Associated Press, stated that a North Sea fight between German minesweepers and British speedboats had "developed in our favour."

RAIL, BUS FARES MAY BE RAISED AGAIN

Main line railway and London Transport bus and underground fares may go up again soon.

An application from the railway companies for an increase equivalent to about 6.8 per cent. on the present rates and fares will be the subject of a public inquiry in London on August 26.

If the railway companies' application is successful this increase—with the 10 per cent. already granted—would make a total increase of 17½ per cent. on pre-war fares.

It would mean another ½d. in every shilling on main line railway fares. A 10s. season ticket would cost 10s. 8d., a £1 13s. season ticket £1 17s. 4d. A 2s. 6d. fare would be increased to 2s. 8d. L.P.T.B. bus and underground fares would also be increased.

A further sum of £15,000,000 is required by the railway companies and L.P.T.B. undertakings by September 30, 1941.

S.E. COAST SHELLED?

HEAVY fragments of grooved steel picked up at the scene of four mysterious explosions on the south coast were being examined by authorities last night.

It is believed by some people in the district that the fragments were pieces of shell, and reports of the shelling of the British coast from France were "front-paged" by the American newspapers yesterday.

One of the south-east explosions wrecked houses.

Two people were killed and some were reported injured.

The metal splinters were said to resemble shell pieces rather than bomb splinters. People living near the scene of the explosion heard no sound of falling bombs.

No plane had been visible or audible.

The two people killed were a woman aged thirty-nine, an A.R.P. first-aid worker, and a man thirty-nine, married, a member of the A.R.P. service at a mill.

The woman's husband, an A.R.P. ambulance driver, turned a corner and saw her lying dead. He cried: "My wife" and fainted.

We Raid 1,000 Mile Line

AS German air raiders again swarmed over the Channel yesterday, British bombers swept out to hit back as enemy air bases on a 1,000-mile front from Jutland to the Bay of Biscay.

The R.A.F. bombers fiercely attacked Northern France aerodromes, from which the Germans are launching their squadrons against Britain and her shipping.

Other targets pounded by the R.A.F. raiders included the German-occupied airfields at Waalhaven and Hingene.

But from these widespread and daring raids twelve of our bombers did not return.

Sheeted in Ice

Not many hours before, the R.A.F.'s night raiders had again ranged over North-West Germany and occupied territory in France and Holland.

Some of our heavily-laden bombers found a temperature of 20 deg. below zero prevailing up to a height of three miles.

The machines were sheeted in ice as they sped to their objectives.

When the German anti-aircraft guns began to fire, the pilots found that the extra weight of the ice on the planes made them unable to climb out of danger.

So the bombers roared on, defying the gunfire, until they had unloaded their bombs on their targets.

From the night raids four of our bombers did not return.

100 TRAPPED IN RAID FIRE—ALL ESCAPE

Trapped in a shelter beneath a blazing furniture depository, 100 people escaped as firemen turned hoses on the debris during yesterday's raid on Southampton.

They were marshalled out through a back exit. No one was hurt.

The depository was struck by a heavy high explosive bomb. A glass window was shattered and a man was blown out after, and dropped twenty-five yards away in the road unhurt.

4d. a Day More for Service Women

Sir Kingsley Wood, Chancellor of the Exchequer, announced last night that the increase to women in the Forces will be 4d. a day, representing two-thirds of the pay of corresponding ranks of the men's services. Cost of the increase will be about £6,000 a year for each thousand women.

The Soldier's 6d.

Mr. Eden, War Minister, stated that the increase of 6d. a day in their pay would not increase the soldiers' compulsory allotment to dependents.

Nervous Headache?

Genasprin kills pain QUICKLY
—time it!

Keep 'Genasprin' handy always — ready for every nerve-testing emergency. It is pure. It is harmless. It works quickly. That is why your doctor recommends it.

Sold only by qualified chemists.
3d., 6d., 1/3, 2/- and 3/6.

At every time of strain or pain 'GENASPRIN' sees you through

MIRROR, Saturday, August 17, 1940

Daily Mirror

AUG. 17

No. 11,448 ONE PENNY
Registered at the G.P.O. as a Newspaper.

RAIDERS BOMB LONDON SUBURBS AND GUN STREETS

The King to the RAF

The whole nation and Empire will join with the King in the message he sent yesterday to the gallant men of the R.A.F., congratulating them on their heroic feats of the past week.

The message, sent to the Secretary for Air states:—

"Please convey my warmest congratulations to the fighter squadrons, who, in recent days, have been so heavily engaged in the defence of our country.

"I like all their compatriots, have read with ever-increasing admiration the story of their daily victories. I wish them continued success and the best of luck."

GOERING'S BLITZ RAIDERS STRUCK FOR THE FIRST TIME AT LONDON LAST NIGHT. THEY DROPPED BOMBS IN SOUTH-WESTERN SUBURBS.

Several points on the Thames Estuary were also attacked, including Tilbury and Northfleet.

As the German Press and radio screamed that daring Nazi squadrons were wrecking military objectives round Britain's capital, the raiders' bombs were in fact falling on civilian property and one railway station.

And the day's raids cost Goering's Air Force at least SEVENTY machines. Seventeen British fighters were lost, but ten of the pilots were saved.

The bombers swooped to machine-gun the streets in hit and run attacks. Bombs caused damage in several areas, but casualties were comparatively small.

Waves of bombers dived from the clouds and rained bombs on residential districts in the south-west suburbs of London.

One of the bombs fell on the booking office of a railway station and killed a number of people, some of whom had gone to seek shelter. Others were injured.

Rows of houses, shops, a club, two stores and a garage were either wrecked or badly damaged. A church was smashed and a mission hall cut in two. Some trolleybus lines were destroyed.

Train Attacked

In one suburb more than thirty bombs were dropped.
There were miraculous escapes. Crowded trains were running when bombs dropped close to the Southern Railway line.

"I threw myself flat on the floor as a bomber dived," said a signalman. "The train was just passing the box as the raider came down within a few feet and released a bomb. The back coaches of the train were riddled with shrapnel. It was a deliberate attempt to bomb the train. The windows of my cabin fell in on me, but I escaped without a scratch."

Half a dozen bombs were dropped within a few yards of the line. One landed near a concrete lodge.

The windows of nearly every shop in one street were shattered, and scores of people sustained minor injuries from glass which flew in every direction. A bomb dropped on the pavement in the street.

"Murderous Thing"

"It was a murderous thing," one woman said. "I saw only one bomber—he seemed to have broken adrift from the others, and he dived right along the street. He released his bombs and then, not satisfied, he tried to machine-gun A.R.P. men at their post."

"I saw a black mass in the sky as the Germans swooped from the clouds," said one man. "They swooped down like lightning. I had got my wife and two kiddies in a club-room when the shrapnel started to fly. It got so hot that I pushed them under the billiard table.

"Thank God I did, because huge lumps of shrapnel pierced the walls

Cont'd. on Back Page, Col. 3

Orphanage Boy Wins Naval V.C.

SON of a sailor who was killed at sea, a boy entered the Royal Merchant Seamen's Orphanage on his father's death. The sea was in his blood, too.

Last night the sailor's son, now Lieutenant Richard Been Stannard, R.N.R., of H.M.S. Arab, was awarded the second naval V.C. of the war for "magnificent gallantry."

During five days of bomber attacks at Namsos, Norway, he saved his ship and many lives and eventually brought his damaged ship to England.

This is the story of his feat as told in last night's *London Gazette* which announced the award "for outstanding valour and signal devotion to duty."

"When enemy bombing attacks had set on fire many tons of hand grenades on Namsos wharf, with no shore water supply available, Lieutenant Stannard ran Arab's bows against the wharf and held her there.

He Fought Five

"Sending all but two of his crew aft, he then endeavoured for two hours to extinguish the fire with hoses from the forecastle. He persisted in this work till the attempt had to be given up as hopeless.

"After helping other ships against air attacks, he placed his own damaged vessel under shelter of a cliff, landed his crew and those of two other trawlers and established an armed camp.

"Here those off duty could rest while he attacked enemy aircraft which approached by day, and kept anti-submarine watch during the night.

"When another trawler nearby was hit and set on fire by a bomb, he, with two others, boarded Arab and moved her 100 yards before the other vessel blew up.

"Finally, when leaving the fiord, he was attacked by a German bomber which ordered him to steer east or be sunk. He held on his course, reserved his fire till the enemy was within 800

Contd. on Back Page, Col. 1

Lieutenant Richard Been Stannard, V.C. Other pictures on page 3.

SWEDEN: FUTURE UNCERTAIN

Sweden's desire to "contribute to the organisation of Scandinavia" was affirmed by M. Gunther, Swedish Foreign Minister, in a statement on foreign affairs to both chambers of the Riksdag today.

Reviewing developments in Europe he said the situation with regard to Sweden was calm, but none could say what the future would bring.—Reuter.

GOEBBELS WHOOPS IT UP

THE German Press and radio said at 6 o'clock last night that special squadrons had been sent out to bomb all military targets on the edge of London.

"The German Air Arm will prove today that no power in the world can prevent it dropping its bombs where it wants to. Anywhere in England, even, should its be necessary, over the City," it was declared.

Then started a running commentary. It was a spate of exaggerations and lies designed to excite the German people and give them the impression of an all-conquering German Air Force.

"The squadrons are now over the Channel . . . they have met British fighters . . . they are driving towards their objectives . . ."

"While part of the German fighters are battling over the south coast of England, the next wave of German planes rushes up.

"Like Gnats"

"Now another wave of German bombers is approaching—the dreaded Stukas. They swoop down on their prey, yelling and howling.

"The fighters are dancing over London fog like gnats over a swamp. Their numbers seem infinite. As far as the eye can see, Hurricanes, Spitfires and Messerschmitts are locked in battle of death.

"Arsenals, warehouses and refrigeration plants were main objectives. Huge fires were raging on both sides of the Thames and columns of smoke were rising everywhere. Hit after hit was observed, the wind driving a black pall over London's eastern slums.

"Air raid alarm on air raid alarm, the howling of sirens and the thunder of guns is in London today."

The German announcements claimed that hangars, oil depots and shelters were hit at Rochester and Maidstone, a power station near Enfield bombed, aerodromes in Kent attacked, and that at Gosport and Lee-on-Solent hangars and wharves were fired.

FORD TO MAKE PLANES

The Ford Motor Company will manufacture 4,000 Pratt-Whitney aircraft engines under a contract with the United States War Department. Mr. Henry Ford recently refused to make Rolls-Royce engines for Britain, basing his objection on pacifist grounds.—British United Press.

Croydon Avenged: Not One Got Back

Further details about Thursday's big action in which 169 enemy aircraft were destroyed yesterday were received yesterday. The best was this:

Not a single one of the enemy formation which attacked Croydon on Thursday evening got home to tell the tale.

It ought to be **PLAIN** to you

Here's a handy food for quick energy, that hasn't gone up in price—Bournville PLAIN Chocolate at only 2d a packet. It's full of cocoa beans and makes you feel full of beans—just the thing you need for life to-day. Many people prefer the tang of Bournville Plain to Cadbury's famous Dairy Milk Chocolate. Try Bournville to-day.

TWOPENNY BLOCKS

CADBURY'S BOURNVILLE PLAIN FLAVOUR CHOCOLATE

Daily Mirror, Monday, August 19, 1940.

Daily Mirror

AUG. 19

No. 11,449 — ONE PENNY
Registered at the G.P.O. as a Newspaper.

140-16: R.A.F.'s BIGGEST VICTORY

THE GERMAN AIR FORCE, RENEWING MASS RAIDS ON SOUTH AND SOUTH-EAST ENGLAND YESTERDAY AFTER SATURDAY'S LULL, LOST AT LEAST 140 MACHINES. ONLY SIXTEEN R.A.F. FIGHTERS WERE LOST; EIGHT PILOTS WERE SAFE.

Declared the Air Ministry early today: "Having regard to the numbers employed, this represents the heaviest defeat the enemy has yet suffered at the hands of our fighters and ground defences."

The grand total of enemy planes shot down since he began attacking Britain and our shipping has now soared to at least 1,033.

More than 600 machines were used in the mass raids yesterday. The R.A.F.'s work reached new heights of brilliance. Whole groups of raiders were wiped out in combats at equal odds.

Twice the Germans were beaten off as they tried to penetrate London's defences. During the second raid, in the evening, there were terrific combats over the Thames.

Londoners for the first time heard their anti-aircraft guns open fire. Seventy German bombers paid our A.A. gunners the biggest compliment in their power—they turned back.

Driven off from the city, German planes dived to bomb and machine-gun towns on the southern outskirts of London, and attacked areas in Kent and other parts of the south-east and south.

This was another attempt at "terror" raiding on civilians. More delayed action bombs were dropped.

Attacks on several R.A.F. aerodromes killed and injured some service personnel.

Just after 1 p.m. came the first attacks. Raiders crossed the Kent coast.

Shot Down the Lot

A squadron of Spitfires tackled bombers which were about to attack their aerodrome in Surrey, and in a few minutes destroyed eleven.

At the same time a Hurricane squadron was shooting down eight over Hampshire.

Another squadron of Hurricanes on patrol, sighted five Messerschmitt fighter-bombers at 21,000ft.

Over Kent a crack Spitfire squadron which is approaching its century of successes attacked eighty enemy planes flying "in a huge rectangle," shot down three and damaged nine.

Nine Hurricanes went up and shot down nine Nazis.

An hour later eleven Spitfires

Continued on Back Page

U.S., CANADA FIX JOINT DEFENCE

PRESIDENT ROOSEVELT and Mr. Mackenzie King, Prime Minister of Canada, have agreed that "a permanent joint board on defence shall be set up at once by the two countries," it was announced last night in a joint statement.

The Board will begin the immediate study of "sea, land and air problems," and consider "in a broad sense" the defence of the northern half of the Western Hemisphere.

Four or five representatives of each country, mostly from the armed Services, will comprise the Board.

A statement by President Roosevelt on the sale of American destroyers to Britain is expected within the next fortnight.

Indirect Sale?

It is understood if the deal materialises it will be through Canada after the ships have been to the manufacturers as surplus, thus avoiding the direct sale by the United States to belligerents, which is illegal.

A counterblast from Isolationist Senators is inevitable, but regarded as likely to be ineffective.

In view of Mr. Wendell Willkie's speech yesterday, once President Roosevelt has reached a decision an organised Republican opposition is not expected.—British United Press and Associated Press.

See **U.S.-Canada Talks Begin**, Page 2.

U.S. WARNED BY GERMANY

"IN view of the German warnings, the trip of the American Legion can only be described as criminal folly, and the U.S. Government bears the sole responsibility for any incidents."

So declared the Nazi radio last night on the subject of the U.S. troop transport, American Legion, which left Petsamo on Friday, and, says Berlin, has chosen a course which takes her into the "mine-infested war zone north of the British Isles."

"The U.S. Government is providing Churchill with a splendid opportunity for another torpedo shot similar to those which sank the Athenia and the Greek cruiser Helle," the announcer said.

"Churchill still hopes to find new Allies by such knavish tricks.

"The German note, however, has warned the world of the possibility of another crime."—Reuter.

Business as Usual

A bomb did a little shop-breaking in this south-west suburb of London ... but the owners of this general store didn't put up the shutters (if there were any left!). ...

Business as usual was the order of the day—

—But the Bremen Radio said last night, "Since the raid on Croydon, 8,000,000 Londoners are in effect trembling day by day in their air-raid shelters."

More raid pictures on the back page.

NO RIGHT TO REFUSE SHELTER

AIR raid wardens in London have refused to allow people into a public air raid shelter because they had no gas mask with them.

Air-raid wardens in charge of public shelters refused to allow people living near to enter the shelter; ordered them to return home.

In both cases, typical of a number of complaints received by the *Daily Mirror*, the air-raid warden was exceeding his authority, it was stated officially by the Ministry of Home Security.

There is no law compelling a person to carry a gas mask other than the law of commonsense, it was added.

Regarding the public shelters near shopping centres, of the type at which local residents at Edgware were refused admission, it was said that a warden should use his discretion.

If the shelter is half empty local people living near the shelter should be allowed in.

MOTORISTS CAN AID AFTER RAIDS

PRIVATE motorists can do a great deal to get people home after evening air raid warnings in London and other big cities.

Thousands of office and other workers, already an hour late, had to wait in queues for their buses after last Friday's all clear.

The authorities suggest that if motorists kept help handy in their cars a notice, "I am going to ——," they could exhibit it on their windscreens and lead up with pedestrians going home in their direction.

It was done in the General Strike. Why not in this greater national emergency?

RAF FIRE FRENCH HARBOUR

THREE tons of high explosive bombs and showers of incendiaries were dropped on Boulogne Harbour and enemy ships and formations of seaplanes assembled in the basin.

An Air Ministry communique issued last night says that the raid was made at dusk on Saturday by Fairey Battle bombers of the Coastal Command escorted by Bristol Blenheim fighters. All our planes returned.

The English coast shook with the rumble of the explosions. The harbour was bombed on all sides from a low height. The main pier at the entrance was hit several times, but most of the bombs fell plumb among the ships and seaplanes in the basin.

One of the seaplanes which was struck came up above the smoke of the explosions in a thousand pieces.

Fighters reported that when the attack ended, the Boulogne Basin was ringed and criss-crossed by spreading flame.

Besides this raid, oil plants, munition factories, aircraft stores and railway targets in Germany were bombed and attacks were made on twenty-six aerodromes in North-West France, Holland and Belgium.

And not a plane was lost.

'TORPEDOED' SOS

Mackay radio reported late last night having intercepted an SOS shortly after 11 p.m. B.S.T. from a ship reporting that she had been torpedoed 300 miles west of Ireland.

Mackay radio stated that the call letters "O N V P" indicated that she was one of the ships formerly owned by the U.S. Lines and sold to a Belgian firm. The crew was in the boats.

Daily Mirror

DAILY MIRROR, Thursday, August 22, 1940.

AUG. 22

No. 11,452 — ONE PENNY
Registered at the G.P.O. as a Newspaper.

PLANES DIVE TO GUN WOMEN

MORE civilians were deliberately machine-gunned in the streets yesterday as the Germans, finding mass attacks too expensive, launched hit-and-run raids on England by single machines or small groups.

As women were shopping in the main street of a south-east coast town a raider dived out of the clouds and fired four bursts at them. Bullets pattered on roofs and slashed through bushes. But there were no casualties.

Machine-gunning of a "residential area" was put on record last night in a communique by the Air Ministry and Ministry of Home Security.

In one of two raids on a south-east town an aerial torpedo is believed to have been used. It smashed eight of a row of working-class cottages to pieces.

It was officially stated early today that thirteen enemy planes were destroyed yesterday. Two R.A.F. fighters were lost; but one pilot is safe.

Two single raiders attacked the south-east town where the aerial torpedo was believed to have been used. Diving suddenly out of the clouds, the first dropped two heavy screamer-bombs, one of which blotted out an allotment garden, the other making a huge crater in a field.

Later came the second raider. What is thought to have been an aerial torpedo hit a street of working-class houses. After the smoke had cleared all that could be seen of what had once been several cottages was a huge crater full of debris.

Many other houses were damaged. It is feared that a number of people lost their lives.

Blew Her Over Wall

Last night three bodies had been recovered from the wreckage and several people taken to hospital.

The blast of the bomb blew one woman who was in her garden clean over the wall, but she escaped with bruises and shock.

One man fifty yards away crouched against a wall as pieces of debris flew round him. When he got up he saw his shape outlined on the wall with brick dust.

One of the victims was an eighty-year-old woman who had just been put to bed in her upstairs bedroom by her son. As he reached the foot of the stairs the house was blown to pieces. He crawled through the debris unhurt except for bruises.

A young girl was playing a piano in a house opposite when the blast blew in all the windows. But she escaped injury.

People leaving their shelters after an alarm at another south-eastern town last night looked up to see five German airmen descending by parachute from their blazing plane.

One of the airmen came down in the middle of a street and was captured by a dustman who was busy carting victory salvage.

Another of the Germans was a youth of eighteen. Said a special constable: "The poor kid was scared stiff. When I reached him a Home Guard was trying to cheer him up."

When a raider dropped bombs on shops in a south-west town residential area last night, A.R.P. men who rushed to the spot were horrified to see it strewn with the bodies of men, women and children. Then they realised that the bodies were tailors' dummies.

Mr. Frederick William Landray, aged thirty-one, who was in his garden, was killed in the raid. He leaves

Continued on Back Page

R.A.F. BOMB DESTROYERS, DAMAGE ONE

AIRCRAFT of the Coastal Command attacked two enemy destroyers in the North Sea and damaged one of them, the Air Ministry announced last night.

"We suffered no losses in these operations," the Ministry added.

A later communique told of another R.A.F. encounter with the enemy in the North Sea yesterday.

A Hudson aircraft of the Coastal Command, while on reconnaissance duty off Denmark, found two German ships. A dive-bombing attack was going on when seven Messerschmitt 109s swooped on the Hudson.

During a running fight lasting thirty-five minutes the British pilot skimmed the sea-surface most of the time manoeuvring his aircraft so that all its guns were brought into action in turn as the Messerschmitts assailed him.

Got Home

Continued bursts of fire were registered on each of the German fighters, and at least one was shot down in the sea.

The Hudson was repeatedly hit by machine-gun fire and cannon-shells, and two members of the crew were wounded. The hydraulic landing gear was jammed, but after flying the aircraft 250 miles back to his base the pilot landed it safely.

The Ministry also announced that owing to adverse weather conditions no bombing operations were carried out over Germany on Tuesday night.

"Daylight attacks were carried out yesterday and today on aerodromes in enemy-occupied territory," the communique added.

All German radio stations were off the air last night—presumably because of widespread raids.

EGYPT WILL FIGHT IF ATTACKED

Egypt will declare war if her territory or her army is attacked, the Egyptian Premier said this morning. He had summoned Press representatives to hear his statement.

The Premier's statement was made after a five-hour debate on Egyptian war policy in a crowded Chamber of Deputies.—Associated Press.

'FRONT LINE' ON HOLIDAY

IT is wrong for Parliament to adjourn while the Battle of Britain is in progress. It is our job to stay in the political front line of the war and set an example to the democracies of the world.

Despite that call by Mr. E. L. Granville, M.P. for Eye, Suffolk, Parliament decided last night to adjourn today until September 5.

Mr. Granville was backing an amendment to the formal holiday motion proposed by Mr. Attlee, Lord Privy Seal.

Sir Henry Morris-Jones (L.-N., Denbigh) said the adjournment should be until Wednesday next, August 28.

The coming fortnight was a most important fortnight from the point of view of Hitler's attack.

Sir Henry urged that Parliament should not adjourn until the cause for which we stood had been triumphantly vindicated.

Mr. Attlee, resisting the amendment, pointed out that power had already been taken to bring back the House at any time if necessary.

It was not true, even in war-time, that people did their best work without any holiday.

EVACUATION: NO HUN GUARANTEE

AN indication that Germany will not give a guarantee of safe passage for American ships evacuating children from Europe is contained in a semi-official statement issued in Berlin last night.

"No belligerent Power can give guarantees in respect of ships passing through mine-infested zones," says the statement. "Even the British Government has recognised this fact by cancelling its own plans for the organised evacuation of children.

"In the circumstances the American legislation cannot be made effective, although the humanitarian motives which inspired it are not questioned."—Reuter.

After next Monday these are the only kind of loaves you will be able to buy; and they will be sold by weight.

Left to right they are: The Sandwich, Large Tin and Danish loaves. In front are rolls (not over 2ozs.) and a Vienna loaf.

WAR CABINET CHANGES?

BY OUR POLITICAL CORRESPONDENT

MR. CHURCHILL wants to make his War Cabinet more active, more capable of cutting red tape and getting things done quickly.

He may remodel his team of Ministers during the Commons recess.

If so, Mr. Neville Chamberlain, Lord Halifax and Mr. Arthur Greenwood may leave the War Cabinet.

These are possible changes:—

Mr. Ernest Bevin, now Minister of Labour, to change places with Mr. Arthur Greenwood, Minister without portfolio.

Mr. Anthony Eden, War Minister, to replace Lord Halifax at the Foreign Office.

Beaverbrook Again

Mr. C. R. Attlee to become Lord President of the Council in place of Mr. Chamberlain.

Mr. Lloyd George is mentioned as the new Lord Privy Seal.

M.P.s believe that Mr. Churchill has a new War Minister in mind. The appointment will cause a surprise.

And Lord Beaverbrook is thought so highly of that M.P.s anticipate he will be made Minister "for the speed-up of armament production," with a roving commission to get things done quickly.

Mr. Chamberlain and Lord Halifax are expected to pass quietly into retirement. The ex-Premier would be certain to follow Earl Baldwin to the Upper House.

Air Raid Death Roll Policy

★ Total air-raid casualties in Britain for the past month will be announced shortly. The large-scale German raids mean there will necessarily be more casualties to record than hitherto.

It would perhaps be as well to read them in the light of the 701 German aircraft and 1,500 German pilots and bomber crews which have been lost since August 8.

★ Because of exaggerated rumours about the Croydon raid, names of London raid victims may be posted outside police stations, as in the provinces.

Croydon Rumours -- Back Page.

Mass Meals Boss

A CONTROLLER of Communal Feeding is shortly to be appointed under the Ministry of Food.

There is no question of setting up State communal feeding centres yet except in an experimental way. The Government, however, is preparing for any eventuality, however remote.

There are already experimental centres run by local bodies. Some may be taken over.

The system, in every instance, will be examined by experts to find the one best designed for national use.

A reminder is issued to caterers by the Ministry of Food that the Ministry should be informed at once of the seating and cooking capacity of their establishments in connection with arrangements that might have to be made in an emergency.

There has been, it is stated, a certain lack of response to a questionnaire on this subject issued last month.

While the Ministry has power to obtain the particulars by other means, it is considered preferable that the trade should furnish this information voluntarily to the local food executive officers without further delay.

'Special Drene is my favourite'
SAYS
NORA SWINBURNE
Brilliant Star of Stage and Screen

"FROM the first moment I had a Special Drene Shampoo, I knew I'd found a winner! Never before had my hair taken on such sparkle — such richness. Never before had it been so easy to manage, right after shampooing. And I like Special Drene Shampoo too, because it's so easy to use. My hairdresser tells me it can't ever leave the sticky film that dulls hair and hides its natural lustre. I always insist on special Drene Shampoo."

GLAMOROUS HAIR CAN BE YOURS TOO... WHEN YOU USE

SPECIAL
drene
SHAMPOO
— 6d., 1/6 & 2/6 —

DAILY MIRROR, Saturday, August 24, 1940.

Daily Mirror

No. 11,454 ONE PENNY
Registered at the G.P.O. as a Newspaper.

AUG. 24

2 MORE VCs

A young second lieutenant, twice wounded in battle in France, and a company sergeant-major who has died of his wounds, are two new V.C.s announced last night, making the total for the war nine.

Second-Lieutenant R. W. Annand, V.C

N.Z. NAVY IS HUNTING RAIDER

NEW ZEALAND naval and air forces are searching for a raider which attacked the British steamer Turakina in the Tasman Sea.

This was announced by Mr. P. Fraser, New Zealand's Premier, last night.

The 8,706-ton Turakina wirelessed on Tuesday night saying she was being fired on by a raider.

She gave her position, but no more news has been received from her, said Mr. Fraser. She was due at a New Zealand port on Thursday night.

The Turakina is owned by the New Zealand Shipping Company and registered at Plymouth.

Swedish Disguise?

The lone Nazi raider which has been operating in the Atlantic has been reported to be a fast 10,000-ton vessel named the Narvik.

She is said to be disguised as a Swedish merchantman and to carry disappearing six-inch guns.

Last heard of her was at the end of July, when she was badly damaged by the British armed merchant cruiser Alcantara in the South Atlantic.

She is known to have sunk two British ships (says Reuter).

R.A.F. ATTACK ON GUNS

FLASHES of German A.A. guns in the direction of Boulogne were seen from the south-east coast late last night.

They began shortly before ten o'clock and dotted the French coastline along a length of several miles, indicating that an R.A.F. raid of unusual proportions was in progress.

Occasionally more diffused flashes, believed to be caused by bombs, lit up the sky.

A single searchlight beam swept the sky midway along the French shore towards Calais, but was switched off after a few minutes.

Guns Reply to Channel Bombardment—Page 3.

Sugar Up ½d. Monday

The price of sugar is to be increased by ½d. per lb. on Monday.

The increase is blamed on rising cost of freight and raw materials.

The new prices are: "Granulated sugar, 5d. per lb.; cubes, 5½d.; refiners' castor, 5½d.; soft brown, 4½d.; preserving, 5½d.; grocery West India, 5½d.

C.S.M. George Gristock, V.C.— above: the picture of himself he liked best. The umbrella belonged to his Commanding Officer. The men were often amused by the C.O. walking in the trenches with the umbrella up when they were under fire!

Right: Gristock engaged in a favourite pastime.

SAVED BATMAN IN A BARROW

THE family of Second-Lieutenant R. W. Annand, Durham Light Infantry, whose home is at Carnaby, Bridlington, knew that he had done "something pretty fine" in France.

"He just roared with laughter and wouldn't say a word about it," Lieutenant Annand's guardian, Colonel Robert Chapman, of Cleadon, near South Shields, High Sheriff of Durham, told the "Daily Mirror" last night.

The family got to know last night when the story was told with the announcement of the award of the V.C

The award is for "most conspicuous gallantry on May 15-16, when the platoon under his command was on the south side of the River Dyle astride a blown bridge."

During the night a strong attack was beaten off, but about 11 a.m. the enemy again launched a violent attack and pushed forward a bridging party into the sunken bottom of the river.

Second-Lieutenant Annand, who is twenty-five and 6ft. 2in., attacked this party, but when ammunition ran out he went forward himself over open ground, with total disregard for enemy mortar and machine-gun fire.

Reaching the top of the bridge he drove out the party below, inflicting more than twenty casualties with hand grenades. Having been wounded, he rejoined his platoon, had his wound dressed, and then carried on his command.

During the evening another attack was launched, and again Second-Lieutenant Annand went forward with hand grenades and inflicted heavy casualties on the enemy.

When the order to withdraw was received, he withdrew his platoon, but learning on the way back that his batman was wounded and had been left behind, he returned at once to the former position and brought him back in a wheelbarrow, before losing consciousness as the result of wounds.

"That is typical of him," said Colonel Chapman when he heard the story. "He is amazingly strong-minded."

BAGGED MACHINE-GUN

SECOND V.C. announced last night was awarded to C.S.M. George Gristock, Norfolk Regiment, of Harts Leap-close, Sandhurst, who died of wounds after destroying a German machine-gun nest.

A close friend who was with him in France said that in wiping out the machine-gun nest Gristock had one leg shot away, the other badly wounded.

But he managed to drag himself towards his post where he manned a machine-gun. Afterwards he had his second leg amputated.

"I am O.K., boys. Just carry on," he told his comrades.

C.S.M. Gristock showed "most conspicuous gallantry" on May 21, when his company was holding a position on the line of the River Escaut, south of Tournai, says the official report.

After a prolonged attack, the enemy broke through beyond the company's

Continued on Back Page

You too should make it **PLAIN**

Here's a handy food for quick energy, that hasn't gone up in price—Bournville PLAIN Chocolate at only 2d a packet. It's full of cocoa beans and makes you feel full of beans—just the thing you need for life to-day. Many people even prefer the tang of Bournville Plain to Cadbury's famous Dairy Milk Chocolate. Try Bournville today.

TWOPENNY BLOCKS

CADBURY'S BOURNVILLE
PLAIN FLAVOUR
CHOCOLATE

Daily Mirror

SEPT 2

DAILY MIRROR, Monday, September 2, 1940.

No. 11,461 — ONE PENNY
Registered at the G.P.O. as a Newspaper.

CHILDREN'S SHIP TORPEDOED—ALL SAVED

A MERCY SHIP CARRYING 321 BRITISH CHILDREN TO CANADA HAS BEEN TORPEDOED, BUT NOT ONE OF THE CHILDREN WAS HARMED.

Singing popular songs, the children landed at a British port last night.

Only casualty was the purser, killed in an accident after the attack.

Thus Hitler has fulfilled his threat that Germany would not guarantee a safe conduct to ships carrying child evacuees.

The children—most of them between the ages of five and fifteen—were in bed by 7.30 on Friday evening after a happy day in which they had been playing games on deck.

The youngest of all was six weeks old. The child's parents had just taken " one more peep at baby " when there was a terrific explosion.

The ship had been torpedoed between the first and second holds by a submarine that had been ranging the sea in search of just such prey as this.

The alarm bell rang, but nobody was afraid. The children, who earlier had been enjoying their boat drill, behaved as if this was just another practice.

Within three and a half minutes of the alarm every child was at the boat stations, each wearing a life-jacket and an overcoat.

Darkness was over all, but the children were no more afraid of the dark than they were of Hitler's submarine.

They obeyed orders promptly and coolly filed into the lifeboats.

"Act of God"

Rescue ships were there immediately. Within an hour and a half all the children and other passengers had been taken safely aboard.

Some of the lifeboats got alongside a rescue vessel whose crew hauled the children up two or three at a time in banana baskets.

All the time the children sang popular songs—" Oh, Johnnie " and " Roll Out the Barrel " seemed to be the favourites.

When more than seventy of the children were landed at a British port they were still singing, and most of them were clad only in their pyjamas.

Mr. Geoffrey Shakespeare, Dominions Under-Secretary, who welcomed the children, said, " Their escape is an act of God. There was a very special guardian angel watching over them."

The children had sailed under the supervision of Mr. C. H. Hindley, headmaster of Stoke School, Gosport. Mr. Hindley said that the crew treated them as though they were the salt of the earth.

" The way those children behaved proved that they were," he added.

" There was an eight-year-old youngster in my boat who said, ' We don't

Contd. on Back Page, Col. 2

ACTED LIKE GUARDS ON PARADE

Smiling . . . blankets over their nighties . . . one very young one among them being carried . . . they come ashore at a British port from the ship that was taking them to safety in Canada, a ship that a U-boat torpedoed. As the children were ushered into the lifeboats they laughed and sang ' Roll Out the Barrel." No panic, perfect order, as good as the Guards on parade, is the sailors' description of these British children.

OTHER PICTURES ON PAGE 3.

Murder in the Air

A second instance within a few days of a British pilot, descending by parachute, being deliberately machine-gunned by a Nazi fighter is reported from the south-east.

After a fight with three Messerschmitts on Saturday the British pilot baled out.

Eye-witnesses say that an enemy plane circled round him and fired a machine-gun burst. When the airman landed it was found he had been shot through the heart.

FOUR RAIDERS DIVE BOMB TOWN

FOUR Nazi bombers, breaking from their formation, which was being held by A.A. barrage dived low over a south-east town yesterday and bombed a thickly populated area

There was no panic, only tremendous heroism, not only by the A.R.P. services, but by the ordinary public, who went to the rescue, though a battle was raging over head.

Three fires that were started were soon put out.

The raid had scarcely ended when eight Stukas swooped from the clouds. Swerving to dodge a blast of anti-aircraft fire, they dropped sixteen bombs a mile from their objective in open country.

Two Messerschmitts from a group broken up by Spitfires shot down a barrage balloon.

Out for Airfields

Twenty-five enemy planes were shot down during yesterday's raids. Fifteen of our planes were lost. Nine of the pilots are safe.

Eighty-five aircraft were bagged on Saturday—seventy by the R.A.F., fifteen by A.A. guns. We lost thirty-seven fighters, but the pilots of twenty-five of these are safe.

Enemy planes made a determined attack on a south-west town last night, and dropped many H.E. bombs in residential districts far from any military objective.

A fire started almost in the centre of the town. Some shops were burned out. Minor fires were started and the fire brigade and all the A.F.S. services were in action. Several "whistlers" also were dropped.

German bombers and fighters made more attempts yesterday to destroy aerodromes in Kent, Surrey and Essex. Three times 100 or more raiders crossed the Kent coast and three times Fighter Command pilots and anti-aircraft gunners drove them back.

One squadron of Spitfires saw enemy aircraft marking a target in advance for the oncoming bombers. A line of smoke was laid over an Essex aerodrome.

But the Spitfires were waiting for the Heinkels when they arrived, with two tiers of Messerschmitts above. Three of the Messerschmitts were shot down.

In the third attack the raiders confined themselves to Kent coast aerodromes. Single-seater Messerschmitt 109 fighters dropped bombs. They have been put to this use before, but yesterday it was noticed that they were used as dive bombers.

Five Spitfire pilots caught a close-flying formation of Dornier bombers at 15,000ft. over Maidstone. The

Contd. on Back Page, Col. 4

500 BOMBS ON CIVILIANS

FIVE hundred bombs, mostly high explosives, were dropped by the German Air Force in their mass attack on Ramsgate a week ago. Most of the bombs fell on seaside boarding-houses and workers' homes.

Direct hits destroyed many houses, and many more were made uninhabitable. Nearly 1,000 houses have been wrecked, as Mr. Churchill reveals in a message to our Bomber Command (in page 2).

Casualties were a few killed and injured, although some people are still reported missing.

Some of those made homeless are still being fed at a communal centre, where meals are served by members of the Women's Voluntary Service.

MIRROR, Wednesday, September 4, 1940

Daily Mirror

SEPT 4

No. 11,463 — ONE PENNY
Registered at the G.P.O. as a Newspaper.

BRITAIN GETS 50 DESTROYERS: U.S. 8 BASES

BRITAIN is to get fifty American destroyers immediately to reinforce the Royal Navy. In exchange the United States will get ninety-nine-year leases of eight naval and air bases on British possessions in the North and South Atlantic.

This historic defence agreement between the two greatest democracies was announced last night—on the anniversary of the outbreak of Britain's war against Nazi Germany.

The first eight of the destroyers, which are all fully armed and equipped for action, will be ready for delivery to Britain next Friday. They are now at Boston, and will be sent to Canada. British crews who have already been sent over will man the vessels and bring them to Britain.

Two or three further groups of eight will be released at fortnightly intervals, and the remainder will be ready when asked for.

The destroyers are handy and speedy craft, a first-rate type for convoy and patrol work. Under changed names they will operate as British destroyers to keep open the Empire's vital sea routes.

They will release big, modern Royal Navy destroyers from routine work, and leave them completely available for battle duty.

Said the First Lord of the Admiralty, Mr. A. V. Alexander, in a statement last night: "They come at a time when the strain upon our destroyer fleet has been very great, and they will be of inestimable value to us, not only for escorting convoys, but also for protecting our coasts from threat of invasion.

"Apart from the immediate advantage to both our own naval defence and that of the U.S.A., this event will strengthen the feeling of good will and friendship between our two great peoples."

Churchill's Pledge

The United States gets bases in Newfoundland, Bermuda and British Guiana, and at five points in the West Indies—the Bahamas, Jamaica, St. Lucia, Trinidad and Antigua.

Said President Roosevelt in a message to Congress: "The right to bases in Newfoundland and Bermuda are gifts generously given and gladly received. The other bases have been acquired in exchange for fifty of our over-age destroyers."

He added: "It is an epochal and far-reaching act in preparation for the defence of the Continent (North America) in face of grave danger.

Later, talking to the Press, he appeared to hint at other far-reaching steps.

The U.S. State Department revealed that the British Government had given America this assurance: "Never to surrender or sink the British Fleet in the event of the waters surrounding the British Isles becoming untenable for his Majesty's ships."

This, it was added, is the Government's settled policy.

An authorised Nazi spokesman said last night: "The Anglo-American agreement is a question of conceivably vast import. The German attitude cannot be defined before a thorough-going study of the international law involved."

The American people think the U.S. has got a good bargain.

SAILOR DIED AT HIS GUN —V.C.

"Between his bursts of fire he had time to reflect on the grievous injuries of which he was soon to die; but his great courage bore him up till the end of the fight, when he fell by the gun he had so valiantly served."

THIS is a sentence from the official announcement last night of the gallantry which has won Acting Leading Seaman Jack Foreman Mantle, the V.C.

His left leg was shattered by a bomb as he stood at his pom-pom gun when a warship was attacked by a plane. He went on firing...

The ship's electric power failed—he fought his gun with the hand-gear....

Wounded again in many places he still kept on. Then as the action ended he fell dead.

Many Wounds

The official announcement of the award added:—

"Leading Seaman Jack Mantle was in charge of the starboard pom-pom when Foylebank was attacked by enemy aircraft on July 4, 1940.

"Early in the action his left leg was shattered by a bomb, but he stood fast at his gun and went on firing with hand-gear only; for the ship's electric power had failed.

"Almost at once he was wounded again in many places."

ITALIANS PLAN TO GRAB SYRIA

BRITISH official quarters in Cairo believe that the Italians are planning to occupy Syria.

This would bring Axis troops dangerously near the Mosul oilfields, whose output is now available to the British Forces in the Near East.

Britain has asserted that she will not tolerate hostile occupation of Syria and the decision of leaders of various French African colonies to continue the war against Hitler and Mussolini is likely to stiffen French resistance in Syria.—Associated Press.

RED MARSHALS' 31 DIAMONDS

Marshals of the Red Army are to wear a five-pointed star consisting of thirty-one diamonds in a gold and platinum mounting.—Reuter.

Do 30 Knots—Ready for Action

The fifty destroyers are of the 1,200-ton class, can do thirty knots, and carry 4in. guns, A.A. guns, and 21in. torpedo tubes—the size used by the British Navy. They have been recently reconditioned and are in good condition and ready for action.

An expert stated that they are particularly easy to manoeuvre, which means that with their depth-charges they will take heavy toll of the U-boats.

Some of the destroyers U.S. has transferred to us.

BID TO KILL CAROL FAILS

An attempt to assassinate King Carol failed last night, the Associated Press reports from Bukarest, Rumanian capital.

Three men broke through the heavily guarded palace gates and fired seven shots at the brightly lighted windows of the building.

It was reported later that one of three would-be assassins had been killed.

The men were stated to have taken the guards by surprise and reached the drive leading to the palace before being surrounded and overcome.

The three men jumped from a motor-car and ran through the gate firing at the open windows and shouting, "Long live the Iron Guard."

Spectators said that the guards rushed at the men with bayonets, firing at the assailants as they ran.

In the palace grounds the attackers threw out manifestos reviewing the Transylvanian situation.

(Peasants March Against Axis—page 2.)

Berlin Had Air Raid Alarm After Midnight

A.A. GUNS ROUT RAID

A TERRIFIC barrage of anti-aircraft fire barred the way to enemy raiders over a S.E. England town last night.

The raiders, flying high, were caught and held in the searchlights, and forced to flee. The noise of bombs could be heard between the gunfire.

Raiders appeared last night over four south-east towns, as well as in the south-west, north-east and north-west.

The score for this round was once more in Britain's favour.

London's third warning sounded at 11.34 p.m. and lasted for only sixteen minutes.

Three hundred German warplanes attempted to reach London during the first of yesterday's raids—on the anniversary of the start of the war. In five minutes the R.A.F. had routed the bombers.

Shoppers See Fight

A few bombs, the communique added, were dropped in Kent and Essex, causing little damage. A few casualties were reported, several fatal.

The second warning was due to the presence of high-flying raiders over south-east England. Bombs were dropped at one south-east town and in the surrounding district.

Shoppers in a south-east market town saw R.A.F. and the raiders clash above their heads and dived for shelter during the big morning battle.

Whirling planes glinted in the sun during the terrific battle between the rival fighters.

One Spitfire, in escaping from a

Continued on Back Page

25 Down

Twenty-five enemy aircraft are known to have been destroyed in yesterday's raids.

Fifteen of our aircraft are missing, but the Air Ministry announces that eight of the pilots are safe.

88

Daily Mirror

DAILY MIRROR, Thursday September 5, 1940.

SEPT 5

No. 11,464 — ONE PENNY
Registered at the G.P.O. as a Newspaper.

Hitler Launches New Night Blitz—and

LONDON BARRAGE BEATS ATTACKS

Jack Mantle, V.C., NEVER SHIRKED

"A quiet, unobtrusive boy who never shirked his duty." That description of the Navy's first lower-deck V.C. of the war—Acting Leading Seaman Jack Foreman Mantle, aged twenty-three—was given to the "Daily Mirror" yesterday by his old headmaster, Mr. F. J. Hemmings.

The V.C.'s parents, Mr. and Mrs. Lisle John Mantle, live at Malvern Cottage, Malvern-road, Shirley, Southampton. He was one of six children.

"Naturally, we are tremendously proud of him," Mrs. Mantle told the "Daily Mirror." He loved the Navy. Gunnery was both his job and his hobby.

LONDON'S anti-aircraft guns roared into action and flung up a wall of flame against German raiders last night only a few hours after Hitler had threatened new "night after night" blitzkrieg in answer to the R.A.F.'s raids.

The city's defences met the challenge with the fiercest opposition yet. Londoners going to their shelters saw a terrific sky battle.

The German Air Force had already lost forty-five machines —thirty-three of them bombers—in raids earlier in the day. Eleven of our fighters were lost, but five pilots are safe.

And the Air Ministry revealed that Berlin had been bombed again. This time the R.A.F. men fired forests north of the German capital after concealed war objectives had been heavily attacked.

The story of how our bombers dived to smash the Berlin targets is told fully on the back page.

Battle Over City

IT was just after the London area had got its third warning of the day that the anti-aircraft guns opened their barrage last night.

Scores of weaving searchlights, flashes from the terrific gunfire and flares dropped by the raiders lit up the sky.

Londoners going to their shelters in one district could see a big sky battle in the distance.

Over one south-east district at least 100 searchlights swept the sky, while the A.A. barrage could be heard for miles. Windows and doors shook continuously.

The raiders dropped red, blue, green and white flares. Then heavy bombs fell.

Shells soared and flashed all around the raiders. A tremendous burst of light enveloped one machine. It dived steeply to the ground.

Later it was stated that a raider was shot down in the London area. Searchlights and shells pursued the raiders as they fled.

The sky looked like a gigantic fireworks display. Huge planes looked like burning barrage balloons.

Three bombers were caught together in the beams of searchlights over one S.E. area, where the A.A. gunfire was so heavy that raiders appeared to turn back.

It was the biggest night barrage so far.

The warning was sounded at 9.21, and the all-clear came an hour and thirty-seven minutes later.

Earlier in the day an air battle raged for an hour over a hundred miles of English countryside.

After losing seven Messerschmitt fighters in their familiar eight to

Continued on Back Page

SUMMER TIME this year will end on the night of Saturday-Sunday, Nov. 16-17.

"Special Drene Shampoo keeps my hair right in the Spotlight"
SAYS
PAT KIRKWOOD
Now playing in Georgo Black's "Top of the World" at the London Palladium.

"I DEPEND on Special Drene Shampoo to keep my hair full of fascinating highlights," continues Miss Kirkwood. "Ordinary shampoos left my hair dull and lustreless. Then I discovered Special Drene Shampoo—and my hair was left shining and silky—and manageable — right after shampooing. There's none of that sticky film residue either. That's why it's Special Drene Shampoo for me every time!"

GLAMOROUS HAIR CAN BE YOURS TOO ... WHEN YOU USE

SPECIAL
drene
SHAMPOO
6d., 1/6 & 2/6

WIND BROUGHT GOOD NEWS

ON holiday in Devonshire, Miss G. Elliott, of Trimley, Suffolk, picked up a newspaper which had blown across the sands to her feet as she sat on the beach.

Glancing through it, she read that her fiance, Eric Richard Stewart, twenty-two, of Clarkson-street, Ipswich, had been awarded the Military Medal.

That was the first she knew of it. Miss Elliott wrote to Stewart's parents. "It was news to us, too," his mother, Mrs. J. Stewart, told the *Daily Mirror* yesterday.

MINESWEEPER LOST

The Secretary of the Admiralty regrets to announce that H.M. minesweeping trawler Royalo (temporary skipper W. D. Warford, R.N.R.) has been sunk by an enemy mine.

SHORE GUNS ROUT SEAPLANE

HEAVY explosions which shook south-east England coast town last night were understood to have been caused by British guns attacking a German seaplane.

Two loud detonations were followed in quick succession by two others from the direction of another battery of long-range guns several miles away.

Mist limited visibility to mid-Channel, so the effects of the firing could not be observed.

However, it was seen that the seaplane fled.

89

DAILY MIRROR, Monday, September 9, 1940.

Daily Mirror

No. 11,467 — ONE PENNY
Registered at the G.P.O. as a Newspaper.

SEPT 9

SECOND NIGHT IN BATTLE OF LONDON

THE battle for London was on again last night, when Hitler once more launched his bombers at the city. Bombs crashed in the London area.

All day long London had been coolly "patching up" the damaged spots left after the heavy and prolonged attacks made on Saturday—the first day of the battle.

Immediately after last night's warning—it was London's second of the day—a fierce anti-aircraft bombardment opened up. It started in one outer district, shaking doors and windows, but in a few seconds the Central London guns were in action.

There was the sound of a screaming bomb and an explosion.

Raiders approached London from the north-west. Several planes droned over a suburb.

A second wave came toward the East London area three-quarters of an hour after the warning.

The German machines approaching from the south-east could be seen at a great height. A.A. shells burst round them and they changed their course.

Some bombs were dropped on a suburb, including incendiaries, which started a blaze.

Fires Their Guide

Some of the German machines appeared to turn over another district owing to the fierce A.A. gunfire and flew back toward the coast without, apparently, reaching their main objective.

It was evident that the German airmen had used the smouldering fires of Saturday's raids to guide them, for the attacks were directed at the same area—London's dockland.

The first hour of the attack was considerably less formidable than Saturday's raid—fewer enemy planes were penetrating the intense defensive barrage from the coast to London. At the end of an hour there was a hushed lull.

Ten minutes passed—then, "like all hell let loose," the whole of London's defence barrage roared and crashed into action, heralding the return of the raiders.

Dull menacing crunches, whining and quivering reverberations were heard. Livid flashes leapt across the darkened sky as the planes dropped their bombs.

A.A.'s 3 in Minute

The London area's first warning sounded as formations of raiders attempted a daylight attack.

As one big formation emerged from clouds over a south-east area, three Dorniers were blown to pieces within a minute by A.A. fire. The brilliant marksman was a gunner aged twenty-two.

When the planes were hit their bombs were released and fell over a wide area. Shops and cottages were badly damaged, but all the occupants escaped injury.

The bombs set light to a schoolroom at a boys' home and the matron's house. A master gave the alarm and the elder boys fought the flames.

Members of the Home Guard, disbanding after a church parade, captured one of the airmen who had baled out. He told them that four others were close.

The Air Ministry said that during London's raid alarm some houses and

Continued on Back Page

99

German raiders were shot down during Saturday's battles, the Air Ministry stated last night. A.A. guns got twenty-one.

TROOPS REACH EGYPT

BRITAIN'S determination to defend Egypt and the Middle East at all costs has been proved by the arrival in Egyptian ports of huge convoys of ships carrying men and material from England, Rhodesia, India and Australia.

Not a periscope of a submarine broke the surface of the sea, not a single enemy aircraft was sighted, not a gun was fired from the enemy coast.

Large liners transported many thousands of technicians, infantrymen, whole hospital staffs and R.A.F. pilots, with quantities of munitions and tanks.

With the harbour a solid mass of shipping, the great liners anchored outside alongside smaller vessels to which they were lashed, while soldiers and white-uniformed nurses crossed the gangplanks to take up their berths for the last stage of their journey.

Not a Casualty

Heavy equipment was swung aloft, munitions were transferred without a single casualty or loss.

Since the beginning of the war many great convoys have loomed on the horizon, but nothing like this. Mast after mast appeared from sunrise onwards until the roadsteads could hold no more, and still they came.

Many disembarked and throughout the day the town rang with cheers as trains, loaded with waving soldiers, many of whom had seen fighting in France, passed through the centre of the town towards the desert, on their way to Cairo, Palestine and elsewhere.

Waiting For It

The Australian Air Force pilots were a particularly cheery lot. One man told Reuter that he had been waiting impatiently since the beginning of the war for this moment.

A special message from the Commander-in-Chief in the Middle East, General Sir Archibald Wavell, was posted up in each ship.

In it the General told the troops that "by serving here in the Middle East you are doing as much for the defeat of our enemies, Germany and Italy, as if you were defending your homes in the United Kingdom."

LONDON PORT CARRIES ON

The Port of London is carrying on in spite of Saturday night's bombing raid.

An official of the Port of London Authority told the *Daily Mirror*:

"While damage by fire at the docks is considerable, discharging and loading berths are intact, and all services of the Port will be maintained.

"Though some warehouses have been damaged, the losses of food-stuffs relatively small," he added

Actg.-Sergeant Ian Blair, D.F.M.

COULDN'T FLY —SAVED PLANE

ALTHOUGH his flying experience was practically nil, a twenty-two-year-old navigator took the place of his dead pilot and flew a bomber 250 miles back to the base.

He said he found it easy until the time came to land, when, in his own words, "he began to sweat." But that didn't prevent him from making a nearly perfect landing.

He is Ian Blair, of St. Vincent-street, Glasgow, who has been awarded the D.F.M., it was revealed in Cairo last night.

The bomber in which Blair was navigator, was attacked by two Italian fighters. A bullet went through the glass panel, killing the pilot and going out on the other side.

Blair saw the pilot's head go forward and the bomber started to dive.

Blair rushed to the control column and, helped by the air gunner, removed the pilot's harness and safety belt and lifted him from his seat.

Then the air gunner went back to watch for Italian fighters and Blair set out for his base.—British United Press.

PRESIDENT IS AIR VICTIM

General Jose Felix Estigarribia, President of Paraguay, has been killed in an aeroplane accident, according to a dispatch from Asuncion, quoted by Reuter.

★ All London's Fires Out But One ★

By seven o'clock last night London Fire Brigade announced that all fires caused by air raids have been overcome or extinguished, with the exception of one which was in hand.

The Air Ministry and Ministry of Home Security issued this communique yesterday:—

Further particulars can now be given of the heavy attacks directed on London by the enemy during yesterday (Saturday) evening and continued on a smaller scale in the night.

Bombing was widespread and in the later part of the attack appeared to be indiscriminate. Damage was severe but, judged against the background of the war, is not serious.

✦ ✦ ✦

The major weight of the enemy's offensive was concentrated on both banks of the Thames east of the City, especially on the riverside, where three extensive fires and a number of others were caused.

Much damage was done, and a number of persons were rendered temporarily homeless, but were removed from the danger area and given food and shelter.

Bombs also fell on a utility plant in this area and some of the services were seriously interfered with.

Many bombs were dropped in the docks of the Port of London Authority, and a large fire was caused in the docks south of the river. Elsewhere some warehouses were damaged and several barges were set on fire.

The attacks in other parts of London were not comparable in magnitude, but many bombs were dropped. In South London two schools were seriously damaged, a fire was caused in Central London, and houses were demolished.

✦ ✦ ✦

Throughout all these areas the Civil Defence Services are speedily and successfully dealing with the tasks imposed upon them, which have included the evacuation of several hundred civilians from one area rendered dangerous by fire; assisting to restore road and rail communications which suffered considerable interruption, although trunk lines have not been seriously affected; and more particularly fire fighting, which has imposed a very heavy task upon the fire service, many of whom carried on their work under bombardment.

In Great Britain, outside the London area, the only report of major damage comes from an oil installation on the Lower Thames, where a large fire was caused.

✦ ✦ ✦

These attacks much exceeded in scale any that have preceded them. There is evidence from all areas of the high courage with which the civil population have accepted this challenge.

'ALL EARNED V.C.'

By JOHN WALTERS
NEW YORK, Sunday.

"All Londoners deserve the V.C."

THIS was the comment of an American broadcaster to-day.

He was paying a moving tribute to the courage of Londoners in Saturday night's raid. Many other radio speakers and newspaper correspondents used similar expressions.

This is what the *New York Times* correspondent said:

"One simply cannot convey the spirit of the British people. Adversity only angered and strengthened them. They're tough in a way we Americans seldom understand."

Wave of Sympathy

Millions of Americans are expressing horror and disgust at the murderous Nazi attacks, and a wave of sympathy for Britain is sweeping the country.

It is predicted in Washington that this merciless bombing will result in increased aid for Britain.

Congressmen are receiving thousands of telegrams urging greater help.

Americans, led by President Roosevelt, today said special prayers for peace in churches in all towns and villages. At hundreds of services prayers were said for a British victory. Many worshippers wore British war relief buttons and miniature Union Jacks.

GUNNED ON PARACHUTE

"It was sheer, cold-blooded murder," said an East End stevedore, describing how two German planes again machine-gunned the pilot of a Spitfire as he descended by parachute during the first raid on Saturday.

"The Spitfire,' he said, "was shot down in flames, and the pilot baled out. As he floated down two German fighters passed and re-passed him, pouring burst after burst of machine-gun fire into him.

"We could see the pilot sag in his harness, and then he fell on top of a barrage balloon.

"The crew hauled the balloon in, and they got the pilot down.

DAILY MIRROR, Saturday, Sept. 14, 1940.

Daily Mirror

No. 11,472 — ONE PENNY
Registered at the G.P.O. as a Newspaper.

KING AND QUEEN IN PALACE, BOMBED

The King's Resolution

AFTER the attacks on Buckingham Palace and Downing-street, the following telegrams passed between the War Cabinet and the King:—

The War Cabinet to the King:
"The War Cabinet offer their hearty congratulations to their Majesties on their providential escape from the barbarous attack made on their home and royal persons."

The King to the Prime Minister:
"The Queen and I are so grateful to the War Cabinet for their kind message.
"Like so many other people, we have now had a personal experience of German barbarity, which only strengthens the resolution of all of us to fight through to final victory."

DAYLIGHT RAIDER DIVED THROUGH CLOUDS YESTERDAY AND DROPPED FIVE BOMBS ON BUCKINGHAM PALACE, ALREADY SLIGHTLY DAMAGED BY A TIME-BOMB. THE KING AND QUEEN, WHO WERE IN THE PALACE, ARE UNHARMED.

After the "All clear" sounded, quite unshaken by their experience, they left on a tour of other bombed areas.

The Palace chapel, where the Princesses were christened, was damaged. Nearly all the windows on the south side of the inner quadrangle were broken. Bomb fragments pitted the walls. Three of the Palace staff were injured.

Incendiary bombs fell in Downing-street, but did no damage.

News of the Palace bombing was released by the Ministry of Information yesterday towards the end of London's longest day raid warning yet.

After a night of limited air activity in which the Nazis were repelled by a mighty A.A. barrage—a barrage which met enemy planes in the provinces also—London had several day warnings.

The first, just over an hour and half after the all clear following the eight and a half hours' night raid, was short, but soon after a further warning was given which lasted over four hours.

Deliberate Attack

During these day raids enemy planes—dodging in between clouds—were seen from all parts of London.

A.A. fire broke out from time to time and a number of bombs, the majority incendiaries, were dropped.

There are reports of a number of enemy planes being shot down, and at some points observers saw enemy airmen baling out from their crippled craft.

The Air Ministry and Ministry of Home Security issued this communiqué:

"Following last night's ineffective attacks in which bombs were dropped in London at random through heavy clouds, a small number of enemy aircraft have today deliberately bombed a number of conspicuous buildings in various parts of London irrespective of their nature.

In Downing-st.

"It is feared that the enemy has succeeded in killing and injuring a number of civilians.

"Buckingham Palace was attacked, several bombs falling within the precincts, one of which damaged the palace chapel.

"Their Majesties were in residence but fortunately escaped injuries. Three members of the staff of the Palace were injured.

"Incendiary bombs also fell in Downing-street, but did no damage."

Continued on Back Page

The altar in the private chapel at Buckingham Palace. Generations of British Kings and Queens have worshipped in this chapel; the sons of Kings have been married in it under The Cross. The cross of Nazi-ism has wrecked it in moments.

WATCH FOR FIRES: THEY HELP RAIDERS

THE danger arising from outbreaks of fire in unattended buildings is stressed in an urgent warning issued by the Ministry of Home Security.

R.A.F. "Leaves" Made Him Shiver

The new British "incendiary leaf" was shown to the Berlin correspondents of Spanish newspapers at the Nazi Ministry of Propaganda.

The correspondents were told that the leaf is composed of a paste of celluloid, cotton and phosphorus and the slightest contact is sufficient to turn them into "perilous tongues of fire."

The correspondent of the newspaper "Ya" states that thousands of these leaves have been dropped in Berlin and Hamburg. "I give you my word that these leaves make me shiver," he adds.—Reuter.

It is pointed out that if an outbreak occurs in such a building, the fire may not only involve a serious call on the local fire services through not having been detected at an early stage, but may also serve as a beacon to raiding aircraft.

A single person in the building could at least summon the fire brigade at once, even if he could not extinguish the fire before it got a hold.

The main classes of premises to be considered are factory and warehouse buildings and timber yards. Occupiers of all such premises are strongly urged to arrange that at least one person is always on the premises for the purpose of giving an alarm in case of fire, and also to provide simple fire-fighting equipment for use until the brigade arrives.

FIRE BOMBS ON ULSTER

INCENDIARY bombs were dropped on a Northern Ireland coastal town yesterday and houses and shops set on fire, according to an official statement issued in Belfast.

The announcement stated:—

"A single enemy aircraft made an unsuccessful attack on shipping off the coast of Northern Ireland. Subsequently a small number of incendiary bombs were dropped on a coastal town.

"A few fires were caused which were soon brought under control by the local fire brigade and A.F.S. The damage was slight and there were no casualties."

AMBULANCES FROM N.U.R.

The National Union of Railwaymen are to provide four ambulances for the British Red Cross Society and a mobile canteen for the Forces.

Bournville Cocoa down in price!

now costs **5d** PER QTR. LB.
9½d per ½ lb. 1/6½ per lb.

— NOW CHEAPER THAN BEFORE THE WAR

Bournville Cocoa is down in price. By cheaper packings, economies in distribution and the withdrawal of Coupon Gift Schemes, savings have been made which, according to our practice, we are at once passing on to the public.

Cocoa is a concentrated food; and thus this action is in line with Lord Woolton's appeal to manufacturers to find means of making the price of staple foodstuffs as low as possible.

QUALITY UNCHANGED
A CUP OF COCOA IS A CUP OF FOOD

Daily Mirror

SEPT 19

No. 11,476 — ONE PENNY
Registered at the G.P.O. as a Newspaper.

R.A.F. BAG 46 IN 5 ATTACKS

GOERING flung five separate waves of bombers and fighters over the south-east coast yesterday in new attempts to wear down our fighter strength and clear the path to London. The tactics failed at a cost of forty-six machines—forty-five shot down by the R.A.F. and one by A.A. fire.

Time after time between 9.30 a.m. and 8 p.m. Spitfires and Hurricanes slashed big enemy formations. Few German planes reached the London area. Yet the R.A.F. lost only nine machines, and the pilots of five of them are safe.

London had seven daylight raid warnings—including its hundredth since the war began. Then, at black-out time, came the eighth. The night raid was on.

Once more Goering's night bombers landed high explosives on the West End. Heavy bombs crashed in the area just before midnight.

Bombs fell in the same place in a South-West London suburb for the fifth time in five weeks.

Two houses damaged in the first raid were hit again, this time being completely demolished.

A nearby public shelter, full of people, was rocked by the explosions. Rescue parties immediately started a search of the buildings for victims.

A plane flying at a great height over a north-west suburb dropped a low calibre bomb. Searchlights went into action as A.A. batteries opened heavy fire.

"Camping" in Tubes

Simultaneously the great barrage over London broke out at full force.

Through the roar of the guns occasionally came the sound of enemy planes.

"Star bursts" of anti-aircraft fire in the drifting clouds lit up the sky.

The noise of the barrage and of falling bombs echoed along almost deserted streets.

Hundreds of homes were as empty as the streets. Their occupants were "camping" in the safety of the tubes.

They were in rows two deep along the platforms at some stations. Babies slept peacefully in nooks found by their mothers. Family parties played cards or chatted before going to sleep. Those without rugs and cushions found the "bed" hard. But they slept, nevertheless.

The fifth raid of the day produced a terrific air battle, and revealed

Contd. on Back Page, Col. 2

MEDALS WAITED AS POLES FOUGHT RAID

General Sikorski, Polish Commander-in-Chief, was pinning decorations yesterday on twenty airmen of a famous Polish fighter squadron when an air raid alarm sounded.

Only about half of the airmen had received their medals. But all of them jumped into the machines and took off to tackle the raiders.

General Sikorski waited until the squadron returned. Then the pilots lined up again, and the awards were completed.

They had just arrived back from a fight when the ceremony started.

In eighteen days this squadron has destroyed with certainty seventy-one German machines, and probably twelve more.

They received the Polish equivalents of the D.S.O. and the M.C.

M.M. for a Home Guard

First Home Guard to win a military decoration ... Volunteer Glyn Jones, who has been awarded the Military Medal. He was defending a vital point when the post was bombed and one man was killed and another seriously wounded. After he had carried the wounded man to safety, Jones continued on guard, though bombs and debris were still falling around him.

FRENCH SHIPS ALLOWED TO SAIL TO DAKAR

The French warships which recently passed through the Straits of Gibraltar are now at Dakar.

Before they passed through the Straits a message was sent to the British authorities announcing their intention and destination. Britain is not at war with France, and the ships were allowed to pass.

London "Worse Than Rotterdam"

"Military air attaches and correspondents who went to ground under a blizzard of bombs in Warsaw, Barcelona and Madrid, agree that London has already taken more punishment than any other city—even Rotterdam—in eleven days of intensive bombing."

This was part of a dispatch from London to the Associated Press in New York, in which Drew Middleton gave an account of various interviews he had had with expert neutral observers on Londoners' reaction to the raids.

"Despite these attacks," Middleton said, "they declare that the Luftwaffe has failed to achieve the raids' two main purposes and that the prospects of invasion diminish. The bombs are failing to disorganise London's communications so that supplies and reinforcements could not be sent to areas where the invasion is planned."—Associated Press.

Mr. Robert E. Sherwood, the American playwright, vouched for the accuracy of British claims in the air fighting over and around Britain in a broadcast from Boston last night.

He said he had recently learned from U.S. Government circles in touch with American military and diplomatic observers in Britain that, amazing as they seemed to be, the R.A.F. successes were "certainly not exaggerated."

TRAPPED 17 HRS. WITH DEAD WIFE

AFTER he had been trapped for seventeen hours with his dead wife in a taxi buried under tons of wreckage, a man was last night pulled to safety.

He had been conscious the whole time as rescuers strained to reach him.

He was fed with tea through a tube and after part of the debris had been removed, a slim nurse was able to squeeze beneath three girders to wash his injuries and ease his head with a pillow.

For fifteen hours without a break the man, Herbert Ernest Reaves, thirty-three-year-old taxi-driver, of Astley-road, Islington, N., was attended by Dr. J. Lister Boyd.

Before he was rescued Reaves wrote a note on a piece of newspaper: "Don't tell my mother." But his mother and sister had already arrived and stood by as the rescuers worked.

The taxi was at the bottom of a huge shell-hole in a bombed West End garage, and the injured man had to be pulled to safety up a chute of planks, with a score of workers pulling on a rope to relieve the pressure of a girder.

Wed Few Weeks

The body of Reaves's wife was brought out of the wreckage a few minutes before he was rescued.

A friend told the "Daily Mirror": "Bert has been married only a few weeks. His wedding reception was held near the garage where he was trapped.

"His wife worked in a restaurant about thirty yards from the bombed garage, and carried on working there owing to staff shortage after the marriage.

"I suppose he must have called at

Contd. on Back Page, Col. 5

BOMB NEAR U.S. EMBASSY

A time bomb fell near the American Embassy in Grosvenor-square, London, W., during a recent raid.

The building was not damaged, and the Embassy staff carried on work.

EARTHQUAKE HITS JAPAN

An earthquake shook a wide area of Eastern Japan on Tuesday, it was learned yesterday, says Reuter.

PLAIN JANE'S CAR GROUSE

Plain Janes everywhere and the "not so young" business women are protesting because pretty girls get preference when it comes to hitch-hiking to and from work.

In after-raid rushes for transport, motorists are inclined to put beauty before age, say these pavement wall-flowers.

"It is really most unfair" one thirty-five-year-old city secretary said to the *Daily Mirror* yesterday.

"I have seen motorists creep along the kerb, ignoring requests from older and less attractive women till they come across a pretty one, to whom they offer a lift immediately."

But motorists do not agree. The not-so-youngs and not-so-pretties are being unreasonable they say.

"From my experience motorists make no distinction," said an official at the R.A.C.

HUN PORTS BLAZE

TERRIFIC flashes of flame lit up the French coast last night in the region of Boulogne as the R.A.F. launched a great attack on the German invasion ports.

The raid, which appeared to be the most violent yet carried out by the R.A.F. on Boulogne, began soon after nine o'clock. As it developed, many miles of the French coast seemed to be ablaze.

As the R.A.F. raid developed fresh waves of British bombers spread the attack to Calais where big fires broke out.

Flaming onions cut through the searchlight beams and shell bursts studded the sky, but the almost continuous bomb flashes showed that the British pilots were pressing home their attack with determination.

It was revealed last night that the R.A.F. have sunk two big ships, one thought to be a destroyer in an attack on Cherbourg.

It was also stated last night that one of the biggest forces of British bombers so far used in the war struck new blows at the German-held Channel ports during Tuesday night.

In the brilliant moonlight the heavy guns near Cap Gris Nez were clearly picked out and pounded with bombs. Our pilots could see explosions well within the target area.

R.A.F. Hammer Channel Ports—Page Seven.

"EVAN WILLIAMS"
—the choice of millions

These millions of women, coming as they do from every grade of life, can't be wrong in their choice and their loyalty to this perfectly blended shampoo. After all ... "Evan Williams" is of no mushroom growth; there is behind it a tradition of service in the cause of hair beauty lasting more than 40 years, evidence of dependability and worth which must make "Evan Williams" Shampoo the choice of every thoughtful woman.

EVAN WILLIAMS *Shampoo*

Still only 4d. per packet

DAILY MIRROR, Monday, Sept. 23, 1940.

Daily Mirror

SEPT 23

No. 11,479 — ONE PENNY
Registered at the G.P.O. as a Newspaper.

83 CHILDREN DIE AS HUNS SINK LINER IN STORM

HERO OF A SHIP

Chatting to Derek and Sonja Bech in the picture below is Edward Colin Ryder Richardson (centre) of Monmouthshire.

Hero of the children's ship that Germany torpedoed.

"His spirit never went down," the ship's carpenter said of him. "His cheery little voice could always be heard above the moaning of passengers. When a nurse in a lifeboat cried that she was dying, little Edward held her head in his lap, and told her that rescue ships were coming."

Derek and Sonja Bech (of Bognor Regis) were twelve hours with mother on a raft.

EIGHTY-THREE out of a party of ninety children being taken to Canada died along with 211 other passengers and crew when a British liner was torpedoed and sunk by the Huns in an Atlantic storm.

Seven out of nine adults who were escorting the children were also drowned.

A U-boat committed this crime against civilians when the liner was 600 miles from land. The ship sank in twenty minutes.

Huge seas swamped some of the boats which the crew managed to launch. In other boats people sat waist deep in water and died of exposure.

Many of the children were killed when the torpedo struck the ship.

The disaster was revealed last night when it was stated officially that the number of missing was 294.

There were 406 people in the ship, a crew of 215 and 191 passengers, including the ninety children, who were being evacuated by the Overseas Reception Board.

The 112 survivors included thirty-six Lascars.

Two of the children who were drowned were making their second attempt to reach safety in Canada. They were rescued from the first evacuee liner to be torpedoed—the Volendam. They were still eager to cross the Atlantic and were embarked on the next available ship. This time they did not escape the Huns.

Apart from those in the party of ninety evacuee children a number of children travelling privately with their parents are among the missing.

M.P. Among Dead

Among the passengers who went down with the ship was Colonel James Baldwin-Webb, M.P. for Wrekin, Shropshire. He was on a special Red Cross mission to Canada.

When last seen he was bleeding from a wound, and refusing to go into a lifeboat until all the women and children had been got away safely.

The survivors, haggard, worn,

Continued on Back Page, Col. 1

NIGHT RAIDERS MAY HAVE NEW WEAPON

TWO high explosive bombs fell in south-west London last night.

Flares were dropped by the raiders to light their targets.

It seemed as if a new weapon were being used by the Nazis, for several times in quick succession there was a yellow glow which lasted for a couple of seconds.

A Nazi plane dropped a high explo-

Continued on Back Page Col. 5

BROADCAST BY THE KING TONIGHT

The King will broadcast to listeners at home and overseas at 6 p.m. today.

The speech will be broadcast on all B.B.C. transmitters and for listeners in this country on the additional short wave length of 48.82 metres.

Deep Shelters for Six Million?

Sir John Anderson is to be asked by Mr. R. R. Stokes (Lab., Ipswich) if he is aware that engineers consider deep bomb-proof tunnels could be dug in London for the whole of the population of six million for a total cost of £120,000,000, and if he will have this work put in hand at once, in view of the Government's declared opinion that the war will last three years.

HOMELESS—LOSE FIVE

THEIR home smashed by Nazi bombers.... Five of their twelve children lost in the sinking of the evacuee ship by a U-boat.

That is what the Germans have done to the Grimmond family, of Lilford-road, Camberwell.

Just before the children were due to leave London for the embarkation port, bombers reduced their home to a mass of debris.

The family were safe in their shelter, but all the new clothes that had been bought for the little evacuees were destroyed.

"I decided it would be impossible for them to go and thought of asking for a postponement of the evacuation," said Mr. J. E. Grimmond, a general labourer.

"I wish to God I had done so now, but the authorities told us fresh equipment would be provided for my children."

The children who are missing are Leonard, aged five, Violet, aged eleven, Constance, aged ten, Edward, aged eight, and Augusta, aged thirteen.

A letter confirming his children's deaths arrived by the same post as last letters from the children themselves.

"Dear Mum and Dad," wrote Augusta from the evacuee ship, "we are starting off on the boat today at half-past one. We came on the boat yesterday.

"Eddie and Lennie are shearing a cabin, and Connie, Violet and me are shearing a cabin.

"It is very lovely. I wish you were with us, the cabins are all furnished.

"Connie and Violet are shearing a big wardrobe, and I have got a single, we have got dark servants

Continued on Back Page, Col. 5

DAILY MIRROR, Tuesday, Sept. 24, 1940.

Daily Mirror

No. 11,480 — ONE PENNY
Registered at the G.P.O. as a Newspaper.

SEPT 24

SAVE SICK IN RAID

DOCTORS and nurses at a hospital in a south-east town moved patients from some of the wards last night when incendiary bombs fell on two blocks of the building.

A fire was quickly put out by staff and firemen.

Patients in other parts of the hospital had been moved, as it was feared that there was an unexploded bomb nearby. Families in houses near the spot have been evacuated.

Two bombs were dropped by a raider in a south-western district of London last night.

The roar of a plane flying fairly low was heard in Central London. A.A. guns opened fire and the raider quickly made off.

Two banks, a post office and a block of luxury flats were damaged when a high explosive bomb dropped in a North-West London district early today.

Earlier in the evening a raider flew over a North-East London suburb. A.A. guns opened fire. Some bombs were dropped.

What appeared to be a "Molotov breadbasket" was dropped on a Northern suburb.

The incendiaries from "the breadbasket" fell on and around the new wing of a school which has been used as an ambulance station. All the ambulances were removed to safety and no one was injured.

More than 200 incendiary bombs fell in an open space, and lit it up like a gigantic fireworks display.

A.R.P. wardens put out the flames. The fire bombs were followed up by several high explosives. A fierce A.A. barrage was put up by the guns, from which the raiders turned.

It was announced last night that in fights during the day eleven German planes were shot down. The R.A.F. lost eleven planes, but seven of our pilots are safe.

Giant Plane Fled

A new giant four-engined bomber, surrounded by a cloud of Messerschmitt fighters, crossed the Kent coast yesterday in a vain bid to reach London.

The monster raider was followed by three formations each of nine bombers. All flew at a great height.

A police officer said: "I looked through binoculars, and when the bomber was caught in the sunlight I was astonished at the huge size of its wing span.

"The Messerschmitt escort looked like dots beside it."

The enemy was scattered by Spitfires and Hurricanes.

Last seen, the bomber was speeding Channelwards with Spitfires in pursuit.

Eastbourne Bombed

An armed trawler shot down a German plane which tried to attack it in the Channel in the afternoon.

A lone raider dropped twenty-eight bombs on Eastbourne.

Casualties are believed to be about twenty, with none fatal.

The bombs fell in a working-class district. There was widespread damage to small houses in about eight roads.

A Messerschmitt 110 dived towards the cliffs between Dover and Folkestone and hurtled seawards, a Spitfire racing after it Spitfire's machine-guns blazed. The German just cleared the Mole at Folkestone harbour and, badly hit by bullets, plunged into the sea with a terrific crash, sending up a column of water.

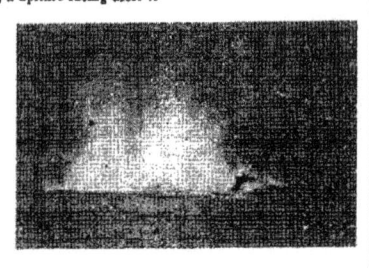

When the splash had died away the tail of the Messerschmitt could be seen from the cliffs sticking out of the water

★ THEN... THE VICTORY ROLL

From above the Spitfire pilot watched the result of his fire. Then his machine rolled over and back....

The Victory Roll, telling the shore watchers of his success.
★

DE GAULLE LEADS SWOOP ON PORT: NAVY OPENS FIRE

GENERAL DE GAULLE, AT THE HEAD OF A FORCE OF FREE FRENCHMEN AND BRITISH TROOPS, YESTERDAY ARRIVED IN A BRITISH SQUADRON OFF FRANCE'S VITAL WEST AFRICA PORT OF DAKAR, SENEGAL, TO LEAD A REVOLT AGAINST THE PETAIN AUTHORITIES THERE.

LYONS RADIO LAST NIGHT SAID THAT AFTER THE FRENCH AUTHORITIES HAD REFUSED DE GAULLE'S ULTIMATUM TO SURRENDER THE TOWN, THE BRITISH SQUADRON OPENED FIRE.

The British Ministry of Information announced De Gaulle's move —one of the most sensational of the war.

Last night, says British United Press, it was reported in Vichy that at least sixty had been killed and sixty seriously injured in the bombardment of Dakar, which was still continuing after four hours.

It was stated that seven French warships, including the Richelieu, damaged in an earlier British attack, were returning the fire of the British ships.

Latest reports received in Vichy, says Reuter, indicate that the British squadron consists of two battleships, four cruisers, six auxiliary cruisers and a number of destroyers.

Dakar is the seat of the General Government of French West Africa. The port is a vital point affecting the British Empire's Cape route, which could be cut or seriously hampered if enemy air and naval forces were established there.

De Gaulle's expedition has forestalled Nazi plans to grab Dakar.

Rally to the Flag

Declared the Ministry of Information statement:

"General de Gaulle arrived off Dakar and has summoned his followers to rally to the flag of Free France.

"Resistance seems to have been encountered, but the situation is not as yet fully clear.

"General de Gaulle's Free French force is accompanied by a British force, which will lend him full support."

Petain's Cabinet met at Vichy last night.

It was stated that the British action did not call for a French declaration of war on England but, "wounded as she is, France is still capable of defending herself, and of replying to blow with blow."

The Petain Government ordered "the strongest possible military action" against the British Fleet.

Later it was stated that the British Fleet opened fire there had been no news from Dakar, as the radio station was damaged.

King's "V.C." for Civilians

THE King has instituted two new decorations for Home Front gallantry—a civilian V.C. to be known as the George Cross, and a George Medal.

The George Cross will rank second only to the Victoria Cross. The Empire Gallantry Medal, which was the second highest honour, will be absorbed, and present holders of that medal will have it replaced by the new decoration. It may be awarded posthumously.

For the George Medal, the standard will be high, though it will be awarded more freely than the Cross.

These new decorations are for men and women in all walks of life.

They are intended to meet the need for an award for civilian gallantry arising out of enemy action. But they will be awarded also for other brave deeds.

There will be a small military division of the Cross for members of the fighting Services who perform acts coming within the terms of the warrant.

Admiral of the Fleet Lord Chatfield has been appointed to watch over the award of the new decorations.

In a broadcast speech last night announcing that he had created these new decorations, the King declared that men and women who carry on the nation's work after the raid sirens sound take their place among the heroes of this war.

The King, who said he was speaking Continued on Back Page, Col. 1

BERLIN LONGEST RAID—3 HOURS

Berlin was kept awake by its longest raid last night.

British planes circled overhead for more than three hours and bombs crashed in the central district.

All sizes of anti-aircraft guns were in action in the most concentrated barrage ever heard in Berlin.

The noise of the raid penetrated to shelters throughout the city, reports Associated Press.

"Fire Leaves" on Berlin—Back page.

Daily Mirror

MIRROR, Thursday, Sept. 26, 1940.

No. 11,482   ONE PENNY
Registered at the G.P.O. as a Newspaper.

SEPT 26

BID FOR DAKAR ABANDONED

THE De Gaulle expedition against Dakar has been abandoned.

The British Ministry of Information stated last night:

"The Forces of General de Gaulle attempted to make a landing which was not successful, and when it became plain that only a major operation of war could secure the fall of Dakar, it was decided to discontinue hostilities, as it had never been the intention of H.M. Government to enter into serious warlike operations against those Frenchmen who felt it their duty to obey the commands of the Vichy Government.

"General de Gaulle himself was most anxious that he should not be the cause of bloodshed to his fellow countrymen.

"The forces concerned are therefore now being withdrawn from the region of Dakar."

It was revealed that the British warships sustained hits and casualties when forced into a duel with the shore batteries—which were themselves hit.

And the Navy sank two out of three French submarines which, despite a warning, made attacks.

The French Admiralty at Vichy stated last night that a violent British attack on Dakar started yesterday at 10 a.m. There was a fierce battle off shore and British planes repeatedly flew over the city.

It was claimed that two British battleships were torpedoed and that one withdrew from the action.

It was further claimed that on Monday, French cruisers scored several hits on the Barham and the Resolution and a cruiser of the Kent type.

The British Ministry of Information statement said that the expedition was sent because General de Gaulle, from information received, believed that a large proportion of the Frenchmen in Senegal (of which Dakar is the capital) would welcome him

What Navy Did

He therefore proposed to his Majesty's Government that he should proceed there with some of the troops at his disposal, with the good will and support of Great Britain. His Majesty's Government were all the more ready to afford General de Gaulle this support as information had reached them that German influence was spreading to Dakar," said the statement.

Meanwhile, while the expedition was on passage, the Vichy Government dispatched three cruisers from Toulon which passed through the Straits of Gibraltar and eventually arrived at Dakar.

"It is no part of the policy of his Majesty's Government to interfere with the movements of the French men o' war, so long as they are not destined for any ports in German control. For this reason, no hindrance was put in the way of the vessels in question passing through the Straits of Gibraltar.

"When having done so, they pursued a southerly course they were permitted to proceed.

"They therefore reached Dakar without interference. When later they put to sea again, steaming south, it was thought that they might be intending to interfere with the situation existing in French Equatorial Africa which had already declared for General de Gaulle.

"Ships of the Royal Navy intercepted their passage and insisted upon their reversing their course, which they eventually did, two of them returning to Dakar, and the third, which was suffering from engine trouble, being escorted by

Continued on Back Page, Col. 4

German Troops in Spain

GERMAN troops and equipment are moving into Spain, according to a reliable neutral witness who crossed the Spanish frontier yesterday.

This man, who has been living in Spain for twenty-five years, told British United Press that about a fortnight ago he saw about 500 German armoured cars, with full complements, arrive at Bilbao, where they were detrained and crossed the city southwards.

Their destination was unknown. According to Italian reports and Berlin hints, Spain is coming into the war against Britain.

Gibraltar—to be taken with German help—part of French Morocco and Madagascar are to be Spain's share of the spoils.

Japan, in return for a free hand in the East, will come into the plot, say the same sources, by stirring up trouble to keep the U.S. too busy to come in on Britain's side

Ceremony Plans

Hitler had an hour's talk yesterday with Ramon Serrano Suñer Spanish Minister of the Interior

The Rome radio yesterday suggested that Ciano (Italian Foreign Minister), Ribbentrop and Suñer may meet soon for some sort of ceremony. This is expected to be the signature of the pact with France.

It is known that the protocol office in the Wilhelmstrasse is preparing for some kind of ceremony, but German officials refuse to say what the ceremony will be.

Ciano left Rome yesterday for Berlin. Before he left he was said to have had a talk with the Japanese Ambassador in Rome says Associated Press

7-HOUR RAID ON CALAIS

A seven-hour raid on Calais causing thirty fires and smashing many barges, was included in one of the R.A.F.'s "systematic attacks" on enemy invasion ports carried out throughout Tuesday night.

A series of terrific explosions from the other side of the Channel were heard on the south-east coast late yesterday morning.

They were heavier than any heard since the outbreak of war, and the whole of the English coastline seemed to be shaken.

Last night the Air Ministry issued the following communique: "Throughout Tuesday night our bomber forces continued their systematic attacks on enemy invasion ports, including Delfzijl, Ostend, Calais, Boulogne, Cherbourg and Le Havre Many fires and explosions resulted.

"An aircraft of the Coastal Command attacked a convoy of enemy vessels off Terschelling last night. One of the vessels was hit by three bombs and left sinking. Two of our aircraft were lost in the night's operations."

(R.A.F. Raid Berlin—page 7.)

FOOD: BE CAREFUL

LORD WOOLTON, Minister of Food broadcasting last night, said that Britain has stored food for today and for the days to come

"I beg of you to keep careful watch how you use this store, which is enough to meet our needs," he added.

"Let me warn you of this. During the second year of war you must not expect all the things you had in the first year.

"You will have enough to eat, but you must be prepared for changes If you cannot have one thing, we will give you another we must be flexible

"When you realise that quite suddenly we lost all the supplies of butter, eggs, bacon and condensed milk that used to come from our main sources of supply—Holland and Denmark—you will agree that during this last year we have had everything we could expect

These Grand People

"We now have to bring butter from the Southern Hemisphere instead of Denmark. Supplies begin to arrive about November and stocks are running down a bit.

"So I ask you to use a little more margarine until the new stocks arrive."

Lord Woolton paid tribute to dock labourers who worked magnificently in bombed ports, warehousemen and the men of the rail and road transport who had stuck to their jobs during raids; wholesalers, who had seen to the distribution, and to the shopkeepers and assistants.

"My heart goes out to the small shopkeepers in the bombed areas," he added.

"They will rise again, these grand people I want to thank them for their service and their fortitude."

(Butter Ration Cut—page 3.)

NAZIS DEPOSE KING HAAKON

American radio stations stated yesterday that Germany has issued a decree deposing King Haakon and forbidding for ever any of the Norwegian Royal Family to enter Norway.

U.S. Arms Pouring Into Germany

American industrialists are secretly supplying Germany and Italy with £2,500,000 worth of vital war materials a month, according to an investigation made by the New York "Daily News."

Vast quantities of ore (including copper), machinery and cotton which is essential in the manufacture of explosives are entering Axis territory through Arctic Ocean ports, Spain, Portugal and Russia. Some goes via Cuba and Mexico.

These five nations are co-operating with American business men, who have made profitable contacts with Axis agents in all parts of the world.

The "Daily News" reveals that powerful Axis friend Juan March — who was France's financial backer—has a desk in the offices of Francis Du Pont, which has connections with the huge Du Pont arms and gunpowder firm at Wilmington, Delaware.

Another desk in the same office is occupied by Avelino Montes, who is an expert at getting secret shipments through Mexico.

Yesterday's Score—

THE Air Ministry announced last night that twenty-three enemy planes, including fifteen heavy bombers and three fighter-bombers, were shot down during the day. Four of our planes were lost, but three pilots are safe.

Twenty of the enemy were destroyed by our fighters between Bristol and the English Channel. A.A. guns got the other three.

This was the R.A.F.'s biggest bag for a week.

Last Wednesday they shot down forty-eight enemy planes with the loss of twelve planes, nine of whose pilots escaped.

The Huns renewed their night attacks on London Searchlights, shells and flaming onions were flung up against them, and several of the early raiders were unable to penetrate the barrage.

Early this morning in the middle of the London barrage a direct hit was apparently scored on a bomber over a south-west area. The sound of the engine ceased and there were violent explosions, followed by silence.

Several shops were damaged in a North-West London suburb when a bomb crashed in a main street, but there were no casualties

Parachutist Dead

Yesterday the German formations were the biggest they have sent over since their crushing defeat on Sunday September 15, when they lost 185 planes.

Between 100 and 200 bombers and fighters flew north-west in a variety of formations just before noon.

During the day raids crowds who had watched a brilliant attack by a few Spitfires on a German formation of fighters and bombers were present at the final act of the drama, which took place in a smoke-filled chine near Bournemouth.

In a space of seconds, two of the raiders, one a bomber and the other a Messerschmitt fighter, were seen diving out of control.

Three forms were seen leaving one plane. One German was hanging with his head and feet down and suspended by the waist from his parachute.

He was dead when he landed on a railway embankment at Parkstone.

Another black object twirled over and over as it fell. It was the body of a German whose parachute had failed

Continued on Back Page, Col. 3

300 FRENCH BOMBS ON GIB.

A HUNDRED French planes again attacked Gibraltar yesterday, dropping about 300 bombs of various sizes, wires British United Press from the Rock.

In this heaviest some of the bombs fell on buildings, roads and the old defences, causing considerable damage to private property and Government offices and killing a number of people. Three raiders were shot down.

A small ship in the harbour was hit and sunk.

Vichy claimed that the Renown was hit and had to leave harbour. (Story in page 2.)

23 to 4

'Special Drene Shampoo keeps my hair sparkling'

JEAN COLIN
Fascinating Star of Stage and Screen.

MISS Colin goes on to say—" It's really quite miraculous how easy my hair is to set right after a shampoo with Special Drene Moreover, no other shampoo gives my hair such thrilling, dazzling beauty All my friends agree — Drene gives them really glamorous hair

GLAMOROUS HAIR CAN BE YOURS TOO... WHEN YOU USE

Special drene SHAMPOO
6d., 1/6 & 2/6

DAILY MIRROR, Saturday, Sept. 28, 1940.

Daily Mirror

SEPT 28

No. 11,484   ONE PENNY
Registered at the G.P.O. as a Newspaper.

FLYER V.C. AT EIGHTEEN

V.C. hero at eighteen is Sergeant John Hannah, of Glasgow, who put out a fire caused by a direct hit on the bomb rack of his machine and made it possible for the pilot to land safely.

He is the youngest V.C. of the war.

The award was announced yesterday. On the night of September 15, 1940, Hannah was the wireless operator-air gunner in an aircraft engaged in a successful attack on enemy barge concentrations at Antwerp.

It was then subjected to intense anti-aircraft fire and received a direct hit from a projectile of an explosive and incendiary nature which apparently burst inside the bomb compartment.

A fire started which quickly enveloped the wireless operator's and rear-gunner's cockpit; and as both the port and starboard petrol tanks had been pierced, there was grave risk of the fire spreading

Sergeant Hannah forced his way through the fire to obtain two ex-

Contd. on Back Page, Col. 4

Hit Back, Arms Workers

To the workers in the arms factories, Mr. Herbert Morrison, Minister of Supply, issues this "Order of the Day"—

You are front line fighters in the battle for freedom. While the Nazi barbarians rain down their bombs on our people, yours is the proud task of counter attack.

Alone among the troops of our civilian army, you can do more than suffer and endure in grim patience —you can hit back.

You are the men and women of whom Hitler is afraid, for your hands are forging the weapons of victory

Every hour of working time that he can keep you idle is a gain to him; every hour that you can defy his bombers and remain at your posts is one more blow struck in defence of your homes and families, one more step towards victory.

That is why the whole nation welcomes the new policy of working on after air raid warnings until danger is imminent.

Within a few days the arms industry of the country will have adopted it. This is a victory for courage and common sense alike.

Stand to your jobs, then, men and women of the arms industry.

You provide the best of all protection for your families. Victory will crown your efforts.

PACT MAY SWAY U.S.

As soon as President Roosevelt learned yesterday of the pact between Japan and the Axis he called his defence chiefs, State officials and Lord Lothian, British Ambassador for special conferences.

Berlin and Rome officials openly boasted that the ten-year military, political and economic pact would keep the United States out of the war by facing her with the threat of attack from Japan.

The pact was carefully studied at yesterday's meeting of the U.S Cabinet

Washington officials, cables John Walters, predicted last night that the ultimate effect of the pact will be to make the United States a fully-fledged ally of Britain.

U.S. Doomed If—

"It must at last be obvious, said one in an interview which he said must be taken as official, "that if Britain is defeated the United States will fall a prey to the powerful forces of Germany and Japan. Unless we back Britain to the full we may be doomed."

New York is fully prepared for war after many months of secret preparations

Air-raid shelters have been designed for each resident, plans for the evacuation of two million children perfected, and constant food shipments have been assured

Measures have been taken to protect water, heat and power. Hundreds of posters have been prepared urging the population to keep calm. Anti-gas propaganda is being printed

Send All Quickly

Lord Lothian, British Ambassador to the United States, after a conference with President Roosevelt yesterday, said that Britain would welcome from America all kinds of supplies sent with the great possible speed.

Asked what was Britain's greatest need, Lord Lothian replied, "More of everything, and quick."

Shortly before Lord Lothian arrived at the White House, Mr. Roosevelt received a large delegation urging further immediate aid for Britain

NEW SHELTER POWERS

Wide powers have been given to local authorities under new defence regulations to provide air-raid shelters. The authorities can order opening of shelters of any premises by day and night

130 DOWN IN DAY WAR

ONE hundred and thirty raiders shot down. That was last night's official estimate of Germany's air losses yesterday.

Fierce battles raged as R.A.F. fighters ambushed mass formations of daylight raiders over the London area and many parts of South England.

Thirty-four of our fighters were missing last night but the pilots of fifteen are safe.

Watchers on the coast near Beachy Head saw a Spitfire pilot deliberately sacrifice his life rather than allow a Junkers 88 to escape. He rammed the bomber, tearing off its tail. The Junkers dived headlong and crashed.

One of the crew was taken prisoner and two were killed. The Spitfire pilot died also.

Sixty planes fought it out over Redhill, Surrey. For an hour a battle raged over Kent. There was a fight over Somerset—another over Dorset.

The King and Queen watched an afternoon air battle over London during a tour of bombed areas. Standing on the edge of a huge crater in North London they saw A.A. shells bursting and British fighters pursuing a German formation.

4-Engine Plane Down

A fight which ended with the destruction of one of Germany's latest four-engined bombers was seen by many people at East Grinstead, Surrey.

The raider was flying low, with Spitfires diving at him from all angles. He came near crashing when he banked over a railway station. A final burst of machine-gun fire sent the big blue bomber crashing into a house, where it caught fire.

The occupier's wife and children had run out of the back of the house as the bomber hit the front. They escaped unhurt.

The enemy came over in four waves—three directed against London and south-east England, and the fourth against Bristol. Each time fighters met them well before they reached their objective, shot down many and drove the rest home.

Over 1,000 enemy aircraft have been destroyed in air attacks on this country since September 1. In August over 1,000 were destroyed.

In a morning battle over the London area at least ten raiders were destroyed

Four of the London raiders met their doom in a south-west district

Contd. on Back Page, Col. 2

Sergeant John Hannah, who at eighteen becomes the youngest V.C. of the war

DICTATOR FOR HOMELESS

DICTATOR appointed to care for the air-raid homeless in London is Mr Henry Willink, K.C.

He will see that they are fed, clothed and rehoused as quickly as possible.

His official title is Special Commissioner.

Mr. Willink has been known to his friends as Happy Harry since his Army days when, at the age of twenty-two, he commanded a battery, won the Military Cross and the Croix de Guerre

He became M.P. for North Croydon last June with a majority of 12,718.

Appointment of a second dictator —to rebuild road and rail services damaged by enemy action—was also announced last night.

This Special Commissioner is Sir Warren Fisher who in a recent speech said:

"Of all foul and dirty fighters the German is the foulest and dirtiest we must give 'hem hell in every sort of war

He will also supervise the clearance of salvage

IF IT'S CHOCOLATE THEN IT'S FOOD

CADBURY'S

BOURNVILLE

PLAIN FLAVOUR

CHOCOLATE

for quick energy

★

Bournville backs you up — gives you an instant supply of energy when you're feeling low. This famous plain chocolate — containing sunshine Vitamin D, iron and other minerals — is also abundantly rich in carbohydrates, for quick, immediately available energy. Look for the famous red packet.

Daily Mirror

DAILY MIRROR, Tuesday, Oct. 1, 1940.

No. 11,486 — ONE PENNY
Registered at the G.P.O. as a Newspaper.

Japs Say Britons Are Spies

SEVEN out of fifteen British residents in Japan who were arrested as alleged spies two months ago have been indicted and found guilty of breaking Japanese defence laws—including the "Military Secrets Protection Law."

Three other Britons have been indicted and the other five are being examined.

This was officially announced in Tokio last night.

The Japanese news agency, stating that one Japanese had been indicted for aiding the British residents, declared that scores of people in high Japanese society, as well as statesmen, had been questioned.

Business Chiefs Held

The names of the ten Britons either found guilty or indicted were given as follow:

1. Captain O. H. N. James, fifty-six, representative of the Federation of British Industries;
2. Michael C. Ringer, twenty-seven, of the Uriu Shokai Shimonoseki Steamship Agency;
3. Vanya Ringer, twenty-five, Nagasaki agent of the Uriu Shokai;
4. H. C. MacNaughton, fifty-four, honorary Consul for Greece, and owner of the MacNaughton Company, woollen dealers in Kobe;
5. H. C. W. Price, twenty-nine, managing director of the Clifford Wilkinson Tansan Mineral Water Company in Kobe;
6. J. F. James, fifty-seven, general manager, Nickel and Lyons, Ltd., freight brokers, Kobe;
7. B. W. James, O.B.E., fifty-two, managing director, Cameron and Co., import and export firm, Kobe; president of the Osaka and Kobe Foreign Chamber of Commerce;
8. A. F. Drummond, sixty, manager of the Osaka and Kobe branches of Frazar and Co.;
9. William Philip Charles de Trafford, fifty, lecturer at the Nagasaki Higher Commercial College;
10. L. T. Woolley, fifty, chief statistician of the Rising Sun Petroleum Company Yokohama.

Scare Report

Earlier in the day the Japanese news agency put out a report that Japan's Embassy in London had instructed 750 Japanese residents in London to leave for home.

Then Associated Press said the Japanese Foreign Office had confirmed it.

But an official at Japan's Embassy in London stated: "There must be some mistake. We definitely have not done so."

Nazi officials, stating that the Japanese liner Ushimu Maru was to be sent to Liverpool to embark the "evacuees," spoke of the "daily worsening of Anglo-Japanese relations."

Basis of the scare report, states Reuter, was probably a request to Tokio by the Japanese Consul-General in London for a boat to evacuate seventy employees of Japanese firms who are reducing their staff to a "skeleton" basis owing to shrinkage of business and air-raid risks.

SCHOOL FIRST AID PLAN

ELEMENTARY first aid teaching for every senior schoolchild in the country, "as a matter of urgency," was requested last night by the Board of Education.

A memorandum calls on all local education authorities to start courses in their schools at once as a wartime measure.

Pupils over sixteen will be taught the full first aid course taken by A.R.P. casualty services and members of St. John Ambulance Association and the British Red Cross.

So many air raid casualties have been found to be caused by flying glass and similar minor causes that it is possible for a person with rudimentary knowledge of handling wounded people to save life or prevent aggravated injuries.

One of the most important lessons in the course will be the study of pressure points, by which critical arterial bleeding can be stopped immediately with a deft touch.

To have this finger-tip knowledge at the finger tips, casualty authorities stress, will possibly cut down fatalities considerably.

Another lesson will teach the elementary alleviation of shock.

The two principal first-aid bodies last night welcomed the Board of Education's plan and promised full co-operation.

There is no intention of incorporating the children, when trained, in the A.R.P. services.

THE FIRST "G.M."

FIRST man to get the George Medal—one of the two new decorations for civilian gallantry—is an air raid warden.

He is Patrick King, aged thirty, of Wark-avenue, Shiremoor, Northumberland, who rescued a sixty-year-old blind woman, Miss Mary Wilson, when bombs were still falling in a raid.

Miss Wilson's house received a direct hit on the night of August 26 and she was buried in the debris.

Week-old Award

It was on Monday of last week that the King, in a broadcast, told his people that he had instituted two new decorations, chiefly for civilian gallantry. They are the George Cross—the civilian "V.C." which ranks second only to the Victoria Cross—and the George Medal.

News of the honour reached Mr. King yesterday in a telegram from the North-East Regional Commissioner, Sir Arthur Lambert.

It said: "Your coolness and courage in action have brought renown and honour to the civil defence services in this region and all will join with me in offering you congratulations upon this well won recognition."

??? French Warships Again Pass Gib.

Two French destroyers, and a third destroyer which was escorting two French merchantmen, passed through the Gibraltar Straits yesterday without the British Patrol attempting to interfere, according to a British United Press message from Tangier.

But according to another British United Press message from Madrid, the Cifra (Spanish) News Agency says that British warships were in pursuit of the ships when they were n

HUNS LOSE 47 IN 6 BREAK-THROUGH BIDS

SIX times German raiders in an attempt to break through to London and six times the attacks were smashed. Last night it was announced forty-seven Nazi planes had been shot down. We lost twenty-two fighters but twelve of our pilots are safe.

Only isolated planes managed to slip through the defences and drop bombs in the western suburbs. Damage was done and there were casualties.

Enemy planes were met by fighters over Surrey, and machines crashed near Oxted, Godstone, Tadworth and Ealing. As many as 150 Germans crossed the coast in one attack.

Heavy machine-gunning could be heard. The battle continued for about twenty minutes until our fighters drove the enemy back and followed them away southwards.

People at Tadworth heard the battle, but could see nothing of it until after one long burst of machine-gun fire a plane dived to earth in flames.

Several places in the South-East, notably Bexhill and Hastings, were hit and damaged, and casualties, some fatal, caused at both towns.

The pilot of a German fighter who descended by parachute in Dorking was badly burned and there is small chance of his recovery. His plane crashed in the Kingswood district.

A.A. gunners in the Thames Estuary area who opened fire on a Messerschmitt fighter hit it twice and it was seen to stagger and swoop down. It fell in a potato field at Strood. The pilot was unhurt and when police helped him

Contd. on Back Page, Col. 4

WOMEN, CHILDREN TO QUIT BERLIN

A general evacuation of women and children from Berlin has been ordered, according to the Columbia Broadcasting Station in New York. The evacuees are to be sent to rural areas where bombing is unlikely.

Earlier it had been officially announced, says Associated Press, that parents of children who may suffer in health from the nightly R.A.F. raids on Berlin would be given the opportunity of sending them out of the city.

"If parents are fairly well-to-do they must meet any expenses of the evacuation, which is purely voluntary," it was stated.

"For the poor, welfare organisations will supply funds to meet the cost of a temporary home for the children."

TOWN PROUD OF HIM

"Mad Wally, the warden." That is how people of one of London's most heavily-bombed districts refer to one of their civil defence workers. Because of his self-sacrificing heroism, his calculated defiance of all that Hitler pits against us in this battle for Britain.

Wally Oldfield's bravery is described on page 3. Other towns and villages have their Wally Oldfields, too. The "Daily Mirror" believes that their heroism should be brought to light.

If, then, you know of any special acts of bravery by any air-raid warden, A.F.S. man or Red Cross girl in your district—or by any other defence worker—write to us. The facts in your story must be vouched for by an officer of the organisation. Address your letters to the "Daily Mirror," Geraldine House, Fetter-lane, London, E.C.4, and mark your envelope "Unsung Heroes."

IN SIX MONTHS WE HAVE SPENT £1,610,135,776

In the first six months of this financial year, Britain's expenditure has reached the colossal figure of £1,610,135,776. Last year in the same period—which included less than a month of the war—we spent £562,026,216.

Our total ordinary revenue in the past six months is £452,518,411—that is £1,157,617,365 behind our expenditure. Treasury returns revealed this last night.

DAILY MIRROR, Wednesday, Oct. 2, 1940.

Daily Mirror

No. 11,487 — ONE PENNY
Registered at the G.P.O. as a Newspaper.

OCT 2

FIRST WOMEN TO WIN GM

Three A.R.P. women have won the new George Medal for Valour.

Three—whose honour is the honour of the thousands of women who, by day and night, in the towns and villages, go unfearingly, unflinchingly amid falling bombs, to their self-imposed duty.

Their deeds unsung, often unknown...

Valiant Women of England.

Mrs. Jane Bessie Hepburn (left) and Mrs. Dorothy Clarke, Aldeburgh (Suffolk) ambulance workers, who have been awarded the George Medal for rescuing a man who was injured in an explosion.

RAIDERS CHECKED

GERMAN night raiders over London again had to run the gauntlet of terrific anti-aircraft fire, and in the early stages of last night's attack big guns turned some of the bombers off their course.

Two which came in from the north-west were forced to swing south before they had reached Central London.

So fierce was the opposition that London had an unexpected All Clear before midnight—the first since the blitzkrieg started.

The lull had lasted more than an hour.

One of twelve incendiary bombs dropped on a North-West suburb fell near a shelter entrance. A man rushed from the shelter, picked up the bomb, which was then alight, and hurled it into the roadway out of danger.

A sixteen-year-old grocer's boy and his brother coolly threw sand and water over other bombs and stamped them out before the fire brigade arrived.

Several German attacks on southern England and London were smashed during daylight, and four enemy planes were shot down. Three British machines are missing.

The King paid his first visit since his accession to the Colonial Office during the afternoon.

An air raid warning was in operation when he arrived, but the "All clear" was sounded during his visit, which lasted nearly an hour.

At Poole, Dorset, fighters shot down three out of a large formation of raiders.

A Messerschmitt 109 came down completely wrecked on a farm on the northern outskirts of Brighton. The pilot was dead.

Two other enemy fighters were so damaged by Spitfires in this battle that though they escaped in the clouds their return home is unlikely.

Miss (Air Raid Warden) Sonia V. C. Straw, of Caterham (Surrey), one of the first three women to win the new George Medal. Only nineteen years old, she volunteered, and attended injured women and children while bombs fell round her.

GIRL, 19, AIDS VICTIMS 13 HOURS

FOR thirteen hours a Titian-haired girl of nineteen, a part-time A.R.P. volunteer, helped to save the lives of more than a dozen people injured in a raid.

She had had no practical experience of first aid, but her work won the admiration of experts.

Miss Sonia Straw, of St. Michael's-road, Caterham Hill, Surrey, is one of the first three women to be awarded the George Medal.

The two other heroines are Mrs. Dorothy Clarke and Mrs. Jane Bessie Hepburn, ambulance workers at Aldeburgh, Suffolk.

Sonia Straw is a shorthand typist. She works in a solicitor's office.

Her first-aid training was not finished when she was called out for duty.

After skilfully dressing the wounds of people injured by bombs near her home, she went out into the darkness during a raid—against the advice of fellow A.R.P. workers—to search for a woman missing among wreckage.

She's Qualified Now

She would not give up until the woman had been traced.

Sonia has since qualified in first-aid tests and is now a fully-fledged warden.

"I did no more than anyone else could have done," she told the *Daily Mirror* last night.

"I came across several people lying badly injured. With whatever I could find I bandaged them up.

"I used to think I would be scared at the sight of blood, but all those feelings leave you when you see pain and distress.

"Three soldiers brought water and bandages for me, and I soon had all the injured fairly comfortable. They were mainly women and children.

"After I had finished someone telephoned to say they could not trace their mother, who had been in the bombed part of a flat.

Midnight Search

"With another warden I helped search for her till after midnight. When we found her she was dead under a bed."

Sonia was having a cup of tea when the sirens sounded. Immediately she rushed to her post. An injured woman with a wound in her head was her first patient. The woman was lying in a damaged Anderson shelter.

Sonia lives in digs at Caterham, goes to work at 9.30 every morning and finishes at six.

"Then I go home for supper and off to the wardens' post," she said.

Continued on Back Page, Col. 4

GUARD ON BRIDE

BY A SPECIAL CORRESPONDENT

AFTER she had received two anonymous letters warning her not to go through with her marriage, a bride at Tchidy, Cornwall, had her home set on fire on the wedding eve.

The bride, Miss Ida Hosking, aged twenty-four, of Collingwood House, was asleep in the house with her mother and two friends, but neighbours saw the blaze soon after midnight and warned them.

When the wedding took place next day police were on guard outside the chapel. Mr. Leonard Lawry, of Kehelland, Cornwall, was the bridegroom.

Police investigating the mystery believe jealousy was the fire raiser's motive. Before she left for the wedding they interviewed the bride in her bridal gown.

Dog Didn't Bark

The bride's mother told the *Daily Mirror*: "We had been in the house preparing for the wedding until eleven o'clock. Someone must have waited to see the lights go out, then crept across the garden. Neither I nor my daughter can think of anyone who would want to harm her.

"She had been going out with Mr. Lawry for six years and had been engaged to him for three.

"Whoever started the fire must have been known to us, as the dog was outside in the porch and would have barked at a stranger.

"It was a miracle we were not burned to death. We were fast asleep and it was only when our neighbours, Mr. and Mrs. Ashton, knocked heavily at our window that we awoke. They had been playing chess in the house next door and saw the blaze. At first they thought an incendiary bomb had dropped.

"Fortunately, nothing untoward happened during the ceremony. Bride and bridegroom have now gone to St. Austell on their honeymoon."

DAILY MIRROR, Thursday, Oct. 3, 1940.

Daily Mirror

No. 11,488 ONE PENNY
Registered at the G.P.O. as a Newspaper.

OCT 3

CHAMBERLAIN TO LEAVE WAR CABINET

GOVT. STOPS MERCY SHIPS

EVACUATION of children overseas was stopped by the Government last night until further notice.

This does not mean that the Children's Overseas Reception Scheme has been abandoned.

Storms now raging in the Atlantic make safe passages uncertain even in convoy.

"Recent loss of children in the liner City of Benares illustrated the dangers to which passenger vessels are exposed in the weather conditions prevailing at this time of the year in the Atlantic," it was stated in London last night.

"The Government have come reluctantly to the conclusion that during the winter season of gales and heavy seas, they cannot take the responsibility of sending children overseas under the Government scheme."

Still Want to Go

"Although operation of the scheme is suspended for the time being, it has not been abandoned."

The *Daily Mirror* was told:—

"Despite the Government's decision, the American committee, which arranges private evacuation of children overseas will continue to function.

"We shall continue to accept the names of children for registration and to arrange for the transport of those already registered.

"Our records do not indicate that there have been any withdrawals as a result of the loss of the City of Benares."

The number of children who had been approved as suitable for overseas evacuation under the C.O.R.B. scheme reached 24,130 a fortnight ago. Of these, 2,650 children have already gone overseas.

TELL THE POLICE OF RENT PROFITEERING

The rent ramp, which has been a sequel to the arrival in Oxford of thousands of refugees from London, is to be ended.

Following prompt action by the emergency committee to safeguard victims of any profiteering landlord and landlady, the town clerk of Oxford asked yesterday that people overcharged for either furnished or unfurnished rooms should get in touch with the police, giving full particulars, so that proceedings could be taken. ("Rent Ramp to Stop."—See Page 11.)

Miss Mabel Manning carried a policeman to safety.

CARRIED P.C. ON HER BACK

A WOMAN, 5ft. 2in. tall, carried an injured policeman, a man of over 6ft., down a blazing staircase; another—a doctor—crawled down a tunnel under the ruins of bombed houses to aid raid victims.

The stories of these two heroines were told yesterday.

The first—Miss Mabel Manning, a canteen worker at a London police station—was badly cut by flying glass.

Despite her own injuries, she hoisted the wounded policeman on her shoulder and carried him down the burning stairs to safety after a bomb had set light to the building.

Then, as other injured were brought in, she tended to their wounds and bandaged them without a thought for her own injuries.

When morning came she went to her own home, in a block of flats. There she found that an incendiary bomb had burnt out her flat.

"Wonderful"

A police officer who saw her gallant work told the *Daily Mirror*:

"Miss Manning was really wonderful. I don't know how she managed to carry that man down the stairs. He was a big fellow.

"Now she is suffering from shock brought on by this affair."

A detective-inspector had just left the building when the bomb fell. As fire broke out he raced back and,
Continued on Back Page, Col. 1

IMMEDIATE changes in the War Cabinet are anticipated. Mr. Neville Chamberlain is expected to leave the War Cabinet and Mr. Ernest Bevin is to join it.

Lord Halifax is also affected.

Mr. Churchill will probably choose another Foreign Secretary when he reshuffles the War Cabinet within the next few days.

Mr. Chamberlain has come to the conclusion that for health reasons it would be wise to give up office as Lord President of the Council.

Mr. Bevin, one of the outstanding successes in Mr. Churchill's Government, may change from his present office of Minister of Labour for one in the War Cabinet with more scope but less responsibility.

Mr. Eden was named last night as the successor of Lord Halifax.

Duff Cooper to Go?

Lord Halifax has been so much identified with Mr. Chamberlain's policy that it would be almost impossible for him to remain in the War Cabinet if Mr. Chamberlain went.

Mr. Duff Cooper was mentioned last night as a member of the Government who will be found another office.

He has had a difficult and rough time as Minister of Information, having faced much criticism in Parliament.

NEW U.S. ATLANTIC FLEET

Confronted with the new alliance of Germany, Italy and Japan, the U.S. Navy plans to establish a "newly organised force" of over 125 ships in the Atlantic, in addition to the present big fleet in the Pacific.

This announcement was made by the Navy Department last night, says Associated Press.

RAID HOMELESS MUST REGISTER

IF you have lost your home in an air raid, you must register with the local authorities.

The Minister of Health (Mr. Malcolm MacDonald) has sent a circular to local authorities in the London Civil Defence Region asking them to notify the London Council of Social Service of the names, former addresses and new addresses of all people who have lost their homes and for whom the local authorities have found fresh accommodation in billets or houses.

The London Council of Social Service is setting up a register of people notified to them in this way.

Friends and relatives of people in Greater London who have lost their homes should, if they cannot get in touch with them, inquire at the town hall or Citizens' Advice Bureau of the area in which the family lived before, or write direct to the secretary of the London Council of Social Service, 7, Bayley-street, Bedford Square, London, W.C.1.

Help Came

Tended by a stretcher bearer is a woman suffering from bomb shock.

A bomb dropped in S.W. London, within 200 yards of a "Daily Mirror" Cameraman.

He raced to the spot, but the stretcher workers were before him even in that short time. His pictures, the best pictures of London's war, which appear in our middle pages, are a tribute to the men and women who are serving, heroically, in the air raid services.

Traffic Gunned

GERMAN fighter planes swooped on a small south-east town in daylight yesterday and blazed away at people and houses with their cannon and machine-guns.

Mrs. D. Chesterman, aged seventy-three, received three wounds when a cannon shell exploded in her room. She was taken to hospital.

This new "frightfulness" was paralleled in an Essex town, where a Dornier bomber machine-gunned traffic and made shoppers dive for shelter.

Bullets fell like hail as the raider fired continuously across a street. Then his high explosive bombs wrecked a maternity hospital, garage and hit a road.

But it was the bomber's last attack. Hurricanes on their way home after a patrol over the North Sea intercepted it and shot it down.

One of these British pilots, who later landed near the wrecked Dornier, was Flying-Officer Hart Massey, 4ft. 3in. cox of the Oxford crew which lost to Cambridge in the 1939 boat race.

Son of the High Commissioner for Canada, he is one of the smallest pilots in the R.A.F.
Continued on Back Page, Col. 3

"I'm all for Special Drene Shampoo— always!"

SAYS **POLLY WARD**
Glamorous Star of Stage and Screen

"I WAS thrilled to find how truly radiant my hair became after a Special Drene shampoo. Another thing I like about Special Drene Shampoo is that no special rinses are necessary. And my hair is so easy to set in a smart hair style right after the shampoo. Special Drene is wonderful!"

GLAMOROUS HAIR CAN BE YOURS TOO ... WHEN YOU USE

SPECIAL **drene** SHAMPOO

6d., 1/6 & 2/6

DAILY MIRROR, Saturday, Oct. 5, 1940.

Daily Mirror

OCT 5

No. 11,490   ONE PENNY
Registered at the G.P.O. as a Newspaper.

Nurseries at Arms Works

Mr. Ernest Bevin, Minister of Labour, in reply to a Parliamentary question, says that where it is necessary in munition works to employ married women with young children, day nurseries should be set up if children cannot be suitably provided for otherwise.

These day nurseries, Mr. Bevin explains, do not cover children of school age. In their case, he has asked the Board of Education to increase the provision of school meals.

AIR CHIEF'S N.Z. POST

Air Marshal Portal.

AIR Chief Marshal Sir Cyril Newall, fifty-four-year-old chief of the British Air Staff and a key man in the great expansion of the R.A.F., has been appointed Governor-General of New Zealand.

His appointment was officially announced last night. He succeeds Viscount Galway, whose term of office expires in February, 1941.

Sir Cyril's appointment caused considerable surprise in aviation circles, it was stated last night.

Sir Cyril is succeeded as Chief of the Air Staff by Air Marshal Sir Charles Portal, Chief of the Bomber Command, who is only forty-seven and a keen pilot.

"Made" R.A.F.

Sir Cyril Newall has been a successful Chief of Air Staff since his appointment in September, 1939, and has shown great tactical organising gifts. He has borne the brunt of the struggle and the success of the R.A.F., both in the defence of this island and in its hammer strokes on the Continent.

The modern R.A.F. is, indeed, partly his own creation, for he has been Chief of the Air Staff throughout most of the tremendous expansion which has taken place, and he has forged a formidable weapon.

Air Chief-Marshal Portal is Commander-in-Chief of the Bomber Command, whose communiques tell with almost monotonous regularity of the battering of Nazi bases and key-points.

JAPAN THREAT OF WAR ON U.S.

JAPAN'S Foreign Minister threatened the United States with war yesterday if America enters the European conflict or even so much as opposes Japanese ambitions in the Pacific.

As Hitler and Mussolini were making new plans in the Brenner talks, the Japanese Minister—Yosuke Matsuoka—bluntly admitted that Japan and the Axis entered into alliance to frighten America out of any war move.

"I fling this challenge to America," he declared, in a sensational interview given to the New York Journal American in Tokio.

Apparently carried to record heights of Japanese insolence owing to the pact with the Axis, Matsuoka told the United States:—

If America is going to stick to the existing position in the Pacific, we shall fight her.

Then he added: "It is better to perish than to maintain the status quo. Frankly, Japan and the Axis made a pact to prevent America from becoming involved in the present European war."

Matsuoka's challenge to America was no personal outburst. It was backed by his Premier, Prince Konoye.

"If U.S. Refuses—"

Konoye declared at a Press conference in Tokio.

"Should the United States recognise Japanese-German-Italian leadership in East Asia and Europe, the three Powers would logically recognise United States leadership in the Western Hemisphere."

"If the United States deliberately refuses to understand the intentions of the Japan-Axis pact, considers it hostile, and challenges the three Powers, we are ready to accept the fight to the finish.

"War or peace in the Pacific depends on the extent to which Japan and the United States can undertake to respect each other's interests respectively in the Eastern and Western Hemispheres."

Konoye then added that Japan, despite her pact with the Axis, "did not intend to provoke the United States without grounds."

He revealed that although they would not compromise with Communism, the Japanese Government hoped to minimise every source of conflict between Japan and Russia."

Daily Mirror, British United Press, Associated Press, Reuter.

BRENNER PLOTS

NEW YORK reports last night stated that Hitler and Mussolini, at their Brenner meeting yesterday, discussed the possibility of a final peace settlement with Petain by which France would join in the war against Britain.

Said Rome radio: "Hitler and Mussolini discussed the military and political programme of the present war against Britain, which has now reached a decisive stage.

"The world will soon see the outcome of the conference. One thing is sure. There was no plotting against any nation which is not involved in the present war.

"The leaders of the two nations do not intend to fix the date of the final common victory. The two nations will achieve this victory whenever and wherever the decision may come."

An official communique after the talks, which were held in an armoured car with fighter planes patrolling overhead, merely said:

"Within the framework of the ordinary exchange of ideas, the Duce and the Fuehrer met for a cordial reunion conducted within the sphere of the Axis.

"The two chiefs, during three hours, examined in the presence of Count Ciano and Von Ribbentrop, all problems concerning the two countries. General von Keitel (Commander-in-Chief of the German

Continued on Back Page

"I've Been Bombed Out of Two Homes"

Twelve-year-old Albert West, shyest of a family of eight, was telling everyone yesterday: "The King spoke to me today. When the King walked into a room at the Wilton Way L.C.C. Rest Centre at Hackney, he found Albert there alone, guarding the family's possessions. The King talked to him for several minutes, but all Albert could remember was that the King asked if he were comfortable.

"I told him that I wouldn't mind staying here until the war is over," said Albert.

Albert's family has been bombed out of two homes.

The King was on a tour of shelters, and hardly a minute before he reached a half in Central London there was a whistle from the clouds which sent hundreds scurrying from the streets. The King arrived on schedule almost before the whistle of the bomb had died away.

SWAM THROUGH BLAZING PETROL

AN aeroplane crashed into the sea near an English coast town. It floated upside down, surrounded by blazing petrol.

Two soldiers swam through the burning oil of the plane, and arriving before the rescue boats, tried gallantly but unsuccessfully to rescue the occupants.

The soldiers were Lance-Sergeant W. Joynson and Corporal G. Goodwin, both of the King's Regiment.

A similar act, this time successful was performed by four privates.

They swam out in the darkness and rescued an R.A.F. sergeant who had come down by parachute.

The four privates, all of the Border Regiment, were R. M. Collins, J. Hodgson, J. Mitchell and R. V. Eldren.

The names of these four, as well as those of the two N.C.Os. have been brought to notice by the Commander-in-Chief, Home Forces, for "gallant and distinguished service," the War Office stated yesterday.

WHICH IS THE 5-STAR COCOA?

★ **EXTRA FOOD VALUE.** Bournville Cocoa is rich in body-building proteins, and natural cocoa butter and carbohydrates to give you energy. So remember, a cup of Bournville — the 5-Star Cocoa — is a cup of food.

★ **IRON — THE BLOOD ENRICHER.** The rich iron content of Bournville Cocoa tones up the corpuscles in your bloodstream, makes you feel stronger.

★ **PHOSPHATES — FOOD FOR NERVES.** Bournville Cocoa is rich in the various phosphates and calcium. These help your nerves, build up bone and muscle, strengthen teeth.

★ **AID TO DIGESTION.** Bournville Cocoa is particularly digestible, helps digestion of other foods and so makes every meal go further.

★ **VITAMINS—VITAL TO HEALTH.** Remember that every tin of Bournville Cocoa contains the natural sunshine Vitamin D, specially necessary for kiddies' healthy teeth and straight, strong bones.

Bournville Cocoa, Britain's favourite quick-to-make hot drink, starred five times for health value and all-round excellence — is actually down in price! Now only 5d per ¼ lb. with the quality unaltered, it is more than ever the real household economy drink. Meal times, and odd times, and especially when the siren goes, 'go to it' and stir up a nice hot cup of Bournville Cocoa. It's fine for morale!

BOURNVILLE
THE 5-STAR
COCOA
DOWN TO
5d per qtr lb
COSTS LESS THAN PRE-WAR

A.R.P. CYCLIST GETS G.M.

Although blown off his bicycle by two bombs which exploded on either side of him, an A.R.P. cyclist insisted on going on to deliver his messages.

For his bravery, it was announced yesterday, he is to get the George Medal.

He is William Joseph Jenkins, aged twenty-seven, of Stepney-street Swansea.

Soon after he had set off, on his bicycle to deliver a dispatch he crashed into a pile of debris But he got up and went on.

Soon afterwards bombs fell around him. They blew him off his bicycle and he was thrown unconscious to the ground

First aid men came along and after he came round they advised him to go to hospital.

"No," he answered, "I am going to get the dispatch through."

The bicycle was damaged, the tyres flat, but Billy mounted it and finished his journey before he would accept medical attention.

DAILY MIRROR, Monday, Oct. 7, 1940.

Daily Mirror

OCT 7

No. 11,491 — ONE PENNY
Registered at the G.P.O. as a Newspaper.

HE REFUSED TO FUNK—FIRED BY GOVT.

[Ministry of Labour and National Service Unemployment Insurance form excerpt, Local Office Camden Town]

This man, during air raids, refused to enter a shelter. The standing orders at the time were that all trainees must take cover in shelters provided. His attitude had a bad effect on other trainees, who wished to follow his example. He was warned of the consequences but stated that he would never obey the order to enter a shelter. He was, therefore, dismissed.

Above is the official report why Mr. Dickson was dismissed—because he "had a bad effect" on the other men by wanting to continue work during an air raid "alert."

"Goering Reorganising Air Force" Report

The German Air Force is being reorganised, according to the Berlin correspondent of the Columbia broadcasting system, speaking to New York yesterday.

LONGEST LONDON SILENCE

LONDON had its best sleep for weeks last night when hour after hour passed into early morning without an alert.

The break in the raids was the longest all clear period at night since the intense attacks on London began.

Just before this silence London had one of its shortest night warnings.

The silence was strange. For hours the usual nightly roar of A.A. guns, drones of planes and crump of bombs were absent.

During the day ghost raiders sneaking in and out of the clouds made attacks at random in the London area and in a number of places in the provinces.

Nearly twenty places in the Home Counties were visited.

A Bren gunner shot down a bomber between Harrow and Ruislip after a bomb had been dropped in a field.

A German fighter was reported to have been bagged in an air battle over South-East England.

A few people were injured by machine-gunning. Six adults and two children were injured by a bomb in Central London.

Stated the Air Ministry last night: "During today enemy aircraft, flying singly or in small formations, have made attacks at a number of places in South-East England and in the London area.

"A few bombs were dropped in the
Continued on Back Page, Col. 5

Wanted to Work Through Siren

By Bill Greig

WHILE the Government makes frantic — and feeble — efforts to undo the harm of its earlier "run to the shelter" policy, which almost stopped the wheels of the war machine, it is being baulked by its own departments.

Having encouraged the people for nearly a year in the idea that a "Maginot-mind" meant safety, it now is using nothing but fine words to encourage the workers to remain at their posts.

"Set Bad Example"

It is failing because the example and the lack of any evidence of whole-heartedness are missing.

Today I can reveal the story of veteran soldier William Dickson, who has been dismissed from his job by the Ministry of Labour.

HIS OFFENCE, GIVEN IN COLD PRINT ON OFFICIAL NOTE-PAPER, IS THAT HE SET A BAD EXAMPLE TO HIS FELLOW WORKERS BY DESIRING TO

The Queen Suffering from Slight Cold

The Queen did not go to church as usual yesterday, as she is suffering from a slight cold. Her Majesty is expected to be out again in a few days.

CARRY ON AT HIS MACHINE DURING AIR RAIDS.

This is then, the example set to workers of Britain—to our second line of defence—by a factory under direct control of the Ministry.

William Dickson was dismissed a few hours after Mr. Bevin, the Minister of Labour, had made an impassioned wireless appeal to the workers of Britain to "carry on," despite sirens, unless there was danger directly overhead.

Gratitude

Here is the amazing story of William Dickson and what a "grateful" Government department has done for him.

Years ago he joined the 5th Dragoon Guards, and the early days of 1914 found him in France.

There was to be little peace for him, and succeeding years found him fighting in many parts of the world.

By 1922, when his time as a soldier had expired, he had collected seven wounds and four medals. Not bad going, so he thought.

The beginning of this war found him still eager to do his bit. Too old for the British Army, he volunteered to go to Finland in that army which never sailed.

He Was Happy...

Despite these setbacks, William Dickson decided that he must help in the war effort. He was accepted by the Ministry of Labour for training as an acetylene moulder and sent to the Park Royal training centre.

There he took his place at the benches with hundreds of other men, many of them ex-soldiers grimly anxious to take part in this war in some form or other.

For the first eight of the sixteen weeks which the course should last, William Dickson was happy.

He liked the work and he felt
Continued on Back Page, Col. 2

Mr. Dickson, the dismissed man.

Daily Mirror

DAILY MIRROR, Friday, Oct. 11, 1940.

No. 11,495 — ONE PENNY
Registered at the G.P.O. as a Newspaper.

RAF Defy Snow

DEFYING heavy rain and snowstorms extending up to 10,000ft., Coastal Command Blenheims dropped three tons of heavy bombs in a brisk raid on Boulogne on Wednesday night.

Fires were started at the rate of one a minute.

The railway station and storehouses on quays near the Port de Maree were in flames. One pilot saw on the water near the quay two black masses which looked like barges tied bow to stern. They received the full weight of his salvo and another blaze started.

German destroyers in the harbour at Brest were bombed by Albacore aircraft of the Fleet Air Arm operating with the Coastal Command. The Albacores had to face intense anti-aircraft fire, but the warships were methodically attacked with patterns of bombs laid across the harbour. Other salvoes damaged jetties and buildings in the old French seaplane base.

ST. PAUL'S BOMBED

★ Where you see the heap of rubble and masonry in the picture on the left is the spot where stood the great High Altar of St. Paul's Cathedral, wrecked by a bomb which came through the roof. ★

U.S. ACT TO FOIL NAZIS

PRESIDENT ROOSEVELT yesterday issued a decree which shows that the United States now regards Rumania as just another country over-run by Germany.

The decree freezes Rumania's funds in the U.S. The funds, amounting to £25,000,000, cannot be withdrawn except by special licence from the U.S. Treasury, and are lost to Rumania's German masters.

Similar orders have already been made for the funds of the other countries occupied by Germany and Russia.

Two other moves made by the U.S. yesterday will cause the Axis Powers disquiet. It was announced that Mr. Alexander Kirk, U.S. Charge d'Affaires in Berlin, has been recalled.

Mr. Edward Reed, Rome Charge d'Affaires, has also been recalled. They are returning to give Presi-

Continued on Back Page

NIGHT BOMBS ON 50 AREAS

FIFTY districts, mostly in the London area, were bombed last night after a day of attacks on South-East England.

At least one night bomber was shot down by A.A. fire in or just beyond a London district.

During a day air battle over Maidstone a Spitfire crashed out of control.

As the machine hurtled towards the ground it appeared that the pilot was doing his best to avoid the town.

Just before the machine crashed the engine roared, and the plane turned towards open ground, but it was too low and struck the rear of a shop, completely demolishing a house, damaging several others and burying itself into a cellar.

The buildings burst into flames, but the fire was soon under control.

It is feared there are a number of fatal casualties, including a mother and several children who were buried in a cellar.

Several attacks were made on coastal towns in Kent and Sussex and in the Thames Estuary.

A few bombs were also dropped in one part of London. There were few casualties.

In these attacks four enemy aircraft were destroyed. Four of our fighters were lost, but the pilot of one is safe.

U.S. MAY TRAIN EMPIRE AIRMEN

THE Empire air training scheme is being expanded, and should it be enlarged beyond Canada's capacity to handle it, it may be necessary to send some of the future pilots to flying schools in the United States.

This was stated by the Canadian Air Minister, Mr. Charles G. Power, in Ottawa yesterday. He emphasised however, that no decision as to whether it would be necessary to send men to the United States had yet been reached.

He said that President Roosevelt had agreed that there were no objections to Canadian pilots attending flying schools in the United States, providing they did not wear uniform.
—British United Press.

EVENSONG was sung in the crypt of bombed St. Paul's Cathedral yesterday.

Choir men assembled in the shadows of the crypt under the wreckage of the high altar, hit during a recent attack on London.

Canon Alexander, who had escaped injury, held the service.

As the bomb fell he was sleeping in the crypt immediately beneath the altar.

"After the crash I hurried upstairs, but the place was so thick with dust that for a time I could see nothing," he said yesterday. "I suppose the damage might have been worse but it was quite bad enough.

"The cross and candlesticks went from the high altar. The cross was particularly beautiful."

Crucifix Untouched

The main fabric of the cathedral was not affected, nor was the choir damaged and no one was injured, according to a communique issued by the Air Ministry and Ministry of Home Security.

The bomb exploded on the double eastern roof of the cathedral a little distance from the great dome.

It ripped a hole through the upper roof of lead and rafters, and tore away great blocks of masonry from one of the arches of the main roof.

These blocks crashed ninety feet and obliterated the black-and-gold marble high altar, which dates back to the 1880s.

The pediment of the stone reredos suffered, but the crucifix and the other figures were untouched.

In the Jesus Chapel the picture over the altar, "The Doubting of Thomas," was gashed and pitted by flying stones which holed the stained-glass windows.

NAZIS ON DANUBE

Six German troopships steamed down the Danube past Belgrade, Yugoslavia, on their way to Rumania yesterday.

As they sailed, Berlin unofficially announced that "a few units" of the German Air Force had arrived in Rumania.

Acting on the advice of German Army officers, the Rumanian Cabinet voted the call-up on November 20 of youths whose military training would normally begin next year.

And an Axis spokesman in Bukarest said the rupture of diplomatic relations between Britain and Rumania was only a matter of hours.

Britons Leaving

The British Legation said the Rumanian Government's replies to questions raised by the British Minister, Sir Reginald Hoare, were unsatisfactory.

The legation was reported to have begun to destroy secret documents.

It has now advised not only Britons in the oilfields, but also all Britons in any way connected with the oil industry to lose no time in leaving Rumania.

Another decision taken by the Rumanian Government was the immediate construction of large A.R.P. shelters in various cities.

Associated Press, British United Press.

Lieut. K———, of the ——— Regiment, stationed at ———, says

When I've only a minute for a stand-up meal it's

Fry's SANDWICH CHOCOLATE

2D AND 4½D

Daily Mirror

No. 11,497 — ONE PENNY
Registered at the G.P.O. as a Newspaper

OCT 14

NAVY FIGHT NEAR MALTA

FIERCE naval fight near Malta was revealed yesterday when Italy admitted the loss of three vessels, but claimed that a British cruiser had been sunk.

This followed a report from Berlin of a sea fight off the Isle of Wight between British and German naval forces.

The Malta fight, stated an Italian communique yesterday, took place in the Sicily Channel during the night of October 11-12.

Italian planes hit a British aircraft carrier and damaged another British cruiser, it was claimed.

"One British cruiser, probably of the Neptune class, was sunk. Other enemy units which made off were also hit," added the communique.

"We lost two torpedo boats of 600 tons each and one destroyer of 1,600 tons. Most of the crews were saved.

"In the early hours of the next morning our air force sighted the enemy making for the Levant and submitted them to an intense bombardment.

"Despite violent counter-action by enemy naval guns and the intervention of British fighters which had taken off from an aircraft carrier, and despite unfavourable weather conditions, a British aircraft carrier was hit astern by a heavy bomb and a heavy cruiser was hit."

The naval fight in the Channel between British and German vessels was reported to Nazi sources in Berlin.

The fight, said the report, took place off the Isle of Wight, when a German torpedo boat flotilla, putting out from an unnamed Continental port, was met by British submarines, destroyers and torpedo boats.

The result of the action was not disclosed.—Associated Press, British United, Press and Reuter.

Russia May Join Us—Bevin

Russia, in her own defence, may be forced to join Britain and America, Mr. Ernest Bevin, Minister of Labour, said on Saturday.

"I may be wrong, but watch it," he told trade unionists at Ashton-under-Lyne, Lancs.

He recalled that at the Trades Union Congress in 1934 he protested that when the clash came Russia and Germany would be found in the same camp.

"I was stormed at for saying it at the time. Now I take a different view," he went on.

It had been Russia's determination throughout that if ever the Western Powers got at each other's throats she would take the chance to readjust her geographical and strategic position.

"On the other hand, if Germany ever wanted to attack us, she would try to keep one frontier clear. So the two interests of the two countries had coincided at that point.

"But I can see a new orientation now," said Mr. Bevin.

"The time will be, with the spread of the Axis to Japan and the drive East, when it will be to Russia's interest to join with America and us on grounds of self-preservation."

Bribe to Work On in Raids

BY A SPECIAL CORRESPONDENT

A STEP has been taken which may add 50 per cent. to the cost of Britain's war effort.

Without reference to Parliament, but with the knowledge of the Ministry of Labour, the Baking Trade Board has asked all employers in the trade to pay time-and-a-half rates to workers who carry on during air raid warning periods.

If this principle has been accepted by one trade, it is unlikely that workers in other industries will be satisfied unless they receive the same treatment.

Without consultation with the nation's leaders, the principle of bribing men and women to remain at their posts has been established.

Immediately the decision was made public I asked the Ministry of Labour if they considered it in the national interest to allow one of the boards under their control to take such a step.

"The Minister has no control over recommendations made by trade boards," was the answer. "Had they chosen to make it an order it would have required the sanction of Mr Bevin but in the present case he has no authority to act."

Asked if, in view of the vital principle involved, the matter could not have been referred to Parliament for discussion, the Ministry replied that they could not interfere.

A prominent industrialist with whom I discussed the matter last night stated that he was "staggered" by the fact that the Ministry of Labour had not interfered.

Continued on Back Page, Col. 3

BIG BOMBS ON KRUPPS' WORKS

High-explosive bombs dropped by the R.A.F. on the Krupps armament factory at Essen on Saturday night included several of the heaviest calibre yet carried into Germany.

The attack on Krupps lasted almost two hours, and the works buildings, which cover many acres, were repeatedly hit.

"The factory seemed to be working at full pressure when we arrived," said the navigator of one of the British aircraft.

In all, bombs were dropped on forty separate military objectives in the course of the night's widespread raids.

Tons of bombs on Berlin—page 3.

Princess Elizabeth at the microphone. She made her first broadcast yesterday to the children of the Empire. By her side is Princess Margaret—who joined her sister in saying "Good-night."

PRINCESS SAYS "IT'S UP TO US"

PRINCESS ELIZABETH last night spoke to the children of the Empire. She spoke with deep sincerity, and though this was her first broadcast, she faced the ordeal without a tremor.

Her voice came through clear and resolute—the voice of English girlhood. Not once did she hesitate or falter.

Many who have heard her mother broadcast were struck by the resemblance of their voices.

To children everywhere the warmth and friendliness of her speech made it seem that the Princess was speaking just to them. It was as though she knew, and felt with them, their home-sickness, their fears and their worries.

There was understanding in her tones as she told how she and her sister, Princess Margaret Rose, knew what it means to be away from loved ones.

"When Peace Comes..."

There was pride in her voice, too, as she declared: "And when peace comes, remember it will be for us, the children of today, to make the world of tomorrow a better and happier place."

Princess Elizabeth made her broadcast from a room near to her own apartments. Her speech opened the Children's Hour.

As she sat before the microphone waiting for the red signal light to flash and tell her she was "on the air" for the first time in her life, the King and Queen stood in the room near her.

Princess Margaret was there, too. All listened intently, and then, as Princess Elizabeth neared the end of her speech, came the biggest surprise of the broadcast.

She turned to Princess Margaret and said, "My sister is by my side and we are both going to say goodnight to you. Come on, Margaret."

The listening world heard a sweet childish call, "Good-night, children."

Then Princess Elizabeth concluded with: "Good-night and good luck to you all."

She had rehearsed her speech several times, but in case of a slip of memory she had her manuscript in front of her.

Afterwards B.B.C. officials—they were in an adjoining room with "Uncle Mac"—congratulated her on a perfect broadcast.

Her speech lasted three minutes. Hundreds of British children sat by their radio sets in the United

Continued on Back Page, Col. 4

The Speech

The Princess said:

In wishing you all "Good evening" I feel that I am speaking to friends and companions who have shared with my sister and myself many a happy Children's Hour.

Thousands of you in this country have had to leave your homes and be separated from your fathers and mothers.

My sister Margaret Rose and I feel so much for you, as we know from experience what it means to be away from those we love most of all.

To you living in new surroundings we send a message of true sympathy, and at the same time we would like to thank the kind people who have welcomed you to their homes in the country.

All of us children who are still at home think continually of our friends and relations who have gone overseas—who have travelled thousands of miles to find a wartime home and a kindly welcome in Canada, Australia, New Zealand, South Africa and the United States.

My sister and I feel we know quite a lot about these countries. Our father and mother have so often talked to us of their visits to different parts of the world. So it is not difficult for us to picture the sort of life you are all leading.

But I am sure that you, too, are often thinking of the old country. I know you won't forget us. It is just because we are not forgetting you that I want, on behalf of all the children at home, to send you our love and best wishes—to you and to your kind hosts as well.

We children at home are full of cheerfulness and courage.

We are trying to do all we can to help our gallant sailors, soldiers and airmen, and we are trying, too, to bear our own share of the danger and sadness of war.

We know, every one of us, that in the end all will be well. For God will care for us and give us victory and peace.

And when peace comes, remember it will be for us, the children of today, to make the world of tomorrow a better and happier place.

Got a COLD coming?

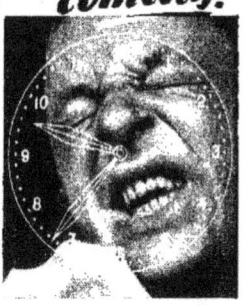

Genasprin
kills colds QUICKLY
—time it!

Take 'Genasprin' at the first sign of a cold—a sneeze, sore throat or slight temperature. Take two more when you go to bed. In the morning your cold will be gone. Buy some 'Genasprin' today.

At every time of strain or pain 'GENASPRIN' sees you through

DAILY MIRROR, Thursday, Oct. 17, 1940

Daily Mirror

No. 11,500   ONE PENNY
Registered at the G.P.O. as a Newspaper.

I WON'T LET THEM HURT YOU

The Story of a Great Picture

BY A SPECIAL CORRESPONDENT

MRS. MARY COUCHMAN, twenty-four-year-old warden in a small Kentish village, sat smoking a cigarette in the wardens' post. She was resting between warnings.

★

Suddenly the sirens sounded again.

She saw her little boy, with two friends, playing some distance away.

The cigarette still in her hand, Mrs. Couchman ran out of the post. Bombs began to fall as she ran.

The children, Johnnie Lusher, aged four, Gladys Ashsmith, aged seven, and her four-year-old son Brian, stood i the street, frightened by the scream and thud of the bombs.

Gathering them in her arms, she huddled over them, protecting them with her own body.

Bombs were still thudding down only a short distance away.

There she crouched, to save the children from flying shrapnel and debris.

★

A "Daily Mirror" photographer was on the spot when the incident occurred.

He took this picture.

Afterwards, when the planes had passed over, he told Mrs. Couchman, "You are a brave woman."

"Oh, it was nothing. Somebody had to look after the children," was her reply.

★

THE NAVY WIPES OUT A CONVOY, AND BLASTS DUNKIRK

—See Page Three

Daily Mirror

No. 11,502 — ONE PENNY
Registered at the G.P.O. as a Newspaper.

DAILY MIRROR, Saturday, Oct. 19, 1940. — OCT 19

No Silk Stockings (Real) After Nov. 30

Shops will get no more silk stockings or silk undies after November 30.

Manufacturers and wholesalers have been forbidden by the Government to supply silk hosiery to the retailers after that date.

But the order applies only to real silk. Women will still be able to buy—and keep on buying—artificial silk stockings and underwear.

The retail price of real silk stockings today varies from 3s. 11d. a pair to a guinea or more, according to quality.

The order means that Britain will soon be back to the days when pure silk stockings were seen only on the legs of well-to-do women.

The President of the Board of Trade yesterday met representatives of the Hosiery Trade Federation and told them that the prohibition of home sales after November 30 was due to increased Service requirements of silk.

To Go Overseas

Every effort would have to be made, he said, to divert to overseas markets stocks of silk stockings and other silk hosiery previously intended for the home market.

The term "silk hosiery" is used by the Board of Trade, and until the position is clarified it will not be known if it applies to blouses and other garments.

Hosiery is a term used in the industry itself to cover all types of goods, including scarves, jumpers and blouses, in addition to stockings and underwear.

No Surprise

The Board's decision has not come as a surprise to the trade. For some weeks there has been a shortage of pure silk. More artificial silk, better known as rayon and lisle, will take its place.

The bulk of our raw silk comes from Japan. Since the outbreak of war its price has risen greatly.

At present rayon is being mixed with real silk to keep down the price. Compared with the production of silk stockings, the production of silk underwear in this country is small. Most of it is made at Nottingham, Belper (Derbyshire) and Leicester.

It is estimated that 99 per cent. of the silk used in these two types of hosiery goes to the production of silk stockings.

Not real silk after November 30.

JAPS BOMB BURMA ROAD

THE Japanese last night bombed the Burma Road, now reopened by Britain for war supplies to China.

Meanwhile, discouraging news about Japan's oil supplies came from New York.

Japan, it was stated, has forced the American and Netherlands-British oil companies in the Dutch East Indies to supply her with about 40 per cent. of her total oil needs.

At his Press conference yesterday, Mr. Cordell Hull, the U.S. Secretary of State, stated that he had no information on the subject.

Supplies will be sent for the next six months, the "New York Times" stated.

While Japan is getting this aid, China is likely to obtain a loan of £15,000,000 for the purchase of supplies in the U.S.

China is also likely to receive fighting planes to beat off constant Japanese air attacks on Chungking and on the Burma Road.

The Japanese liner Durhan Maru has been held by British units in the

(Continued on Back Page)

RUMANIA LOOTED OF ARMS

GERMANY is looting modern British and French arms and other war equipment supplied to Rumania.

Nothing is known of the fate of fourteen Blenheim bombers which were flown by Rumanian pilots from England to Rumania in September, 1939, when King Carol was making a belated attempt to rearm.

★ Eden for Turkey? ★

Two radio stations gave forecasts yesterday about the plans of Mr. Anthony Eden, War Minister, after he ends his tour in Egypt.

New York Radio stated that Mr. Eden will go to Ankara, Turkey but Budapest Radio gave his destination as Greece.

The deal appears to be a good one for Rumania. Actually it is the Nazi version of new lamps for old.

Reports in Bukarest yesterday stated that Germany had ordered the Rumanian General Staff to scrap all guns, shells and other war materials bought in recent years from Britain and France.

Specialists Arrive

The equipment, the Nazis say, will be sent to Germany, to be melted down. Rumania, in return, will get German-type equipment.

German specialists are arriving daily to assume direction of the production of munitions.

At the same time the Rumanian Council of Ministers issued several decrees, designed to turn the country into a totalitarian State, with its economy supplementing rather than competing with that of Germany.

Industrial, agricultural and marine life will be reorganised.

Envoy Recalled

Industrial reorganisation will attempt to eliminate needless plants, while an extensive campaign will be undertaken to increase agricultural production.

Various ministries are assuming strict control of food, and shipping in the Danube and the Black Sea will be placed under sweeping powers given to the Ministry of Marine.

Interest was aroused in diplomatic circles by the announcement that Radu Ginvara, the Rumanian Minister to Greece, had been recalled. —Associated Press.

AXIS WILL SHARE TRADE

A trade conference between Germany and Italy concluded in Berlin yesterday, decided that the two countries will in future share trade, industry and foreign currencies on an equal basis, reported the Beromunster (Swiss) radio last night.

6,954 DIED IN RAIDS

DURING September 6,954 civilians were killed and 10,615 seriously injured in air raids on Britain, it was officially announced last night.

This death roll is slightly more than four times the total for the preceding three months.

These figures were: June, 336; July, 258; August, 1,075—a total of 1,669.

A week ago Mr. Churchill told Parliament the Government had expected 3,000 civilians to be killed and 13,000 injured in one night by raids.

September's figures, so far as classified, were divided as follows:

KILLED. — 1,820 men, 2,210 women, 694 children under sixteen; 3,629 women, 675 children under sixteen.
SERIOUSLY INJURED. — 4,178 men, 3,629 women, 675 children under sixteen.

Of the remaining 2,130 killed, 1,157 were men and 973 women.
Of the other 2,133 seriously injured, 1,231 were men and 902 women.

R.A.F. SMASHED INVASION PLAN

REPORTS from reliable neutral sources leave little doubt that the day chosen by Hitler for his invasion of England was September 16.

The factors in his favour were the harvest full moon—high tides, a powerful air force, and an enormous fleet of barges and other vessels.

Against him was the R.A.F.

Came September 15 and his air advance guard which, in massed formations, attempted raids on a colossal scale.

The R.A.F.'s reply was to bring down at least 185.

A report now reaching official quarters in London states that, on September 16 many German troops were embarked at invasion ports but were later taken off the ships.

The R.A.F. began its own blitz on the Channel hide-outs of the would-be invaders, and the invasion plans, it is now learned, were not adopted because of the "sustained offensive by the R.A.F."

Raid chaos in Germany—page 2.

SHELTER FOOD PLAN

MORNING and evening meals will be on sale at canteens to be started in London's public air-raid shelters this winter.

That is Dr. J. J. Mallon's idea of the job he has been given by Lord Woolton, Minister of Food.

The appointment of Dr. Mallon, warden of Toynbee Hall, London, to be the Minister's "adviser on the provision of food and refreshments in London's shelters" was announced last night.

Dr. Mallon said "The great need will be for tea and sandwiches and things of that sort, and the Ministry of Food will see that tea is available."

600,000 Bunks

Meanwhile 12,000 tons of steel have been released for the construction of shelter sleeping berths. This will produce another 600,000 berths.

Delivery of the 1,000,000 timber berths already ordered by the Ministry of Home Security will begin today and will be completed within a month.

The 1,600,000 berths thus provided are to be increased by others ordered locally by local authorities.

A proportion of the total will be allotted to the big shelters in the East End of London and others to surface shelters intended as communal domestic shelters.

A FOOD AT LESS THAN PRE-WAR PRICE

Weekly budgets down, now favourite food-drink reduced in price

CADBURY'S famous Bournville Cocoa — always an economy drink — is DOWN IN PRICE to 5d per ¼lb! To-day housewives who want to cut down those rising bills are making full use of Bournville as a *food*. For instance, if you make it with milk, a cup of Bournville costs just over 1d, but contains the value of 2 eggs. And even made without milk you get a steaming cupful of energy-giving food that makes the family meals go further.

● You get twenty-eight cups (6 ozs.) of Bournville Cocoa out of every 1 lb. tin. That's enough for a family of four, every night, for a week's cocoa drinking!

It's the 5-STAR Cocoa!

★ EXTRA FOOD VALUE. *Bournville Cocoa is rich in body-building proteins, and natural cocoa butter and carbohydrates to give you energy. So remember, a cup of Bournville—the 5-Star Cocoa—is a cup of food.*

★ IRON — THE BLOOD ENRICHER. *The rich iron content of Bournville Cocoa tones up the corpuscles in your bloodstream, makes you feel stronger.*

★ PHOSPHATES — FOOD FOR NERVES. *Bournville Cocoa is rich in the various phosphates and calcium. These help your nerves, build up bone and muscle, strengthen teeth.*

★ AID TO DIGESTION. *Bournville Cocoa is particularly digestible, helps digestion of other foods and so makes every meal go further.*

★ VITAMINS — VITAL TO HEALTH. *Remember that every tin of Bournville Cocoa retains the natural sunshine Vitamin D, specially necessary for kiddies' healthy teeth and straight, strong bones.*

BOURNVILLE
THE 5-STAR COCOA

QUALITY UNALTERED

DOWN TO **5d per qtr lb**

DAILY MIRROR, Wednesday, Oct. 23, 1940.

Daily Mirror

OCT 23

No. 11,505 ONE PENNY
Registered at the G.P.O. as a Newspaper.

FIGHT BRITAIN —HITLER TO FRANCE

LIMPING SPY SOLD RUMANIA

FROM DAVID WALKER
BELGRADE (Yugoslavia), Tuesday.

Junkers 87s circled low over the railway station as I left Bukarest yesterday after eighteen months in Rumania.

Two Gestapo agents followed me to the train to see that I went.

I passed Jilava Prison, in whose cells are imprisoned Rumanian Cabinet Ministers now awaiting trial by men who look on murder as an incident. The Rumanian tragedy is complete.

In his rich mansion in Bukarest an aged cripple rubs his hands with pleasure. Clubfoot Conradi, Nazi criminal who enjoyed German Legation protection, brought off the rape of Rumania.

Moonfaced Minister

His right-hand man is the moon-faced German Minister, Fabricus. What Fabricus could not do in the open Conradi did secretly. It was to Conradi that the Fuehrer cabled praise.

When police visited Conradi's cellars they found no wine—only stacks of Thompson guns and millions of rounds of ammunition. The little cripple blandly explained he was the Rumanian representative of Krupps. These were his business samples.

He was right—his business is death. Police saluted and withdrew.

This sinister cripple and the German Minister conquered Rumania between them. It fell like a plum into Hitler's hands at a cost of only 2,000 lives—the lives of Rumanian Legionaries, whose organisation they had bought with Nazi gold.

Gestapo Everywhere

Now the Gestapo are everywhere. One of their first acts was the arrest at Brasov of the former Polish Foreign Minister, Colonel Beck.

It is they who organised the torture of British oil workers, they who had hundreds of shots fired at apartments of British Legation officials, and who systematically are driving the few remaining Englishmen from Rumania.

The German troops now in occupation are happily gorging. One officer at the Ambassador Hotel ordered and ate two whole chickens himself on arrival.

Rumanians have not yet been told that 40,000 hungry German children will be quartered on them for the winter.

Germans Hated

Before leaving I dined with a great Rumanian industrialist. "Germany," he said, "is moving heavy industry east, away from British bombers. Germany will steal our greatest firm, Malaxa, and make it a second Skoda working night and day to feed the German war machine."

The mass of the Rumanian people hate the new overlords.

But Rumania, in a fantastic atmosphere of hidden death and persecution suffers in silence and shame at the Gestapo occupation.

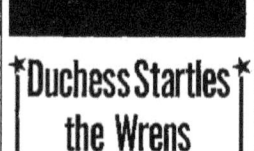

Duchess Startles the Wrens

All W.R.N.S. could talk about after being inspected by their commandant, the Duchess of Kent, was her hair style.

There was nothing elaborate about it. From beneath her tricorn hat the Duchess's hair reached down to her tunic collar in a smooth page boy bob. But that was the cause of the discussion—it reached down to her collar. W.R.N.S. regulations say that the hair must be worn off the collar. And all the W.R.N.S. had their hair cut short when they joined the Service.

BOMBERS TURN BACK

Three raiders were destroyed when a large formation was intercepted by our fighters after crossing the Kent coast yesterday evening.

At least 100 planes took part in a fierce battle, and after the formation had been broken, Spitfires and Hurricanes hunted them down as they tried to penetrate inland, and forced them back over the Channel.

This battle, the dark night and heavy A.A. fire, kept bombers away from London, and the "raiders passed" signal was sounded before midnight.

During the day, too, air attacks were on a small scale.

A few raiders penetrated to the outskirts of London, where they were pounced on by British fighters and driven back down the Thames Estuary.

Passengers flung themselves on the floor of a bus when a bomb-carrying Messerschmitt fighter swooped down to machine-gun the vehicle as it climbed a steep hill on the Kent coast.

As the plane dived to the attack, the young conductor warned inside passengers, and, as he ran to the upper deck, the raider roared down to within a few hundred feet and opened fire.

Bullets kicked up a shower of dust alongside the bus, but it was undamaged, and there were no casualties.

Six of our fighters were lost during yesterday's air actions, but the pilots of two of them are safe.

FRANCE must declare war on Britain. Hitler was reported to have delivered this ultimatum to Laval, French Vice-Premier, when they met in France last night.

Terms for an "easy peace" were dictated by Hitler in the presence of Ribbentrop, Nazi Foreign Minister, New York radio said.

The French Fleet would operate with the Italians and Germans to deliver the final blow to Britain.

For this Germany would return to France all occupied territory excepting Alsace Lorraine and probably Nice, Tunis and Jibuti.

But in Berne, Switzerland, it was stated that the meeting was accepted at Vichy as meaning "the final settlement may be near but not at the price of active French participation in the war against Britain."

German sources said it was doubtful whether the Fuehrer and his Foreign Minister would have received Laval publicly unless some form of future German collaboration with the Vichy Government had already been arranged during the Vichy Vice-Premier's talks with Abetz, German envoy in Paris.

News of the meeting created a sensation in America.

French co-operation against Britain was at once said to be Germany's peace price to Vichy.

Berlin officially announced the meeting but did not say where.

Vichy reported it as taking place in or near Paris.

War Ludicrous

Berlin officials threw no light on the meeting. They said it took place during the day, but where, what was discussed, and who was present with Laval in the French party they did not know.

Foreign reports that France might re-enter the war were referred to by Baudouin, French Foreign Minister, yesterday. France was out of the war, was looking ahead to the peace, and was willing to collaborate with Germany in post-war reconstruction, he said.

"The post-war status of Alsace-Lorraine will have an important influence on future relations between France and Germany," he added.

Later an official Government spokesman in Vichy said:

"The French Government denies in the most formal manner the report that M. Laval has gone to Paris to negotiate the declaration of war by France against England.

"This report is simply ludicrous. Laval has gone to Paris to discuss questions of a general nature concerning immediate Franco-German relations."—British United Press and Associated Press.

Earlier reports—Page 2.

'UNDERGROUND' NEWS ROUTE

By underground sources, the Committee of Union of the French Socialists in Britain have received a manifesto from the French Socialist Party "somewhere in France."

"The Socialists of France," it is stated, "salute with admiration the resistance of the British people, and feel sure that in this they are at one with almost the whole of the French population."

DORNIER RIDDLE

WHILE every road in East Suffolk was being watched yesterday for four German airmen from a Dornier 17 which crashed on the mud flats of the River Stour, near Ipswich, three nights ago, police in Wiltshire were looking for a German plane belonging to four airmen they had captured.

The puzzle for the police in these two distant counties was to connect the two reports.

All day Chief Constable Staunton of the East Suffolk police, waited for a phone call from the Wiltshire police to hear if their German prisoners were from this Dornier.

It is 160 miles flight from Wiltshire, and it does not seem possible that an empty Dornier could have blindly flown all that distance without any mishap.

But it did. The four airmen baled out from their Dornier at Chilmark East Knoyle, Hindon and Wylye—villages in the Wiltshire countryside.

Saw No Parachutes

Their machine flew on just so far as its petrol kept the engines turning. It came down at midnight nine miles from here hardly damaged, except for one or two bullet holes in its side.

A naval rating was first on the spot when the German plane crashed on the edge of the River Stour.

He saw no goggles or helmets or parachutes.

One or two bullet holes had penetrated the grey fabric here and there, but there is nothing to show that the Dornier had been hit by anti-aircraft fire.

People in a village four miles away heard the plane flying very low. No one saw airmen baling out.

He brought out a suitcase from the pilot's compartment inside which were papers giving the pilot's name—Lieutenant Heinrich Werdemann.

Hours later, when questioned by the Wiltshire police, the officer of the German prisoners said he was Werdemann.

EDEN NOT FOR ANKARA

A German report that Mr. Anthony Eden, Foreign Secretary, is to visit Ankara, either next week or in the future, was denied yesterday.

Italian Warship Blown Up In Red Sea

The British destroyer Kimberley blew up the Italian destroyer Francesco Nullo and silenced two of three shore guns when a British convoy was attacked in the Red Sea.

This was announced by the Admiralty in an official communique last night.

Kimberley was hit, but no other ship in the convoy was damaged.

Earlier, Italy claimed that six ships in the convoy were sunk and a British cruiser disabled.

The Admiralty communique stated: "During the night of October 20-21 one of our convoys in the Red Sea was attacked by two Italian destroyers who fired torpedoes at the escorting vessels and shelled the convoy.

"Our escorting vessels immediately opened fire on the enemy and gave chase.

Stranded, Torpedoed

"Contact was temporarily lost, but H.M.S. Kimberley (Lieutenant-Commander J. S. M. Richardson, R.N.) regained touch at daylight and engaged one enemy destroyer, identified as the Francesco Nullo.

"After an action lasting forty minutes the Italian destroyer, having been heavily damaged, ran ashore and was blown up by a torpedo fired from the Kimberley.

"Kimberley came under fire of a shore battery of three guns and received one hit splinters from which damaged a steam pipe and reduced her speed.

"Kimberley succeeded, however, in silencing two out of the three shore guns.

Three Wounded

"In this spirited action Kimberley sustained three wounded and the next of kin will be informed as soon as possible.

"No other ship, either escorting vessel or in the convoy, received any damage."

Kimberley, the last of the "K" Class destroyers, was launched at Southampton in 1939.

She took part in the second sea battle of Narvik in which seven German warships were routed, three being sunk.

Francesco Nullo, with a displacement of 1,058 tons, had a speed of thirty-five knots and carried 142 men.

Italy made the usual exaggerated claims in a communique which (says Reuter) stated that "a fierce engagement was fought until dawn.

"By this time one of the British cruisers—a cruiser of the Sydney class—came within range of our shore batteries on the Red Sea Islands.

"It was soon hit by the accurate fire.

"She subsequently came to a standstill while other British ships came to her aid.

"During the action six British ships were sunk and others were damaged.

"Despite the fierce battle only one of our ships was hit. A torpedo boat was seriously damaged but reached safety."

DAILY MIRROR, Saturday, Nov. 2, 1940.

Daily Mirror

NOV 2

No. 11,514 ONE PENNY
Registered at the G.P.O. as a Newspaper.

NAVAL CHIEFS IN GREECE

BRITISH Naval officers have arrived in Athens and in a number of Greek islands, it was learned this morning.

They are working at full speed preparing for co-operation with the Greeks, which owing to the perfectly correct neutrality of the Greek Government in the past had not previously been possible.

Turkey is studying the Mediterranean situation in collaboration with Britain and is ready to defend her " independence, security and land."

They Win the M.M.

One of the first three women in the Services to win the Military Medal in this war— Corporal Elspeth Candlish-Henderson, of Edinburgh.

She has now been promoted Acting Assistant Section Officer.

Biggest Night Bag: 5

Five enemy bombers were brought down during the night, it was announced shortly after 1.30 this morning.

This is the largest number destroyed on any night since the war on Britain began.

Altogether fourteen enemy planes were brought down yesterday. Six of our fighters were reported lost, but the pilots of two are safe.

In the night raids, first came news of a plane coming down at Glaseby, Yorks, a few miles inland from Whitby. It burst into flames, and is believed to have been brought down by A.A. fire.

Another plane, a Junkers 88, was forced down at Storrington, Sussex, and three others crashed in the area of the Thames Estuary, one coming down in flames at Hornchurch, Essex.

TEARING with their hands at the debris, A.T.S. girls helped to free people trapped beneath shattered masonry when a high explosive bomb hit a London cinema in last night's raid.

Although light streamed from the cinema through the broken wall and there was constant danger of further bombs falling, the girls insisted on helping with the rescue work.

Two more bombs fell in the district, but the girls still carried on.

One pretty, fair-haired A.T.S. girl pillowed the head of a man trapped by debris. She gave him a cigarette and tried to comfort him by talking to him.

He was in pain, but he smiled at her as he said: "This is almost worth being bombed."

Not until demolition squads and ambulances arrived did the girls consent to leave. Even then they pulled broken doorways from the heaps of rubble to form stretchers for the injured.

Men who were in the cinema when the bomb fell helped to prevent a panic.

They led women into the streets and then returned to release their friends trapped beneath the debris.

A Roman Catholic priest hurried to
Continued on Back Page

Her relations with Russia have taken a " friendly turn." These were the main points in a statement yesterday by the Turkish President, Inonu.

And last night Italy was claiming an advance of thirty-five miles from the Albanian border into the Janina region. They claim to control a Greek region of seventy-nine villages and 35,000 inhabitants.

The Turkish President, whose statement was made to the Assembly, described Soviet policy "in the face of a dark world" as one of "greatest security."

"While thinking of our own welfare, we will remain loyal to our friendships and obligations. Our ties and collaborations are unshakeable." he said.

Two Bombers Bagged

The Yugoslav Government issued a declaration of neutrality yesterday.

According to the Rome radio, the British Legation in Yugoslavia has advised British citizens to leave the country within forty-eight hours.

The Italians were attacking heavily yesterday in the mountain passes of Northern Greece in an effort to break through to Florina.

According to one report they had advanced only a mile and a quarter when they were halted by Greek fire. Forty-nine were taken prisoner.

Two Italian bombers were shot down by Greek anti-aircraft batteries
Associated Press, British United Press and Reuter.

SON OF A DEAD HERO

A Narvik hero's wife has given birth to a son seven months after her husband's death.

She is Mrs. Geraldine Cross, wife of Lieutenant C. P. W. Cross radio officer in H.M.S. Hardy who was killed when the British destroyer led the world-famous attack on German warships in Narvik Fiord last April.

He died at the side of his commander, Captain Warburton-Lee, who himself died of wounds.

Mrs. Cross already has a little boy, Denis Charles, who is two and a half years old.

MEALS FOR SHELTERERS SOON

Mr. H. G. Nightingall, the catering manager appointed by Westminster City Council to supervise meals in public shelters, set about the job yesterday, and within ten days hot meals night and morning are expected to be available.

Local firms are to supply hot soups and drinks, sandwiches and snacks, etc., at night, and hot breakfasts in the morning.

Sergt. Joan E Mortimer, M.M.

Sergt. Helen E. Turner, M.M.

MARKED OUT LIVE BOMBS

WHEN enemy bombers heavily attacked an R.A.F. Fighter Command station, a twenty-eight-year-old W.A.A.F. sergeant was on duty in the station armoury. Though a large amount of ammunition was stored near her office, she manned the telephone, passing instructions to the various defence posts.

She shouted words of encouragement to the airmen in the building, and when the raid was over, calmly went outside and began to peg out with red flags all the places on the aerodrome where unexploded bombs were buried.

Her commanding officer said of her afterwards: "Her exceptional courage and coolness had a great moral effect on all those with whom she came in contact."

Her name is Joan Eugene Mortimer, and her identity is revealed today in the official announcement that she had been awarded the Military Medal.

Two other W.A.A.F.S. in the same station also receive the Military Medal for their courage during another bombing attack.

First Awards

They are: Assistant Section Officer (then Corporal) Elspeth Candlish Henderson, age twenty-seven, whose home is in Edinburgh, and Sergeant Helen Emily Turner, whose home is in London.

This is the first time a military decoration like the Military Medal has been awarded to women members of the Royal Air Force.

Corporal Henderson and Sergeant Turner were on duty in a building which received a direct hit during a September raid. Sergeant Turner was the switchboard operator, and Corporal Henderson had charge of a special telephone line.

Bombs were falling around the building, but both airwomen carried on with their jobs, though they knew there was only a light roof over their heads. When the building received a direct hit both continued working till it caught fire, and they were ordered to leave.
Continued on Back Page

4 MILLION TONS WORLD SHIP LOSS

The destruction of British merchant tonnage through enemy action during the first year of war is stated to be 395 ships of 1,561,000 gross tons —an average of about 30,000 tons a week.

Taking into account natural obsolescence, and enemy ships operating under the British flag, we can assume a total casualty figure of round about 4,000,000 tons (says Burntisland Shipyard Journal).

If the extent of British losses during the second year of war do not exceed those of the first, our shipyards should have no difficulty in making losses good.

It is estimated that in the first year Allied and neutral countries have lost 363 ships (1,235,000 tons). Enemy loss by capture, scuttling and sinking is about 330 ships (1,300,000 tons).

This makes a world total of 1,089 ships amounting to 4,096,000 tons.

BAGGING MORE NIGHT RAIDERS

Last month A.A. gunners and R.A.F. fighters brought down twenty-six German bombers during night raids, and one was brought down by the balloon barrage.

This is two more than were destroyed during September, but as many more came over in September our October success was comparatively greater.

A FOOD AT LESS THAN PRE-WAR PRICE

Weekly budgets down, now favourite food-drink reduced in price

CADBURY'S famous Bournville Cocoa — always an economy drink — is DOWN IN PRICE to 5d per ¼lb! To-day housewives who want to cut down those rising bills are making full use of Bournville. For instance, if you make it with milk, a cup of Bournville costs just over 1d, but contains the value of 2 eggs. And even made without milk you get a steaming cupful of energy-giving food that makes the family meals go further.

● You get twenty-eight cups (6 oz.) of Bournville Cocoa out of every ¼lb tin. That's enough for a family of four, every night, for a week's raid warnings!

It's the 5-STAR Cocoa!

★ **EXTRA FOOD VALUE.** Bournville Cocoa is rich in body-building proteins, and natural cocoa butter and carbohydrates to give you energy. So remember, a cup of Bournville— the 5-Star Cocoa — is a cup of food.

★ **IRON—THE BLOOD ENRICHER.** The rich iron content of Bournville Cocoa tones up the corpuscles in your bloodstream, makes you feel stronger.

★ **PHOSPHATES—FOR HEALTHY GROWTH.** Bournville Cocoa is rich in the various phosphates and calcium. These build up bone and muscle, strengthen teeth.

★ **AID TO DIGESTION.** Bournville Cocoa is particularly digestible, helps digestion of other foods and so makes every meal go further.

★ **VITAMINS—VITAL TO HEALTH.** Remember that every tin of Bournville Cocoa retains the natural sunshine Vitamin D, specially necessary for kiddies' healthy teeth and straight, strong bones.

BOURNVILLE
THE 5-STAR
QUALITY UNALTERED
COCOA
DOWN TO 5d per qtr lb

DAILY MIRROR, Monday, Nov. 4, 1940.

Daily Mirror

NOV 4

No. 11,515   ONE PENNY
Registered at the G.P.O. as a Newspaper.

The King of Greece is a cousin of the Duchess of Kent. So, yesterday, the Duchess attended a Service of Intercession in the Greek Cathedral, London. Picture shows her arriving.

TOWN CUT OFF BY GREEKS

An Italian division was in danger of being cut off, the town of Koritza, seven miles inside Albania, was encircled and 1,200 Italians captured by the Greeks yesterday after an all-day battle.

News of this Greek success was flashed from Belgrade, Yugoslavia, where Axis influences are strong. It was not confirmed in Athens or London. Fall of Koritza, the report added, was believed to be imminent.

FROM DAVID WALKER

ATHENS, Sunday.

THE sparrow still defies the vulture in this fantastic fight. The Greek Air Force, outnumbered by 100 to one in front line machines, still gaily invites death rather than dishonour.

For example, Captain Demetriou who, when his ammunition was exhausted, rammed a huge three-engined Italian plane in mid-air yesterday.

CRETE BASE FOR BRITAIN

British army, naval and air units are in Crete.

This news was reported by the Greek Press yesterday when referring to Mr. Alexander's broadcast (reported on page 11).

Greek morale, already high, rose still higher on hearing this.

The Greeks have great faith in Britain, believing that she will use to the full Greek's stand against aggression.

Rome radio last night reported that British warships appeared near the island of Leukas, thirty-six miles south-east of Corfu.

While British aid mobilises to strike, the Greeks are doing their utmost to hinder the Italians with harrying tactics.

"Italian troops are finding themselves up against a well fortified line of resistance," Rome radio admitted.

Greek troops, passing the lower end of Lake Prespa in small boats at night,
Continued on Back Page Col. 4

HITLER PEACE MOVE?

Reports circulated in diplomatic quarters in Washington last night that Hitler planned in the "next day or two" to present the terms on which Germany is willing to end the war.—Associated Press.

King George visited Captain Couzuyani's hospital here last night and promoted him to Major in one of his brief moments of consciousness.

The Greeks are ready to sacrifice their Air Force pending the arrival of British machines—the smallest and greatest suicide squad the world has ever known.

Greek blood is boiling at the cowardice of the Italian attacks.

The large death roll at Salonika consisted mostly of children. The working-class quarter is a shambles. Greek hatred is mingled with contempt.

For instance, I saw Greeks yesterday hurry out of a restaurant during an alarm waving plates of macaroni at the Italian machines.

Italians Ran

Recruiting offices are besieged by every type.

A bearded priest wearing clericals went to join up when he learned his mother was killed at Salonika. He is determined to fight.

Another large group of Albanians applied to fight yesterday.

The biggest jest in Athens today was the Rome radio claim that Piraeus was heavily bombed.

The Italians fled at the first glimpse of three Greek fighters.

The Italian story of heavy floods and torrential rain at the front line is also amusing, since the Greek trenches are bone dry.

The only low-altitude Italian attack made was against rocks where machine-guns were suspected but none existed.

Nine machines were valiantly attacking a deserted hillside.

Italy Loses 2 Submarines

Italy admitted the loss of two submarines in yesterday's official communique, which also claimed to have hit a warship in an air raid.

"Two Italian submarines," it was stated, "have not returned to their bases.

"A large British naval formation off the Egyptian coast was overtaken by our torpedo-carrying aircraft and one British ship was hit."

"Our Air Force has carried out numerous bombing actions, effectively hitting military objectives at Corfu, where numerous explosions were caused, particularly in Porto Novo," the communique said.

"The Port of Patras was also bombed, where a fire was caused in the station at Samandrea, and where a factory and military barracks were hit.

"In addition, Larissa, Janina and Salonika were bombed. During these actions an enemy fighter was probably shot down.

"In addition, Navarino was bombed and a fire was caused there. Canea also figures in the list of towns bombed by the Italian Air Force, and the port installations received a number of hits.

"Two Italian planes have not returned."

BRIDE SWORN TO SILENCE

An English officer's American fiancee has been sworn to silence about her wedding plans by the British authorities.

Her lover is overseas, and an indiscreet word about where he is stationed might imperil him and his men.

Hush-hush bride whose romance could betray military secrets is Miss Dorothy West, niece of Governor Leverett Saltonstall, of Massachusetts.

She is on her word of honour not to reveal, even to her relatives, the date and place of the wedding.

She herself is at present unaware of her fiance's whereabouts, because the authorities refuse to reveal it. And now she has sailed from America to an undisclosed destination to marry Captain T. Desmond Butler, a native of Somerset, who is with his regiment somewhere in Africa.

Her sister, Miss Mary West, said in New York yesterday: "Dorothy, a fine horsewoman, met Captain Butler while hunting in Ireland five years ago.

Captain Butler is thirty-five.

AIR CHIEF'S NEW JOB

Appointment of a new Vice-Chief of Air Staff—Air Chief Marshal Sir Wilfrid Freeman—was announced by the Air Ministry last night.

He succeeds Air Marshal Sir Richard Peirse, who has recently taken up the appointment of Air Officer Commanding in Chief Bomber Command.

Great tribute to Sir Wilfrid Freeman was paid by Lord Beaverbrook, Minister for Aircraft Production in July. He said:

"Sir Wilfrid, more than any other single man, had provided the R.A.F. with planes whose superiority over the enemy has been proved in battle."

VICHY ENVOY TO NAZI FRANCE

M. Fernand de Brignon has been given a roving mission to the authorities in the occupied territories with the rank of Ambassador, it was announced yesterday.—Reuter.

LONDON TO DIG MORE TUBES AS RAID SHELTERS

New tunnelling, "spokes" from the present Underground system — more and better surface communal shelters — more large Andersons and enlargement of smaller ones to take bunks — use of above-ground rooms in modern buildings—tunnelling in suitable provincial areas.

THESE are among Mr. Herbert Morrison's plans for shelter accommodation as he outlined them in a broadcast yesterday, his "interim report" after three weeks as Minister of Home Security.

"Anything like a universal policy of deep shelter, for the whole population or the greater part of it," he said, "is beyond the bounds of practical possibility. This fact I cannot alter.

"To attempt to build more than a limited amount in suitable places would mean providing deep shelter for a given number at the cost of leaving a much larger number with no good shelter.

"No appreciable amount of this deep shelter, even in the most favourable event, can be ready until this winter is over. This fact, too, I cannot alter.

"In some places, and in some circumstances, the construction of deep shelter is practicable and will be undertaken.

"Be on Your Guard"

"The deep shelter provided in London by the Tubes will be extended by tunnelling.

"In other parts of the country, where the slope of the ground and the nature of the soil make tunnelling relatively easy, work will also be begun.

"I tell you the truth as I see it, knowing you to be not a set of faint hearts longing for fairy tales about absolute safety, but a great people standing erect fighting for its life.

"Be on your guard against all who seek to make this deep shelter cry a means of defeatist agitation.

"Political schemers who seek to destroy our will to take risks for freedom are playing Hitler's game.

"He knows that if our people could be stampeded into putting personal safety before success he would win."

Want Fresh Air

The men, women and children of Britain had done magnificently, said Mr. Morrison. The world was electrified to see the civil defence army and police stand up to the rain of fire and death.

Britain was arming for the offensive. For that steel, cement and bricks were needed for munition and aircraft factories and aerodromes.

Thus the person who clamoured for all material and labour to be devoted to passive defence made a great mistake.

"A great many people," the Minister
Continued on Back Page, Col. 1

BLITZ RECORD BROKEN

Germany's record of nightly bombing on the London area was broken last night.

For the first time since the attack on London began fifty-six days ago, nightfall did not bring an Alert. Up to early this morning the sirens had not sounded, and there was no report of enemy air activity anywhere in the country.

Weather conditions at German air bases are believed to be responsible for this.

During an early evening Alert bombs fell in a residential area of London, and rescue squads were sent to two houses.

But the "raiders passed" signal was soon given.

Raider Shook Fist

During a daylight Alert in London, people in a street gunned by a lone raider saw one of the crew lean out and shake his fist at them from a height of 50ft.

This plane, a fighter-bomber with a crew of three, was one of several which swept low out of cloud and mist to machine-gun districts in London and East Anglia.

It dived to within 30ft. of the ground before opening fire with machine-guns and a cannon.

Then, banking, it came 30ft. lower. The crew did not fire again, but the man behind the pilot shook his fist.

A dive-raider narrowly missed housetops in another London area. People in the streets and in a park ran for shelter. None was hurt.

Bomb in Room

Several bombs were dropped. People returning from church were in the streets of these two districts. There were several casualties.

Houses were demolished by bombs and there were casualties, some fatal.

A plane, flying a few feet above the roof tops, machine-gunned several streets in a working-class district of an East Anglian town.

Bullets and broken glass flew into scores of rooms where families were having their teas, but no one was seriously injured.

The bullets spluttered into the hedge row by the side of the vehicles.

After A.A. and machine-gun fire, the raider began to lose height rapidly.

The Air Ministry said one enemy bomber was destroyed during the day. One R.A.F. fighter was lost.

Daily Mirror

Friday, Nov. 8, 1940. NOV 8

No. 11,519 ONE PENNY
Registered at the G.P.O. as a Newspaper.

EIRE WOULD FIGHT FOR HER BASES

IRELAND WILL FIGHT RATHER THAN GIVE UP THE BASES BRITAIN NEEDS FOR CRUSHING THE U-BOAT MENACE IN THE ATLANTIC.

Mr. de Valera stated this in the Dail yesterday in referring to Mr. Churchill's speech about ports in Eire.

"So long as this Government remains in office," Mr. de Valera said, "we shall defend our rights in respect of these ports or any part of our territory against whoever may attack them."

Mr. de Valera said he did not know if every one of them was prepared to take Mr. Churchill's statement, as he was prepared to take it, as a symbol, perhaps a natural expression of regret, or whether it portended something more.

"Our Cause Is Just"

As he had often said before, they wanted friendly relations with the people of Britain and with other people, but naturally they wanted to be friendly with Britain because she was nearest to them.

"I want to say to our people," he said: "We may be—I hope not—facing a grave crisis. If we are to face it we will do it knowing our cause is just and right.

"There can be no question of the handing over of these ports so long as this nation remains neutral.

"Bloodshed If—"

"There can be no question of releasing these ports and there can be no question of them being handed over on any conditions whatever.

"Any attempt to bring pressure to bear on us by any of the belligerents—by Great Britain—would only lead to bloodshed."

Mr. de Valera said it was a lie to say that German submarines or any other submarines were being supplied with fuel or provisions in their ports.

It was not only a lie, but is known to be a falsehood by the British Government themselves.

Must Keep Out

Mr. de Valera said that all the outstanding differences between Eire and Britain have been settled with the exception of the question of partition.

Up to the present it had not been suggested that they were not entitled to act as they acted on remaining out of the war.

He was anxious that they should still continue to remain neutral.

That policy of neutrality had been endorsed by the Dail and by the people themselves.

GERMANS SAY RAIDER GUNS NEWFOUNDLAND

"The coast of Newfoundland is being shelled by a German battleship," Berlin radio announced yesterday in a broadcast picked up in New York.

The announcement also declared that two British steamships—the City of Cornish and a vessel of 16,000 tons—are in distress 100 miles off Newfoundland.

The City of Cornish was one of the ships announced as attacked on Tuesday. Another vessel mentioned then was the 16,698-ton Rangitiki.

ROOSEVELT TO BROADCAST

President Roosevelt will make a nation-wide broadcast at 11 a.m. on Armistice Day, it was announced at the White House yesterday.—Reuter.

BRITISH TAKE A TOWN

Britain took the offensive against Italy yesterday, capturing a colonial town, bombing a key sea base, and warning her that Rome can be bombed as well as London.

1 British and Indian troops swooped on Gallabat, important centre in the Sudan near the Abyssinian frontier, and captured it in three-quarters of an hour.

Planes, tanks, armoured cars and artillery made a smashing attack on the town at dawn.

The Italians, taken by surprise, were driven out.

A number of prisoners were taken. The Italians suffered many casualties.

Later, the Italians counter-attacked but were beaten off. Two air raids did little damage.

Gallabat adjoins the Italian frontier town of Mettema and is eighty-five miles north-west of Lake Tsana, source of the Blue Nile.

News of this British success was given in an official communique issued at Cairo.

2 R.A.F. Bomb Brindisi

British bombers aided Greece by heavily bombing Brindisi, Italian port used for sending reinforcements to Albania.

"The naval dockyard, a destroyer, submarine pens, the main railway junction and railway sidings were attacked," stated an R.A.F. communique issued last night in Cairo.

"Many bombs were seen to burst in the target area and a fire was started between the naval dockyard and the railway terminus which continued to burn steadily.

Brindisi is one of the most important centres from which Italy is waging war on Greece.

It is one of Mussolini's main naval and seaplane bases and an embarkation point for troops and supplies for Albania.

3 Rome Can Be Bombed

The British Government have taken note of the Italian statement that Italian men and aircraft have participated in the bombing of London, and they must accordingly reserve full liberty of action in regard to Rome.

That important announcement regarding the war in the air was made by Mr. R. A. Butler, Foreign Under-Secretary, in a written Parliamentary answer yesterday.

When the Italians entered the war they announced that they had moved all troops out of Rome.

Tyler Kent, former U.S. Embassy clerk, who was sentenced at the Old Bailey yesterday with Anna Wolkoff, Russian Admiral's daughter, for secrets offences. Kent goes to penal servitude for seven years.

SEA CHIEFS' MUDDLE: M.P.

Sensational allegations of muddle at the Admiralty were made in the House of Commons last night by Commander R. T. Bower, Conservative M.P. for Cleveland, Yorks, who attacked the naval chiefs and particularly the First Sea Lord Sir Dudley Pound.

Referring to the evacuation of Narvik—in which H.M. aircraft carrier Glorious and her two escort destroyers were sunk with great loss of life, Commander Bower said:

"The evacuation was considered to be such a secret that none of the higher naval officers was told it was going to take place.

"Naturally, an operation of that sort in normal circumstances would involve the closest co-operation between the Admiralty, the Coastal Command, the vice-admirals, submarines and other high officers.

"But such co-operation never took place."

Commander Bower also declared:

"There is very grave disquiet about the Board of Admiralty and about the First Lord in particular. Years ago, when Admiral Keyes was Commander-in-Chief, the First Sea Lord was chief of staff and I was a junior.

"There was no finer man in the world, but there is such a thing as anno domini.

"He is sixty-three, he is suffering from not the best of health, and everybody who knows him says the same thing: 'He's not the man he was.'"

First Lord's Silence

The Commander claimed that, after speaking to the First Lord of the Admiralty about naval officers' misgivings over the Narvik operations, he had been victimised by being given a "most inferior command."

He opened his speech by confirming everything said by Mr. Stokes (Lab., Ipswich), who had raised the question of the Glorious disaster.

Mr Stokes made several allegations in the form of questions:

"Was it a fact that the ship had been relieving aircraft from Narvik and was cluttered so that she could not get her flights up?

"Was it true that 1,000 and more men were on rafts for three nights and two days?

"Was a proper search made for them and were the rafts provided with proper illumination?"

Did Admiral Sir Charles Forbes,

Continued on Back Page Col. 4

NAVAL PACT WITH U.S.A.

A new naval agreement between Britain and the United States has been completed, according to reports from various U.S. sources last night.

Radio stations said that the agreement concerns the further transfer of American warships to the British Navy.

There are still 115 destroyers of the same age as the fifty already sent to Britain, and, said one announcer, "many of these ships will certainly be available for Britain in addition to twenty-five flying fortresses."

Bases in Pacific

American Press reports last night said that the broad outline of an agreement in principle for defence collaboration in the Pacific has been reached between Britain, the U.S., and Australia.

The reports add that it would not be surprising if, without any formal advance commitments, an understanding were reached whereby, under certain contingencies, bases in Australia and Singapore would be made available to the United States.

Mr. Purvis, head of the British Purchasing Commission in the U.S., is to fly to Britain and will "doubtless return with more orders for war materials."

She was Spy for Haw Haw

BY A SPECIAL CORRESPONDENT

A RUSSIAN Admiral's daughter who tried to send a secret message in code to Lord Haw Haw was sentenced to ten years' penal servitude at the Old Bailey yesterday.

Anna Wolkoff, thirty-seven, tall and handsome daughter of a Czarist Admiral, flushed deeply as Mr. Justice Tucker said in a voice full of emotion:

"You, a Russian subject, who in 1935 became a British subject, at a time when this country is fighting for her very life and existence, sent a document to a traitor who broadcasts from Germany for the purpose of weakening the war effort of this country."

Her more serious offence, the Judge said, was trying by secret means to send a letter addressed in code to "Joyce" in Berlin.

The traitor "Joyce" referred to by the Judge is William Joyce—Lord Haw-Haw, who broadcasts in English from Zeesen.

Once intensely patriotic, Joyce became Fascist after leaving the Conservative Party. Later he was a founder of the National Socialist League.

Wolkoff was found guilty of committing offences contrary to the Official Secrets Act, 1911, and also of

Continued on Back Page Col. 1

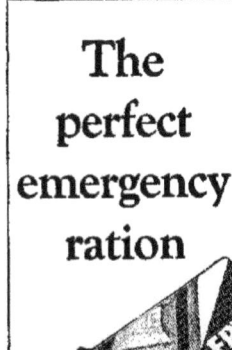

The perfect emergency ration

Fry's Sandwich Chocolate

2d AND 4½d

Daily Mirror, Thursday, Nov. 14, 1940.

Daily Mirror

No. 11,524 — ONE PENNY
Registered at the G.P.O. as a Newspaper.

The man who said, last week: "We will hit them (Italy) hard and in many places." —And some of the type of Fleet Air Arm machines which hit so hard at Taranto that they halved Italy's battleship strength in one blow.

NAVY HIT ITALY TWO SMASHING BLOWS

BRITISH NAVAL FORCES SCORED TWO VICTORIES AGAINST ITALY IN ONE NIGHT. FLEET AIR ARM BOMBERS, IT WAS ANNOUNCED YESTERDAY, HUNTED DOWN MUSSOLINI'S FIGHT-SHY NAVY, WHILE WARSHIPS TRAPPED A CONVOY. AND THIS IS WHAT THEY DID TO THEM:

The Fleet Air Arm smashed half of Italy's Battle Fleet in one blow.

Three of her six battleships and two of her cruisers are out of action.

The warships intercepted four supply ships. One was sunk, two set on fire and almost certainly sunk.

The fourth escaped, but one of the two escort destroyers which fled was hit.

"This glorious episode," was how the Premier described Britain's biggest naval victory of the war to the House of Commons yesterday.

"This result," Mr. Churchill said, "while affecting decisively the balance of naval power in the Mediterranean, also carried with it reactions upon the naval situation in other quarters of the globe."

M.P.s cheered loudly

"The Royal Navy has struck a crippling blow at the Italian Fleet," he said.

The total strength of the Italian Battle Fleet was six battleships, two of the Littorio class, which had just been put into service and are, of course, among the most powerful vessels in the world, and four of the recently-reconstructed Cavour class.

"This fleet was, of course, considerably more powerful on paper than our Mediterranean Fleet, but it had consistently refused to accept battle.

"On the night of November 11-12, when the main units of the Italian fleet were lying behind their shore batteries in their naval base at Taranto, our aircraft of the Fleet Air Arm attacked them

Beached—Under Water

"The reports of our airmen have been confirmed by photographic reconnaissances.

"It is now established that one battleship of the Littorio class is now so badly down by the bows that her fo'c'sle is under water and she has a heavy list to starboard (Cheers.)

"One battleship of the Cavour class has been beached and her stern up to and including the after turret is under water.

"This ship is also heavily listed to starboard.

"It has not yet been possible to establish the fact with certainty, but it appears probable that a second battleship of the Cavour class has been severely damaged and beached.

"In the inner harbour of Taranto two Italian cruisers are listed to

Continued on Back Page

MOUSE MEANT HOPE

BY A SPECIAL CORRESPONDENT

After a sleepless vigil of forty-eight hours beside the wreckage of a bombed London building under which her husband lies buried, a bride of three weeks stood yesterday fondling a tiny mouse, which soldiers had discovered while digging in the debris.

Her tears fell on the trembling creature in her hand.

"You poor little thing," she said. "He has sent you to me. I know he is alive. Oh, if you could only speak."

With a sigh she wrapped the mouse in a handkerchief, and turned to watch the soldiers digging, trying to find human life in the twisted mass which was once a printing works.

The bride was twenty-year-old Mrs. Nicky Irish. Her husband, a Canadian, and an ex-ballet dancer, was employed at the works as an engineer. It was a young soldier of the Pioneer Corps who gave her the mouse which had found its way out of the debris.

Brought Comfort

Up to last night, when she was persuaded to go home, Mrs. Irish had been watching the spot where her husband was trapped since Monday night. She had refused to leave, and had neither eaten nor slept.

Sympathetic A.R.P. workers provided her with a chair, on which she sat, a tragic, lonely figure.

Last night they told her that rescue work was still going on at the other side of the debris. When she left, she took with her the mouse.

"The little animal seems to have brought her comfort," Mr. Westwood, a brother-in-law, told the "Daily Mirror."

"The shock almost killed her when she heard the news. Only an hour or two before the bomb fell she and her husband, Francis, had a meal together at the works. Then she hurried home to prepare a late dinner at their little home.

"Soon after she left, the place was bombed."

Pictures—back page

2 TOWNS HAVE DAY OF BLITZ

The south-east coast had a hectic day yesterday. Two towns were dive-bombed; there were terrific dog-fights overhead; explosions shook the towns as British long-range guns fired several salvos across the Channel; and more heavy explosions were heard from the other side of the Channel where the R.A.F. were believed to be making a surprise daylight attack on German-occupied ports.

Messerschmitt fighter-bombers raiding the south-east coast arrived soon after the gun explosions, apparently carrying out a reprisal.

In their attack on one of the towns they banked low over the cliffs.

Two farm labourers ploughing a field at the cliff edge flung themselves face downwards between the shafts of their horse-drawn plough. They saw a large bomb fall from the underside of one of the machines and drop over the side of the cliff on to houses below

Fierce Air Battle

Soon after the raids on this town the Messerschmitts dive-bombed the second town. Their bombs fell in the centre of the town. Several shops were wrecked and people were killed and injured.

Spitfires streaked across the sky to reinforce Hurricanes which had intercepted the raiders over the Straits of Dover. A fierce air battle was fought out among the clouds.

Watchers saw three raiders fall to the British fighters and a fourth was chased and shot down.

A formation of raiders, some of which were believed to be Italians, crossed the Kent coast yesterday, but were turned back and scattered by the A.A. barrage and attacked

YEAR'S SHIP LOSSES—406

BRITAIN lost 406 merchant ships, including fishing vessels, by enemy action in the first twelve months of the war. The total tonnage amounted to 1,611,842 gross tons.

This was stated by Mr. A. V. Alexander, First Lord of the Admiralty, in a written answer yesterday.

In addition to the British losses, he added, our Allies lost 103 ships (474,816 tons) and neutrals 253 ships (769,212 tons) during the same period.

Crews and passengers numbered 3,327 lost, 15,636 saved, and 1,100 taken prisoner or interned.

Enemy losses for the first twelve months of the war, as far as known, were 261 ships of about 1,260,000 tons. The number of crews and passengers lost and saved was not known.

6 MORE IN PORT

Six more ships of the Jervis Bay convoy have reached port safely. They are the St. Gobein, Stureholm, Cetus, Trefusis, Puck and Sovac.

As the Jervis Bay, the British liner that fought a German battleship for three hours to save a convoy, was sinking, her master, Captain E. S. Fogarty Fegen, was seen on the bridge. He had one arm shot away.

Blood streamed from his wounds, but to the last he was seen bellowing orders from the bridge.

The story was told yesterday when the sixty-five survivors of the Jervis Bay landed at an Eastern Canadian port. Some of the men suffering from shrapnel wounds were taken to hospital.

The Admiralty stated last night that none of the sixty-five is seriously injured, but that owing to the worsening of the weather it is unlikely that there are more survivors. Next of kin of casualties will be informed as soon as possible.

The Jervis Bay's gallant fight saved twenty-nine of her convoy of thirty-eight ships.

An officer said of Captain Fegen, who was an Irishman: "He was a magnificent hero, worthy of the best traditions of his nation."

The ship's flag had been shot away, but one of the crew ran up the rigging with a new ensign, and fastened it there.

An officer told how the cargo ships in convoy scattered and the Jervis Bay got between them and the raider, laying a smoke screen as she approached the enemy.

"Never a moment did Captain Fegen hesitate," he said.

DAILY MIRROR, Friday, Nov. 15, 1940.

Daily Mirror

No. 11,525 — ONE PENNY
Registered at the G.P.O. as a Newspaper.

NOV 15

Fought in Blazing Plane: V.C.

Flight-Lieutenant James Brindley Nicolson, who refused though wounded, to jump from a blazing Hurricane till he had destroyed his enemy, has been awarded the V.C.

This is the thirteenth V.C. of the war, and the first to be awarded to a fighter pilot.

Nicolson, who is twenty-three, is one of the tallest pilots in the R.A.F.—he is 6ft. 4in. His father, who lives in Buckingham-road, Shoreham, Sussex, was an airman in the last war.

The exploit which won him the V.C. was his first fight.

He was out on patrol with his squadron, No. 249, over the Southampton area in the afternoon of August 16 when he was detailed to chase a Junkers 88.

"Manners, You Hun"

Suddenly four cannon shells from a Messerschmitt 110 tore into his plane. He was wounded in the foot and left eye. His spare petrol tank exploded, setting his plane on fire.

Then he found that the Messerschmitt had overtaken him and was right on his gun sight. As both planes dived at about 400 m.p.h. he pressed his gun button.

"When I saw the Messerschmitt in front of me, I remember shouting out, 'I'll teach you some manners, you Hun,'" he said later. "I am glad I got him. I did not think of anything at that time but to shoot him down.

Pretended To Be Dead

"Curiously enough, although the heat inside must have been intense, in the excitement I did not feel much pain. In fact, I remember watching the skin being burnt off my left hand. All I was concerned about was keeping the throttle open to get my first Hun."

The Messerschmitt zigzagged, trying to avoid the stream of fire, but in vain. Eye-witnesses saw it crash into the sea.

Nicolson then baled out. As he floated down another German fighter screamed past, and he pretended he was dead.

After fifty minutes in the air at the end of his parachute he landed a quarter of a mile inland.

"Sorry Darling"

He was suffering agonies of pain, but to the people who came to his help he insisted on dictating a telegram. It was to his wife, and said:

"Sorry. Shot down, darling. Slight injuries. All my love. Nic."

Those "slight injuries" were so serious that doctors had to fight for his life for forty-eight hours, but he has now almost recovered.

Nicolson's wife, who lives at Kirkby Wharfe, Yorkshire, gave birth to a son a month after the fight.

"Important Baby"

She proudly displayed to the "Daily Mirror" the tattered tunic and charred boots of her husband, and said:

"I could not kiss him and tell him how delighted I was about the V.C. because he is still in hospital in the south of England."

"So when I heard about it I rushed home and kissed baby. I just said, 'You are the most important baby in the world today.' He laughed and chuckled as though he knew all about it."

NAZI AIM: BULLY TURKS

GERMANY is trying to bully Turkey into allowing German troops to pass through the Dardanelles to attack in the Near East.

Berlin officials turned on the propaganda machine full blast last night after Molotov, Soviet Premier, left Germany for Moscow.

Hints of a sensational Red-Nazi decision were given by the usual "well-informed" Berlin sources to foreign newspaper men.

Moscow was silent about an agreement.

An official twenty-four-word communique stated that Ribbentrop and Molotov had a "final conference"—and nothing more.

Turkey will be the next Axis victim if she does not obey Germany.

But, stated the usual well-informed Berlin sources quoted by Associated Press:

The Dardanelles would not be taken from Turkey provided she "behaved in a manner non-inimical to the Axis and Russia."

Russia's Place

Molotov and Hitler, the same sources added, decided Russia's place in the plans of the totalitarian nations for a new world order.

What this place will be was not clearly stated. This point was definitely stated:

Europe and Africa must stand under Axis leadership.

Turkey received the Berlin threats calmly.

"If the decision of the Berlin meeting is unfavourable," an official stated in Ankara last night, "Turkey will not be taken unawares."

Late last night Berlin admitted that there was no question of a new pact having been signed.

NEW C.-IN-C. AT SINGAPORE

Air Marshal Sir Robert Brooke-Popham, newly-appointed Commander-in-Chief of the Far East Forces, arrived in Singapore yesterday by air.—Associated Press.

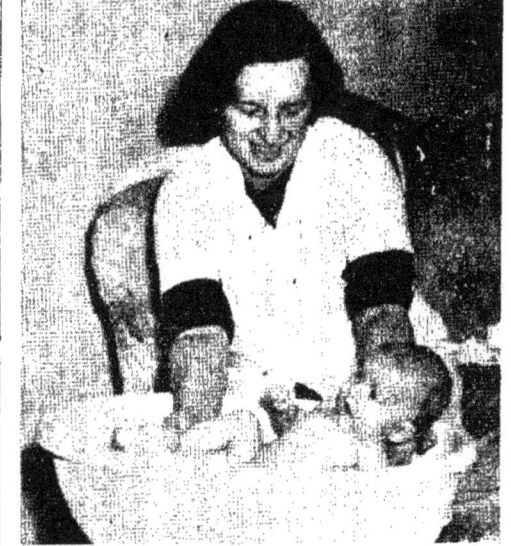

Bath-time for a hero's son. Mrs. Nicolson, wife of Flight-Lieutenant J. B. Nicolson, the new V.C., and their six-week-old boy.

R.A.F. BAG 19 IN DAY

The R.A.F. bagged nineteen enemy planes with the loss of two fighters yesterday. Both pilots are safe.

A London hospital during last night's raid received a direct hit on a block in which were aged sick women, and some were killed.

Fifteen of the enemy planes downed were destroyed by twenty Spitfires, which encountered forty Junkers 87's on their way to dive-bomb Dover Harbour.

Twelve Spitfires of one squadron accounted for thirteen of them—and a Messerschmitt 109 fighter. One pilot shot down three.

The dive-bombers were seen approaching Deal in regular formation at 14,000 feet, with about sixty Messerschmitt escorts dodging in and out of cloud at 18,000ft.

Suddenly, in the middle of the raiders, a Spitfire appeared. Then

Continued on Back Page

Sub Leader ———, stationed at ———, says

When I've only a minute for a stand-up meal it's

Fry's SANDWICH CHOCOLATE

2ᵈ AND 4½ᵈ

DAILY MIRROR, Saturday, Nov. 16, 1940.

Daily Mirror

NOV 16

No. 11,526 ONE PENNY
Registered at the G.P.O. as a Newspaper.

70 Nazis Down in Week: We Lost 5—

that was the R.A.F. score for the past seven days. We lost only three pilots. Yesterday nineteen German planes were destroyed at the cost of one fighter and one pilot. (Story on back page)

RUSSIA SNUBS BRITAIN

The Soviet Government has made no reply to certain proposals submitted by Britain through our Ambassador in Moscow as long ago as October 22.

The proposals, which were submitted to M. Vishinski, Deputy Commissar for Foreign Affairs, included an offer of the de facto recognition of the incorporation of the Baltic States in the U.S.S.R.

Other proposals were a guarantee that Russia would be a participant in any peace settlement which might be concluded after the war, and an assurance that Great Britain would not be associated in any attack against Soviet Russia.

COVENTRY RAIDERS RETURN

EVERYONE TO FIGHT HITLER

THIS IS GOING TO BE A MORE UNCOMFORTABLE WAR. MANY THINGS YOU THOUGHT WERE NECESSITIES ARE TO DISAPPEAR. BUT YOU ARE GOING TO LIKE IT BECAUSE IT WILL BE YOUR OWN PRIVATE WINTER CAMPAIGN AGAINST HITLER—A CAMPAIGN WHICH WILL SHORTEN THE WAR.

THE PRESIDENT OF THE BOARD OF TRADE, MR. OLIVER LYTTELTON, SAID THAT IN LONDON LAST NIGHT WHEN HE ANNOUNCED THAT A NEW ORDER IS TO BE ISSUED INTENSIFYING THE RATIONING OF GOODS TO THE SHOPS. IT WILL AFFECT FIFTY-TWO INDUSTRIES AND ABOUT 800 MAIN PRODUCTS, LUXURIES AND "NEAR NECESSITIES."

IN SUBMITTING TO THESE NEW "INCONVENIENCES AND HARDSHIPS," YOU WILL BE PUTTING PLANES, TANKS, RIFLES AND ALL THE APPARATUS OF WAR INTO THE HANDS OF THE SERVICES. BECAUSE "SELF-DENIAL IN PURCHASES" WILL RELEASE RAW MATERIALS, PLANT CAPACITY AND WORKERS FOR THE ARMAMENTS INDUSTRY.

All that remains of Coventry's famous fourteenth century cathedral. The beauty of its nave has been reduced by the Germans' bombs to a heap of rubble. Another picture of Coventry after the raid is on the Back Page.

BY A SPECIAL CORRESPONDENT

As refugees from the first big night blitz on the provinces streamed from Coventry last night the raiders struck again.

Advance enemy warplanes circled the city, guided by fires still raging, and the guns barked again.

One thousand people had been killed or injured in a raid by 500 planes on the city which began at dusk on Thursday night and ended at dawn yesterday.

Coventry's beautiful fourteenth century cathedral was destroyed, and many buildings, including churches, a school, hotel, four public shelters and a police station were destroyed.

Pathetic streams of refugees, men, women and children were trekking to the safety of the countryside when darkness fell last night.

Every road out of the city, which had had a bomb rained on it at the rate of one a minute, was filled with the same tragic procession.

GUN KILLS TWO AT EXHIBITION

A boy and a youth were killed and a woman, her daughter and another boy wounded when an anti-tank gun—part of an exhibition of war weapons—exploded at the City Hall, Sheffield, yesterday.

The gun was being demonstrated to a crowd of visitors to the exhibition, which was being held in connection with the city's War Weapons Week, when it went off accidentally.

The two dead were Gordon Strange, fourteen, of Hartley Brook-road, Sheffield, and Allan L. Tucker, twenty, of Sheffield-road, Woodhouse. The injured are: Mrs. Ethel Sykes, forty-two, of Raisen Hall-road, Sheffield (arm wound); her daughter, Ethel, sixteen (wounded in thigh); and Allan Tame, fourteen, of Alder-lane, Handsworth, Sheffield (leg wound).

Immediately after the accident the building was cleared and placed under guard

Thousands Stay

All day long this had gone on. By nightfall there were still thousands of people who had stayed behind to the last minute in the hope of salving more of their treasured belongings.

Mothers pushed perambulators filled with household goods, their babies lying on top.

Fathers carried elder children on their shoulders and bundles of clothing under their arms.

In the darkness I walked seven miles from Coventry with the silent army of homeless.

Alongside me, at times holding my

Continued on Back Page

Schoolchildren to Get Christmas Holidays

Schoolchildren are to have their usual Christmas holidays. But the Board of Education asks reception area authorities to discourage children from returning to danger areas.

And the authorities are asked to arrange to keep the children happily occupied and off the hands of householders as much as possible.

Teachers in reception areas are to have holidays in turns, so that some can supervise recreation in the schools.

"RAMILLIES SUNK," ITALIANS CLAIM

The Italians claimed on Rome radio last night that their submarine Capponi had sunk the British battleship Ramillies, which had been struck by three torpedoes.

It was also claimed that a torpedo had struck an aircraft carrier, but the name of this vessel was not given.

Nothing is known in official circles in London to confirm the Italian claims.

Mr. Lyttelton emphasised that there will be no scarcity in essentials.

Further limitations of supplies, now announced, mainly apply to the same industries and categories as those covered by the existing Limitations of Supplies Order, and continue a policy begun nine months ago.

Fewer Toys

Here are examples of the effect of the new Order:—

The quota of corsets, garters, and surgical goods, 50 per cent.; mattresses and similar articles, 25 per cent.; pottery, 50 per cent.; carpets, 33 1-3 per cent.

Willow or cane furniture, 33 1-3 per cent.; cameras, fancy goods, perfumery, goldsmiths' and silversmiths' ware, toys and other articles, 25 per cent.

The quota for silk goods and aluminium hollow-ware is nil.

As the percentages will be calculated by value, the higher prices will make the reductions heavier than they at first appear.

Infants knitted or crocheted wearing apparel, vacuum flasks, and shaving creams are among the articles to which the restrictions will not now apply.

Help for Poor

"I am paying particular attention both to the needs of the poor and to the needs of those who are in distress because they have been bombed out of their homes," said Mr. Lyttelton.

"Officers will keep the Board of Trade in close touch with supply and demand of the cheapest lines of goods covered by the Order and to ensure that fair distribution is being carried out.

"If unemployment is caused by the Order, the Board of Trade is confident that it would be absorbed in a reasonably short time."

Mr. Lyttelton emphasised, too, that the Board was watching carefully to prevent people with money rushing out and getting in large stocks.

THE 5-STAR FOOD DRINK
is down in price!

WHAT a comfort to know that this comforting food is actually down in price—down to 5d a quarter-pound! Cadbury's Bournville Cocoa is a balanced food in itself. And made with milk, Bournville Cocoa gives you the food value of two fresh eggs and costs you less than a quarter as much.

WHY FIVE-STARS?

★ **EXTRA FOOD VALUE.** Bournville Cocoa is rich in body-building protein, and natural cocoa butter and carbohydrates to give you energy. So remember, a cup of Bournville — the 5-Star Cocoa — is a cup of food.

★ **IRON — THE BLOOD ENRICHER.** The rich iron content of Bournville Cocoa tones up the corpuscles in your blood-stream, makes you feel stronger.

★ **PHOSPHATES—FOR HEALTHY GROWTH.** Bournville Cocoa is rich in phosphates of lime and calcium. These build up bone and muscle, strengthen teeth.

★ **AID TO DIGESTION.** Bournville Cocoa is particularly digestible, helps digestion of other foods and so makes every meal go further.

★ **VITAMINS—VITAL TO HEALTH.** Remember that every tin of Bournville Cocoa retains the potent anti-sterility Vitamin D, specially important for kiddies' healthy teeth and straight, strong bones.

BOURNVILLE
THE 5-STAR
QUALITY UNALTERED
COCOA
DOWN TO
5ᴅ PER QTR. LB.

DAILY MIRROR, Wednesday, Nov. 20, 1940.

Daily Mirror

No. 11,529   ONE PENNY
Registered at the G.P.O. as a Newspaper.

1941's VITAL JOB FOR THE H G

"THE Home Guard cannot act as a substitute for the Army, but it can release an important element of the Field Army to go and fight elsewhere —and that is the role we hope to see the Home Guard play in 1941," Mr. Anthony Eden, War Minister, told the House of Commons yesterday.

"In the Government's view the role of the Home Guard this winter and in the campaign of 1941 must be as important as, if not more important than, it has been up to the present.

"The danger of invasion is not over. The German armies are still there—massed in the Channel ports and in Flanders—and Hitler is not likely to forget that as long as Britain stands the gains he has won elsewhere are in great and growing jeopardy.

"That being so, his desire to humiliate and overthrow us, as he can only do finally by invasion, is not likely to have passed away. So it is the Government's view that the threat of invasion stands, and we shall be foolish indeed to relax our efforts in any respect."

Commander Aged 56

Mr. Eden was speaking in a debate in which Sir Edward Grigg, Under-Secretary for War, had denied that the Regular Army had adopted "a stepmotherly attitude" to the Home Guard.

Sir Edward announced that fifty-six-year-old Major-General T. R. Eastwood, former Commandant at Sandhurst, has been appointed Director-General of the Home Guard.

"In appointing a young commander to the post of Director-General, the Regular Army is endeavouring to give the Home Guard of its best," he commented.

Major-General T. R. Eastwood was formerly Inspector-General of the Guard.

In the last war he fought in Gallipoli, Egypt and France, won the D.S.O., the M.C., and was five times mentioned in despatches. He joined Lord Gort's staff in France on the outbreak of this war.

With 1,200 battalions, 5,000 companies and 25,000 platoons, the Home Guard was an enormous force five or six times as great as the Territorial Army, and all the instructors could not be found from the Regular Army, said Sir Edward Grigg.

The Commander-in-Chief would facilitate training in the lower commands and, in addition to instructors training at the Home Guard School, there would be a permanent staff of one instructor to each battalion.

"Let no one imagine," Sir Edward said, "that the danger of invasion had ceased to exist."

Continued on Back Page, Col. 3

Maj Gen. T. R. Eastwood

In Error

Captain Lyttelton, President of the Board of Trade, corrected himself yesterday about a statement he made during the week-end that the Government wish to sell stockings at a high price, "especially at Christmas time."

The Board of Trade stated yesterday that "some misunderstanding seems to have arisen."

"No decision has yet been reached"

GREEKS CRY FOR PLANES

"We must have planes—planes, planes!" M. Nicoloudis, Greek Press Minister, told foreign correspondents yesterday

"We appeal," he said, "to Allied and neutral opinion, while there is yet time, that aerial aid be given to Greece without delay.

"America and Britain must not be satisfied only with epic messages announcing epic victories of the Greek army. There are also the dangers and sacrifices to which the Greeks are exposed.

"During the last few days, in view of Koritza, the Greek army was attacked by 400 Italian planes. It advanced in spite of them.

"But although this is the first example of any army in 1940 advancing before an enemy without the support of aircraft while the enemy smites us with his powerful aviation both at the front and over our undefended towns, that does not mean it can last indefinitely."

Appeal to U.S.

Greece has appealed directly to the U.S. for planes and arms. In Washington last night it was stated that the appeal was being considered, but that difficult problems were in the way. Foremost was whether arms could be spared without impairing U.S. aid to Britain.

Greek wounded and Italian prisoners arriving at Athens testify, cables David Walker, to the almost incredible heroism of Greek fighter pilots.

Solitary fighters take off to face a sky black with Italian planes.

All the Greek soldiers say the same—"Send us planes and we'll push them into the sea before Christmas."

Koritza last night was still holding out, but Greek reports said the Italians were being slowly pressed out of the entire zone.

"Daily Mirror," British United Press and Reuter messages.

WAR WORK FOR 500,000 WOMEN

BY A SPECIAL CORRESPONDENT

EVERY unemployed woman in the country will be given the chance of training as a munition worker under a new Ministry of Labour scheme to put 500,000 women into the arms industry.

They will get the same pay and allowances as men while training.

Mr. Ernest Bevin, referring to the scheme in Parliament yesterday, said he would tell employers of the need for giving as many jobs as possible to women.

"The demands of the armed Forces for men," said Mr. Bevin, "are already becoming so great that it is manifest that women must be employed in all forms of production in ever-increasing numbers."

The only initial qualifications for women trainees will be average intelligence and physical fitness. There is no age bar.

Even grandmothers may apply so long as they are hale and hearty.

"We need 500,000 women for our armament factories by next August, Miss Caroline Haslett, Adviser to the Minister of Labour in the training and employment of women, told the Daily Mirror yesterday.

"The scheme will absorb almost the whole of the large number of unemployed women of all ages.

"Women accepted for training courses of eight weeks' duration will be sent to technical colleges and engineering works in London and the provinces," she added.

"One of the most important points in the scheme is that the women will receive the same payment and allowances as men get while in training."

What They Will Get

"For the first time it has been recognised that women may have elderly relations to support just as men may have."

Girls aged eighteen to twenty will receive 20s. a week if training locally, plus an allowance of 15s. for an adult dependant upon them.

If they go away to train, they will get a lodging allowance, 5s. pocket money and 30s. for an adult dependant.

Women over twenty-one will get 24s. per week, plus 15s. a week for an adult dependant if training locally.

When training away from home they will get a lodging allowance, usually 19s. a week, plus 7s. pocket money and 30s. for an adult dependant.

Unemployed women are urged by the Ministry to register for the scheme at once.

Training courses will start very soon, and a continual stream of

Continued on Back Page, Col. 2

WE GET MORE U.S. WARSHIPS

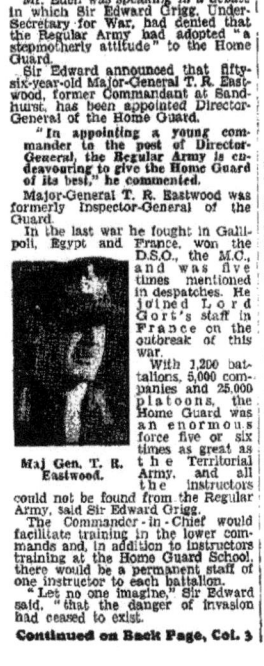

The transfer of twenty-five or thirty more over-age American destroyers to Britain is believed in well-informed Washington circles to be imminent, John Walters cables from New York.

COVENTRY: ONE GRAVE

The death roll from the bombing of Coventry increases as further bodies are recovered from beneath tons of debris in shattered buildings. Already the total is more than 250.

A mass funeral takes place today at a local cemetery. A fleet of lorries will carry their tragic loads beneath Union Jacks which will form their pall.

The interment will begin in a common grave over which a memorial will be placed when the war is over.

Compulsory billeting is now in operation, and as soon as accommodation can be prepared the homeless who have been evacuated will be able to return.

One a Minute Blitz on Midlands

A mass attack on the Midlands was made by German bombers last night when the blitz again moved to the provinces.

One Midlands town had its heaviest and longest raid of the war.

Planes arriving at one a minute did considerable damage to property. A large number of shops and other premises, as well as houses, were demolished.

Damage to industrial buildings was reported to be small, however.

A.A. fire was the heaviest the town has known.

Many of the planes would not

★ ★ ★

"THOUSANDS OF BOMBS ON BIRMINGHAM"—NAZIS

Informed German sources in Berlin said early today that large-scale aerial attacks were proceeding against "war essential targets" in an unnamed city in the Midlands.

Later the Nazis announced: "Birmingham apparently suffered the same fate as Coventry, as thousands of bombs of all calibres were dropped on armament and supply centres in that city."
—Associated Press.

★ ★ ★

face it, jettisoned their bombs and turned tail.

Many fires were started, which acted as a guide to successive waves of bombers.

Bombs of almost all types were dropped in nearly all parts of the town.

Three other Midlands towns were attacked, and at two of them many casualties are feared.

Liverpool had three raids, and enemy activity was also reported from another north-west town, south-east and north-east Scotland, Wales, north-east England and East Anglia.

Continued on Back Page, Col. 3

Mrs. Ray Blake and Mr. Patsy Blake (left pair), and Mrs. Nellie Edwards and Mr. William George Edwards, four of the family of twenty-two who were trapped and killed in their basement shelter when a bomb demolished the business premises above. The picture was taken at their double wedding. (Story on back page.)

Daily Mirror

DAILY MIRROR, Monday, Nov. 25, 1940.

No. 11,533 — ONE PENNY
Registered at the G.P.O. as a Newspaper.

How Captain Whitehead, survivor of a torpedoed ship, looked from a British aircraft which sighted him on his upturned lifeboat and brought help.

Threaten Duce's Air Bases

WITH Greek cavalry and motorised units still thrusting after them, the retreating Italian forces are trying to reform their line of battle deep in Albanian territory.

It was reported in Athens that a strong Greek force yesterday entered Pogradets, the Albanian town at the southern end of Lake Ochrida, on which the Italians were retreating from Koritza.

Greek cavalry are also reported to have entered Moscopole, ten miles west of Koritza, and to be continuing their advance.

The quick successes have cut down the danger of counter-attacks by the Italian Air Force. The three enemy aerodromes at Koritza are in Greek hands.

Another report said the Greeks had occupied the heights dominating Argyrokastro, main Italian base in South Albania.

The aerodrome at Argyrokastro is threatened, while the air bases at Tirana, Albanian capital, and Valona, have been heavily attacked from the air.

R.A.F.'s Bullseye

British planes scored a direct hit on a bridge across the Devoll River which the Italians were crossing in their retreat from Northern Greece.

The bridge had been so heavily mined by the retreating Italians that the explosion was terrific.

Greek soldiers said Italian tanks were blown to pieces.

Meanwhile, Mr. Churchill has sent a message to General Metaxas, Greek Dictator, in which he says: "We are all inspired by this feat of Greek valour against an enemy superior in numbers and equipment. This recalls the classic age. Long live Greece."

LORD TRYON, EX-P.M.G., DEAD

Lord Tryon who, as Major G. C. Tryon, was Postmaster-General from 1935 until his resignation in April this year, died yesterday from heart failure at Liddle Court, Sunningdale, Berks. He was sixty-nine.

"Lord Tryon had a heart attack last night and died peacefully. His illness was quite sudden," Lady Tryon told the "Daily Mirror."

Lord Tryon, who received a peerage in April, was the son of the late Vice-Admiral Sir G. Tryon and the Hon. Lady Tryon, sister of the first Earl of Ancaster.

He joined the Grenadier Guards in 1890, and served in the South African War.

He began ministerial service in 1919 when, at the age of forty-eight, he was appointed Under-Secretary for Air.

AXIS DRAG IN SLOVAKS

Thousand Incendiary Bombs on Berlin

A thousand incendiaries were showered on the Putlitzstrasse and Lehrter railway yards in Berlin by the R.A.F. before eight o'clock on Saturday night. Huge explosions followed the dropping of high explosive bombs, and in one phase of the attack ten large fires raged fiercely.

At Essen a tremendous explosion lasting ten seconds followed a heavy onslaught on the Krupps arms works.

At the other end of the Axis, the arsenal and the Fiat works at Turin were raided.

One pilot counted twenty-three explosions at the arsenal. Another pilot counted twenty-eight fires as he left the city.

There is no doubt the arsenal was severely damaged, says the Air Ministry.

Details of the night's raids on page 7.

MILK TO GO UP A HALFPENNY

Milk prices go up another halfpenny a pint next Sunday.

This is the second halfpenny a pint increase since war began.

In announcing this increase, which all goes to the farmer, the Ministry of Food says its aim is to meet the higher cost of production.

The increase, says the Ministry, will probably continue for six months.

Expectant and nursing mothers and children under five years of age will still be entitled to a pint a day at twopence, or free, according to their circumstances.

Schoolchildren will continue to be eligible for a daily allowance of a third of a pint a day at a halfpenny.

HITLER dragged another of his vassal States into the Three-Power Axis pact at Berlin yesterday—Slovakia. Every effort was made to represent this adherence of a two-year puppet as an imposing contribution to the Nazi plan for a "New Order" in Europe.

But Mussolini's newspapers, anxious to speed up the diplomatic campaign against Greece and Turkey, and cover up the Italian defeats in Albania, revealed the new Berlin ceremony as another attempt to stampede Yugoslavia and Bulgaria.

The entire Italian Press urged the Yugoslavs to join the pact—which would open one of the roads for German aid to the Italian forces—or "declare their real intentions."

And it chorused a forecast that Bulgaria would join the "Three Power Pact tomorrow or Wednesday"—which would mean another threat to Greece—and to Turkey.

Said the Voce d'Italia: "One may consider that Bulgaria has already ranged herself on the side of the Axis Powers, not as a neutral Power but as a non-belligerent."

According to the New York radio yesterday Belgrade reports say that Bulgaria has postponed the departure of her statesmen to Berlin to join the Axis because she wants to make sure of Soviet Russia's attitude on this move.

Week-end reports stated that Russia had warned Bulgaria against following Hungary and Rumania into the Axis Pact.

Papen Gets Busy

Von Papen, Hitler's Ambassador to Turkey, getting busy on his return to Ankara, saw the Turkish Foreign Minister, M. Sarajoglu, and his deputy.

In face of the threat of German troops passing through Bulgaria, the Turkish Press shows no weakening in confidence that Turkey can defend her independence.

Turkey is keeping a move ahead by means of defence measures, including martial law in her European territory.

Slovakia's adherence to the Axis pact was staged in Hitler's Chancellery where Bela Tuka, Slovak Premier, made a pompous speech after putting down his signature.—Reuter, British United Press, Associated Press, Exchange.

"SHELLS US" SOS

"BEING shelled by raider" was the message picked up by Mackay, New York, radio yesterday from the British vessel Port Hobart (9,430 tons).

The position of the Port Hobart, which is owned by Port Line, Ltd., and registered in London, was given as "off the West Indies," approximately 500 miles north-east of Puerto Rico.

Another intercepted message was from the British steamship Trehata.

It stated that she had sighted a "suspicious vessel" about 500 miles west of Ireland, in waters where three ships were attacked on Saturday.—*Daily Mirror* and Associated Press.

FIGHTERS SHOOT DOWN BOMBER IN CHANNEL

An enemy bomber was shot down by our fighters in the English Channel yesterday—a day on which enemy activity over Britain was reported as "slight."

Several formations of fighters and fighter-bombers crossed the S.E. coast during the morning in the direction of London.

They were met and dispersed by our fighters. A few bombs were dropped at several points in Kent. Little damage and very few casualties were reported.

DRIFTED ALONE ON WRECK— IS SAVED

TORPEDOED in the Atlantic—his ship went down in less than a minute—a skipper grabbed a piece of wreckage in the darkness and hung on.

For eight hours he clung to the drifting wreckage, waiting for daylight. When dawn broke he found he was the sole survivor out of thirty-six men. Near him, tossing about upside down, was one of the ship's boats. It was his only hope.

To right it was a hopeless job, but he swam across to it and climbed on to the upturned keel.

There he sat, hungry and shivering, waiting, hoping, as the boat drifted helplessly far out of sight of land or ship.

For four more hours he drifted along. Then he spotted a plane.

Whether it was British or enemy he did not know, but he must attract its attention. He got to his feet, balanc-

Continued on Back Page

'GENASPRIN' soothes QUICKLY—time it!

GENASPRIN
The SAFE Brand of Aspirin

turns an UNEASY DOZE into RESTFUL SLEEP

Let 'Genasprin' give you deep, sound sleep the moment your head touches the pillow. Two tablets will soothe your jangled nerves, do away with that period of tossing, turning and twitching. Remember that doctors all over the world recommend 'Genasprin' for its quicker action and greater purity. Buy a bottle of 'Genasprin' to-day and be absolutely sure of sound sleep to-night.

Sold only by qualified chemists.

At EVERY time of strain or pain 'GENASPRIN' sees you through

The word 'GENASPRIN' is the registered trade mark of Genatosan Ltd., Loughborough, Leicestershire.

DAILY MIRROR, Tuesday, Nov. 26, 1940.

Daily Mirror

NOV 26

No. 11,534 — ONE PENNY
Registered at the G.P.O. as a Newspaper.

HANG A LOOTER

HANG A LOOTER, AND STOP THIS FILTHY CRIME.

Fines and imprisonment have done nothing to stop the ghouls who rob even bodies lying in the ruins of little homes.

Looting, in fact, is on the increase. There have been more than 450 cases in London alone during the past ten weeks. Yesterday brought another crop.

A war reserve policeman was found guilty of looting in a bombed London house. He had been stationed there as a guard—against looters. And the articles he took belonged to a woman killed by the bomb which wrecked her home. He got five years' penal servitude.

At bomb-scarred Coventry, three A.F.S. men who were drafted in to help the city got six months each for looting in a shop. A gang was gaoled for looting in houses.

The heaviest penalty imposed so far has been five years' penal servitude. It has not stopped looting.

But the law, under the Defence Regulations, can sentence to death.

ENFORCE THAT LAW.
HANG A LOOTER.

The country demands that this crime be stamped out.

Home Guards, helping with rescue work, have had to stop their mercy task to guard neighbouring shops to save them from looters.

Impose It Now

To cover themselves the thieves often mingle with a rescue squad, pretending to help, so that they can get nearer to their prey.

A.R.P. workers have had to interrupt their work to make sure the beasts are not among them.

Judges and magistrates have hinted that a death sentence will have to be passed.

Mr. F. O. Langley the Old-street magistrate, told the *Daily Mirror*: "I have had a fair experience of looters by now and I have sought to make an example.

"It may well be that the death penalty will have to be imposed."

Impose it now before looting increases still more.

HANG A LOOTER.

STAY PUT DEC. 25

THE Government have planned a "stay-put" Christmas for you. There are to be no extra travel facilities either then or at the New Year.

War workers are asked to take only one day off—either on Christmas Day or New Year's Day.

As already forecast, there will be no Bank Holiday on Christmas Day in Scotland or on Boxing Day in England, Wales and Northern Ireland.

The Ministry of Labour announced last night:

"The flow of production for war purposes is great and ever increasing in spite of the efforts of the enemy to impede it, but this is not the moment for any slackening off.

"The more the flow of production is accelerated the earlier will be the day of final victory.

"The Government, therefore, call on all managements and workers engaged on war work to continue production during the coming Christmas and New Year season with not more than one day's break either Christmas Day or New Year's Day.

"On Christmas Day in England and Wales, and on New Year's Day in Scotland normal Sunday services will in general be run."

Christmas Buying Is Patriotic.—Back Page.

BRITISH HARASS ITALIANS

British "harassing operations" in the Sudan, east of the recently-captured village of Gallabat, are continuing, it was reported in the G.H.Q. communique issued in Cairo yesterday.—Associated Press.

TARANTO—

Here is the first picture of the havoc we did to the Italian Navy at Taranto—a Cavour class Italian battleship (23,622 tons) beached in harbour.

Musso said we only slightly damaged one ship. Well, this picture was taken two days after the attack, from a height of 6,000ft. The R.A.F. said yesterday they believe the ship to have been abandoned, because her starboard side and her stern is under water, and there is no activity of any kind round her. She is only 300 yards from the beach, where there is not enough water to float her. In the words of the Air Ministry, "she may as well be given to Lord Beaverbrook for scrap."

Other pictures on page 7.

GREEK PUSH ON WHOLE FRONT

THE Greeks were still pushing forward yesterday. They advanced along the entire front in pincer formation after having occupied Pogradetz, the town to which the Italians fled on their way from Koritza.

The fall of Argyrokastro, main Italian southern base in Albania, was expected, according to dispatches from the front.

These messages said that Greek advance units had already entered the outskirts of the town.

Heavy fighting was reported to be going on south-west of Argyrokastro, where the Greeks were threatening to push to the coast, isolating a large force of Italians.

Additional Greek columns were threatening Premeti, north-east of Argyrokastro.

The Greeks announced their occupation of Moschopolis yesterday as the enemy abandoned Mount Ostrovitza to the south of the town.

Here the Italians had strong positions solidly fortified. They are now fleeing from the 8,000ft. Mount Tomori and have abandoned Fracheri.

9,500 Prisoners

After the Greek High Command had reported 1,500 prisoners taken during the mopping-up operations round Koritza, it was announced in Athens last night that another 8,000 Italians had been captured.

The enemy forces are falling back to Elbasan, presumably to hold a line from that town to the port of Valona.

Italian prisoners say that no one in Italy wants the war.

According to a Rome report the Fascist leader Farinacci, writing in the *Regime Fascista*, criticises the Italian General Staff for lack of foresight and military preparedness and a badly chosen season for operations.—Exchange, Associated Press, Reuter.

SHIP SOS—'ATTACKED'

"Being attacked by submarine," was the dramatic S O S sent out yesterday by the British steamer Temple Inn.

Mackay Radio, New York, intercepted the message, which gave the Temple Inn's position as 56.15 latitude N. and 8.40 longitude W. This is roughly off the west coast of Scotland.

Mackay Radio also reported (says Reuter) that the Swedish steamer Anten, which was torpedoed off the Irish coast on Saturday, sent out an S O S at 11.12 a.m. G.M.T. yesterday saying she was still afloat and drifting in a position between Ireland and Iceland.

V.C.'s Family Share Palace Honour

An R.A.F. hero had his own private investiture at Buckingham Palace yesterday.

And with him in the Palace, sharing this honour, were his young wife, his mother and his two sisters.

He is twenty - three - year - old Flight-Lieutenant J. B. Nicolson, and the King decorated him with the V.C. he won when he dived at 400 m.p.h. in a blazing fighter plane to shoot down a German machine.

The King chatted with the flight-lieutenant for several minutes about that heroic attack.

RAIDER SHOT DOWN IN SEA

AN enemy bomber crashed into the sea off Dover yesterday after it had been attacked by a Spitfire.

The pilot, flying at 5,000ft., first saw the raider—a Dornier 17—7,000ft. above him when fifteen miles off Dover.

He climbed to attack and fired two short bursts at 350 yards' range. Pieces from the bomber fell in the sea before the machine itself crashed.

Two bungalows were demolished and two houses damaged when two Messerschmitt fighter-bombers dive-bombed a south-east coast town.

One man was slightly injured. His wife, who sheltered under a table, was dug out from the wreckage of her home unhurt.

During the afternoon, enemy planes were reported near a western town.

DAILY MIRROR, Saturday, Nov. 30, 1940.

Daily Mirror

NOV 30

No. 11,538 — ONE PENNY
Registered at the G.P.O. as a Newspaper.

IRON GUARDS KILL 2,000

BOY KING FLEES

With his country terrorised by an Iron Guard murder campaign which has already caused 2,000 deaths, nineteen-year-old King Michael of Rumania was last night reported to have fled from his capital.

While his Premier, General Antonescu, struggled to keep control of the country, Michael was said to have either headed for the Yugoslav border, or to be hiding outside Bukarest to await events.

Iron Guard Legionaries broke loose from their leader, Horia Sima, to exact revenge on former opponents. They are estimated to have murdered 2,000 people, mostly Jews, in the last three days.

But more than a murder campaign was indicated by reports seeping through the Rumanian censorship. These said that the Legionaries planned a coup for last night but struck earlier when the Government learned of their plans.

At Turnu-Severin, Caiova and Brasov, reports said, the Legionaries sought to seize power and there was heavy loss of life in fighting for the possession of public buildings.

While Sima, the Iron Guard leader, sped to Ploesti, town in the oilfields, in an attempt to check the mounting revenge killings there, Legionaries made a gangster attack on his Bukarest headquarters.

Hitler May Step In

They swept past in a car and poured a hail of machine-gun bullets into the building, killing and wounding several men.

Antonescu ordered several divisions of the Rumanian Army to Bukarest—and sought the aid of Maniu, respected peasants' leader, to prevent the unrest spreading to the population.

There were indications that Hitler would take a hand to end the Rumanian turmoil.

King Michael's mother, Queen Helen, who fled the country recently went to Rome yesterday, then returned to Florence.

It was learned last night that the greater part of the Rumanian Legation staff in London has resigned.

The resignations, which are being forwarded to Bukarest, are stated to be because of "recent shootings."—Foreign messages: Reuter, British United Press, Associated Press.

London Blitz Comes Back
—Story on Back Page

THE KING'S PILOTS

Listening to last-minute instructions to night bomber crews is the King, Marshal of the Royal Air Force. The picture was taken in the briefing room at a Bomber Command Station, where the King spent a wakeful night. Wishing his flyers "Good Luck," the King dined at the aerodrome and waited for their return, some of them from Cologne. Then he questioned them with keen interest as they reported on the night's work over enemy territory.

ACTION STATIONS

ACTION on sea, land and in the air ... British warships, British guns and British bombers provided this news yesterday:

Navy Shells an Italian Port

A British warship, with aircraft co-operating has successfully bombarded targets at Ras Alula, near Cape Gardefui in Italian Somaliland.

Considerable damage was done to depots and two large fires were started, says the Admiralty. No damage or casualties were sustained by our force.

And the Fleet's Air Arm have pounded Mussolini's sea base at Leros, in the Dodecanese, and Tripoli, Libya. At Leros, Italian ships, one probably a warship, were attacked, and big dockyard fires started. At Tripoli, the quayside and a ship were hit.

R.A.F. Bombs on Baltic Ports

R.A.F. bombers roared over to the Baltic on Thursday night. They planted bombs on the naval shipyards at Stettin and on a synthetic oil plant in the port of Politz.

Twenty fires were started in the Politz plant, one of Germany's biggest.

They also visited Dusseldorf and Mannheim where they attacked gas works, communications and armament factories, and they attacked the invasion ports of Antwerp, Boulogne and Le Havre. We lost two planes

5 Nazi Raiders Shot Down

Five German raiders were shot down in day raids on Britain yesterday. Two of our planes were lost, but both pilots are safe.

Four lone bombers were shot down over the Channel, and an Me 109 was destroyed over Dungeness.

Small forces of German machines crossed the south-east coast, and bombs were dropped in South London. The Air Ministry said the damage was small and the casualties few.

Warships Clash in Channel

BRITISH and German light naval forces clashed in the Channel early yesterday.

An Admiralty statement last evening said the result of the engagement was not yet known.

The enemy fled at high speed towards Brest, pursued by our ships. "It is known that one of our units sustained damage," it was stated, "and a report has been received that damage was inflicted upon the enemy."

The Nazi radio claimed that two British destroyers were torpedoed.

BRITISH WOMEN TO DIE
—Nazi Sentence

Two British women have been sentenced to death in Paris by a German Military Court, according to a message from France to New York last night.

The women, Winifred Harle and Florence Frickard, were charged with distributing pro-British and anti-German propaganda.

The U.S. Embassy is trying to win reconsideration of the case.

Repeatedly members of foreign colonies in France are being placed in confinement on charges of attempting to help British war wounded to escape.

SO GOOD!
SO GOOD FOR YOU
— and actually down in price!

WHY FIVE STARS?

★ **EXTRA FOOD VALUE.** Bournville Cocoa is rich in body-building proteins, and natural cocoa butter and carbohydrates to give you energy. So remember, a cup of Bournville — the 5-Star Cocoa — is a cup of food.

★ **IRON — THE BLOOD ENRICHER.** The rich iron content of Bournville Cocoa tones up the corpuscles in your bloodstream, makes you feel stronger.

★ **PHOSPHATES — FOR HEALTHY GROWTH.** Bournville Cocoa is rich in the various phosphates and calcium. These build up bone and muscle, strengthen teeth.

★ **AID TO DIGESTION.** Bournville Cocoa is particularly digestible, helps digestion of other foods and so makes every meal go further.

★ **VITAMINS — VITAL TO HEALTH.** Remember that every tin of Bournville Cocoa retains the natural sunshine Vitamin D, specially necessary for kiddies' healthy teeth and straight, strong bones.

IT'S amazing, but it's true, that one food is actually *down* in price! It's Cadbury's famous Bournville Cocoa — always a favourite standby in every kitchen cupboard, and now a big new help to proper feeding at an economical cost. Down in price to 5d per quarter-pound, and a natural food in itself. But suppose you make it with milk — a cup of Bournville Cocoa gives you the nourishment of two whole fresh eggs and costs you less than a quarter as much.

BOURNVILLE
THE 5-STAR
COCOA
QUALITY UNALTERED
DOWN TO
5D PER QTR. LB.

DAILY MIRROR, Tuesday, Dec. 3, 1940.

Daily Mirror

No. 11,540   ONE PENNY
Registered at the G.P.O. as a Newspaper.

PROFITEERS IN DEATH

HARDER LIVING AHEAD

Cuts in Meat Bacon

THE meat ration is to be cut in the near future. There will probably be less bacon.

Lord Woolton, Minister of Food, announced this last night. His Christmas Box to the people will be a postponement in cutting down the meat ration.

He also said: "I cannot afford any longer to use ships for things not essential for the prosecution of the war. So I have with great regret decided, on the best scientific advice, that I shall have to cut out all fruits, except oranges, from the public diet. Practically all tinned fruits will have to go."

Lord Woolton warned the country that in future we should have to live harder.

"But," he added, "do not think when I say that it means that you must tighten your belt. That is a wrong phrase to use, because it means you must go hungry and you will not go hungry.

"We shall live on our home produce as far as possible and for the rest we will import the foods that we have already bought, and which now lie over the world ready for us to collect.

"The call is for ships, ships and more ships—and to increase their usefulness by 10 per cent."

That was why he must ask the nation to use its shipping with greater care. That was why he had cut out most of the fruit.

"And I may find from time to time that I shall be able to give you even less bacon than you are getting now," he added.

"It would not be jannock to cut down the meat ration for Christmas," he said.

Lord Woolton said that he would not impose unnecessary sacrifices for the sake of sacrifice.

★ —This Is Why

5 Ships Lost in 4 Hours

Renewed raids against shipping in the Atlantic off the Irish coast were indicated by several distress calls heard yesterday by Mackay Radio, New York.

Five British steamers were torpedoed within four and a half hours in the Atlantic yesterday, 400 to 600 miles off the coast of Ireland, according to some of these messages.

Here is the list of the radio calls for help:—

1. —SOS was picked up by Mackay Radio Station at 4.15 a.m. (British Summer Time) from the LADY GLANELY, 5,497-ton ship owned by the Tatem Steam Navigation Company.

2. —NINETY minutes later another British vessel reported that she had been attacked near the same spot, but her identity could not be established in New York from her call letters—GKIF.

3. —THE GOODLEIGH (5,448 tons), also owned by the Tatem Steam Navigation Company, was the third ship torpedoed. The attack was made less than 150 minutes after the Lady Glanely was hit.

4. —LESS than two hours after the message from the Goodleigh, the Mackay Station intercepted a report from the VICTOR ROSS (12,247 tons), owned by the British Mexican Petroleum Company.

5. —TWENTY-FIVE minutes later a fifth ship, the LOCH RANZA (4,958 tons), of Glasgow, had been torpedoed, was sinking, and she had the crew of another wrecked ship on board.

...ll we know about the girl in the picture is that her pet name is "Cynth."

And the mother of the man she loved asks us to publish the picture, in order that she can trace "Cynth," and tell her that her boy has died a hero's death; and so that they can meet and talk of him together.

(See story on middle pages.)

SLAVS ARE HITLERED

YUGOSLAVIA into the Axis next, say German reports.

Hitler is said to have had a secret conference at the week-end with Cincar Markovitch, Yugoslav Foreign Minister.

There Hitler put on the screws and prepared the way for Yugoslavia's signature to the Tripartite Pact.

A report in diplomatic quarters in Budapest says that the conference took place in Germany and "arranged the preliminary details for Yugoslavia to follow Hungary, Rumania, and Slovakia in joining the Axis alliance."—Daily Mirror and Associated Press.

✦ Hitler pouring four more divisions into Rumania.—Back page.

370 CASUALTIES AT SOUTHAMPTON

The Air Ministry announced late last night that there were 370 casualties in the week-end raids on Southampton.

"Casualties were not heavy taking into account the scale of operations," says the Ministry.

For the two raids on Saturday and Sunday they are known to be about 370, which includes both killed and seriously injured.

Germany claimed yesterday that Southampton smoke could be seen from Cherbourg.

✦ Homeless trek from blitz town.—Page 3.

MORE WAR WORK HOPE

The Ministry of Supply is to make a survey of Wearside's idle works and factories which might be employed in turning out munitions.

ITALY EXECUTES "PACIFISTS"

FROM OUR CORRESPONDENT
LISBON, Monday.

Neutral travellers from Genoa declare that mass trials are going on in Italy and hundreds of people are being executed for alleged "pacifism."

It will be recalled that in his last speech, on November 18, Mussolini said the Fascist Party must "fight its battles on the home front."

"A certain kind of pacifism of an intellectual and international tint," he said, "must be closely watched and fought."

PROFITEERING IN DEATH . . . Wembley Corporation exacts the last legal penny of its rights when it allows an air raid victim to be buried in its Alperton Cemetery.

Three weeks ago the "Daily Mirror" printed the story of the Baptism of Monica Mary—the christening party at which Monica Mary, her father and mother, her grandfather and grandmother, and her great-grandmother, were killed by a German bomb.

Today it prints the bill that had to be paid to the Wembley Corporation for the burial of the child, her father and mother, and her grandfather and grandmother.

They were all buried in one grave, at a cost of £28 9s. for burial alone. Monica Mary was buried in her mother's arms—a fact that was duly noted.

TO THE BILL FOR BURYING THE MOTHER WAS ADDED 7s. BECAUSE THE BABY WAS LAID IN THE SAME COFFIN.

Although all were buried in one grave, Wembley Corporation charged for four separate burials, sent in four separate bills. Here they are:—

The 7s. Extra

Mr. James Holt (Monica Mary's grandfather):
Exclusive right of interment .... £6 6s.
Interment .... £5 5s.
Minister .... 15s.
Right of numbering grave .. 1s.
                          £12 7s.

That bill would have been the same had Mr. Holt been buried alone.

Mrs. James Holt (her grandmother):
Interment .... £4 10s.
Minister .... 15s.
                          £5 5s.

Then similar bills for Mr. George Young (her father) and Mrs. Young (her mother).

Except, of course, that 7s. addition to the bill for Mrs. Young.

And there was also the bill for the burial of Mrs. Louisa Thorning, Monica Mary's great-grandmother, buried in her husband's grave in the same cemetery. It was £4 2s. 6d., including 7s. 6d. for the minister.

In all, fees for the minister at this single funeral amount to £3 7s. 6d.

The Rev. J. G. Weatherston, of St. Nicholas's Church, Perivale, took the

Continued on Back Page, Col. 2

5 MEN LOST IN SUNK DESTROYER

H.M. destroyer Sturdy has been lost.

She ran ashore on the Scottish coast in thick weather. Five ratings were lost.

Sturdy was one of the "S" destroyers completed in 1918-19 as part of the emergency war programme. She had a displacement of 905 tons and carried a peace time complement of ninety-eight.

ITALIAN LINE IS SMASHED

A VICTORY described as "without exaggeration, of exceptional importance" was claimed by the Greeks last night.

The Greeks say that they captured 5,000 Italian prisoners—the largest claim yet made—and made a huge gap in the centre sector of the Italian line on the northern front.

"The enemy line in this sector has been destroyed and all danger to us eliminated," said an Athens spokesman.

Military authorities forbade the mention of the exact location of the victory.

The surrender of the group of prisoners is reported to have been the signal for a general retreat by other Italian forces in the same area.

Reports said that the Italian commander surrendered his force after the Greeks had surrounded it. It was claimed that the captured men included an elite corps which had fought in the Spanish War.

R.A.F. Success

A "successful" attack by R.A.F. bombers on Italian reinforcements on a road in south-western Albania was announced in Athens yesterday as the Greeks continued their advance along the whole sixty-mile front from the coast to the shores of Lake Ochrida.

In the eastern sector Greek troops are reported to have captured new positions north of Pogradets—the town they took on Saturday.

On the coast, according to a Greek spokesman, the enemy's resistance is being broken and the Italians are yielding strategic positions. In the central sector further progress has been made in the region of Premeti.

In the eastern sector the Italians are caught between two fires, says a dispatch from the Yugoslav frontier.

The Greeks are pursuing them relentlessly towards Elbasan. In the neighbourhood of that town

Continued on Back Page, Col. 4

DAILY MIRROR, Wednesday, Dec. 4, 1940.

Daily Mirror

DEC 4

No. 11,541 — ONE PENNY
Registered at the G.P.O. as a Newspaper.

NAZIS CLAIM 19 SUNK IN ONE DAY

THE Germans yesterday claimed the sinking of nineteen vessels and the "probable" sinking of another two, on one day—Monday.

An attack by U-boats on one convoy was said to have accounted for fifteen ships, an escorting 17,000-ton auxiliary cruiser, and the two "probables."

The auxiliary cruiser was first said to have been the 17,046-ton Caledonia. Then the Germans remembered that the Admiralty reported the loss of the Caledonia—which was renamed the Scotstoun — in June. So they took the ship's name out of the claim.

A German High Command communique stated:

"On December 2 our submarines, with particular success, attacked and dispersed a large convoy sailing for Britain.

"In spite of heavy protection by cruisers and destroyers and violent defence, which started at once, fifteen ships with a total tonnage of 110,000 tons, and the British auxi-

19 in One Week

Nineteen British and three Allied ships—tonnage of 87,975—were lost in the week ended November 24-25. See page 2.

★ ★ ★

liary cruiser Caledonia, 17,046 tons, which formed part of the escort, were torpedoed and sunk.

"Two more ships totalling together 16,000 tons were probably sunk.

"The U-boat commanded by Lieutenant Mengersen alone sank five vessels."

Then the communique claimed the sinking by a U-boat of two armed freighters totalling 21,247 tons, "one of them being the modern British motor-ship Victor Ross of 11,247 tons."

This made a total of eighteen definite sinkings claimed by the enemy.

And the High Command communique declared: "Thus our U-boats alone yesterday sank a combined total of over 160,000 tons."

The official German news agency brought the total to nineteen with the claim that on Monday Nazi bombers sank a freighter in the Channel.

Following Monday's U.S. reports of S O S calls from five British ships being attacked in the Atlantic off the Irish Coast, the Mackay Radio of New York received a distress call from another vessel yesterday.

Attack by Plane

The message said that the steamer Alvonia had been attacked by a plane at 11.47 B.S.T. 300 miles west of Ireland yesterday.

There is no vessel named Alvonia listed in Lloyd's Register of Shipping. Extension of the war on shipping was claimed by the German radio yesterday.

It declared that German surface raiders are now successfully operating in the Pacific and Indian Oceans, and that "Britain has not enough ships to hunt them."

It was added that the British liner Empress of Russia had been requisitioned by the Admiralty when about to leave Hong Kong and transformed into an auxiliary cruiser to protect shipping in the Pacific.

'WOPS' WHITE HELL

The Greeks were reported yesterday to be pushing deeper into Albania. Santi Quaranta, Mussolini's most southerly port, is threatened. The Greeks have driven a wedge between Argyrokastro and Santi Quaranta.

In the central sector the Greeks have captured the 6,800-ft. Polita Politzani, in face of strong Italian positions.

In the north the Italians, after making a stand north of Pogradetz, on the shore of Lake Ochrida, are again in retreat. Farther west a vigorous Italian counter-attack was smashed with great loss.

FROM DAVID WALKER
ATHENS, Tuesday.

SWIRLING snowstorms are tearing through the ravines and gorges of the vast Pindus Mountains which are now the scene of the fiercest fighting of this war.

Down in the valley, bogged Italian tanks are merging into the landscape under a blanket of snow, while the long mule and donkey columns of Greek supplies stand out sharply black against the white background.

From ruined Pogradetz in the north to the newly bombarded roads of Santi Quaranta, Mussolini's port in the south, the Greeks are fighting with unbelievable frenzy. Many units outrun their ammunition, forging ahead with bayonets and rifle butts.

In certain sectors, despite the bitterest cold, and blizzards, the Greeks are covering twenty miles a day to reach the front. They trudge past huge Italian Fiat trucks already bogged, snowed up, deserted.

Landing Crashes

Half finished meals in Italian quarters give proof of the incessantly relentless Greek pressure which is not allowing the Italians rest or sleep.

The Italian Army in the north, which had brought flags and mistresses for a triumphal trip to Athens, is now deserting both.

The first cases of serious infectious disease are now reported among the Italian prisoners.

Tremendous scenes are reported from Koritza, where life has been restored to normal; gramophones are playing long-hidden Greek records.

It is now revealed that the final storming and taking of heavily-defended Pogradetz was achieved after the Greeks' ammunition was

Continued on Back Page, Col. 2

Earns £3-£4 a Week at 15—Got Drunk

Two boys aged fifteen, stated to be earning good money, one of them between £3 and £4 a week in a war production factory, were accused at Windsor Juvenile Court yesterday of being drunk and disorderly.

They told the Court they had been celebrating the departure of a school friend on active service. They got drunk and fell out among themselves. In a fight one of them who had a knuckle duster missed another boy's face with a punch, but smashed a plate-glass window valued at ten guineas.

The boys were fined £1 each for being drunk. One was ordered to pay ten guineas damages for breaking the window.

CANTEEN HEROISM

While firemen fought serious fires at oil depots in London during the early days of the blitz two girls in the London Fire Service cheered and strengthened them by supplying hot drinks and food from a mobile canteen van.

The girls are Woman Auxiliary Winifred Mary Eustace, of Crowborough - road, Tooting, and Section Officer Millicent Pennington, of Rivell - road, Cheam, Surrey, whose gallantry has won them the medal of the Civil Division of the Order of the British Empire, it was announced last night.

Each night of the blitz they worked for twelve hours on end. Incendiary and high explosive bombs were raining down all the time, and several times splinters hit the canteen in which they were working.

Their outstanding coolness was a great example to the men.

Both are stationed at Southwark Bridge Fire Station, but more recently Miss Eustace has had experience of the blitz further afield.

George Cross for Bomb Hero—back page.

Miss Pennington.

NO EXTRA LEAVE

The Army is to have no extra leave for Christmas or New Year.

Asked in the Commons about it yesterday, Mr. Law, Financial Secretary, War Office, said the present percentage of leave was on as generous a scale as operational needs would allow and this would be continued over Christmas.

"The industrial population is making sacrifices in this respect," he said, "and I am sure the Army would not wish to do less."

Captain W. J. S. Fletcher.

BATTLE OF LONDON'S FIRST M.C.

An officer's wife sat lonely in a little house at Beaconsfield, Bucks, last night. She had just put her two children to bed. And she was sitting wondering—as so many wives have done since the war began—how her husband was faring.

Suddenly the 'phone rang. It was her husband speaking.

"Darling," he said, "they've just given me the Military Cross!"

Thus did Second Lieutenant (Acting Captain) John Stapylton Fletcher, of the Royal Artillery, announce to his wife that he had earned the distinction of being the first winner of the M.C. in the battle of London, "for gallant conduct in action with the enemy."

During intensified day and night air attack on London in September he was site commander in the centre of a heavily-bombed area.

"Responding readily to the example, leadership and military bearing of Captain Fletcher," says the War Office, "the troops, although the site was frequently ringed with bombs, never wavered.

"He encouraged them in every way

Continued on Back Page, Col. 5

Briton Toured U-Boat

BY A SPECIAL CORRESPONDENT
LISBON, Tuesday.

A BOY of seventeen is probably the only British seaman to have been on a conducted tour of an enemy submarine in this war.

He is Robert Timarco, of Penny-street, Skelmersdale near Ormskirk. Robert, who is in the merchant navy, was shown the workings of the Italian submarine which shelled and sank his ship.

After the submarine had seen the crew of the ship take to the boats it disappeared. For two days and nights Robert helped his fellows bale out the lifeboat to which they had rigged some sails. They fed on dry biscuits.

The sea got rough and the improvised mast went through the bottom of the boat. As she was sinking the Italian submarine reappeared and took the men on board.

Robert asked the Italian second officer: "What did you want to sink us for?" The officer replied: "You shouldn't ask that. We are at war. But I can tell you that no good Italian wants war."

Then, because of Robert's pluck, the officer took him over the submarine, showed him how it was built and worked.

The British crew were in the submarine for four days, then they were landed in the Azores, whence they came by ship to Lisbon.

Racked with Rheumatism?

Genasprin kills pain QUICKLY —time it!

Just two tablets of 'Genasprin' —that's all you need for instant relief from rheumatism, neuritis, neuralgia, and all types of nerve pain. Doctors everywhere recommend 'Genasprin' for its extra purity. Buy some from your chemist to-day.

Sold only by qualified chemists.

At every time of strain or pain 'GENASPRIN' sees you through

Daily Mirror

DAILY MIRROR, Thursday, Dec. 5, 1940.

No. 11,542 ONE PENNY
Registered at the G.P.O. as a Newspaper

DEC 5

XMAS AT THE FIRESIDE

THIS will be a fireside Christmas. There's no compulsion about it. But if you insist on going away as usual, travel will be very uncomfortable.

Colonel Moore-Brabazon, Minister of Transport, made this clear in the House of Commons yesterday

He was asked whether the public would be warned that there would probably be great congestion on the railways at Christmas

He replied that it was quite understood that there would be no extra trains and there was no encouragement for travelling at that time

Stay Put—but not Stay Glum
There are many ways you can enliven Christmas. Even local authorities are doing it. They are:—

Holding Treats for Evacuees

A CONFERENCE of London evacuation authorities has recommended the pooling of contributions from their own funds to enable reception area authorities to provide Christmas entertainment for children

Mr E C H Salmon, Clerk to the L.C.C. said yesterday that the conference considered that contributions should be on a uniform basis for each child evacuated and merged in a common fund to be administered by a small representative committee.

"The representative committee," he said, "will co-operate with authorities in the reception areas in the best use of the money made available, so as to ensure that Christmas 1940 shall be for the young people away from home as happy an occasion as possible in the circumstances."

While the local bigwigs are giving the evacuees a spot of whoopee, you too, can do your bit by entertaining the lads in uniform. But don't be surprised if you find the—

Troops Are Shy Diners-Out

YOU wouldn't think the average soldier was shy—but he is, according to Welfare Officers in charge of the scheme for getting the men Christmas hospitality near their camps and barracks.

"One of our greatest difficulties is to make the soldiers realise that they will be really welcome in the homes which have been offered in large numbers in the Eastern Command." Lord Nathan, the Command's Chief Welfare Officer, told the *Daily Mirror*. "Many of the men are shy about going to strange homes for their Christmas dinner."

FINANCE ENVOY SENT TO THE U.S.

Sir Frederick Phillips, Under-Secretary of the British Treasury, arrived in New York by Transatlantic plane yesterday to place the latest information on British finances before the U.S. Treasury.

The visit, it was revealed, was one of the chief factors prompting the meeting of Government and defence leaders on Tuesday.

This conference was thought to indicate that the United States was planning to set up a committee to work with the commission which Britain was reported to be sending to America to survey the financing of British war purchases.

Ford Changes Tune

Henry Ford, the American car magnate, said that if Britain needed money, he favoured "giving them all they want."

"It will end the war in a hurry," he said. "We did it before and we might as well do it again."

Some months ago Ford refused to make aeroplane engines for Britain.

U.S. advocates of aid for Britain were strengthened last night by further news of the success of the aid already given.

It was an American plane from which were taken the photographs of the Taranto raid.

The reliability of U.S. engines has long been proved. Lockheed Hudsons have taken part in hundreds of bombing raids from the Bay of Biscay to Norway.

(British United Press and Reuter

HUNGARY RECALLS ENVOY

The Hungarian Government has recalled its Ambassador to Washington, reports the Beromunster, Swiss radio.

Zog's Men Rule in Koritza

A new Albanian Government has been set up in Koritza, the town recently occupied by the Greeks in Albania.

This was reported last night by New York radio.

Friends and followers who have been living in exile with King Zog formed the Government.

Midlands Raid: Fire Quelled

When German planes again raided the Midlands last night the attack was centred on one West Midlands town, but it was of comparatively short duration and not very intense.

High explosive bombs and incendiaries were dropped, and there were some casualties. Among the buildings damaged were a church and a police station, where one policeman was slightly injured.

People were trapped in basement shelters when houses were demolished. Fires started early in the raid, but none was serious and all were quickly put out.

In another Midland town one house was demolished and others damaged. There were six slight casualties.

A bus ran into a bomb crater in a rural district, but no one was hurt.

Wave after wave of enemy bombers passed over an East Midlands town, flying south.

Bombs of various calibres were dropped on a small town.

A stick of bombs was dropped along a road in a London district.

A school for incurable children was

Continued on Back Page

CEMENT WRIT AGAINST BISHOP

MEMBERS of the Cement Federation have issued a writ against the Bishop of Birmingham (Dr Barnes) in respect of a speech he made at Birmingham last Saturday.

During his speech the Bishop referred to production of air-raid shelters, and criticised what he described as "a cement ring"

DUCE'S ARMY QUITS 3 TOWNS

THE Italians are evacuating three towns—Santi Quaranta, Argyrokastro and Premeti—a Greek Government spokesman stated in Athens last night.

On all fronts, he added, the Italians were withdrawing.

Greek forces were pushing forward in the Central and Northern sectors despite bad weather and Italian counter-attacks.

Greek patrols were late last night reported to be already in the outskirts of Santi Quaranta, base port for the Italians in Southern Albania.

A Greek victory after a fierce battle which lasted throughout the darkness of a bitter winter's night enabled them to push on to Argyrokastro.

They captured the Forest of Bouna and cut to pieces the so-called "Death Battalions" of the Italian Ferrara Division.

The Italians offered stubborn resistance, but the Greek victory was decisive.

R.A.F. Bomb Road

R.A.F. planes heavily bombed the road from Lin (on the western shores of Lake Ochrida) to Elbasan for seven hours yesterday.

The Italians have been unable to use the road since Monday, according to frontier reports.

The annihilation of an Italian artillery regiment in the Suhas Ravine is described by a correspondent on the Argyrokastro sector of the Albanian front.

The Greeks, pushing up this mountain valley through deep snow, were met by heavy fire from the Italian gunners. They retreated slowly, leaving many dead.

This gave the Evzones time to reach heights on both sides of the ravine, and from there they attacked the Italians with hand grenades, rocks, machine-gun fire, until they broke and ran.

Silk Stockings

Eleven hundred prisoners were taken, as well as several batteries of mountain guns.

Yesterday's Italian communique claimed that the Greek advance had been halted.

The Greeks, cables David Walker from Athens, expected to find ammunition in a number of cases captured in the northern sector, but when opened these revealed large supplies of women's silk stockings, presumably gifts intended for Greek women.

The R.A.F. communique issued in Athens said that in addition to four Italian aircraft shot down on Monday, our fighters have since destroyed two reconnaissance aircraft.

Reuter, British United Press and Exchange.

WARN HUNS TO IMPROVE CAMPS

A MAJOR GENERAL wants Britain to warn Germany that unless conditions are improved in camps for prisoners of war, German captives in England will be treated in the same way.

He is Sir Alfred Knox, Conservative M.P. for Wycombe.

Sir Alfred will ask Mr. Eden, the War Minister, if he knows that British prisoners in Ofling VII C a notorious internment camp are sleeping twenty-seven in a room 16 to 17ft. square.

Banking in War Time

The Midland Bank stands just as ready in war as in peace time to offer you an extensive range of banking services. You may have moved your home or business premises and require banking facilities in a new locality. Even in the absence of such a change you may still feel the need of a banking account.

This applies to the man who has not hitherto availed himself of the facilities offered by the Midland Bank; who temporarily has joined one of the defence forces or become a civil servant; who, separated from his family, wishes to make regular financial provision for their benefit.

Whatever your station in life, you may rely upon the Midland Bank to conduct with efficiency and tact all business you decide to entrust to its care. Every description of banking service in England and Wales is placed at your disposal at branches so spread that an office is easily accessible to you or within reasonable distance.

You may discuss in strict confidence with a Midland Bank branch manager questions of banking services as they affect you. He will gladly explain the facilities offered by this great bank, established over a century ago but ever modern in its methods and vision.

A 32-page illustrated booklet, "The Service of the Midland Bank," is obtainable at any branch or from the Head Office, Poultry, London, E.C.2.

MIDLAND BANK
LIMITED

NAZI PACT WITH RUMANIA

A ten-year agreement for the "economic reconstruction" of Rumania was signed in Berlin yesterday by Germany and Rumania.

The effect of the pact is to place Rumania's oil, industrial and agricultural resources at the disposal of Germany.

Germany promises to give Rumania the capital and equipment to develop her resources.

In return, the Reich will buy all her products at fixed prices "independent of economic crises."

Rumania promises to develop her railways, roads and oil pipelines.

The Rumanian newspaper "Curentul," often referred to as the Axis mouthpiece in Rumania, said that the Axis plans to use the armies of the small European nations for "the final stage of the war," beginning in April.

The newspaper warned Rumanians to take seriously their promise of military assistance to the Axis.

It did not state against whom the war will be waged in the spring

The Editor, writing from Rome, said: "Axis diplomacy is preparing a huge coalition of all European nations which will involve the participation of their armies and the free use of their territories and transportation facilities."

Germany, he added, was planning a new "league of nations," with headquarters at Vienna.—Reuter and Associated Press.

Rumania Seizes Oil Wells—Page 11.

Daily Mirror

DAILY MIRROR, Friday, Dec. 6, 1940.

No. 11,543 — ONE PENNY
Registered at the G.P.O. as a Newspaper.

Italians' New Worry

As if their worries were not enough, the Italians are now fighting in the northernmost sector in country inhabited by hostile highland clans, who are turning the Italian retreat into a constant hell.

For example, the Clan Clementi, which successfully defied the entire Ottoman Empire, and collected taxes by cutting off the noses and arms of all who did not pay up.

SHIPS SAVE ITALIANS IN RETREAT

14 Day Raiders Down

FOURTEEN day raiders were destroyed yesterday. A.A. guns accounted for one.

Two of our fighters were lost. One pilot is safe.

A Spitfire squadron shot down eight Messerschmitt 109s in the sea off the Kent coast without loss to themselves.

Pilot-Officer H. M. Stephens, D.F.C. with Bar (picture below), shot down one and shared another. Thus he became the first pilot in the squadron to shoot down twenty of the enemy.

A Hurricane pilot, flying in cloud off South-West England, gave a Dornier 17 bomber one three-second burst. It crashed in the sea.

A Hurricane squadron, about to return to refuel after a patrol over South-East England, saw fifteen Messerschmitt 109s at 20,000ft. One was shot down in the sea. The rest made for home.

THE Greeks yesterday fought their way into Santi Quaranta, Italian base port in Southern Albania, as the Italians evacuated remnants of their beaten battalions by troopship.

This latest victory of the Greeks in their drive towards the sea was reported from several sources yesterday.

Athens had not officially confirmed the occupation of Santi Quaranta last night, but earlier reports from the Greek capital indicated that the port was completely cut off from the rest of Albania.

R.A.F. bombers aiding the Greek advance scored a direct hit on an Italian destroyer just off the port and left it listing heavily.

Ten Planes Downed

British fighters fought a fierce battle over the Italian lines on Wednesday, and shot down a large number of the enemy—the Greeks say ten—without loss to themselves.

Argyrokastro was threatened by renewed Greek attacks at dawn yesterday. It was reported in Athens.

One report declared that the radio station at Argyrokastro had been silent since last night, shortly after it was officially stated in Athens that the Italians were withdrawing from the city towards Tepeleni.

Only Italian rearguards are now holding Argyrokastro and the Italians are trying to form a new line some miles farther back it was learned in Athens today.

New Line on Heights

Isolated Italian units are reported to be covering the retreat from the whole coastal sector.

The eleventh Army Corps is taking up the new line, which runs along the heights eighteen miles north of Argyrokastro.

Italian barracks at Tepeleni crowded with reinforcements were hit by Greek dive-bombers, who also bombed the only serviceable bridge across the Blousa River, thus further disrupting Italian communications.

Along the entire front in Albania the Greeks are grimly occupying one snow-covered peak after another.

Continued on Back Page

R.A.F. BLITZ TURIN

R.A.F. bombers, flying from England, have again heavily attacked the Royal Arsenal and Fiat works in Turin, Italy's vital arms centre.

The double trip to make the attack took nine hours.

Our bombers were over the arsenal for nearly two hours, beginning soon after 9 p.m. on Wednesday. Many fires and explosions broke out.

Seven minutes after the last raider had left for home, there was another fierce blast, causing flames seen for fifty miles of the journey.

The official story of the raid across the Alps says that much was done to reduce the arsenal's output of guns, gun carriages, shell cases and tanks.

Large fires were started in the Fiat works. A subsidiary factory, which makes cars and also engines, was also raided.

The Air Ministry says one of our planes was lost over Italy.

The Italians (according to Reuter) state that wool factories and a carpet factory were hit.

Other R.A.F. bombers were making a concentrated attack on Dusseldorf in the Rhineland.

Railway yards, the Mannesmann Rohrenweke arms works (where 6,000 are employed), the quays along the river, and coal gas plants were bombed.

Dozens of "good fires" were started. The damage is described as crippling.

SHE WASTED BREAD—FINED

A housewife was fined five shillings at Ipswich yesterday for wasting bread.

A Food Ministry official said he called at the home of Mrs. E. M. Oxborrow, of Bredfield-street, Woodbridge, and found in the back garden a newly-dug piece of ground. Two feet down he found a bushel of bread.

Mrs. Oxborrow pleaded guilty and gave no explanation.

THEY WON THE KITTY

As the number of enemy aircraft falling to certain fighter aerodrome's credit in the south approached the 600, excitement grew intense.

Shooting 'em down is their business. BUT THERE WAS A KITTY AT STAKE, SUBSCRIBED BY THE AERODROME PERSONNEL.

And above are the two pilots who've raked it in—Flight Lieutenant J. C. Mungo-Park, D.F.C. (in cockpit), and Pilot Officer H. M. Stephens, D.F.C. and Bar.

They shot a Messerschmitt 109 down between them.

BULGARS CLOSE FRONTIER

It was learned in official circles in Bukarest last night that the Bulgarians had closed their frontier.

The explanation given was that Bulgaria had decided that the entire number of emigres allowed to enter Southern Dobrudja under the Craiova agreement had already crossed.

Meanwhile, the official Ankara radio said that it was "indicated" that Germany had promised to return to Rumania some of the territories which Rumania had already lost.

The broadcast was apparently warning Bulgarians about the Dobrudja, says Associated Press.

By 341 to 4

— Mr. J. McGovern's peace aims amendment was rejected by the Commons yesterday. M.P.s of all parties agreed that to sue for peace now would only bring a "Petain Peace." Page 3

SOMEONE SHOULD HANG

"HANG a looter" was the advice given to the authorities by the *Daily Mirror* recently as the best means of stamping out this beastly crime against air raid victims.

One of the worst cases of looting is being investigated by a London council. It occurred in a block of shopping and residential property.

When the evacuated people returned they found that their shops had been cleared out of everything that could be taken away.

A hairdresser lost his entire stock. Houses had even the tea and sugar rations, suits of clothes and other personal belongings stolen.

Live chickens from the back yards were also taken.

HANG A LOOTER!

The perfect emergency ration

Fry's Sandwich Chocolate

2ᴅ AND 4½ᴅ

DAILY MIRROR, Tuesday, Dec. 10, 1940.

Daily Mirror

No. 11,546 — ONE PENNY
Registered at the G.P.O. as a Newspaper.

DEC 10

BRITISH LAUNCH DESERT ATTACK, TAKE 1,000 WOPS, KILL C.-IN-C.

Barked SOS to Police

BY A SPECIAL CORRESPONDENT

A WHITE dog, barking frantically as she swam around her mistress, guided river police to a mobile canteen which had plunged into Bristol Harbour in the black-out yesterday.

The dog was saved, but her owner — Mrs. Dorothy Furneaux Cook, widow, aged fifty, of Rodney Cottages, Clifton, Bristol — was drowned.

Mrs. Cook was driving one of the Y.M.C.A canteens presented to the King by the T.U.C.

Ever since it arrived in Bristol a fortnight ago it had been in twenty-four hour use.

For several nights in succession Mrs. Cook had driven it to A.F.S. workers' first-aid posts and demolition.

Always she had her pet—Vanka, a Russian Samoyed—with her.

Then on Sunday night she set out on her rounds for the last time.

Her Epitaph

With her were two Sea Scout assistants—Alfred Ayles aged eighteen, of Penfield-street and Peter Carter, aged fifteen, of Denbigh-street, both of Bristol.

They were in the back of the canteen when it plunged into the harbour from an unfenced road.

Flung clear through the unlocked back doors they tried to rescue Mrs. Cook, but they could not find her in the darkness and they swam to safety.

Mrs. Cook's daughter, who lived with her at Rodney Cottages, spoke this epitaph:

"THIS IS HOW MOTHER WOULD LIKE TO HAVE DIED-SERVING HER COUNTRY."

The canteen has been raised. Soon it will be repaired and put back into the service for which Mrs Cook W.V.S. gave her life.

Halifax to Go, Says U.S.

Columbia Radio, New York, reported last night that Britain is on the eve of important Cabinet changes.

"Lord Halifax, Foreign Secretary, and Sir Kingsley Wood, Chancellor of the Exchequer, are to resign," stated the announcer.

"Lloyd George will become a member of the War Cabinet."

The changes, he added, would indicate a more vigorous British war policy.

"Gentlemen, We Attacked at Dawn"

GENERAL Sir Archibald Wavell, Commander-in-Chief of the British Forces in the Middle East, himself gave British, American and Turkish war correspondents the first news of the British attack less than four hours after it started.

Leaning cross-legged against his desk with his hands in his pockets, he said at his Cairo H.Q.:

"Gentlemen, I have asked you here to tell you that our Forces began to carry out an engagement against the Italian Armies in the Western Desert at dawn this morning.

"Two hours ago I received word that we had captured an Italian camp."—Reuter.

BRITAIN GETS A DAY-LONG LULL

Early today no part of the British Isles had had an air raid since the Raiders Passed of the early morning of yesterday.

Many people expected that, with the long hours of moonlight, the Nazis would make a further effort to try a Coventry blitz on London or some other city and took the usual precautions.

But the hours passed raid-free.

Except that an enemy bomber was shot down in the North Sea by fighters yesterday, there was no air activity.

PENNY STAMP THIS YEAR

Christmas cards cannot be sent for a halfpenny and the Postmaster-General reminds the public that unsealed envelopes containing a printed Christmas card must bear a penny stamp.

BRITISH forces captured more than 1,000 Italian troops yesterday in a surprise offensive at dawn against the Italian armies in the Western Desert of Egypt, it was officially announced in Cairo last night.

The R.A.F. and the Royal Navy assisted in the attack, which had immediate success. Within an hour the first objective had been captured—an Italian armed camp near a water well south of Sidi Barrani.

The R.A.F. carried out offensive patrols which machine-gunned and bombed the enemy throughout the day.

Enemy aerodromes were raided to prevent Italian planes taking off for attacks.

Fighting was still continuing last night, when the position was described as "satisfactory." The general officer commanding one of the Italian forces attacked was killed. His second in command was captured.

The moment has been well chosen to make Marshal Graziani fight—after the Italian debacle in Albania.

Britain's attack is on a larger scale than any yet started in Africa since the war began.

The effect of an Italian defeat in the Western Desert would be a terrific blow to Italy's war effort.

The operations are directed mainly against the Italians' right flank along the top of the escarpment fifteen or twenty miles south of Sidi Barrani, Graziani's advanced base on the coast forty miles inside the Egyptian border.

Although the actual attack was made at dawn yesterday, it was set in train on Saturday night.

British Forces Waited Unseen

Mechanised units and infantry moved forward into positions which had been prepared with the utmost secrecy in the eight miles wide no-man's-land separating the British and Italian armies.

Opposite the British lines were some half a dozen strongly-defended Italian camps.

All Sunday the British forces waited in the desert—unseen by enemy reconnaissance aircraft.

Then, under cover of darkness, they moved forward within striking distance, and actually within sound of the Italian outposts.

They struck at dawn—and while the sun was still red and low over the desert their first victory was won.

Two Cairo communiques described the British attack.

The first stated that 500 prisoners

Contd. on Back Page, Cols. 1 & 2

WEDDING DAY HITCH

MS Barbara Lucy Thomas, who was to have married Second Lieutenant, the Hon Peter Aitken, second son of Lord Beaverbrook, on Saturday, spent the week-end at an hotel in Woking.

The wedding was arranged for 11 a.m at Chelsea register office. One guest, the superintendent registrar, and the registrar of marriages waited until the afternoon. Neither the bride nor the bridegroom turned up.

The Daily Mirror traced Mrs. Thomas to an hotel in Woking.

She refused to say whether the wedding had been postponed or was definitely broken off. Nor would she tell who was responsible for its not taking place.

On Friday night, the night before the wedding, Mr. Aitken and Mrs Thomas were driving near Bromley, Kent. Their car was involved in a slight accident there.

Mrs. Thomas, who is thirty, was formerly the wife of Mr. Albert Llewellyn Thomas, a dance band musician. She was granted a divorce in January this year after proceedings in which Mr Aitken was cited as co-respondent.

Mr. Aitken, who was described in the licence as a Second Lieutenant, Royal Fusiliers, is twenty-nine. His former wife, the Hon. Mrs. Janet Murrens Aitken, formerly Miss MacNeill, was granted a divorce in June, 1938.

General Sir Archibald Wavell launches desert attack.

TANK MAN'S NEW POST

AN important new Army appointment — Commander of the Royal Armoured Corps — was announced last night.

The man chosen to fill it is fifty-one-year-old Major-General G Le Q. Martel, whose knowledge of mechanised warfare has been continuously developed since he served on the Staff of the Tank Corps in France for eighteen months in 1917-18.

It was General Martel, who in 1925 invented the one-man tank. He has worked with tanks ever since they were brought into being and has written much about them.

"This appointment marks a definite stage in the policy of rapidly increasing the armoured strength of the Army," said the War Office yesterday.

An appointment of equal importance last night was the promotion of Lieutenant-General the Hon. H. R. L. G. Alexander to be General Officer Commanding the Southern Command.

He succeeds General C. J. E. Auchinleck, now Commander-in-Chief in India.

General Alexander, aged forty-nine, commanded the B.E.F. during the last days of the Dunkirk evacuation and has since been serving as a corps commander.

He went "over the top" thirty times in the last war.

DAILY MIRROR, Friday, Dec. 13, 1940.

Daily Mirror

No. 11,549 — ONE PENNY
Registered at the G.P.O. as a Newspaper.

20,000 More Prisoners Captured in Sidi Barrani

VICTORY

Fighters Meet Night Raiders

R.A.F. fighters met successive waves of raiders which crossed the East Coast for two hours last night.

Activity in this area was greater than for some nights past. Heavy A.A. gunfire inland and many bomb explosions were heard in the distance.

Enemy planes were reported over London, Liverpool and towns in the Midlands, East Anglia, South-West and North-West England and Wales.

Raiders visited an East Midlands town soon after dusk for the second time yesterday.

Bombs were dropped before the planes made off towards other Midlands areas.

A church and a furniture store were destroyed in one town.

When incendiary bombs fell on a North-East Coast town, an A.F.S. messenger boy — Robert Cooper, aged seventeen — put out four of them with his steel helmet.

His Blind Gun

One bomb set fire to a small chapel and others fell on private property. All the fires were soon put out.

Four enemy planes were destroyed during the day.

One was bagged by a Hurricane squadron leader.

Although his gunsight was damaged he closed to within fifty yards of a Messerschmitt 109 fighter, aimed as best he could, and fired a three-second burst.

The Me crashed in the sea.

A town on the South-East Coast was machine-gunned by two Me's, which skimmed the rooftops as they aimed at shopping centres.

Each raider fired six bursts but no one was injured.

Flying at a tremendous height, raiders dropped bombs in two London districts.

EARTH TREMOR TAKEN FOR RAID

Towns and villages in North Wales were violently shaken last night by an earth tremor which lasted for forty-three seconds.

At Pwllheli, where the shock was felt about 10.29, the whole town rocked and windows rattled violently. People ran into the streets in alarm, fearing that a heavy bombing attack was being made.

About ten years ago a similar tremor was felt in the same area.

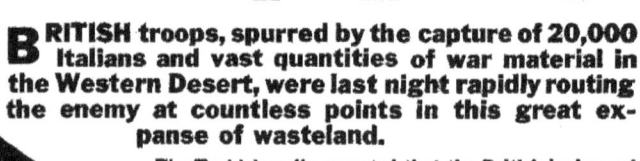

The Three Trumps

GENERAL SIR ARCHIBALD WAVELL (left), fifty-seven, with only one eye, is "the intellectual general." He's a master of desert warfare. One of his greatest friends was Lawrence of Arabia. Wavell is a thinker, a quick one. Became General two months ago, three months after becoming first Commander-in-Chief of Middle East land forces.

♦ ♦ ♦

ADMIRAL SIR ANDREW BROWNE CUNNINGHAM (centre), Commander-in-Chief, Mediterranean. Wiry and alert at fifty-seven. His dash and vision gained him command of destroyer Scorpion in last war. Brought to Whitehall as Deputy Chief of Naval Staff after being in charge of destroyer-flotillas and battle-cruisers in the Mediterranean.

AIR CHIEF MARSHAL SIR ARTHUR LONGMORE, fifty-five-year-old Australian, has been Air Officer Commanding-in-Chief, R.A.F., Middle East, since May. His pilot's licence is the oldest in the Service, dated April 25, 1911. In last war served as naval officer, then with R.N.A.S. Before his present appointment was head of Training Command. Two sons and son-in-law in the R.A.F.

U.S. CALL FOR GRANT TO BRITAIN

"IT would appear that there is nothing in the law to prevent the U.S. Government from giving credit to Britain or making an outright grant-in-aid."

Mr. Winthrop W. Aldrich, chairman of the Chase National Bank, made this statement in a speech at Boston yesterday.

"Neither the Johnson Act nor the Neutrality Act, I am reliably informed, prohibits our Government from giving direct financial aid to Great Britain, though both interpose barriers against private citizens or corporations giving credit," he added.

"Both political parties have declared it to be the American national purpose to give every aid to Great Britain short of war. If that pledge means anything it means that our full industrial and financial strength shall be thrown into the scales on the side of England."

Mr. Morgenthau, Secretary to the U.S. Treasury, declared yesterday that the Treasury would consider lending money to Britain only if Congress consent had been obtained.

"Irrespective of any interpretations lawyers might give of the Treasury's powers to lend money without specific Congress consent, I certainly would not be a party to any loan to Britain or any other country coming under the Johnson Act without the direction of Congress." — Exchange and Associated Press.

SLAVS SIGN PACT

The signing of a Hungarian-Yugoslav pact of friendship yesterday between Count Csaky, the Hungarian Foreign Minister, and the Yugoslav Foreign Minister, M. Cincar Markovitch, was announced by Belgrade Radio last night. — Associated Press.

BRITISH troops, spurred by the capture of 20,000 Italians and vast quantities of war material in the Western Desert, were last night rapidly routing the enemy at countless points in this great expanse of wasteland.

The Turkish radio reported that the British had swept on to Sollum, on the border of Egypt and Libya, and captured it.

Sollum is fifty miles west of Sidi Barrani, the capture of which Mr. Churchill described in Parliament yesterday as "a victory of the first order." (His speech is on back page.)

Blackshirt troops, fighting fiercely on the retreat, were thrown into utter confusion when the R.A.F. heavily machine-gunned the road to Sollum.

Marshal Graziani has thrown into the battle 1,000 motorised units with hundreds of anti-tank guns, according to dispatches from Benghazi reaching Rome last night, in an attempt to stop the British advance.

AN ITALIAN REPORT STATED THAT BRITISH AND ITALIAN MECHANISED UNITS OVERLAPPED EACH OTHER, AND THAT THE CREWS JUMPED OUT AND FOUGHT HAND TO HAND WITH GRENADES.

Outstanding feature of the British drive on Sidi Barrani — bitter, ruthless and swift — was the clocklike co-ordination of moves by the Army, Navy and R.A.F.

The attack began with a rapier-like thrust through the desert to Alam Bibeiwa, an Italian encampment inland on the escarpment.

The enemy were taken completely by surprise, and the encampment fell within a couple of hours of the beginning of the fight. It was here that General Maletti, commander of a flying armoured column, was killed.

During the morning a whole series of small Italian forts fell to the British.

In German Style

Then the British mobile forces made a rush towards the coast west of Sidi Barrani as swiftly as the Germans rushed Boulogne.

The British advance may be likened generally, in fact, to the German advance into France.

The British forces carried out a swift and extensive flanking movement, encircling one enemy position after another, while the Air Force concentrated on keeping the Italian bombers on the air by incessant bombing and machine-gunning of their aerodromes.

The Royal Navy contributed a twelve hours' bombardment of Sidi Barrani and the Air Force bombed it almost continuously for sixteen hours on Monday, inflicting heavy casualties.

And the British troops, after four days of gruelling fighting — sometimes in thick sandstorms — are overjoyed at the successes achieved after months of waiting.

The number of Italian prisoners taken was estimated at 20,000 in yes-

Contd. on Back Page, Col. 3

Evan Williams Shampoo...contains

elements upon which hair thrives. Its regular use will retain all those qualities which make your hair so delightfully charming & attractive

'ORDINARY' for Dark Hair
'CAMOMILE' for Fair Hair

EVAN WILLIAMS Shampoo

Keeps the hair young

Daily Mirror

DAILY MIRROR, Saturday, Dec. 14, 1940.

No. 11,550 — ONE PENNY
Registered at the G.P.O. as a Newspaper.

BRITAIN PILES IT ON

All Mussolini's vital supplies of food and oil for the invasion of Egypt have been captured. They will be of great value to the rapidly advancing British Army.

Several thousand more Italian troops, including two more generals commanding divisions are now British prisoners, it was officially stated yesterday.

Windsor, President Confer on Defence

FROM JOHN WALTERS
NEW YORK, Friday.

THE Duke of Windsor returned to Miami in a naval seaplane tonight after a ninety-minute talk with President Roosevelt about the proposed U.S. defence bases in the West Indies.

"We discussed the naval bases for the whole of the West Indies islands," the Duke said in a statement to the Press.

"We also talked about the economic future of the islands and how America might co-operate with Britain in their development."

The Duke said he could not comment on the rumour that he might become British Ambassador to the United States in succession to the late Lord Lothian.

It was the first time in twenty-one years that the President and the Duke had met. The last occasion was at the Annapolis (Maryland) Naval Academy when the President was Assistant Secretary of War.

Talk on Deck

The Duke boarded the U.S. cruiser Tuscaloosa, in which the President is touring the Caribbean, off Eleuthera Island, fifty-two miles from the Bahamas.

The two sat alone on the deck in deep conversation and had lunch there.

The Duke's departure from Miami followed a night of feverish activity in his suite.

All night, operators on his private switchboard were busy passing calls, one of which is understood to have come from London, and several times during the night messenger boys went to the hospital with cables for him.

The Duke looked worried and excited as he boarded the seaplane.

GOOD-BYE Mr. PICK

MR Frank Pick, Director-General (until yesterday) of the Ministry of Information, has given up the job.

But to the end he maintained the traditions of the Ministry of Information.

For when he was asked to explain what had happened, this message came—through his secretary:

"Mr. Pick is saying nothing.
He is making no statement.
He is not giving any interview."

So in a deep hush goes the sixth Director-General since the war began. The seventh is Mr. Pick's deputy, Sir Walter Monckton.

DUCE RUNS TO HITLER

Hitler and Ribbentrop left Berlin yesterday for an undisclosed destination, but it was believed they were on their way to meet a discomfited Mussolini at a rendezvous in Germany.

In Berlin rumours persisted that Mussolini would go to the German capital soon, but authorised sources declared "emphatically" that nothing was known of any such visit.

"Informed circles" in Rome said a Hitler-Mussolini conference was possible soon, but doubted whether it would occur within the next few days.

The Berlin representative of the New York Columbia radio, broadcasting to America from the German capital, said:—

"There are rumours that Ribbentrop has gone to Athens. But it would be too early to speculate whether he intends to mediate in the Italo-Greek conflict."

Some of the Italian commanders in Albania are in favour of asking the Greeks for an armistice, according to a captured Italian officer in Athens.

Other Italian officers taken to Argyrokastro expressed doubt about Italy's ability to continue the struggle should Klysoura fall. Here they hoped to check the Greek advance.

Rome discredits reports that an armistice is possible.—Associated Press and British United Press.

LESS MEAT— HOMES FIRST

THERE will be less meat in some parts of the country in the next few days, and the Ministry of Food yesterday advised butchers to cut down supplies to restaurants and other caterers rather than see the housewife go short.

Shorter supplies are due to transport difficulties following unexpectedly low marketings of livestock.

"A butcher should not hesitate to reduce his sales to catering establishments, especially those of the non-residential type, if only by these means can he supply the ration to householders, institutions and residential establishments," said the Ministry.

FRANCO SACKS BRITISH OFFICIALS IN TANGIER

At a moment's notice the Spanish authorities dissolved the International administration at Tangier yesterday.

All British, French and Italian employees have been dismissed with immediate effect.

The international police have also been dissolved and replaced by a Spanish security guard.—Reuter.

R.A.F. BLITZES FRONTIER

ONE of the heaviest blitzes, lasting all day and throughout the night, was made on Libya by the R.A.F. Aerodromes, troop and motor transports were bombed and machine-gunned.

Petrol dumps were fired and arms dumps blown up. Meanwhile the British Fleet heavily shelled the Italians.

SWIFT SUDDEN SWOOPS BY OUR BOMBERS DEMORALISED ITALY'S TROOPS. ENEMY AIRCRAFT ON THE GROUND WERE DESTROYED.

"A particularly heavy raid was carried out on Tobruk during the night," the R.A.F.'s Cairo communique stated last night. "Many tons of bombs were dropped on the town and harbour.

"Fires were observed burning fiercely in many places and violent explosions and fires near petrol dumps were seen from Sollum Bay by our aircraft on the return journey. There were also heavy explosions in the vicinity of ammunition stores.

"At El Adem aerodrome, near Tobruk, hangars were seen to be completely gutted by previous raids

Flames 1,000 Feet

"Aircraft on the ground were heavily machine-gunned by our reconnaissance machines.

"Heavy raids were also made on Bardia.

"Bombs caused a violent explosion in a stores dump park which resulted in flames rising to a thousand feet.

"Enemy aircraft on the ground were machine-gunned and three C.R. 42s destroyed.

"At El Tmimi one S 79 was shot up and other aircraft badly damaged.

"In all, over a dozen enemy aerodromes or landing grounds were raided and considerable damage done.

"Fighter aircraft patrolled throughout the day, covering our
Continued on Back Page

NAVY ATTACK IN ADRIATIC?

Reports that the British Navy was attacking Italian transports circulated in Dubrovnik, the Yugoslav port on the Adriatic, yesterday.

Heavy firing was heard off the port all the morning. Later a Yugoslav plane reported that it had sighted a patch of oil on the open sea, but had not seen any ships.—British United Press.

HOW NAVY LET FLY

First story of how the British Fleet scattered the Italian Army is told below by a correspondent who was aboard a British warship off Egypt.

BRITISH warships swinging into action to help the Army's big push against the Italians in the Western Desert, hurled tons of high explosives into Graziani's bases and forced thousands of Fascist troops to flee towards Libya.

Scores of shells pouring into the enemy ranks destroyed the Italian Army's attempts to reinforce the advanced troops.

This warship and other units of the British Navy, sweeping through minefields to within half a mile of the shore batteries, threw everything but their gun turrets at the Italians.

The warships turned their big guns first on Makilla, fifteen miles east of Sidi Barrani, shattering that big armed camp and making the initial British land attack easier

Shelled Sollum

For an hour after dawn the warships pumped shells into the enemy position wrecking motor transports, blasting troop columns out of existence and tearing big gaps in the macadamised coastal road.

This ship flung high-explosive projectiles into the enemy advanced columns and started huge fires at many Italian bases.

Then it swept westwards along the coast to Sollum, seven miles from the Egypto-Libyan frontier to deliver a fresh assault.

Italian batteries at Sidi Barrani and Sollum heavily answered the fire of the British warships.

But the nearest shell dropped some yards away and caused no damage.

Shells from the British warships, landing among the enemy columns and mechanised units started panic among Mussolini's tired soldiers.

They threw down their rifles and packs and turned and ran in the direction of Libya.—Associated Press.

General O'Connor, our Western Desert Commander, holds Italian Silver Medal for Valour.

THE 5-STAR FOOD DRINK
is down in price!

WHAT a comfort to know that this comforting food is actually down in price—down to 5d a quarter-pound! Cadbury's Bournville Cocoa is a balanced food in itself. And made with milk, a cup of Bournville Cocoa gives you the food value of two fresh eggs and costs you less than a quarter as much.

WHY FIVE-STARS?

★ **EXTRA FOOD VALUE.** Bournville Cocoa is rich in body-building proteins, and natural cocoa butter and carbohydrates to give you energy. So remember, a cup of Bournville—the 5-Star Cocoa — is a cup of food.

★ **IRON—THE BLOOD ENRICHER.** The rich iron content of Bournville Cocoa tones up the corpuscles in your bloodstream, makes you feel stronger.

★ **PHOSPHATES—FOR HEALTHY GROWTH.** Bournville Cocoa is rich in the various phosphates and calcium. These build up bone and muscle, strengthen teeth.

★ **AID TO DIGESTION.** Bournville Cocoa is particularly digestible, helps digestion of other foods and so makes every meal go further.

★ **VITAMINS—VITAL TO HEALTH.** Remember that every tin of Bournville Cocoa retains the natural sunshine Vitamin D, specially necessary for kiddies' healthy teeth and straight, strong bones.

BOURNVILLE THE 5-STAR COCOA
QUALITY UNALTERED
DOWN TO 5D PER QTR. LB.

DAILY MIRROR, Monday, Dec. 16, 1940.

Daily Mirror

No. 11,551   ONE PENNY
Registered at the G.P.O. as a Newspaper.

Pilot Who Has Been 'in Thick of Every Stage of Air War'—Wins D.S.O.

Dapper, smiling Pilot-Officer H. M. Stephen is finding life good.

He was awarded the D.S.O. during the week-end, first D.S.O. on the Home Front.

He had already won the D.F.C. and Bar.

Also he won (with his C.O.) the "kitty" subscribed for the man or men who should shoot down the fighter station's 600th raider.

He has fought enemy planes at Dunkirk, over the sea, and over Britain. In fact, as the Air Ministry says, "he has fought with skill and success in every stage of the air war."

VICHY MEN SACK ALL THEIR M.P.s

PETAIN'S Cabinet at Vichy yesterday took another step toward Fascism. It decided to set up a "consultative assembly" to replace the old Senate and the Chamber of Deputies (the French Commons).

The sacking and arrest — confirmed yesterday— of pro-German Foreign Minister Laval at such a time is explained by the fact that his successor, Flandin, is equally pro-German but a more ardent advocate of Nazism.

Yesterday's Vichy Cabinet meeting was the first since the Cabinet's reorganisation. After the meeting a communique announced that the text will soon be published of a measure to create the new consultative assembly.

The communique clearly stated that the Assembly "will replace the old Senate and Chamber of Deputies, which transferred full legislative powers to Marshal Petain on July 10." This is exactly on Fascist and Nazi lines.

Detention of Laval was confirmed yesterday by a telephone message to a neutral correspondent from Vichy.

As soon as the correspondent started to amplify that message the censor in Vichy cut off the conversation, says British United Press from Zurich.

Strong pressure from the United States was partly responsible for Laval's dismissal, according to diplomatic officials in Washington, cables John Walters.

Refused to Go, Unless—

They say Admiral Leahy, the new U.S. Ambassador to Vichy, refused to go unless he was guaranteed a conference with Petain without the presence of Laval.

One suggestion has been that Laval was plotting to lead France into war against Britain, but authentic information is scarce.

A more probable theory, according to London political circles, is that Petain discovered that Laval, by plot and intrigue, was trying to doublecross him, threw him out, and obtain full power in France for himself.

Laval had been gradually working himself into the position of potential "Gauleiter" of France.

BRITISH CADET OF 15 PRISONER

A cadet aged fifteen was named among British prisoners of war in Germany in a list received "from enemy sources" and issued last night. He was described as Leslie Brown, born April 1, 1925, in Glasgow.

SAYS U.S. WILL SEND SHIPS

When he returns to Washington, President Roosevelt will announce that American merchant ships will carry goods to Britain and will be escorted by American warships, says Moscow radio.

Duchess's Xmas Gift

The Duchess of Windsor's Christmas gift to the Duke will be an old-fashioned barber's pole. The Duke recently had his own personal barber's chair installed in their Bermuda home, and expressed the wish to have a barber's pole to go with it.

The Duchess has returned to bed at Miami for twenty-four hours, but her condition is not serious.

BURIED ALIVE FOR THREE DAYS

People are still being dug out alive after being buried in Anderson shelters and strengthened cellars during last Thursday's raid on Sheffield.

WAVES of enemy bombers made a concentrated raid on a north-east area last night. The bombardment began early and was continuous for some hours.

It is estimated that the raiding force totalled several hundred machines and that at least two were brought down.

There was no interval between the downpours of bombs by each successive squadron flying over this area.

Thousands of people had a terrifying experience while the bombardment lasted.

The raiders used thousands of incendiary bombs.

Air activity over Britain was widespread, but ended early, London and the north-east town both being clear of raiders before midnight.

Relatively few bombs fell in London.

In one Midlands district a school was hit. Another school was hit in the Home Counties.

After some days' respite a south-west town was visited by enemy planes three times yesterday.

Enemy aircraft were also reported over Liverpool, another north-west town, a west town, and East Anglia.

WE INVADE LIBYA—BY BAYONET

ITALIAN troops, falling back in the bloodiest hand-to-hand fighting since the last great war, yesterday were bringing up all their North African reserves in an effort to stem a British advance into Libya, Mussolini's colony that lies to the west of Egypt.

Rome reports last night said that thousands of Australian and New Zealand reinforcements had been thrown into a battle for the Italian strongholds of Capuzzo and Bardia.

In a blinding dust storm, tanks led the invasion, but, according to last night's despatches, the British used the bayonet, too. British casualties are known to be slight.

It was stated in London yesterday and admitted in Rome that British forces have penetrated into Italian territory over the Egyptian-Libyan border.

The Navy and the R.A.F. cooperated perfectly. More aerodromes were bombed and more Italian planes brought down; while the Navy accounted for one more of Mussolini's submarines.

An official communique issued from Cairo last night added that "a heavy dust storm is raging and visibility is bad."

The communique said that "operations are proceeding on the Libyan frontier, where our troops continue to press the enemy."

But the Rome admission said more. Yesterday's Italian communique, after recording that Sidi Barrani had been evacuated, spoke of—

"Bloody encounters from dawn to nightfall in the Fort Capuzzo, Sollum and Bardia zones."

Sollum lies just within Egyptian territory. The Italian port of Bardia and the heavily-shelled ruins of Capuzzo lie across the border in the Italian colony of Libya.

A communique from R.A.F. headquarters, Middle East, yesterday revealed that twenty-six more Italian aircraft were destroyed or damaged.

"Bombing aircraft," said the communique, "heavily raided all Italian landing grounds and aerodromes in the advanced area. In addition, Bardia was selected for a particularly heavy attack.

"Throughout these operations only three of our aircraft failed to return safely. It is probable that at least one is safe."

An Admiralty communique last night gave a report from the Commander-in-Chief, Mediterranean. He said:

"A night bombardment of Bardia was carried out with successful results.

"The Italian submarine Naiade which attempted to interfere with these operations was immediately sunk by our destroyers.

"Fleet Air Arm aircraft successfully attacked Tripoli [Mussolini's Libyan naval base] on the night of 13-14."

Earlier there had been reports that Capuzzo had been captured with 50,000 more Italian prisoners. The reports were not confirmed.

Daily Mirror, Reuter, British United Press, Associated Press.

Musso Asks to See Boss

General von Keitel, Chief of Staff of the German Army, has advised Hitler to break off relations with Italy, according to reports reaching Ankara, Turkish capital.

Ankara radio added that Mussolini has asked for an interview with Hitler.

HOW WE DID IT

A smashing British barrage of 60lb. shells, followed by a sudden rush of tanks, field artillery and lorry loads of infantry. . . .

The tanks crashing onward, the infantry, now on foot coming on behind, ready for a charge with bayonets, rifles and machine-guns. . . .

And in front of all this, crack soldiers of the Italian Army, panic-stricken, jumping into holes which speedily became their graves. . . .

THIS was the story, revealed last night, of the opening of the British offensive in the Western Desert.

It began with a surprise attack on Nibeiwa, the strong desert fortress from which the Italians intended to unloose their first thunderbolt against the British lines in Egypt.

Big Surprise

The "battle" for Nibeiwa, which raged for one hour, was described by a captured Italian officer as "the nearest thing to hell ever seen on this earth."

Nibeiwa was selected by the Italians as the base for the "Raggruppamento Maletti," the crack unit especially formed last July to be the vanguard of the Italian push towards the Nile and the Suez Canal.

So great was the surprise element when the British struck at dawn on Monday that the tanks which formed the important part of the Maletti group never went into action.

When the British barrage opened from the east, tanks, field artillery and lorry loads of infantry were then moved in swiftly from the west.

The Italians turned their guns in

Continued on Back Page

DAILY MIRROR, Saturday, Dec. 21, 1940.

Daily Mirror

No. 11,556 — ONE PENNY
Registered at the G.P.O. as a Newspaper.

BARDIA RINGED—
British Are Ready for Last Push
TOLD YIELD
Navy Sweeps Duce's Lake— Blasts Ports

BARDIA was completely cut off last night by British land, sea and air forces. Leaflets dropped by the R.A.F. urged the Italians to yield.

★

FOR five days the Fleet bombarded this key Libyan port, starting fires which are still burning.

THE Navy have forced the gates to the Adriatic—"the Duce's lake"—without opposition from the Italian Fleet.

★

ITALY lost six supply ships—three sunk in Bardia and three by the submarine Truant.

LEAFLETS dropped by the R.A.F. on besieged Bardia gave the numbers of Italian prisoners taken, and mentioned all the captured generals individually.

"Do not provoke further loss of life by continuing to resist," the leaflets stated.

Cairo reports stated last night that a British patrol probed Bardia's defences on Wednesday night, but found some resistance and did not press its attack, leaving Bardia open to the subsequent terrific "pasting" by the R.A.F.

While more British troops were moving up to support the advanced troops, the latter already had engaged the Italians at some points, thrusting them back.

Heavy fighting was said to be going on yesterday.

While the British continue to press on into Libya, and have entirely mopped up Italian resistance in the coastal belt almost to Bardia, one Italian garrison still stands near the border.

It is holding the oasis of Gerabub, 120 miles due south from the coast and about twenty miles west of the Egyptian frontier.

Only a small Italian force is believed to hold the place.

Their line of retreat will eventually be cut off if the British continue to press along the coast.

Enemy Harassed By Shelling

SO heavy was the rain of shells on Bardia—where the Army is closing in—that big fires swept the port on December 15 and are still burning.

"These bombardments played an important part in harassing the enemy and containing the defeated troops in the Bardia area," the Admiralty communique stated yesterday.

"During the whole period our units were repeatedly engaged by the enemy
Continued on Back Page, Col. 1

BIGGEST MERSEY ATTACK

MORE than 100 planes took part last night in the severest air attack Merseyside has experienced.

In Liverpool two big fires were started, but they were mastered within an hour.

The firemen worked at great risk. Incendiaries were showered among them, and one fire engine crashed in a bomb crater.

In Liverpool rescue workers were busy this morning extricating people from bombed working-class houses in the suburbs, but only about six deaths had been reported.

The raiders faced the most intense barrage ever put up on Merseyside. No planes were seen to fall, but it is believed that a number were damaged and were unlikely to reach their bases.

Raiders were also reported over three towns in the North, two towns in the West Midlands, an East Midlands town, a western town, a south-west town, an East Anglian town, a town in Wales, and another in West Scotland.

People in an East Midlands town heard planes pass over in waves—at intervals of less than a minute—in a northerly direction.

Bombs on London

An H.E. bomb fell on a roadway outside a hospital near a north-west town, causing slight damage to property, but no casualties.

Bombs fell in the grounds of a hospital in an East Midlands rural area. Windows were shattered, but no serious structural damage was caused.

One patient and two nurses were scratched by flying glass.

For the first time in three weeks heavy gunfire was heard in an inland town in the north-west.

Guns were frequently in action in several districts in the London area, which had one of its earliest "Alerts." Bombs were reported to have been dropped in one part.

During the day, single raiders were active. A few bombs were dropped in the London area.

They caused a small number of casualties, and damaged buildings, according to the Air Ministry.

ARMOUR FOR R.A.F. PILOTS

FROM JOHN WALTERS
New York, Friday.

Bullet proof armour resembling medieval coats of mail will be worn soon by R.A.F. pilots according to officials at the Breeze armament factories, Elizabeth, New Jersey.

The armour is included in a £250,000 order to be divided equally between the British and American Governments.

Shaped to the human body, it protects bomber pilots from the head to below the knees from machine-gun bullets from pursuit planes, flares out at the side to give elbow-room and fits over the head like a monk's cowl.

Vice-Admiral H. D. Pridham-Wippell, who led the Navy's sweep of the Adriatic, is fifty-five.

His name was included in the list of Flag appointments issued just over a week ago, when it was stated that he had been appointed second in command of the Mediterranean Fleet.

At the start of the last war Admiral Pridham-Wippell was a lieutenant in H.M.S. Audacious. In 1925 he was in command of H.M.S. Enterprise when King George V's illness necessitated the Duke of Windsor's return from Africa.

He was ordered to Dar-es-Salaam and took the Duke, then the Prince of Wales, on board, and made a record trip to Brindisi.

LORD HALIFAX FOR U.S.

THE United States heard over its radio last night that the new British Ambassador to Washington will be Lord Halifax.

New York Columbia Radio reported that the appointment was definite.

A reshuffle in the Cabinet, it stated, would take place.

No indication of Lord Halifax's successor as Foreign Minister was mentioned.

THREE SOLDIERS IN CELL DIE

Three of four soldiers taken ill while under detention in a cell at the Shepton Mallet district of Somerset have died, and the fourth is seriously ill.

The inquest on one of them, Harold Smith, aged nineteen, of Manchester,

FOUR MEN SPEED-UP U.S. ARMS

PRESIDENT ROOSEVELT announced last night the formation of a new office of production management for defence to head the enormous programme for rearming the nation while producing arms for Britain.

The office will be directed by Mr. William Knudsen, Chief of Defence Production.

The associate director will be Sidney Hillman, Defence Commissioner.

The President said that the Defence Commission would remain exactly as it is, but implied that it would be superseded in many of its functions by the new office.

No Voting

The long-awaited adjustment of the defence set-up will not become effective until executive orders can be drafted—a task which may require ten days.

The President said that the new office would have full power to make its own decisions, which would be reached unanimously without resorting to votes.

The President said that should any clash arise over the order in which various items are to be delivered the Priorities Board would settle the matter and advise the administration of the production management office.
—Reuter and Associated Press.

"ITALY'S SEA"

The Otranto Straits and the Adriatic Sea (Musso called it "Italy's Lake"), which the Navy swept, without seeing a glimpse of Italy's Navy.

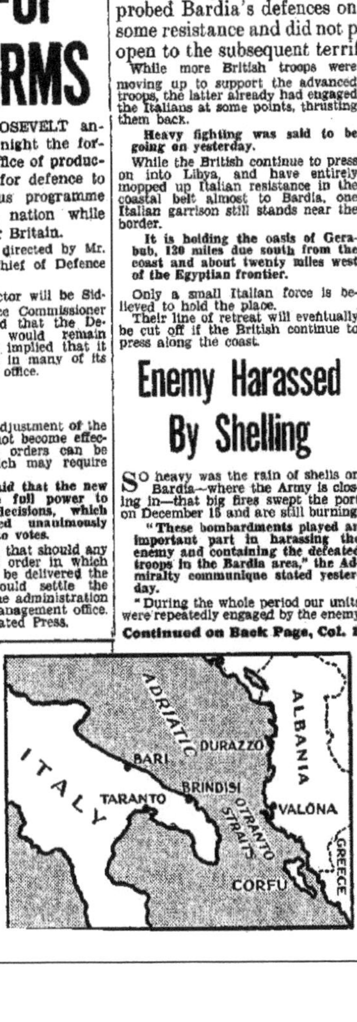

NEW LIVES—NEW NEEDS
ARTIST—toiling night and day in RESCUE SQUAD

This rescue worker, who was an artist, exchanged leisurely hours at his canvas for fearsome change — yet thousands like him have also got to stay the course—sometimes night after night.

IN your strange new Home Front life, remember this, a warming cup of Bourn-vita, still at the old peace-time price, will help you to get the essential body-and-mind-restoring qualities from your SLEEP (even though it is interrupted). Bourn-vita gives scientifically sound sleep, and that's the best thing ever for life to-day.

Bourn-vita is a night food-drink of first-class nourishment value, with special nerve-soothing properties that bring sleep very quickly.

NO SUGAR NEEDED

Get the best out of your sleep with—

CADBURY'S BOURN-VITA

Still at pre-war price — **1/5** PER ½ LB

Daily Mirror

DR, Monday, Dec. 23, 1940.

No. 11,557 — ONE PENNY
Registered at the G.P.O. as a Newspaper.

DEC 23

HALIFAX TO GO TO U.S.

Eden as Foreign Secty.

Surprise for War Office

VISCOUNT HALIFAX has been appointed as British Ambassador in the U.S.A. in place of the late Lord Lothian, it was announced last night. Mr. Anthony Eden is to succeed him as Foreign Minister.

A surprise in the changes was the appointment of Captain the Right Hon. David Margesson, the much-criticised Conservative Party boss, to be War Minister in place of Mr. Eden.

It was also announced that Viscount Cranborne, a firm supporter of Mr. Eden's policy, is to be a baron.

In addition to carrying on his duties as Dominions Secretary, he will act as spokesman for the Foreign Office in the House of Lords.

Appointment of Lord Halifax as British Ambassador to Washington gets him out of the Cabinet with the least political embarrassment to the Prime Minister (writes our Political Correspondent).

Dull and Dated

Halifax is dull and dated. He has been a failure as Foreign Minister.

It will need all his piety and official badges of wealth, breeding and Cabinet rank to reconcile American opinion to this appointment.

On this side of the Atlantic it has at least the advantage of enabling Mr. Anthony Eden to become once more Secretary of State for Foreign Affairs.

Mr. Eden resigned this office under the late Mr. Neville Chamberlain because Mr. Chamberlain thought Mussolini was a great man and ought to be wooed. Mr. Eden said that Mussolini was a weak man and ought to be opposed.

Now Mr. Eden has been proved right and as Mussolini's star is setting, Mr. Eden's is again rising.

Mr. Eden's appointment will

Continued on Back Page, Col. 3

GRAZIANI ADMITS —BRITISH BROKE US

An amazingly frank admission of the "crushing superiority" of the British armoured units which caused Italian positions "to go down one after another in a few hours," is made by Marshal Graziani, the Italian Commander-in-Chief in Libya, in a report to Mussolini, published in Rome late last night.

GRAZIANI claims that his troops fought bravely, and he attempts to put down his defeats in the Western Desert and Libya largely to the failure of tanks to arrive from Italy. But the report makes it clear that the Italians were beaten by the invincible attack of the British units, which included, says Graziani, "the best troops of four continents."

"Against the positions occupied by our troops in the flat desert territory," frankly admits Graziani, "the enemy poured masses of armoured cars, tanks, light and heavy arms supported by mobile batteries and assisted by effective aerial forces.

"As soon as the terrific aerial bombardment ceased, armoured units advanced from all directions against our troops so that in spite of the fiercest resistance, the various positions went down one after another in a few hours."

'Crushing Superiority'

Graziani adds:
"The first point to be attacked was that under General Maletti, who began to withdraw until he was overcome together with the Second Libyan Division.

"Against the armoured mass operating concentrically over a wide front, the opposition of our anti-tank guns and the artillery of our divisions, forced to disperse their fire on a number of very mobile objectives, was ineffectual.

"It is in the crushing superiority of the armoured units employed en masse that the reason for the enemy's initial success is to be found.

"Commanders and troops wrote pages of glory and episodes of epic grandeur were played out during this unequal struggle between the soldiers

Continued on Back Page, Col. 4

BARDIA REINFORCEMENTS

Italian forces in Bardia have been reinforced with heavier tanks and are holding the line at all points, claimed Rome last night.

Wherever the British attacked, this report declares, they used the heaviest type of Morris tanks.

Reinforcements are reaching our troops in the Bardia area, said yesterday's British communique from Cairo G.H.Q.

"COMPLIMENT TO THE U.S."

From JOHN WALTERS
NEW YORK, Sunday.

The report that Britain's new Ambassador to the United States will be Lord Halifax is causing considerable apprehension in Washington.

While the President and State Department have no objection, there is anxiety regarding the effect it would have on the masses who have long linked Halifax with "appeasement."

The New York Times, in a Washington report, says: "Some regret has been expressed that Britain should send such a typical representative of the old English regime....

"On the other side... the Halifax appointment should be construed as a compliment, because he is in a position to acquaint the Administration with the innermost secrets of British war policy.

"It appeared this would be the immediate reaction in high official quarters, but that it might not have the same effect on the public at large."

AIRMEN DOWN IN EIRE

British reconnaissance plane patrolling Northern Ireland border on Saturday night crashed in a field at Dungooley, 500 yards inside the Eire border.

Farmers rescued the two officers in the plane. One was slightly injured and was taken to Dundalk Hospital.

"Just in time for Christmas," was this man's cheerful remark after being rescued from seventeen hours in a vault shelter under a collapsed house in London.

U.S. WAR POSSIBILITY

WAR for the United States is considered to be a "reasonable possibility" by Mr. Jesse Jones, a U.S. Cabinet Minister.

Mr. Jones, who is U.S. Secretary for Commerce, declared at Houston, Texas, yesterday, according to the Associated Press:

"None of us likes the idea of war, but whether we like to contemplate it or not, it would be foolhardy not to realise that war is a reasonable possibility."

A gigantic speed-up in preparedness and arms production will be the reply of the U.S. to Germany's "stop aiding Britain" threats, cables John Walters from New York.

It is understood that President Roosevelt will make a strong reply to the German threats in a broadcast to the American nation.

Gayda, Mussolini's "yes-man," also threatened the U.S yesterday.

He said that continued American intervention would bring about combined action by the parties to the Three-Power Pact between Germany, Japan and Italy.

The proposal to acquire for Britain two German, twenty-seven Italian, thirty-seven Danish and perhaps twenty-eight French ships at present immobilised in U.S. harbours is being studied in Washington.

Woman, resting on a stretcher, after being got out uninjured from a London basement shelter.

JUST IN TIME FOR ← XMAS

BY A SPECIAL CORRESPONDENT

ENTOMBED for more than seventeen hours beneath tons of rubble and brickwork, an elderly London couple were brought out uninjured yesterday through a tiny hole in the pavement.

"Just in time for Christmas," said the man, with a smile, as stretcher men lifted him out.

The couple were Mr. Roderick Peard and his wife Winifred.

They had gone to a vault under house when the air-raid warning sounded. About an hour later a large bomb fell fifty feet away from their refuge and the old house collapsed in ruins above them.

Rescue parties at first thought that there was nobody alive under the great heap of debris. Then voices were heard through a coal hole in the pavement.

Frantically the A.R.P. workers tore away the wreckage and then prized off the lid of the coal hole.

"Are you all right?" they called, and the reply came back in a dazed voice: "Yes, we're all right. Can you get us out?"

Tolled All Night

All through the night the rescue parties toiled, clearing a space round the hole and then lifting paving stones to make an entry into the vault.

While they worked they kept up cheery conversation with the trapped man and woman and stretcher parties passed bread and butter and tea down to them on the end of a rope.

Seventeen hours after the bomb had fallen the rescue party reached them. A stretcher was lowered down the hole and Mrs. Peard strapped to it. Lifting it into a vertical position, the squad hauled it on ropes through the hole into the daylight.

Five minutes later Mr. Peard was out, too.

PREMIER ON AIR TONIGHT

The Prime Minister will broadcast in the Home and Overseas programme at nine o'clock tonight.